A COMPLETE HISTORY OF THE EUROPEAN FIGURE SKATING CHAMPIONSHIPS

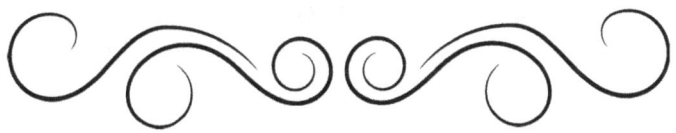

Ryan Stevens

Copyright © 2025 by Ryan Stevens

Print edition published 2025

Independently published
All rights reserved

Library and Archives Canada Cataloguing in Publication

Names: Stevens, Ryan, author
Title: A Complete History of the European Figure Skating Championships / Ryan Stevens
Description: Paperback edition | Ryan Stevens | Halifax, NS : Ryan Stevens, 2025.
Identifier: ISBN: 978-1-997632-02-3
Subject: LCSH: Figure skating [GV.850.4] | BISAC: SPO023000   SPORTS & RECREATION/Winter Sports/Ice & Figure Skating | SPO019000 SPORTS & RECREATION/History

Every reasonable effort has been made to credit all source material included in this book.

If errors or omissions have occurred, they will be corrected in future editions provided written notification and supporting documentation has been received by the author.

TABLE OF CONTENTS

Introduction	1
The Victorian Era	4
The Edwardian Era	22
The Pre-War Era	36
The Roaring Twenties	42
The Great Depression	56
The Age of Austerity	82
The Space Age	104
The Decade of Disco	136
The Decade of Decadence	164
The Age of Globalization	192
The Digital Revolution	244
The Pandemic	304
The New Normal	318
Appreciation	326
Author's Note	327
Other Books	328

GLOSSARY

AND	Andorra
ARM	Armenia
AUS	Australia
AUT	Austria (Austria-Hungary until 1918)
AZE	Azerbaijan
BEL	Belgium
BIH	Bosnia and Herzegovina
BLS	Belarus
BUL	Bulgaria
C/OSP	Compulsory Dances/Original Set Pattern
CAN	Canada
CCP	Compulsory Connected Program
CD	Compulsory Dance(s)
CF	Compulsory (School) Figures
CIS	Commonwealth of Independent States
CRO	Croatia
CYP	Cyprus
CZE	Czech Republic (Czechoslovakia until 1992)
DEN	Denmark
DQ	Disqualified
ESP	Spain
EST	Estonia
FIN	Finland
FD	Free Dance
FRA	France
FRG	Federal Republic of Germany (West Germany)
FS	Free Skating
FS1	Free Skating (1st round)
FS2	Free Skating (2nd round)

GDR	German Democratic Republic (East Germany)
GEO	Georgia
GER	Germany
GRB	Great Britain (United Kingdom)
GRE	Greece
HUN	Hungary
IRL	Ireland
ISL	Iceland
ISR	Israel
ISU	International Skating Union
ITA	Italy
JPN	Japan
LAT	Latvia
LIT	Lithuania
LUX	Luxembourg
MDA	Moldova
MON	Monaco
MNE	Montenegro
NED	Netherlands
NOR	Norway
OD	Original Dance
OP	Original Program
OSP	Original Set Pattern Dance
POL	Poland
QR	Qualifying Round "A"
QRB	Qualifying Round "B"
RD	Rhythm Dance
ROM	Romania
RUS	Russia
S/F	Short Program/Free Skating
SD	Short Dance
SF	Semi-Final
SRB	Serbia

SCG	Serbia and Montenegro
SLO	Slovenia
SOV	Soviet Union
SUI	Switzerland
SVK	Slovakia
SWE	Sweden
(t)	Tie
TP	Technical Program
TUR	Turkey
UKR	Ukraine
USA	United States of America
WD	Withdrew
YUG	Yugoslavia

INTRODUCTION

The European Figure Skating Championships are the oldest figure skating competition in the world, predating the World Figure Skating Championships, figure skating competitions at the Olympics, the International Skating Union, the International Olympic Committee, television and the internet. Yet, if you search this competition online, you will find that much of the information you will find is incomplete and even, at times, inaccurate. This book aims to correct that, by providing accurate records of this competition dating back to the very beginning.

This is a book of historical figure skating records painstakingly and lovingly compiled for figure skating people - nothing more, nothing less.

If you're interested in figure skating history, I believe that you should absolutely be able to walk over to your bookshelf and find the information you're looking for. I hope the results and fascinating facts and figures in this book will be of some interest to lifelong figure skating fans and sports history buffs.

Like people, books are diverse. They all serve different purposes in this world. Cookbooks give us delicious recipes, mystery novels entertain us, and dictionaries give us the definition of words. Every kind of book is valid and serves its own purpose.

Books like this should exist and if you think so too, please take a quick moment to leave a short, honest review.

Figure skating's history matters and I hope this book will enlighten you as to how this historic competition has evolved.

*Eduard Engelmann Jr., European Champion in 1892, 1893 and 1894.
Public domain / Skate Guard Collections.*

THE VICTORIAN ERA

1891 EUROPEAN FIGURE AND SPEED SKATING CHAMPIONSHIPS
Hamburg, Germany, January 23-24, 1891

European Men's Figure Skating Championships:

	CF	FS
1. Otto Uhlig (GER)	1	-
2. A. Schmitt (GER)	2	-
3. Franz Zilly (GER)	3	-
4. Josef Nowy (AUT)	4	-
5. Willi Dinstl (GER)	5	-
6. Fritz Ahrendt (GER)	6	-
7. Wilhelm Schulze (GER)	7	-

European Speed Skating Championships (1/3 mile):

1. Oscar Grundén (SWE)
2. Adolf Norseng (NOR)
3. Klaas Pander (NED)
4. Gustav Landahl (GER)
5. Emil Schou (DEN)
6. Heinrich Ehrhorn (GER)
7. Paul Hille (GER)
8. Albert Schade (GER)
9. J.L. Leonhardt (GER)
10. Jaap Eden (NED)
11. August Underborg (GER)
12. Georg Friebos (GER)
13. Georg Smith (GER)
DNF. Walter Herrmann (GER)
DNF. Otto Traun (GER)
WD Hugo Underborg (GER)

European Speed Skating Championships (1 mile):

1. August Underborg (GER)
2.. Emil Schou (DEN)
3. Adolf Norseng (NOR)
4. Oscar Grundén (SWE)
5. Hugo Underborg (GER)
6. Paul Hille (GER)
7. J.L. Leonhardt (GER)
8. Walter Herrmann (GER)
9. Gustav Landahl (GER)
10. Georg Smith (GER)
DNF. Georg Friebos (GER)
WD. Otto Traun (GER)

European Speed Skating Championships (3 miles):

1. Adolf Norseng (NOR)
2. Oscar Grundén (SWE)
3. Klaas Pander (NED)
4. Heinrich Ehrhorn (GER)
5. Emil Schou (DEN)
6. Jaap Eden (NED)
7. Paul Hille (GER)
8. August Underborg (GER)
9. Georg Friebos (GER)
10. Gustav Landahl (GER)
11. J.L. Leonhardt (GER)
12. Walter Herrmann (GER)
13. Albert Schade (GER)
DNF. Georg Smith (GER)
WD. Otto Traun (GER)

The first European Figure Skating Championships predated the International Skating Union and were organized by the Deutscher und Österreichischer Eislaufverband. Oskar Uhlig made history as the first German skater to win the European Championships. It was also the first time skaters from one country (Germany) swept the medals. Only compulsory figures were skated, as the free skating event was cancelled due to a thaw.

Sources: Allgemeine Sport-Zeitung, February 1, 1891; Seventy-five years of European and World's championships in figure skating, International Skating Union, 1970; Skating Around the World: International Skating Union, the One Hundredth Anniversary History 1892 -1992, Benjamin T. Wright

1892 EUROPEAN FIGURE AND SPEED SKATING CHAMPIONSHIPS (INTERNATIONALE PREIS-WETT-EISLAUFEN)
Vienna, Austria, January 24-25, 1892

European Men's Figure Skating Championships:

	CF	FS
1. Eduard Engelmann Jr. (AUT)	1	1
2. Tibor von Földváry (HUN)	2	3
3. Georg Zachariades (AUT)	3	6
4. Karl Kaiser (AUT)	5	2
5. Jozef Nowy (AUT)	6	5
6. Gustav Hügel (AUT)	8	4
7. Alfred Klement (AUT)	7	7
8. Fritz Ahrendt (GER)	9	8
WD. Carl Sage (AUT)	4	-
WD. Fritz Rehm (GER)	10	-

European Speed Skating Championships (536.5 meters):

1. Hermann Galler (AUT)
2. Franz Schilling (AUT)
3. Heinrich Kern (AUT)
4. Josef Rössler-Ořovský Jr. (CZE)

European Speed Skating Championships (1609 meters):

1. Franz Schilling (AUT)
2. Hermann Galler (AUT)
3. Heinrich Kern (AUT)

4. Josef Rössler-Ořovský Jr. (CZE)

European Speed Skating Championships (4827 meters):

1. Franz Schilling (AUT)
2. Heinrich Kern (AUT)
3. Hermann Galler (AUT)
4. Josef Rössler-Ořovský Jr. (CZE)

Junior Men's Figure Skating:

1. Gustav Hügel (AUT)	1	1
2. Emil Ritter von Meissner (AUT)	3	2
WD. Carl Sage (AUT)	2	-
WD. Karl Perschinka (AUT)	-	-

Speed Skating - Club Run (804.5 meters - only open to club members who didn't participate in other races):

1. K.J. - pseudonym (AUT)
2. Hugo Stein (AUT)
3. Maxime Lurien (AUT)
DNF. L.P. - pseudonym (AUT)

Junior Speed Skating Race (804.5 meters):

1. Paul Krenn (AUT)
2. Heinrich Kern (AUT)
DNF. Karel Reisnér (CZE)
DNF. Albert Titsch (AUT)
DNF. Franz Czernil (AUT)
DNF. Karl Perschl (AUT)
DNF. Leopold Mayr (AUT)
DNF. Karl Schöbl (AUT)
DNF. Heinrich Wiesinger (AUT)
DNF. Paul von Demuth (AUT)
DNF. Hugo Stein (AUT)
DNF. Adolf Tambosi (AUT)

DNF. Adolf Rausch (AUT)

Big Anniversary Speed Skating Race (1609 meters):

1. Franz Schilling (AUT)
2. Thomas Thomas (SWE)
3. H. Ehrhorn (GER)
DNF. Josef Rössler-Ořovský Jr. (CZE)
DNF. Heinrich Kern (AUT)
DNF. Hermann Galler (AUT)

Large Obstacle Skating (804.5 meters, with 8 obstacles not more than 60 meters high and 2 meters wide):

1. Thomas Thomas (SWE)
2. Richard Meidinger (AUT)
DNF. Alfred Klement (AUT)
DNF. Jaroslav Potocky - pseudonym (CZE)
DNF. Franz Czernil (AUT)
DNF. Albert Titsch (AUT)
DNF. Friedrich Pollak (AUT)

Eduard Engelmann Jr. made history as the first Austrian skater to win a gold medal in the European Figure Skating Championships.

Source: Allgemeine Sport-Zeitung, January 31, 1892

1893 EUROPEAN FIGURE AND SPEED SKATING CHAMPIONSHIPS
Berlin, Germany, January 21-22, 1893

European Men's Figure Skating Championships:

	CF	FS
1. Eduard Engelmann Jr. (AUT)*	1	2
2. Henning Grenander (SWE)*	2	1
3. Georg Zachariades (AUT)	4	3
4. Tibor von Földváry (HUN)	3	4
5. Carl Sage (AUT)	5	5

6. Franz Zilly (GER)	6	6
7. Fritz Hellmund (GER)	7	8
8. Johan Peter Lefstad (NOR)	8	7
WD. Alfred Klement (AUT)	-	-

European Speed Skating Championships (500 meters):

1. Julius Seyler (GER)
2. August Underborg (GER)
3. Rudolf Ericsson (SWE)
4. Julius von Salzen (GER)
5. Oskar Fredriksen (NOR)
6. Bernhard Bruzelius (SWE)
7. Walter Herrmann (GER)
8. Franz Schilling (AUT)
9. Otto Schröder (GER)
10. A.G. Beltman (NED)
11. Friedrich Pollack (AUT)
12. Georg Smith (GER)
13. S. Adrian (NED)

European Speed Skating Championships (500 meters final):

1. Rudolf Ericsson (SWE)
2. August Underborg (GER)
3. Julius Seyler (GER)
4. Julius von Salzen (GER)

European Speed Skating Championships (1500 meters):

1. August Underborg (GER)
2. Rudolf Ericsson (SWE)
3. Oskar Fredriksen (NOR)
4. Julius Seyler (GER)
5. Franz Schilling (AUT)
6. Bernhard Bruzelius (SWE)
7. Walter Herrmann (GER)
8. Julius von Salzen (GER)

9. Georg Smith (GER)
10. A.G. Beltman (NED)
11. S. Adrian (NED)
DNF. Otto Schröder (GER)
DNF. Friedrich Pollack (AUT)

European Speed Skating Championships (1500 meters final):

1. Rudolf Ericsson (SWE)
2. Oskar Fredriksen (NOR)
3. August Underborg (GER)
WD. Julius Seyler (GER)

European Speed Skating Championships (5000 meters):

1. Oskar Fredriksen (NOR)
2. Rudolf Ericsson (SWE)
3. August Underborg (GER)
4. Julius Seyler (GER)
5. Bernhard Bruzelius (SWE)
6. Walter Herrmann (GER)
7. Otto Schröder (GER)
8. Georg Smith (GER)
WD. Franz Schilling (AUT)
WD. Julius von Salzen (GER)
WD. A.G. Beltman (NED)
WD. S. Adrian (NED)
WD. Friedrich Pollack (AUT)

This event was sponsored by the Berliner Eislaufverein (Berlin Skating Club) and organized by The German Empire's skating association. At the time of the event, The German Empire consisted of 27 territories, the main one being the Kingdom of Prussia. Austria and Hungary were united constitutionally as the Austro-Hungarian Empire (Austria-Hungary) so technically the judging panel at this event was as stacked as they come.

Two Austrian and two Hungarian judges meant four judges from the Austro-Hungarian Empire were on the panel - to the host country's two. The seventh and final judge on the panel at the event was from Sweden.

Adding to the chaos of a stacked panel, the ISU had only formed the previous year and in its infancy had not yet adopted any universal structure or criteria for judges. The Berliner Eislaufverein (chaired by former champion Oskar Uhlig) named Sweden's Henning Grenander as the winner, whereas the German Empire's Federation named Austria's Eduard Engelmann Jr. as the gold medallist.

Late historian James R. Hines explained, "The discrepancy resulted from different interpretations of the scoring rules, which could result in a tie depending on one's interpretation of them. In point totals, Grenander received 1,988, Engelmann 1,987, but if half-points were considered, the result was a tie. Compulsory figures, which Engelmann won, served as a tiebreaker. The problem was never resolved, but the published record of the ISU lists Engelmann as the champion, with a footnote in the past tense stating that 'The European Championship for 1893 had been declared invalid by the 1895 Congress.' The European Championships for the next two years experienced a marked decrease in participation, perhaps as a result of the scoring debacle."

American skating historian Benjamin T. Wright stated that the confusion "nearly resulted in the demise of the fledgling union." The event sparked considerable debate amongst office holders, so much so that office holders almost resigned. By a mail vote, Swedish sports pioneer General Viktor Balck was elected as ISU President and according to sport historian Ron Edgeworth, "one of his first actions in becoming President was to obtain the adoption of proper rules for the conduct of the competitions in both figure and speed skating at the next Congress."

Sources: Allgemeine Sport-Zeitung, January 29, 1893; The Illustrated Sporting and Dramatic News, February 4, 1893; Figure Skating in the

Formative Years: Singles, Pairs, and the Expanding Role of Women, James R. Hines; *Skating Around the World: International Skating Union, the One Hundredth Anniversary History 1892 -1992*, Benjamin T. Wright; "The Nordic Games And The Origins Of The Olympic Winter Games", Ron Edgeworth, *"Citius, altius, fortius: the ISOH journal"*, vol. 2, no 2, 1994

1894 EUROPEAN FIGURE SKATING CHAMPIONSHIPS
Vienna, Austria, January 28, 1894

European Men's Figure Skating Championships:

	CF	FS
1. Eduard Engelmann Jr. (AUT)	1	1
2. Gustav Hügel (AUT)	3	2
3. Tibor von Földváry (HUN)	2	3
4. Georg Zachariades (AUT)	4	4
5. Carl Sage (AUT)	5	5

Junior Men's Figure Skating:

	CF	FS
1. Emil Ritter von Meissner (AUT)	2	1
2. Josef Fellner (AUT)	1	3
3. S. Brauner (AUT)	5	2
4. R. Gabriel (AUT)	3	4
5. W. Steiskal (AUT)	4	5
6. H. Hermann (AUT)	6	6

Pairs Skating:

1. Christine Engelmann/Carl Euler (AUT)
2. Mitzi Beck/Ludwig Fänner (AUT)
3. Sofie Reininger/M. Deuerling (AUT)

Speed Skating (1000 meters):

1. W. Rowland (AUT)
2. Heinrich Opel (AUT)

Speed Skating (1500 meters):

1. Jaroslav Potocky - pseudonym (CZE)
2. Hermann Galler (AUT)
3. Otto Beyschlag (AUT)

Junior Speed Skating (1000 meters):

1. Otto Beyschlag (AUT)
2. Hugo Stein (AUT)
3. H.S. - pseudonym (AUT)

Large Obstacle Skating (1000 meters, with 8 obstacles not more than 60 meters high and 2 meters wide):

1. Jaroslav Potocky - pseudonym (CZE)
2. Albert Titsch (AUT)

Source: Allgemeine Sport-Zeitung, February 4, 1894

1895 EUROPEAN FIGURE AND SPEED SKATING CHAMPIONSHIPS
Budapest, Hungary, January 26, 1895

European Men's Figure Skating Championships:

	CF	FS
1. Tibor von Földváry (HUN)	1	1
2. Gustav Hügel (AUT)	3	2
3. Gilbert Fuchs (GER)	2	3
WD. Artúr Dezső (HUN)	-	-

European Speed Skating Championships (500 meters):

1. Alfred Næss (NOR)
2. Julius Seyler (GER)
3. Hermann Galler (AUT)
4. Ladislaus Klimkó (HUN)

European Speed Skating Championships (500 meters final):

1. Alfred Næss (NOR)
2. Julius Seyler (GER)

European Speed Skating Championships (1500 meters):

1. Julius Seyler (GER)
2. Alfred Næss (NOR)
3. Hermann Galler (AUT)

European Speed Skating Championships (1500 meters final):

1. Alfred Næss (NOR)
2. Julius Seyler (GER)

European Speed Skating Championships (5000 meters):

1. Alfred Næss (NOR)
2. Julius Seyler (GER)
3. Hermann Galler (AUT)
WD. Ladislaus Klimkó (HUN)

Pairs Skating:

1. Christine Engelmann/Carl Euler (AUT)
2. Carla Edle von Nagy-Bükk/Otto Schwarz (AUT)
3. Mitzi Beck/Ludwig Fänner (AUT)

International Speed Skating (500 meters) - Final:

1. Stefan Szabó (HUN)
2. Eugen Tóth (HUN)
3. Ludwig Grill (HUN)
WD. Ferdinand Däni (HUN)*
DNQ. Richard Meidinger (AUT)
DNQ. Milutin Lillits (HUN)
DNF. Herr Huszmann (GER)

DNF. Friedrich Pollack (AUT)

*This skater withdrew after winning their qualifying heat.

International Speed Skating (5000 meters):

1. Stefan Szabó (HUN)
2. Hugo Stein (AUT)
3. Militun Lillits (HUN)
DNF. Richard Meidinger (AUT)
DNF. Eugen Tóth (HUN)
DNF. Oscar Markus (HUN)
DNF. Herr Huszmann (GER)

Tibor von Földváry made history as the first Hungarian skater to win a gold medal at the European Figure Skating Championships.

Source: Seventy-five years of European and World's championships in figure skating, International Skating Union, 1970

1896-1897
*EVENT NOT HELD**

The European Figure Skating Championships were briefly paused when the ISU began holding the World Figure Skating Championships. Late ISU historian Benjamin T. Wright explained: "The need for a second Championship... quickly [became] apparent, especially when a World Championship might be held abroad, as had already been seen in 1897 in speed skating, when the World Championship had been held in Montreal and the European Championship in Amsterdam... Another reason for re-instituting the European Championship was the ever present possibility of a cancellation due to weather, an event which actually occurred a few years later."

Source: Skating Around the World: International Skating Union, the One Hundredth Anniversary History 1892-1992 (Benjamin T. Wright)

1898 EUROPEAN FIGURE SKATING CHAMPIONSHIPS
Trondheim, Norway, February 26, 1898

European Men's Figure Skating Championships:

	CF	FS
1. Ulrich Salchow (SWE)	1	2
2. Johan Peter Lefstad (NOR)	2	1
3. Oscar Holthe (NOR)	3	3

Speed Skating (500 meters):

1. Peder Østlund (NOR)
2. Edvard Engelsaas (NOR)
3. P. Lindbo (NOR)
4. Martinus Lørdahl (NOR)

Speed Skating (1500 meters):

1. Peder Østlund (NOR)
2. Martinus Lørdahl (NOR)
3. Edvard Engelsaas (NOR)
4. P. Lindbo (NOR)

Speed Skating (5000 meters):

1. Peder Østlund (NOR)
2. Edvard Engelsaas (NOR)
3. W. Hirsch Lund (NOR)
4. Martinus Lørdahl (NOR)
5. P. Lindboe (NOR)
6. J. Johansen (NOR)

Ulrich Salchow made history as the first Swedish skater to win a gold medal at the European Figure Skating Championships.

Sources: Dagsposten, March 1, 1898; Trondhjems Folkebad, March 1, 1898; Seventy-five years of European and World's championships in figure skating, International Skating Union, 1970

1899 EUROPEAN FIGURE AND SPEED SKATING CHAMPIONSHIPS
Davos, Switzerland, January 14-17, 1899

European Men's Figure Skating Championships:

	CF	FS
1. Ulrich Salchow (SWE)	1	2
2. Gustav Hügel (AUT)	2	1
3. Ernst Fellner (AUT)	3	3
4. Martin Gordan (GER)	4	4

European Speed Skating Championships (500 meters):

1. Peder Østlund (NOR)
2. Julius Seyler (SUI)
3. Gustaf Estlander (FIN)
4. Jan Grève (NED)
5. Eduard Vollenweider (RUS)
6. Charles Edgington (GRB)

European Speed Skating Championships (1500 meters):

1. Peder Østlund (NOR)
2. Gustaf Estlander (FIN)
3. Eduard Vollenweider (RUS)
4. Jan Grève (NED)
5. Charles Edgington (GRB)

European Speed Skating Championships (5000 meters):

1. Peder Østlund (NOR)
2. Gustaf Estlander (FIN)
3. Jan Grève (NED)
4. Eduard Vollenweider (RUS)
5. Charles Edgington (GRB)
DNF. Julius Seyler (SUI)

European Speed Skating Championships (10000 meters):*

1. Peder Østlund (NOR)
2. Jan Grève (NED)
3. Gustaf Estlander (FIN)
4. Charles Edgington (GRB)

Speed Skating (1000 meters):

1. Peder Østlund (NOR)
2. Gustaf Estlander (FIN)
3. Eduard Vollenweider (RUS)
DNQ. Charles Edgington (GRB)
DNQ. R. Heinrich (SUI)

Sources: Allgemeine Sport-Zeitung, January 22, 1899; Seventy-five years of European and World's championships in figure skating, International Skating Union, 1970

1900 EUROPEAN FIGURE SKATING CHAMPIONSHIPS
Berlin, Germany, January 21, 1900

European Men's Figure Skating Championships:

	CF	FS
1. Ulrich Salchow (SWE)	1	2
2. Gustav Hügel (AUT)	2	1
3. Oscar Holthe (NOR)	3	3
4. Johan Peter Lefstad (NOR)	4	4
5. Franz Zilly (GER)	5	5
WD. Martin Gordan (GER)	-	-

Pairs Skating for Men (Paarlaufen für Herren):

1. Karl Euler/Gustav Euler (AUT)
WD. Egon Robitsek/Adolph Kleeman (AUT)
WD. Gustav Feix/Anton Steiner (AUT)

Pairs Skating for Men and Ladies (Paarlaufen Dame und Herr):

1. Mizzi/Otto Bohatsch (AUT)
2. Madge Cave/Edgar Syers (GRB)
3. Else Neubeck/Gustav Stahlberg (GER)
4. Fräulein Müller/Herr Gützlav (GER)

Long Jump on Ice (International):

1. Oscar Holthe (NOR)
2. Josef 'Pepi' Weiß-Pfändler (AUT)
3. Richard Meidinger (AUT)
4. Gustav Feix (AUT)
5. Heinrich Bellinger (AUT)

Special Figures (For The Honorary Award of the Imperial Capital and Residence in the City of Vienna):

1. Gustav Euler (AUT)
2. Alfred Klement (AUT)
3. Max Bohatsch (AUT)

Junior Men's Figure Skating:

	CF	FS
1. Edgar Syers (GRB)	1	2
2. Anton Steiner (AUT)	2	1
3. S. Brabant (GER)	3	3

Sources: Neues Wiener Tagblatt, January 24, 1900; Deutsches Volksblatt, January 25, 1900; Allgemeine Sport-Zeitung, January 28, 1900

1901 EUROPEAN FIGURE SKATING CHAMPIONSHIPS
Vienna, Austria, January 13, 1901

European Men's Figure Skating Championships:

	CF	FS
1. Gustav Hügel (SUI)	1	1
2. Gilbert Fuchs (GER)	2	3

3. Ulrich Salchow (SWE)   3   2
WD. Anton Beranek (AUT)   -   -
WD. Carl Euler (AUT)   -   -

Men's Pairs Skating:

1. Carl Euler/Gustav Euler (AUT)
2. Wilhelm Weißmandl/Mony Kleeman (AUT)
3. Egon Robitsek/Adolph Kleeman (AUT)

Ehrenpreis der Stadt Wein (Honorary Prize of the City of Vienna):

1. Max Bohatsch (AUT)
2. Anton Steiner (AUT)
3. Martin Gordan (GER)
4. Adolf Klement (AUT)
5. Gustav Euler (AUT)
6. Ernst Fellner (AUT)
7. Theodore Mészlery (HUN)

Junior Men's Figure Skating:

1. Adolph Kleeman (AUT)
2. Robert - pseudonym (AUT)
3. Leo Geiger (AUT)
WD. Hans Titsch (AUT)

Men's Long Jump on Ice:

1. Richard Meidinger (AUT)
2. Josef 'Pepi' Weiß-Pfändler (AUT)
3. Hans Titsch (AUT)
4. H. Hellinger (AUT)
5. Gustav Feix (AUT)

Though Austrian, Gustav Hügel represented the International Skating Club of Davos at this event, making him the first skater to win a gold medal for Switzerland at the European Championships.

Sources: *Neues Wiener Tagblatt*, January 14, 1901; *Allgemeine Sport-Zeitung*, January 20, 1901

Ulrich Salchow, European Champion in 1898-1900, 1904, 1906-1907, 1909-1910 and 1913. Public domain / Skate Guard Collections.

THE EDWARDIAN ERA

1902-1903
*EVENT NOT HELD**

*The European Championships were awarded to Amsterdam, but were ultimately never held in 1902 or 1903 due to a lack of ice. In 1903, there was an attempt to move the event to Stockholm, but when only one skater entered the Championship event, it was cancelled.

Sources: Skating Around the World: International Skating Union, the One Hundredth Anniversary History 1892 -1992 (Benjamin T. Wright); List of winners of the European Championships, ISU

1904 EUROPEAN FIGURE AND SPEED SKATING CHAMPIONSHIPS
Davos, Switzerland, January 16-17, 1904

European Men's Figure Skating Championships:

	CF	FS
1. Ulrich Salchow (SWE)	1	2
2. Max Bohatsch (AUT)	2	1
3. Nikolay Panin-Kolomenkin (RUS)	3	3
4. Martin Gordan (GER)	6	4
WD. Madge Syers (GRB)	4	-
WD. Heinrich Burger (GER)	5	-

European Speed Skating Championships(500 meters):

1. Rudolf Gundersen (NOR)
2. Coen de Koning (NED)
3. Arend Bouma (NED)
4. Jan Grève (NED)
5. Charles Edgington (GRB)

European Speed Skating Championships (1500 meters):

1. Rudolf Gundersen (NOR)
2. Coen de Koning (NED)
3. Arend Bouma (NED)
4. Jan Grève (NED)

European Speed Skating Championships (5000 meters):

1. Rudolf Gundersen (NOR)
2. Coen de Koning (NED)
3. Arend Bouma (NED)
WD. Charles Edgington (GRB)
WD. Jan Grève (NED)

European Speed Skating Championships (10000 meters):

1. Rudolf Gundersen (NOR)
2. Coen de Koning (NED)
3. Arend Bouma (NED)
WD. Charles Edgington (GRB)
WD. Jan Grève (NED)

European Speed Skating Championships (Overall):

1. Rudolf Gundersen (NOR)
2. Coen de Koning (NED)
3. Arend Bouma (NED)

Pairs Skating:

1. Christine von Szabo/Gustav Euler (AUT)
2. Madge Syers/Edgar Syers (GRB)
3. Phyllis Squire/James Henry Johnson (GRB)

Madge Syers made history as the first woman to skate in an official Championship event at the European Figure Skating Championships. Weather conditions were appalling during the figures, and Syers withdrew thereafter. Nikolay Panin-Kolomenkin became the first Russian to win a medal at the event.

Sources: Seventy-five years of European and World's championships in figure skating, International Skating Union, 1970; Allgemeine Sport-Zeitung, January 24, 1904

1905 EUROPEAN FIGURE SKATING CHAMPIONSHIPS
Bonn, Germany, January 22, 1905

European Men's Figure Skating Championships:

	CF	FS
1. Max Bohatsch (AUT)	1	1
2. Heinrich Burger (GER)	2	3
3. Karl Zenger (GER)	3	2
4. Dr. Kurt Dannenberg (GER)	4	4
5. Martin Gordan (GER)	5	5
6. W.F. (Douglas) Adams (GRB)	6	6
WD. Horatio Tertuliano Torromé (GRB)	-	-

German Men's Figure Skating Championships:

1. Karl Zenger (GER)
2. Heinrich Burger (GER)
3. Martin Gordan (GER)

*This competition was for the national men's figure skating title of the Deutschen Eislauf-Verbandes.

Pairs Skating:

1. Anna Hübler/Heinrich Burger (GER)
2. Frieda Bellinger/Franz Zilly (GER)
3. E. Kolbe/K. Nietz (GER)
WD. Lady Helen Vincent/Karl Zenger (GRB/GER)**

**This team withdrew from the pairs competition, but they gave an exhibition of valsing (waltzing on ice) right after the pairs competition instead.

Junior Men's Figure Skating:

1. Kurt Schmidt (GER)
2. K. Nietz (GER)
3. Dr. Hermann Rüdiger (GER)
4. Alois Wilschek (CZE)
WD. R. Guderacz (GER)
WD. Wilb. Handrich (GER)
WD. Heinrick Neiper (GER)
WD. Otto Fickeisen (GER)
WD. Emil Held (GER)
WD. Fritz Friedlein (GER)

Junior Ladies:

1. Anna Hübler (GER)
2. Fräulein Kolbe (GER)
WD. Lady Helen Vincent (GRB)
WD. Elsa Rendschmidt (GER)

Sources: Allgemeine Sport-Zeitung, January 15, 1905; Neues Wiener Tagblatt, January 23, 1905; Allgemeine Sport-Zeitung, January 29, 1905; Seventy-five years of European and World's championships in figure skating, International Skating Union, 1970

1906 EUROPEAN FIGURE SKATING CHAMPIONSHIPS
Davos, Switzerland, January 28-29, 1906

European Men's Figure Skating Championships:

	CF	FS
1. Ulrich Salchow (SWE)	1	1
2. Ernst Herz (AUT)	2	2
3. Per Thorén (SWE)	3	3
4. Bror Meyer (SWE)	4	6
5. Sándor Urbáry (HUN)	6	4
6. Max Rendschmidt (GER)	5	5

WD. Gilbert Fuchs (GER) - -
WD. Heinrich Burger (GER) - -
WD. J. Hunziker (SUI) - -

World Ladies Figure Skating Championships:

	CF	FS
1. Madge Syers (GRB)	1	1
2. Jenny Herz (AUT)	3	3(t)
3. Lili Kronberger (HUN)	4	2
4. Elsa Rendschmidt (GER)	5	3(t)
5. Dorothy Greenhough Smith (GRB)	2	5
WD. Anna Hübler (GER)	-	-

European Speed Skating Championships (500 meters):

1. Rudolf Gundersen (NOR)
2. Franz Schilling (AUT)
3. Coen de Koning (NED)
4. Steven George Ashe (GRB)
5. Albin Rochat (SUI)
6. Richard Muser (SUI)

European Speed Skating Championships (1500 meters):

1. Rudolf Gundersen (NOR)
2. Franz Schilling (AUT)
3. Coen de Koning (NED)
4. Steven George Ashe (GRB)
5. Richard Muser (SUI)
DNF. Albin Rochat (SUI)

European Speed Skating Championships (5000 meters)

1. Rudolf Gundersen (NOR)
2. Coen de Koning (NED)
3. Franz Schilling (AUT)
4. Steven George Ashe (GRB)
5. Richard Muser (SUI)

6. Albin Rochat (SUI)

European Speed Skating Championships (10000 meters):

1. Coen de Koning (NED)
2. Rudolf Gundersen (NOR)
3. Franz Schilling (AUT)
4. Steven George Ashe (GRB)
DNF. Richard Muser (SUI)
DNF. Albin Rochat (SUI)

European Speed Skating Championships (Final):

1. Rudolf Gundersen (NOR)
2. Coen de Koning (NED)
3. Franz Schilling (AUT)

Pairs Skating:

1. Madge Syers/Edgar Syers (GRB)
2. Anna Hübler/Heinrich Burger (GER)
3. Phyllis Johnson/James Henry Johnson (GRB)
4. Valborg Lindahl/Emil Lindahl (NOR)

Ladies Figure Skating (Internationales Damenlaufen) - Prize of the International Skating Club of Davos:

1. Elsa Rendschmidt (GER)
2. Jenny Herz (AUT)
3. Anna Hübler (GER)
4. Miss Harrington (GRB)
5. Miss Rossel (SUI)

Sources: Feuille D'Avis de Lausanne, January 29, 1906; Neues Wiener Tagblatt, January 30, 1906; Der Bund, January 30, 1906; Allgemeine Sport-Zeitung, February 4, 1906; Seventy-five years of European and World's championships in figure skating, International Skating Union, 1970

1907 EUROPEAN FIGURE SKATING CHAMPIONSHIPS
Berlin, Germany, January 26-27, 1907

European Men's Figure Skating Championships:

	CF	FS
1. Ulrich Salchow (SWE)	1	2
2. Gilbert Fuchs (GER)	2	1
3. Ernst Herz (AUT)	3	3
4. Per Thorén (NOR)	4	4
5. Martinus Lørdahl (NOR)	5	5
6. Martin Gordan (GER)	6	6

Ladies Figure Skating:

1. Elsa Rendschmidt (GER)
2. Phyllis Johnson (GRB)
3. Anna Hübler (GER)
4. Grete Bartel (AUT)
5. Else Bartel (AUT)

International Senior Men's Figure Skating:

1. Gustav Schöning (AUT)
2. Karl Ollo (RUS)
3. Fedor Darlin (RUS)
4. Max Rendschmidt (GER)
5. Oskar Hoppe (AUT)
6. Alois Wilschek (AUT)
7. F. Dreyer (GER)
8. Stolz - pseudonym (AUT)
9. Kurt Schmidt (GER)

Junior Men's Figure Skating:

1. Alois Wilschek (AUT)
2. Erich Gutleben (GER)
3. Adolf Schmidt (GER)
4. O. Aigner (AUT)

5. Ernst Fromm (GER)
6. Gever - pseudonym (GER)
7. A. Vogl (GER)
8. Pulver - pseudonym (GER)
9. H. Tietz (GER)
10. Max Lemm (GER)

Pairs Skating:

1. Anna Hübler/Heinrich Burger (GER)
2. Phyllis Johnson/James Henry Johnson (GRB)
3. Frieda Bellinger/Hans Weber (GER)
4. Grete Bartel/Alois Wilschek (AUT)

Sources: Allgemeine Sport-Zeitung, February 10, 1907; Seventy-five years of European and World's championships in figure skating, International Skating Union, 1970

1908 EUROPEAN FIGURE SKATING CHAMPIONSHIPS
Warsaw, Russian Empire, January 19, 1908

European Men's Figure Skating Championships:

	CF	FS
1. Ernst Herz (AUT)	1	1
2. Nikolay Panin-Kolomenkin (RUS)	2	2
3. Henryk J. Krukowicz-Przedrzymirski (RUS)	3	3

International Men's Figure Skating:

1. Karl Ollo (RUS)
2. Fedor Datlin (RUS)
3. B. Wrobel (AUT)
4. Herr Göbel (RUS)

Sources: Neues Wiener Tagblatt, January 20, 1908; Seventy-five years of European and World's championships in figure skating, International Skating Union, 1970

1909 EUROPEAN FIGURE AND SPEED SKATING CHAMPIONSHIPS
Budapest, Hungary, January 23-24, 1909

European Men's Figure Skating Championships:

	CF	FS
1. Ulrich Salchow (SWE)	1	2
2. Gilbert Fuchs (GER)	3	1
3. Per Thorén (SWE)	2	3
4. Karl Ollo (RUS)	4	4(t)
5. Sándor Urbáry (HUN)	5	4(t)
WD. Irving Brokaw (USA)	-	-
WD. Anton Steiner (AUT)	-	-

World Ladies Figure Skating Championships:

	CF	FS
1. Lili Kronberger (HUN)	1	1
WD. Dorothy Greenhough Smith (GRB)	-	-

European Speed Skating Championships (500 meters):

1. Oskar Mathiesen (NOR)
2. Moje Öholm (SWE)
3. Thomas Bohrer (AUT)
4. Sigurd Mathisen (NOR)
5. Miltiades Mannó (HUN)
6. Franz Schilling (AUT)

European Speed Skating Championships (1500 meters):

1. Oskar Mathiesen (NOR)
2. Thomas Bohrer (AUT)
3. Moje Öholm (SWE)
4. Sigurd Mathisen (NOR)
5. Franz Schilling (AUT)

European Speed Skating Championships (5000 meters):

1. Thomas Bohrer (AUT)
2. Oskar Mathiesen (NOR)
3. Moje Öholm (SWE)
4. Sigurd Mathisen (NOR)
5. Franz Schilling (AUT)

European Speed Skating Championships (10000 meters):

1. Thomas Bohrer (AUT)
2. Oskar Mathiesen (NOR)
3. Moje Öholm (SWE)
4. Sigurd Mathisen (NOR)
WD. Franz Schilling (AUT)

Ladies Figure Skating (Seniorenkunstlaufen):

1. Jenny Herz (AUT)
2. Elsa Rendschmidt (GER)
3. Zsófia Méray-Horváth (HUN)
4. Anna Hübler (GER)
WD. Hermine Kunz (AUT)

Pairs Skating:

1. Anna Hübler/Heinrich Burger (GER)
2. Helene Kuich/Karl Mejstrik (AUT)
3. Ludovika Eilers/Walter Jakobsson (GER/FIN)
4. Hedwig Müller/George Müller (GER)
5. Elsa Lischka/Oskar Hoppe (AUT)
6. Fräulein Beranek/Anton Beranek (AUT)
7. Hedwig Winzer/Hugo Winzer (AUT)
8. Grete Bartel/Alois Wilschek (AUT)
WD. Fräulein Müller/O. Aigner (AUT)

Men's Figure Skating (International Senior Herrenkunst):

1. Andor Szende (HUN)
2. Walter Jakobsson (FIN)
3. Ludwig Richard (AUT)
*. Rudolf Beck (AUT)
*. Herr Wrobt (RUS)
*. Dr. Ernst Oppacher (AUT)
*. Oskar Hoppe (AUT)
*. Henryk J. Krukowicz-Przedrzymirski (RUS)
*. Heinrich Burger (GER)
*. Alois Wilschek (AUT)
*. E. Gutleben (GER)

*Skaters listed are the original entrants in this category. Records from the "Neues Wiener Tagblatt" noted that eight skaters actually competed, but only the top 3 finishers were noted.

Junior Men's Figure Skating:

1. Robert Sander (GER)
2. George Müller (GER)
3. B. Wrobel (AUT)
*. Dr. Ernst Oppacher (AUT)
*. Henryk J. Krukowicz-Przedrzymirski (RUS)
*. Sander - pseudonym
*. O. Aigner (AUT)
*. Herr Farkas (HUN)
*. Seitz - pseudonym
*. Herr Wrobt (RUS)
*. Herr Urban (AUT)
*. Herr Szollás (HUN)
*. Willy Böckl (AUT)

*Skaters listed are the original entrants in this category. Records from the "Neues Wiener Tagblatt" noted that eight skaters actually competed, but only the top 3 finishers were noted.

Junior Ladies Figure Skating:

1. Helene Fräter (HUN)
2. Hedwig Müller (GER)
3. Hermine Proschel-Kunz (AUT)
*. Hedwig Winzer (AUT)
*. Grete Bartel (AUT)
*. Grete Strassila (AUT)
*. Elsa Lischka (AUT)
*. Fräulein Meixner (AUT)

*Skaters listed are the original entrants in this category. Records from the "Neues Wiener Tagblatt" noted that nine skaters actually competed, but only the top 3 finishers were noted.

Sources: Allgemeine Sport-Zeitung, January 24, 1909; Neues Wiener-Tagblatt, January 25, 1909; Pester Lloyd, January 25, 1909; Allgemeine Sport-Zeitung, January 31, 1909; Seventy-five years of European and World's championships in figure skating, International Skating Union, 1970

1910 EUROPEAN FIGURE SKATING CHAMPIONSHIPS
Berlin, Germany, February 10-11, 1910

European Men's Figure Skating Championships:

	CF	FS
1. Ulrich Salchow (SWE)	1	1
2. Werner Rittberger (GER)	2	2
3. Per Thorén (SWE)	3	3
4. John Keiller Grieg (GRB)	4	4
5. Martin Stixrud (NOR)	5	5

International Men's Figure Skating:

1. Fritz Kachler (AUT)
2. Harald Rooth (SWE)
3. Harry Paulsen (NOR)
4. Walter Jakobsson (FIN)
5. Robert Sonder (GER)

6. Karl Mejstrik (AUT)

International Ladies Figure Skating:

1. Elsa Rendschmidt (GER)
2. Fräulein Sonder (GER)

Pairs Skating:

1. Ludovika Eilers/Walter Jakobsson (GER/FIN)
2. Fräulein Sonder/Robert Sonder (GER)
3. Else Weber/Heinrich Weber (GER)

Valsing (Waltzing on Ice):

1. Alexia Schøien/Yngvar Bryn (NOR)
2. Ludovika Eilers/;Walter Jakobsson (GER/FIN)

Junior Men's Figure Skating:

1. Louis Magnus (FRA)
2. Herr Zollner (GER)
3. Herr Bomhardt (GER)
4. Artur Vieregg (GER)

Junior Ladies Figure Skating:

1. Ludovika Eilers (GER)
2. Fräulein Sonder (GER)
3. Grete Štrasilla (AUT)
4. Frau Wolff (GER)

Sources: Neues Wiener Tagblatt, February 11, 1910; Seventy-five years of European and World's championships in figure skating, International Skating Union, 1970

Per Thorén, European Champion in 1911. Public domain / Skate Guard Collections.

THE PRE-WAR ERA

1911 EUROPEAN FIGURE SKATING CHAMPIONSHIPS
February 12, 1911, St. Petersburg, Russian Empire

European Men's Figure Skating Championships:

	CF	FS
1. Per Thorén (SWE)	2	1
2. Karl Ollo (RUS)	1	3
3. Werner Rittberger (GER)	5	2
4. Ivan Malinin (RUS)	3	4
5. Andor Szende (HUN)	4	5

Ladies Figure Skating:

1. Ludovika Eilers (GER)
2. Xenia Caesar (RUS)
3. Lidia Popova (RUS)

Pairs Skating:

1. Ludovika Eilers/Walter Jakobsson (GER/FIN)

Sources: Der Morgen, February 13, 1911; Neues Wiener Tagblatt, February 13, 1911; Die Zeit, February 14, 1911; Sources: Neues Wiener Tagblatt, February 11, 1910; Seventy-five years of European and World's championships in figure skating, International Skating Union, 1970

1912 EUROPEAN FIGURE AND SPEED SKATING CHAMPIONSHIPS
Stockholm, Sweden, February 10-11, 1912

European Men's Figure Skating Championships:

	CF	FS
1. Gösta Sandahl (SWE)	1	1
2. Ivan Malinin (RUS)	2	2

3. Martin Stixrud (NOR)   3   3

European Speed Skating Championships (Overall):

1. Oscar Mathieson (NOR)
2. Gunnar Strömstén (FIN)
3. Martin Sæterhaug (NOR)
4. Ernst Cederlöf (SWE)
5. Otto Andersson (SWE)
6. Petrus Axelson (SWE)
7. Vasily Ippolitov (RUS)
8. Henning Olsen (NOR)
9. Stener Johannessen (NOR)
10. Paul Zerling (SWE)
11. Walter Tvernin (FIN)
12. Paul Poss (SWE)
DNF. Jean Petterson (SWE)
DNF. Albert Berglund (SWE)

*These are the overall results of the speed skating competition, which consisted of 500, 1500, 5000 and 10000 meter races.

Senior Men's Figure Skating:

1. Gillis Grafström (SWE)
2. Olof Hultgren (SWE)
3. Herr Krewitg (SWE)

Senior Ladies Figure Skating:

1. Anna-Lisa Allardt (FIN)
2. Magda Mauroy (SWE)
3. Xenia Caesar (RUS)

Martin Stixrud made history as the first Norwegian skater to win a medal at the European Figure Skating Championships.

Sources: Svenska Dagbladet, February 11 and 12, 1912; Allgemeine Sport-

Zeitung, February 18, 1912; Seventy-five years of European and World's championships in figure skating, International Skating Union, 1970

1913 EUROPEAN FIGURE SKATING CHAMPIONSHIPS
Oslo, Norway, February 1-2, 1913

European Men's Figure Skating Championships:

	CF	FS
1. Ulrich Salchow (SWE)	1	3
2. Andor Szende (HUN)	2	2
3. Willy Böckl (AUT)	3	6
4. Harald Rooth (SWE)	6	1
5. Richard Johansson (SWE)	5	4
6. Martin Stixrud (NOR)	4	7
7. Andreas Krogh (NOR)	7	5

International Men's Figure Skating:

1. Martinus Lørdahl (NOR)
2. Martin Stixrud (NOR)
3. Olof Hultgren (SWE)
4. Arthur Johansen (NOR)

International Ladies Figure Skating:

1. Margit Johansen (NOR)
2. Astrid Nordsveen (NOR)
3. Eva Lindahl (SWE)

Pairs Skating:

1. Alexia Schøien/Yngvar Bryn (NOR)
2. Solveig Andersen/Arthur Johansen (NOR)
3. Fräulein Jensen/Herr Jensen (NOR)
4. Lady Mary Cadogan/Arthur Cumming (GRB)

Speed Skating (1500 meters):

1. Oskar Mathiesen (NOR)
2. Vasily Ippolitov (RUS)
3. Martin Sæterhaug (NOR)
4. Henning Olsen (NOR)
5. Kristian Strøm (NOR)

Speed Skating (5000 meters):

1. Vasily Ippolitov (RUS)
2. Oskar Mathiesen (NOR)
3. Henning Olsen (NOR)
4. Trygve Lundgreen (NOR)
5. Kristian Strøm (NOR)
6. Nikita Naydenov (RUS)
7. Sigurd Syversen (NOR)
8. Gunnar Schou (NOR)
9. Martin Sæterhaug (NOR)

Ulrich Salchow set a record of nine gold medals at the European Figure Skating Championships that has not been matched by any man since.

Sources: Trondhjems Folkeblad, February 4, 1913; Seventy-five years of European and World's championships in figure skating, International Skating Union, 1970

1914 EUROPEAN FIGURE SKATING CHAMPIONSHIPS
Vienna, Austria, February 8, 1914

European Men's Figure Skating Championships:

	CF	FS
1. Fritz Kachler (AUT)	1	5
2. Andreas Krogh (NOR)	4	1
3. Willy Böckl (AUT)	3	2
4. Dr. Ernst Oppacher (AUT)	2	3
5. Ludwig Wrede (AUT)	7	4

6. Josef Oppacher (AUT) 5 6
7. Erwin Schwarzböck (AUT) 6 7

Ladies Figure Skating:

1. Gisela Reichmann (AUT)
2. Paula Zalaudek (AUT)

Pairs Skating:

1. Christine von Szabo/Leo Horwitz (AUT)
2. Helene Engelmann/Karl Mejstrik (AUT)

Men's Figure Skating (Preis de Wiener Eislaufverein):

1. Dr. Ernst Oppacher (AUT)
2. Erwin Schwarzböck (AUT)
3. Josef Oppacher (AUT)
4. Wilhelm Czech (AUT)

Sources: Illustriertes (Österreichisches) Sportblatt, February 14, 1914; Seventy-five years of European and World's championships in figure skating, International Skating Union, 1970

1915-1921
EVENT NOT HELD*

*The European Championships were cancelled during The Great War. Though some European countries continued to hold national figure skating events, the ISU did not resume its Congresses until the spring of 1921. Late ISU Historian Benjamin T. Wright weighed in on the delay thusly: "There is nothing specific in the record to explain the long delay of three years, except the chaotic state of Europe itself, with the defeat and break up of the Central European empires and the formation of new nations resulting from The Treaty of Versailles (signed at the end of June, 1919). In addition, a severe economic depression in Europe after the War had a direct effect on leisure type activities, such as sports."

Source: Skating Around the World: International Skating Union, the One Hundredth Anniversary History 1892 -1992, Benjamin T. Wright

Karl Schäfer, European Champion 1929-1936. APA-PictureDesk / Alamy Stock Photo.

THE ROARING 20s

1922 EUROPEAN FIGURE SKATING CHAMPIONSHIPS
Davos, Switzerland, January 28-29, 1922

European Men's Figure Skating Championships:

	CF	FS
1. Willy Böckl (AUT)	1	3
2. Fritz Kachler (AUT)	2	4
3. Dr. Ernst Oppacher (AUT)	3	1
4. Werner Rittberger (GER)	5	2
5. Martin Stixrud (NOR)	4	5
6. Sakari Ilmanen (FIN)	6	7
7. Gunnar Jakobsson (FIN)	7	8
8. Artur Vieregg (GER)	9	6
9. Dr. Georges Gautschi (SUI)	8	9
10. Wilhelm Czech (CZE)	10	10

World Pairs Skating Championships:

1. Helene Engelmann/Alfred Berger (AUT)
2. Ludovika Jakobsson/Walter Jakobsson (FIN)
3. Margarete Metzner/Paul Metzner (GER)
4. Grete Weise/Georg Velisch (GER)
5. Alexia Bryn/Yngvar Bryn (NOR)

Speed Skating (500 meters):

1. Roald Morel Larsen (NOR)
2. Hellmut Kofler (AUT)
3. Alexander Spengler (SUI)
4. Herr Hermann (SUI)
5. Paul Bombig (AUT)

Speed Skating (1500 meters):

1. Roald Morel Larsen (NOR)
2. Paul Bombig (AUT)
3. Hellmut Kofler (AUT)
4. Alexander Spengler (SUI)
5. Herr Hermann (SUI)

Speed Skating (5000 meters):

1. Paul Bombig (AUT)
2. Hellmut Kofler (AUT)
3. Alexander Spengler (SUI)
4. Herr Hermann (SUI)

Speed Skating (10000 meters):

1. Roald Morel Larsen (NOR)
2. Paul Bombig (AUT)
3. Hellmut Kofler (AUT)
4. Alexander Spengler (SUI)
5. Herr Hermann (SUI)

The Club des Sports d'Hiver de Paris issued a letter directing the French pairs team to pull out of the Championships in protest against the ISU for allowing participants from countries that were not part of the League of Nations.

Sources: Neue Zürcher Zeitung, January 30 and February 3, 1922; Seventy-five years of European and World's championships in figure skating, International Skating Union, 1970

1923 EUROPEAN FIGURE SKATING CHAMPIONSHIPS
Oslo, Norway, January 19-20, 1923

European Men's Figure Skating Championships:

	CF	FS
1. Willy Böckl (AUT)	1	1
2. Martin Stixrud (NOR)	2	3
3. Gunnar Jakobsson (FIN)	3	4
4. Kaj af Ekström (SWE)	4	2

World Pairs Skating Championships:

1. Ludovika Jakobsson/Walter Jakobsson (FIN)
2. Alexia Bryn/Yngvar Bryn (NOR)
3. Elna Henrikson/Kaj af Ekström (SWE)
4. Margit Engebretse/Bjarne Engebretsen (NOR)
5. Randi Bakke/Christen Christensen (NOR

Ladies Figure Skating:

1. Herma Szabo (AUT)
2. Margot Moe (NOR)
3. Ingrid Guldbransen (NOR)

Speed Skating (500 meters):

1. Roald Larsen (NOR)
2. Oscar Olsen (NOR)
3. Theodor Pedersen (NOR)
4. Harald Halvorsen (NOR)
5. Rolf Gihle (NOR)
6. Ole Olsen (NOR)
7. Knut Sundheim (NOR)
8. Hans Thoralf Hansen (NOR)
9. Fridtjof Paulsen (NOR)
10. Ernst Granstrom (NOR)
11. Markus Johansen (NOR)
12. Sigurd Moen (NOR)

13. Fr. Mikkelsen (NOR)

Speed Skating (1500 meters):

1. Roald Larsen (NOR)
2. Ole Olsen (NOR)
3. Fridtjof Paulsen (NOR)
4. Hans Thoralf Hanson (NOR)
5. Sigurd Moen (NOR)
6. Oscar Olsen (NOR)
7. Markus Johansen (NOR)
8. Harald Halvorsen (NOR)

Speed Skating (5000 meters):

1. Ole Olsen (NOR)
2. Roald Larsen (NOR)
3. Fridtjof Paulsen (NOR).
4. Sigurd Moen (NOR)
5. Oscar Olsen (NOR)
6. Rolf Gihle (NOR)
7. Harald Halvorsen (NOR)
8. Alfred Johansen (NOR)
9. Hans Thoralf Hanson (NOR)
10. Theodor Pedersen (NOR)

Speed Skating (10000 meters):

1. Ole Olsen (NOR)
2. Fridtjof Paulsen (NOR)
3. Sigurd Moen (NOR)
4. Roald Larsen (NOR)
5. Rolf Gihle (NOR)
6. Oscar Olsen (NOR)

Junior Speed Skating (500 meters):

1. Bernt Evenson (NOR)
2. Jacob Hansen (NOR)
3. Rolf S. Tandberg (NOR)
4. Einar Fredriksen (NOR)
5. Lorang Andresen (NOR)

Junior Speed Skating (1500 meters):

1. Eigil Hoel (NOR)
2. Jacob Hansen (NOR)
3. Bernt Evensen (NOR)
4. Rolf Larsen (NOR)

Gunnar Jakobsson made history as the first Finnish skater to win a medal at the European Figure Skating Championships.

Sources: Aftenposten, January 20 and 22, 1923; Neue Zürcher Zeitung, February 3, 1922; Seventy-five years of European and World's championships in figure skating, International Skating Union, 1970

1924 EUROPEAN FIGURE SKATING CHAMPIONSHIPS
Davos, Switzerland, January 19-20, 1924

European Men's Figure Skating Championships:

	CF	FS
1. Fritz Kachler (AUT)	1	1
2. Ludwig Wrede (AUT)	2	4
3. Werner Rittberger (GER)	3	5
4. Otto Preißecker (AUT)	4	2
5. Jack Ferguson Page (GRB)	5	3
6. Paul Franke (GER)	7	6
7. Dr. Georges Gautschi (SUI)	6	7
8. Artur Vieregg (GER)	8	8
9. Fritz Schober (GER)	9	9

Speed Skating (500 meters):

1. Clas Thunberg (FIN)
2. Asser Wallenius (FIN)
3. Julius Skutnabb (FIN)

Speed Skating (1000 meters):

1. Clas Thunberg (FIN)
2. Julius Skutnabb (FIN)

Speed Skating (5000 meters):

1. Julius Skutnabb (FIN)
2. Clas Thunberg (FIN)
3. Asser Wallenius (FIN)

A ladies figure skating competition was not held, but Germany's Ellen Brockhöft gave several exhibitions.

Sources: Der Bund, January 20 and 21, 1924; (Wiener) Sporttagblatt, January 24, 1924; Seventy-five years of European and World's championships in figure skating, International Skating Union, 1970

1925 EUROPEAN FIGURE SKATING CHAMPIONSHIPS
Triberg, Germany, February 7-8, 1925

European Men's Figure Skating Championships:

	CF	FS
1. Willy Böckl (AUT)	1	1
2. Werner Rittberger (GER)	2	2
3. Otto Preißecker (GER)	3	4
4. Dr. Georges Gautschi (SUI)	4	5
5. Ludwig Wrede (AUT)	6	3
6. Paul Franke (GER)	5	6

Ladies Figure Skating:

1. Hildegard Thiel (AUT)
2. Elisabeth Böckel (GER)
3. Käthe Wulff (GER)

Men's Figure Skating:

1. Dr. Hugo Distler (AUT)
2. Fritz Schober (GER)
3. Karl Kronfuss (AUT)
4. Herbert Haertel (GER)

Pairs Skating:

1. Else and Oscar Hoppe (CZE)
2. Gisela Hochhaltinger and Georg Pamperl (AUT)

Junior Men's Figure Skating:

1. Karl Kronfuss (AUT)
2. Ernst Baier (GER)
3. Herr Strebel (GER)
4. Bruno Walter (GER)

Sources: Neue Freie Presse, February 9, 1925; Seventy-five years of European and World's championships in figure skating, International Skating Union, 1970

1926 EUROPEAN FIGURE SKATING CHAMPIONSHIPS
Davos, Switzerland, January 30-31, 1926

European Men's Figure Skating Championships:

	CF	FS
1. Willy Böckl (AUT)	2	1
2. Otto Preißecker (AUT)	1	2
3. Dr. Georges Gautschi (SUI)	3	3
4. Jack Ferguson Page (GRB)	4	4

5. Gunnar Jakobsson (FIN)	5	7
6. Robert van Zeebroeck (BEL)	8	5
7. Dr. Hugo Distler (AUT)	7	6
8. Artur Vieregg (GER)	6	8

Pairs Skating:

1. Gisela Hochhaltinger/Georg Pamperl (AUT)
2. Ethel Muckelt/Jack Ferguson Page (GRB)
3. Ilse Kishauer/Herbert Haertel (GER)
4. Marie Schwendtbauer/Gustav Aichinger (GER)

Speed Skating (Overall):

1. Julius Skutnabb (FIN)
2. Teun Hooftman (NED)
3. Franz Schilling (AUT)
4. Willem Kos (NED)
5. Herr Fous (AUT)
6. J. Ruimers (NED)
7. B. Longbloed (NED)
8. L. Wilderbrand de Blaecourt (NED)
9. F. Leicht (SUI)
10. L. Redburn (GRB)
11. Nico Pronk (NED)

Robert van Zeebroeck made history as the first skater to represent Belgium at the European Figure Skating Championships.

Sources: L'Express, February 1, 1926; Neue Freie Presse, February 1, 1926; Der Bund, February 3, 1926; Seventy-five years of European and World's championships in figure skating, International Skating Union, 1970

1927 EUROPEAN FIGURE SKATING CHAMPIONSHIPS
Vienna, Austria, January 22-23, 1927

European Men's Figure Skating Championships:

	CF	FS
1. Willy Böckl (AUT)	1	1
2. Dr. Hugo Distler (AUT)	2	3
3. Karl Schäfer (AUT)	4	2
4. Dr. Ernst Oppacher (AUT)	3	4
5. Paul Franke (GER)	5	5

World Pairs Skating Championships:

1. Herma Szabo/Ludwig Wrede (AUT)
2. Lilly Scholz/Otto Kaiser (AUT)
3. Else Hoppe/Oscar Hoppe (CZE)
4. Hansi Essert/Georg Pamperl (AUT)

Ladies Figure Skating (Jubiläumspreis):

1. Herma Szabo (AUT)
2. Fritzi Burger (AUT)
3. Melitta Brunner (AUT)
4. Elisabeth Böckel (GER)
5. Olga Schiffelers (AUT)

Ladies Figure Skating (Gurschnerpreis):

1. Fritzi Burger (AUT)
2. Elli Winter (GER)
3. Melitta Brunner (AUT)
4. Fräulein Bernhardt (AUT)
5. Ilse Hornung (AUT)
6. Gerda Hornung (AUT)
7. Gerda Veit (GER)

International Men's Figure Skating:

1. Herbert Haertel (GER)
2. Josef Bernhauser (AUT)
3. Herr Schrötter (AUT)
4. Herr Friedel (CZE)
5. Rudolf Práznovský (CZE)
6. Walter Arian (AUT)
7. Herr Hönigschmidt (AUT)

Pairs Skating:

1. Ilse Kishauer/Ernst Gaste (GER)
2. Marie Schwendtbauer/Gustav Aichinger (GER)

Waltzing on Ice:

1. Minna Klingel/Willy Petter (AUT)
2. Fräulein Just/Eugen Richter (AUT)
3. Fräulein Pfeiffer/Karl Zwack (AUT)
4. Fräulein Fischl/Herr Bayerle (AUT)
5. Fräulein Samstag/Fritz Wächtler (AUT)
6. Trude Wintersteiner/Walter Malek (AUT)
7. Herta Baumgartner/Herr Kucharz (AUT)
8. Fräulein Brand/Herr Stöpf (GER)
9. Fräulein Wilpert/Herr Ludwig (GER)

Junior Ladies Figure Skating (Schönheitpreis):

1(t). Melitta Brunner (AUT)
1(t). Olga Schiffelers (AUT)

Sources: Illustrierte Kronen Zeitung, January 24, 1927; Neues Wiener Tagblatt, January 24, 1927; Seventy-five years of European and World's championships in figure skating, International Skating Union, 1970

1928 EUROPEAN FIGURE SKATING CHAMPIONSHIPS
Opava, Czechoslovakia, January 28-29, 1928

European Men's Figure Skating Championships:

	CF	FS
1. Willy Böckl (AUT)	1	2
2. Karl Schäfer (AUT)	3	1
3. Otto Preißecker (AUT)	2	3
4. Ludwig Wrede (AUT)	4	5
5. Rudolf Práznovský (CZE)	6	4
6. Otto Zappe (CZE)	5	6
7. Wilhelm Czech (CZE)	7	7

Ladies Figure Skating:

1. Melitta Brunner (AUT)
2. Edith Hecht (HUN)
3. Gerda Hornung (AUT)

Pairs Skating:

1. Melitta Brunner/Ludwig Wrede (AUT)
2. Else Hoppe/Oscar Hoppe (CZE)
3. Emília Rotter/László Szollás (HUN)
4. Olga Orgonista/Sándor Szalay (HUN)

Ice Dancing:

1. Minna Klingel/Willy Petter (AUT)
2. Fräulein Bosocki-Ronconi/Herr Hanke (AUT)
3. Fräulein Just/Eugen Richter (AUT)

Ice Hockey:

1(t). Troppauer Eislaufverein (CZE)
1(t). Budapester Eislaufverein (HUN)

Sources: Neues Wiener Journal, January 30, 1928; Neues Wiener Tagblatt,

January 30, 1928; Seventy-five years of European and World's championships in figure skating, International Skating Union, 1970

1929 EUROPEAN FIGURE AND SPEED SKATING CHAMPIONSHIPS
Davos, Switzerland, January 19-20, 1929

European Men's Figure Skating Championships:

	CF	FS
1. Karl Schäfer (AUT)	1	1
2. Dr. Georges Gautschi (SUI)	2	4
3. Ludwig Wrede (AUT)	3	2
4. Herbert Haertel (GER)	4	3
5. Josef Bernhauser (AUT)	5	6
6. Paul Franke (GER)	7	5
7. Ernst Baier (GER)	6	10
8. Rudolf Práznovský (CZE)	8	7
9. Dr. Hugo Danzig (GER)	9	8
10. Benno Wellmann (GER)	10	9

Ladies Figure Skating:

1. Melitta Brunner (AUT)
2. Ilse Hornung (AUT)
3. Else Flebbe (GER)
4. Grete Kubitschek (AUT)
5. Lilly Kuhn (SUI)

Pairs Skating:

1. Lilly Scholz/Otto Kaiser (AUT)
2. Melitta Brunner/Ludwig Wrede
3. Gisela Hochhaltinger/Otto Preißecker (AUT)
4. Ilse Kishauser/Ernst Gaste (GER)

Speed Skating (overall)

1. Ivar Ballangrud (NOR)
2. Clas Thunberg (FIN)
3. Roald Larsen (NOR)
4. Rolf van der Scheer (NED)
5. Siem Heiden (NED)
6. Rudolf Riedl (AUT)
7. Otto Polacsek (AUT)
8. Fritz Moser (AUT)
9. Teun Hooftman (NED)
10. István Kauser (HUN)
11. Wim Kos (NED)
12. Haakon Pedersen (NOR)
13. Zoltán Eötvös (HUN)
14. Willy Zipperlin (SUI)
15. László Erdélyi (HUN)
16. Jakob Meng (SUI)

Ice Hockey:

1(t). Berliner Schlittschuhklub (GER)
1(t). Rissersee München (GER)

Curling:

1. Haller Team (GER)

The on-ice events were held as part of a larger multi-sport festival called the Davoser Winterspiele, which also included skiing, ski jumping, bobsled, military patrol and toboggan events.

Sources: Neue Zürcher Nachrichten, January 21, 1929; L'Express, January 21, 1929; Seventy-five years of European and World's championships in figure skating, International Skating Union, 1970

Sonja Henie, European Champion 1931-1936. Everett Collection Inc / Alamy Stock Photo.

THE GREAT DEPRESSION

1930 EUROPEAN FIGURE SKATING CHAMPIONSHIPS*
(men)
Štrbské Pleso, Czechoslovakia, January 18-20, 1930

	CF	FS
1. Josef Slíva (CZE)	1	2
2. Karl Schäfer (AUT)	2	1
3. Otto Gold (CZE)	4	3
4. Otto Hartmann (AUT)	3	4
5. Boh. Sack (CZE)	5	5
6. Verners Auls (LAT)	6	6
7. E. Tubelis (LAT)	7	7
WD. Roman Kikiewicz (POL)	-	-
WD. Zbigniew Iwasiewicz (POL)	-	-
WD. Franjo Avčin (YUG)	-	-
WD. O. Maršálek (CZE)	-	-
WD. Alois Slíva (CZE)	-	-
WD. F. Dité (YUG)	-	-
WD. P. Lejins (LAT)	-	-
WD. Paul Schwab (YUG)	-	-

Immediately following the announcement of the results, there was an uproar. Karl Schäfer, the reigning World Champion, reportedly skated very well, but lost to Czechoslovakian Champion Josef Slíva, whose highest previous finish at an ISU Championship was fifth. A bloc of 3 judges from Czechoslovakia, France and Yugoslavia placed Slíva first. It was later revealed that a second judge from Czechoslovakia, Victor Vašíček, posed as the Yugoslavian judge Ivo Kavsek and judged under his name. Not only was this an ethical issue, but it also broke the ISU's 'one judge per country' rule. A letter of complaint was submitted by the Austrian federation. ISU President Ulrich Salchow issued a letter condemning the incident and he swiftly declared the results of the competition null and void.

It was also announced that a reskate of the event would take place in Berlin the following month. Recalling the scandal, author Emanuel Bosák later remarked that the incident was a "shame, because Josef Slíva... did not need such 'support'." Ironically, one of the supposedly "good" judges at this event, Austria's Hans Grünauer, was suspended for life by the ISU in the 1950s for organizing a calculation office which gave signals to judges to instruct them on what marks to give skaters.

Sources: Wiener Sonn-und Montags-Zeitung, January 20, 1930; Neues Wiener Tagblatt, January 21, 1930; Sports de neige et de glace, February 15, 1930; (Wiener) Sporttagblatt, February 15, 1930; Programme, 1930 European Figure Skating Championships (Štrbské Pleso); Stručný přehled vývoje sportovních odvětví v Československu, Emanuel Bosák, 1969; Seventy-five years of European and World's championships in figure skating, International Skating Union, 1970; Skating Around the World: International Skating Union, the One Hundredth Anniversary History 1892-1992, Benjamin T. Wright, 1992

1930 EUROPEAN FIGURE SKATING CHAMPIONSHIPS
(ladies and pairs)
Vienna, Austria, January 25-26, 1930

European Ladies Figure Skating Championships:

	CF	FS
1. Fritzi Burger (AUT)	1	1
2. Ilse Hornung (AUT)	3	2
3. Vivi-Anne Hultén (SWE)	4	3
4. Lilly Weiler (AUT)	5	4
5. Gerda Hornung (AUT)	2	7
6. Edel Randem (NOR)	6	5
7. Yvonne de Ligne (BEL)	7	6
8. Kathleen Shaw (GRB)	8	8
9. Lilly Kuhn (SUI)	9	9

European Pairs Skating Championships:

1. Olga Orgonista/Sándor Szalay (HUN)
2. Emília Rotter/László Szollás (HUN)
3. Gisela Hochhaltinger/Otto Preißecker (AUT)
4. Ilona Philipovits/Rudolf Dillinger (HUN)
5. Idi Papez/Karl Zwack (AUT)
6. Ridi Jauernik/Pepo Jauernik (AUT)
7. Else Hoppe/Oscar Hoppe (CZE)

Men's Figure Skating (Wiener Eissportklub-Wanderpreis):

1. Dr. Hugo Distler (AUT)
2. Rudolf Práznovský (POL)
3. Rudolf Zettelmann (AUT)
4. Josef Bernhauser (AUT)
5. Otto Hartmann (AUT)
6. Otto Gold (CZE)
7. Heinz Cattani (SUI)

Junior Men's Figure Skating:

1. Marcell Vadas (HUN)
2. Otto Felsinger (AUT)
3. Ewald Büchler (SUI)
4. August Ungethüm (AUT)
5. Kurt Mitter (AUT)
6. Edi Scholdan (AUT)
7. Richard Hammer (AUT)
WD. Heinz Cattani (SUI)

Junior Ladies Figure Skating:

1. Hilde Holovsky (AUT)
2. Helga Schrittwieser-Dietz (AUT)
3. Peri Levitsky (HUN)
4. Olga Hiltner (AUT)
5. Liselotte Landbeck (AUT)

6. Trauti Stolzer (AUT)
7. Fritzi Schobl (AUT)

International Waltzing on Ice:

1. Minna Klingel/Willy Petter (AUT)
2. Fräulein Schneider/Eugen Richter (AUT)
3. Grete Bladyka/Franz Vostanovsky (AUT)
4. Gitta Rimmel/Adolf Rosdol (AUT)
5. Trude Wintersteiner/Walter Malek (AUT)
6. Rosa Cerny/Fritz Wächtler (AUT)
7. Herta Baumgartner/Rolf Stillebacher (AUT)
8. Hilde Kroupa/Oswald Männer (AUT)
WD. Grete Bonlowski/Rudolf Plaside (AUT)

The ladies and pairs events were recognized as the first official European Figure Skating Championships in these disciplines. Fritzi Burger and Olga Orgonista and Sándor Szalay made history as the first Austrian woman and first Hungarian pair to win the titles.

Sources: Die Stunde, January 26, 1930; Pester Lloyd, January 26, 1930; (Wiener) Sporttagblatt, January 27, 1930; Seventy-five years of European and World's championships in figure skating, International Skating Union, 1970

1930 EUROPEAN FIGURE SKATING CHAMPIONSHIPS
(men)
Berlin, Germany, March 15-16, 1930

European Men's Figure Skating Championships:

	CF	FS
1. Karl Schäfer (AUT)	1	1
2. Otto Gold (CZE)	7	2
3. Marcus Nikkanen (FIN)	2	7
4. Herbert Haertel (GER)	3	3
5. Ernst Baier (GER)	4	5
6. Josef Bernhauser (AUT)	5	6
7. Rudolf Práznovský (CZE)	6	4

8. Benno Wellmann (GER)	8	8
9. Otto Zappe (CZE)	9	9
WD. Josef Slíva (CZE)	-	-

International Ladies Figure Skating:

1. Fritzi Burger (AUT)
2. Vivi-Anne Hultén (SWE)
3. Ilse Hornung (AUT)
4. Nanna Egedius (NOR)
5. Yvonne de Ligne (BEL)

International Pairs Skating:

1. Emília Rotter/László Szollás (HUN)
2. Ilse Kishauer/Ernst Gaste (GER)
3. Else Hoppe/Oscar Hoppe (CZE)
4. Ilona Philipovits/Rudolf Dillinger (HUN)
5. Idi Papez/Karl Zwack (AUT)

Josef Slíva of Czechoslovakia, the winner of the annulled European Championships in Štrbské Pleso, reportedly suffered an injury in practice after the competition and was confined to bed for several days. He did not compete in Berlin.

Sources: (Wiener) Sporttagblatt, February 19, 1930; Illustrierte Kronen Zeitung, March 17, 1930; Seventy-five years of European and World's championships in figure skating, International Skating Union, 1970

1931 EUROPEAN FIGURE SKATING CHAMPIONSHIPS
(men)
Vienna, Austria, January 24-25, 1931

European Men's Figure Skating Championships:

	CF	FS
1. Karl Schäfer (AUT)	1	1
2. Ernst Baier (AUT)	2	2
3. Dr. Hugo Distler (AUT)	3	3

4. Marcell Vadas (HUN) 4 5
5. Otto Hartmann (AUT) 5 4
6. Rudolf Zettelmann (AUT) 6 6

Ladies Figure Skating (Wanderpreis des Vereines Kunsteisbahn am Sportsplatz Engelmann):

1. Ilse Hornung (AUT)
2. Helga Schrittwieser-Dietz (AUT)
3. Olly Holzmann (AUT)
4. Annemie Dietze (GER)

Pairs Skating:

1. Idi Papez/Karl Zwack (AUT)
2. Gitta Rimmel/Adolf Rosdol (AUT)
3. Ridi Jauernigg/Pepo Jauernigg (AUT)
4. Helga Schrittwieser-Dietz/Otto Hartmann (AUT)

Sources: Der Morgen, Wiener Montagblatt, January 26, 1931; Seventy-five years of European and World's championships in figure skating, International Skating Union, 1970

1931 EUROPEAN FIGURE SKATING CHAMPIONSHIPS
(ladies and pairs)
St. Moritz, Switzerland, January 29-30, 1931

European Ladies Figure Skating Championships:

	CF	FS
1. Sonja Henie (NOR)	1	1
2. Fritzi Burger (AUT)	2	2
3. Hilde Holovsky (AUT)	3	3
4. Vivi-Anne Hultén (SWE)	4	5
5. Lilly Weiler (AUT)	5	7
6. Yvonne de Ligne (BEL)	6	6
7. Ilse Hornung (AUT)	7	8
8. Else Flebbe (GER)	8	4
9. Reneé Volpato (ITA)	10	9

10. Peri Levitsky (HUN) 9 10

European Pairs Skating Championships:

1. Olga Orgonista/Sándor Szalay (HUN)
2. Emília Rotter/László Szollás (HUN)
3. Lilly Gaillard/Willy Petter (AUT)

Men's Figure Skating:

1. Dr. Hugo Distler (AUT)
2. Marcell Vadas (HUN)
3. Ernst Baier (GER)
4. Herbert Haertel (GER)
5. Jaroslav Hainz (POL)

Junior Men's Figure Skating:

1. Erich Erdös (AUT)
2. Leslie White (GRB)
3. Richard Hammer (AUT)

Junior Ladies Figure Skating:

1. Liselotte Landbeck (AUT)
2. Megan Taylor (GRB)
3. Olly Holzmann (AUT)
4. Annemie Dietze (GER)

Sonja Henie made history as the first Norwegian skater to win a gold medal at the European Figure Skating Championships. Reneé Volpato was the first Italian skater to participate in the event.

Sources: Engadiner Post, January 31, 1931; Neue Zürcher Zeitung, February 1, 1931; Seventy-five years of European and World's championships in figure skating, International Skating Union, 1970

1932 EUROPEAN FIGURE SKATING CHAMPIONSHIPS
Paris, France, January 15-16, 1932

European Men's Figure Skating Championships:

	CF	FS
1. Karl Schäfer (AUT)	1	1
2. Ernst Baier (GER)	2	3
3. Erich Erdös (AUT)	4	2
4. Dr. Hugo Distler (AUT)	5	4
5. Otto Hartmann (AUT)	3	5
6. Jean Henrion (FRA)	6	6
7. Georges Torchon (FRA)	7	7

European Ladies Figure Skating Championships:

	CF	FS
1. Sonja Henie (NOR)	1	1
2. Fritzi Burger (AUT)	2	2
3. Vivi-Anne Hultén (SWE)	3	3
4. Hilde Holovsky (AUT)	4	5
5. Liselotte Landbeck (AUT)	6	4
6. Yvonne de Ligne (BEL)	5	6
7. Joan Dix (GRB)	7	8
8. Gaby Clericetti (FRA)	8	7
9. Reneé Volpato (ITA)	9	9
10. Jacqueline Vaudecrane (FRA)	10	10

European Pairs Skating Championships:

1. Andrée Brunet/Pierre Brunet (FRA)
2. Lilly Gaillard/Willy Petter (AUT)
3. Idi Papez/Karl Zwack (AUT)
4. Margaret Mackenzie/W. Kenneth Ord Mackenzie (GRB)

The European Championships were more often than not held on outdoor ice during this era. In 1932, they moved indoors when they were held at the Palais des Sports in Paris. It was the first time France hosted the European Championships and the first time officially recognized Championships for men's, ladies and pairs were held as part of the same event.

Gaby Clericetti made history as the first French skater to compete in the ladies event. Andrée and Pierre Brunet made history as the first French skaters to win a gold medal at the European Figure Skating Championships.

Sources: Sports de neige et de glace, February 1, 1932; Seventy-five years of European and World's championships in figure skating, International Skating Union, 1970

1933 EUROPEAN FIGURE SKATING CHAMPIONSHIPS
London, England, January 30-31, 1933

European Men's Figure Skating Championships:

	CF	FS
1. Karl Schäfer (AUT)	1	1
2. Ernst Baier (GER)	2	2
3. Erich Erdös (AUT)	3	3
4. Jean Henrion (FRA)	4	4
5. William Clunie (GRB)	5	5

European Ladies Figure Skating Championships:

	CF	FS
1. Sonja Henie (NOR)	1	1
2. Cecilia Colledge (GRB)	2	3
3. Fritzi Burger (AUT)	3	4
4. Hilde Holovsky (AUT)	4	2
5. Yvonne de Ligne (BEL)	5	7
6. Liselotte Landbeck (AUT)	8	5
7. Mollie Phillips (GRB)	7	6
8. Grete Lainer (AUT)	9	8
9. Gweneth Butler (GRB)	6	9
10. Esther Bornstein (DEN)	10	10
11. Margaret W. Thorpe (GRB)	11	11

European Pairs Skating Championships:

1. Idi Papez/Karl Zwack (AUT)
2. Lilly Gaillard/Willy Petter (AUT)
3. Mollie Phillips/Rodney Murdoch (GRB)
4. Violet Supple/Leslie Cliff (GRB)
5. Gertrude Burman/A. Proctor Burman (GRB)
WD. Ethel Muckelt/Jack Ferguson Page (GRB)

Open International Waltzing Competition:

1. Ethel Muckelt/Ronald D. Gilbey (GRB)
2. Violet Supple/Leslie Cliff (GRB)
3. Betty Meakin/Jack Dunn (GRB)

Idi Papez and Karl Zwack made history as the first Austrian pair to win a gold medal at the European Figure Skating Championships. Cecilia Colledge and Mollie Phillips and Rodney Murdoch became the first British medallists in the ladies and pairs events. Esther Bornstein made history as the first skater to represent Denmark at the event.

Sources: Edinburgh Evening News, January 28, 1933; The Scotsman, January 31, 1933; The Leeds Mercury, February 1, 1933; Yorkshire Post and Leeds Intelligencer, February 1, 1933; Programme, 1933 European Figure Skating Championships; Seventy-five years of European and World's championships in figure skating, International Skating Union, 1970

1934 EUROPEAN FIGURE SKATING CHAMPIONSHIPS
(men)
Seefeld, Austria, January 20-21, 1934

European Men's Figure Skating Championships:

	CF	FS
1. Karl Schäfer (AUT)	1	1
2. Dénes Pataky (HUN)	3	2
3. Elemér Terták (HUN)	4	5
4. Leopold Linhart (AUT)	5	6

5. Erich Erdös (AUT)	2	7
6. Jack Dunn (GRB)	6	3
7. Felix Kaspar (AUT)	11	4
8. Ferenc Kertesz (HUN)	7	9
9. Vladimir Koudelka (CZE)	9	8
10. Erwin Keller (SUI)	8	11
11. Jean Henrion (FRA)	10	10
12. Josef Bernhauser (AUT)	12	12
13. Rudolf Zettelmann (AUT)	13	13

Men's Figure Skating:

1. T.C. Patrick Low (GRB)
2. Emil Ratzenhofer (AUT)
3. Adalbert Horosz (ROM)
4. Ernst Fenner (SUI)
5. Lucian Büeler (SUI)
6. Alois Slíva (AUT)
7. Alois Lenhart (AUT)
8. Alois Hauswirth (AUT)

Ladies Figure Skating:

1. Liselotte Landbeck (AUT)
2. Grete Lainer (AUT)
3. Helga Schrittwieser-Dietz (AUT)
4. Gerda Hornung (AUT)
5. Lilly Weiler (AUT)

Pairs Skating (Jubiläumspreis):

1. Herta Baumgartner/Rolf Stillebacher (AUT)
2. Éva Tusák/Zoltán Balázs (HUN)
3. Mlle. Hauser/Erwin Keller (SUI)

Junior Ladies Figure Skating:

1. Emmy Puzinger (AUT)

2. Hertha Dexler (AUT)
3. Bianca Schenk (AUT)
4. Else Bornstein (DEN)
5. Magda Imrédy (HUN)
6. Angela Anderes (SUI)
7. Bessie Alward (AUT)

Sources: (Wiener) Sporttagblatt, January 22, 1934; Seventy-five years of European and World's championships in figure skating, International Skating Union, 1970

1934 EUROPEAN FIGURE SKATING CHAMPIONSHIPS
(ladies and pairs)
Prague, Czechoslovakia, January 27-28, 1934

European Ladies Figure Skating Championships:

	CF	FS
1. Sonja Henie (NOR)	1	1
2. Liselotte Landbeck (AUT)	2	2
3. Maribel Vinson (USA)	3	3
4. Megan Taylor (GRB)	4	4
5. Grete Lainer (AUT)	6	5
6. Nanna Egedius (NOR)	7	6
7. Yvonne de Ligne (BEL)	5	7
8. Esther Bornstein (DEN)	8	9
9. Mollie Phillips (GRB)	9	8
10. Fritzi Metznerová (CZE)	10	10
WD. Liesel Hohlbaum (CZE)	-	-
WD. Libuše Veselá (CZE)	-	-
WD. Jacqueline Vaudecrane (FRA)	-	-

European Pairs Skating Championships:

1. Emília Rotter/László Szollás (HUN)
2. Idi Papez/Karl Zwack (AUT)
3. Zofia Bilorówna/Tadeusz Kowalski (POL)
4. Lucy Galló/Rezső Dillinger (HUN)
5. Herta Baumgartner/Rolf Stillebacher (AUT)

6. Traute Jäger/Fritz Lesk (CZE)
7. Irina Timcic/Alfred Eisenbeisser (ROM)
8. Netty Eisenbeiss/Karl Friedel (CZE)
9. Hildegarde Schwarz/Eduards Goschel (AUT)
10. Libuše Veselá/Vojtěch Veselý (CZE)

The ladies school figures were held during a blinding snowstorm. Liselotte Landbeck made history as the first woman to win a medal in official ISU Championships in both figure and speed skating. After winning the gold medal in the 1933 World Allround Speed Skating Championships in Oslo, she won the silver medal at the 1934 European Figure Skating Championships in Prague. Zofia Bilorówna and Tadeusz Kowalski made history as the first Polish skaters to win a medal at the European Figure Skating Championships. Maribel Vinson made history as the first North American skater to win a medal at the event. At the time, there was a requirement that skaters needed to be a member of a European figure skating club for 3 years to enter. Vinson was a member of The Skating Club of Boston as well as The Ice Club, Westminster in England. She also spent time training in St. Moritz.

Sources: Skating magazine, January 1931 and November 1934; (Wiener) Sporttagblatt, January 22, 1934; Programme, 1934 European Figure Skating Championships (Prague); Seventy-five years of European and World's championships in figure skating, International Skating Union, 1970; Skating Around the World: International Skating Union, the One Hundredth Anniversary History 1892-1992, Benjamin T. Wright

1935 EUROPEAN FIGURE SKATING CHAMPIONSHIPS
St. Moritz, Switzerland, January 23-26, 1935

European Men's Figure Skating Championships:

	CF	FS
1. Karl Schäfer (AUT)	1	1
2. Felix Kaspar (AUT)	4	2
3. Ernst Baier (GER)	2	3
4. Jack Dunn (GRB)	3	4
5. Marcus Nikkanen (FIN)	6	7

6. Erich Erdös (AUT)	5	8
7. Elemér Terták (HUN)	7	5
8. Leopold Linhart (AUT)	8	6
9. Emil Ratzenhofer (AUT)	11	9
10. Lucian Büeler (SUI)	12	10
11. Jean Henrion (FRA)	10	11
12. Herbert Haertel (GER)	9	12

European Ladies Figure Skating Championships:

	CF	FS
1. Sonja Henie (NOR)	1	4
2. Liselotte Landbeck (AUT)	4	2
3. Cecilia Colledge (GRB)	2	6
4. Maxi Herber (GER)	6	1
5. Gweneth Butler (GRB)	3	10
6. Grete Lainer (AUT)	5	5
7. Hedy Stenuf (AUT)	11	3
8. Mollie Phillips (GRB)	12	9
9. Yvonne de Ligne (BEL)	8	13
10. Nanna Egedius (NOR)	9	14
11. Hertha Frey-Dexler (SUI)	13	8
12. Victoria Lindpaintner (GER)	10	11
13. Emmy Puzinger (AUT)	14	7
14. Nadine Szilassy (HUN)	7	16
15. Diana Fane-Gladwin (GRB)	15	12
16. Gaby Claricetti (FRA)	16	15

European Pairs Skating Championships:

1. Maxi Herber/Ernst Baier (GER)
2. Idi Papez/Karl Zwack (AUT)
3. Lucy Galló/Rezső Dillinger (HUN)
4. Ilse Paulsen/Erik Pausin (AUT)
5. Éva Tusák/Zoltán Balázs (HUN)
6. Eleanore Bäumel/Fritz Wächtler (AUT)
7. Violet Cliff/Leslie Cliff (GRB)
8. Traute Jäger/Fritz Lesk (CZE)
9. Gaby Clericetti/Jean Henrion (FRA)

Junior Men's Figure Skating:

1. Herbert Alward (AUT)
2. Günther Lorenz (GER)
3. Richard Hammer (AUT)
4. Ernst Fenner (SUI)
5. Ercole Cattaneo (ITA)
6. Günther Noack (GER)
7. Sidney Croll (AUS)
8. Herr Kunz (SUI)
9. Robert Verdun (BEL)

Junior Ladies Figure Skating:

1. Maria Schweinburg (AUT)
2. Angela Anderes (SUI)
3. Daphne Walker (GRB)
4. Anna Cattaneo-Dubinio (ITA)
5. Martha Mayerhans (GER)
6. Belita Jepson-Turner (GRB)
7. Edlind Weise (GER)
8. Anita Wägeler (SUI)
9. Fräulein Wehrli (SUI)
10. T. Bon (SUI)
11. Susi Demoll (SUI)

Maxi Herber and Ernst Baier made history as the first German pair to win a gold medal at the European Figure Skating Championships. Sidney Croll made history as the first Australian to participate in a figure skating competition held in conjunction with the European Championships.

Sources: (Wiener) Sporttagblatt, January 28 and 31, 1935; Neue Zürcher Nachrichten, January 28, 1935; Neue Zürcher Zeitung, January 28, 1935; Seventy-five years of European and World's championships in figure skating, International Skating Union, 1970

1936 EUROPEAN FIGURE SKATING CHAMPIONSHIPS
Berlin, Germany, January 24-25, 1936

European Men's Figure Skating Championships:

	CF	FS
1. Karl Schäfer (AUT)	1	1
2. Graham Sharp (GRB)	2	3
3. Ernst Baier (GER)	3	5
4. Felix Kaspar (AUT)	4	4
5. Elemér Terták (HUN)	5	2
6. Marcus Nikkanen (FIN)	6	10
7. Toshikazu Katayama (JPN)	7	8
8. Freddie Tomlins (GRB)	8	7
9. Kazuyoshi Oimatsu (JPN)	12	6
10. Robert van Zeebroeck (BEL)	9	12
11. Freddy Mésot (BEL)	11	9
12. Jean Henrion (FRA)	10	14
13. Günther Lorenz (AUT)	14	11
14. Herbert Haertel (GER)	13	13
15. Walter Grobert (POL)	16	15
WD. Tsugio Hasegawa (JPN)	15	-

European Ladies Figure Skating Championships:

	CF	FS
1. Sonja Henie (NOR)	1	1
2. Cecilia Colledge (GRB)	2	2
3. Megan Taylor (GRB)	3	3
4. Liselotte Landbeck (BEL)	6	4
5. Vivi-Anne Hultén (SWE)	4	7
6. Hedy Stenuf (AUT)	5	6
7. Maxi Herber (GER)	8	5
8. Victoria Lindpaintner (GER)	7	9
9. Etsuko Inada (JPN)	11	8
10. Gladys Jagger (GRB)	13	10
11. Mia Macklin (GRB)	9	14
12. Pamela Prior (GRB)	10	15
13. Györgyi von Botond (HUN)	17	11
14. Éva von Botond (HUN)	14	12

15. Věra Hrubá (CZE) 16 13
16. Jacqueline Vaudecrane (FRA) 12 16
17. Anita Wägeler (SUI) 15 17

European Pairs Skating Championships:

1. Maxi Herber/Ernst Baier (GER)
2. Violet Cliff/Leslie Cliff (GRB)
3. Piroska Szekrényessy/Attila Szekrényessy (HUN)
4. Eva Prawitz/Otto Weiß (GER)
5. Stephanie Kalusz/Erwin Kalusz (POL)
6. Louise Contamine/Robert Verdun (BEL)
7. Věra Trejbalová/Josef Vosolsobě (CZE)

The introduction of the Open Marking System dramatically changed figure skating. In previous years, results were not released until the conclusion of the competition and judge's scores were largely shrouded in secrecy. Karl Schäfer and Felix Kaspar both received perfect 6.0's from the judges at the European Figure Skating Championships in 1936. Schäfer received a 6.0 from the Hungarian judge for one compulsory figure and perfect marks for both contents and execution from the Czechoslovakian and Austrian judges in free skating. Kaspar received perfect marks for contents from the German and Finnish judges in the free skating.

For the first and only time, Japanese skaters were represented at the European Figure Skating Championships. The history-making team from Japan consisted of Toshikazu Katayama, Kazuyoshi Oimatsu, Tsugio Hasegawa and Etsuko Inada.

Sources: Skating magazine, November 1935; Wiener Sporttagblatt, January 27, 1936; Programme, 1936 European Figure Skating Championships; Neue Zürcher Nachrichten, January 27, 1936; Seventy-five years of European and World's championships in figure skating, International Skating Union, 1970

1937 EUROPEAN FIGURE SKATING CHAMPIONSHIPS
Prague, Czechoslovakia, February 5-7, 1937

European Men's Figure Skating Championships:

	CF	FS
1. Felix Kaspar (AUT)	1	1
2. Graham Sharp (GRB)	2	2
3. Elemér Terták (HUN)	3	4
4. Freddie Tomlins (GRB)	4	3
5. Herbert Alward (AUT)	5	5
6. Leopold Linhart (AUT)	6	7
7. Marcus Nikkanen (FIN)	7	9
8. Horst Faber (GER)	10	6
9. Jaroslav Sadílek (CZE)	8	8
10. Freddy Mésot (BEL)	11	11
11. Jean Henrion (FRA)	9	12
12. Rudolf Práznovský (CZE)	12	10
13. Paul Schwab (YUG)	13	13
14. Emanuel Thuma (YUG)	14	14

European Ladies Figure Skating Championships:

	CF	FS
1. Cecilia Colledge (GRB)	1	1
2. Megan Taylor (GRB)	2	2
3. Emmy Putzinger (AUT)	3	3
4. Hedy Stenuf (FRA)	4	4
5. Hanne Niernberger (AUT)	6	7
6. Gladys Jagger (GRB)	9	5
7. Věra Hrubá (CZE)	5	8
8. Eva Nyklová (CZE)	11	6
9. Klára Erdős (HUN)	7	9
10. Martha Mayerhans (GER)	8	11
11. Audrey Peppe (USA)	12	10
12. Joy Ricketts (GRB)	10	13
13. Irma Hartung (GER)	14	12
14. Gerd Helland-Bjørnstad (NOR)	13	14
15. Anne-Marie Sæther (NOR)	15	15
WD. Liselotte Landbeck (BEL)	-	-

WD. Lydia Veicht (GER) - -
WD. Lilly Weiler (AUT) - -

European Pairs Skating Championships:

1. Maxi Herber/Ernst Baier (GER)
2. Ilse Pausin/Erich Pausin (AUT)
3. Piroska Szekrényessy/Attila Szekrényessy (HUN)
4. Violet Cliff/Leslie Cliff (GRB)
5. Inge Koch/Günther Noack (GER)
6. Anna Cattaneo/Ercole Cattaneo (ITA)
7. Liese Kianek/Adolf Rosdol (AUT)
8. Věra Trejbalová/Josef Vosolsobě (CZE)
9. Feda Kalenčíková/Karel Glogar (CZE)
WD. Eva Prawitz/Otto Weiß (GER)
WD. Irina Timcic/Alfred Eisenbeisser (ROM)

Cecilia Colledge made history as the first British skater to win a gold medal at the European Figure Skating Championships.

Sources: Wiener Sporttagblatt, February 5 and 6, 1937; Seventy-five years of European and World's championships in figure skating, International Skating Union, 1970

1938 EUROPEAN FIGURE SKATING CHAMPIONSHIPS
(men and ladies)
St. Moritz, Switzerland, January 20-23, 1938

European Men's Figure Skating Championships:

	CF	FS
1. Felix Kaspar (AUT)	2	1
2. Graham Sharp (GRB)	1	2
3. Herbert Alward AUT)	3	3
4. Horst Faber (GER)	8	5
5. Elemér Terták (HUN)	4(t)	6
6. Freddie Tomlins (GRB)	6	4
7. Edi Rada (AUT)	4(t)	7
8. Günther Lorenz (GER)	7	8

9. Per Cock-Clausen (DEN)   9   9

European Ladies Figure Skating Championships:

	CF	FS
1. Cecilia Colledge (GRB)	1	1
2. Megan Taylor (GRB)	2	2
3. Emmy Puzinger (AUT)	4	3
4. Maxi Herber (GER)	3	4
5. Lydia Veicht (GER)	6	5
6. Angela Anderes (SUI)	7	7
7. Gladys Jagger (GRB)	8	8
8. Eva Nyklová (CZE)	5	9
9. Hanne Niernberger (AUT)	9	10
10. Daphne Walker (GRB)	11	6
11. Pamela Stephany (GRB)	10	13
12. Lissy König (AUT)	13	11
13. Nadine Szilassy (HUN)	12	15
14. Susi Demoll (GER)	14	14
15. Inge Manger (SUI)	15	16
16. Jacqueline Vaudecrane Bossoutrot (FRA)	16	12
17. Zdeňka Porgesova (CZE)	17	17
WD. Hedy Stenuf (USA)	-	-

International Pairs Skating (Grossen Preis von St-Moritz):

1. Inge Koch/Günther Noack (GER)
2. Violet Cliff/Leslie Cliff (GRB)
3. Pierrette Du Bois/Paul Du Bois (SUI)
4. Piroska Szekrényessy/Attila Szekrényessy (HUN)
5. Erika Bass/Béla Barcza-Rotter (HUN)
6. Liese Kianek/Adolf Rosdol (AUT)
7. Daphne Wallis/Reginald J. Wilkie (GRB)

Sources: Der Bund, January 21, 1938; La Suisse libérale, January 24, 1938; L'impartial, January 24, 1938; Engadiner Post, January 25, 1938; Seventy-five years of European and World's championships in figure skating, International Skating Union, 1970

1938 EUROPEAN FIGURE SKATING CHAMPIONSHIPS
(pairs)
Opava, Czechoslovakia, January 30, 1938

European Pairs Skating Championships:

1. Maxi Herber/Ernst Baier (GER)
2. Ilse Pausin/Erich Pausin (AUT)
3. Inge Koch/Günther Noack (GER)
4. Piroska Szekrényessy/Attila Szekrényessy (HUN)
5. Stephanie Kalusz/Erwin Kalusz (POL)
6. A. Wächter/Fritz Lesk (CZE)

Men's Figure Skating:

1. Elemér Terták (HUN)
2. Emil Ratzenhofer (AUT)
3. Ferenc Kertesz (HUN)
4. Rudi Schmidtschneider (GER)
5. Erich Schmidtschneider (GER)

Ladies Figure Skating:

1. Nadine Szilassy (HUN)
2. Lilly König (AUT)
3. Anna Pollack (AUT)
4. Liesel Hohlbaum (CZE)
5. Fräulein Beraes (CZE)

Sources: Salzburger Volksblatt, January 31, 1938; Reichspost, January 31, 1938; Seventy-five years of European and World's championships in figure skating, International Skating Union, 1970

1939 EUROPEAN FIGURE SKATING CHAMPIONSHIPS
(men)
Davos, Switzerland, January 27-29, 1939

European Men's Figure Skating Championships:

	CF	FS
1. Graham Sharp (GRB)	1	1
2. Freddie Tomlins (GRB)	3	2
3. Horst Faber (GER)	2	3
4. Edi Rada (GER)	5	4
5. Hans Gerschwiler (SUI)	4	5
6. Bo Mothander (SWE)	7	6
7. Emil Ratzenhofer (GER)	8	8
8. Franz Loichinger (GER)	9	7
9. Hellmut May (GER)	6	11
10. Per Cock-Clausen (DEN)	10	9
11. Tony Austin (GRB)	12	10
12. Ian B. Currie (GRB)	11	12

Speed Skating (1500 meters):

1. Hans Egnestangen (NOR)
2. Ivar Ballangrud (NOR)
3. Michael Staksrud (NOR)
4. Georg Krog (NOR)
5. Charles Mathiesen (NOR)
6. Herr Haraldsen (NOR)
7. Aage Johansen (NOR)
8. Herr Hitveghi (HUN)
9. Jan Langedijk (NED)
10. Roelof Koops (NED)
11. Gedeon Ladányi (HUN)
12. Arthur Ritzi (SUI)

Speed Skating (5000 meters):

1. Ivar Ballangrud (NOR)
2. Michael Staksrud (NOR)

3. Charles Mathiesen (NOR)
4. Hans Egnestangen (NOR)
5. Jan Langedijk (NED)
6. Roelof Koops (NED)
7. Aage Johansen (NOR)
8. Arthur Ritzi (SUI)
9. Georg Krog (NOR)
10. Herr Haraldsen (NOR)
11. Herman Buyen (NED)
12. Piet Zwanenburg (NED)
13. Herr Hitveghi (HUN)
14. Gedeon Ladányi (HUN)
15. Ernö Ladányi (HUN)
18. Josef Rogger (SUI)
29. Herr Wullschleger (SUI)

Ice Hockey:

1. E.H.C. Davos (SUI)
2. E.H.C. Arosa (SUI)

The on-ice events were held as part of a larger multi-sport festival called the Davoser Eisfest, which also included alpine and cross country skiing, ski jumping, bobsled, relay races and military patrol events.

Graham Sharp made history as the first British skater to win a gold medal in the men's event at the European Figure Skating Championships. Freddie Tomlins took the silver, and it was the first time two British men stood on the podium at the event.

Sources: Neue Zürcher Zeitung, January 30, 1939; Neue Zürcher Nachrichten, January 30, 1939; Seventy-five years of European and World's championships in figure skating, International Skating Union, 1970

1939 EUROPEAN FIGURE SKATING CHAMPIONSHIPS
(ladies)
London, England, January 23-24, 1939

European Ladies Figure Skating Championships:

	CF	FS
1. Cecilia Colledge (GRB)	2	1
2. Megan Taylor (GRB)	1	2
3. Daphne Walker (GRB)	3	3
4. Hanne Niernberger (GER)	4	6
5. Emmy Puzinger (GER)	8	4
6. Angela Anderes (SUI)	7	5
7. Eva Nyklová (CZE)	5	9
8. Gladys Jagger (GRB)	6	11
9. Marta Musilek (GER)	10	5
10. Anne-Marie Sæther (NOR)	9	10
11. Britta Råhlén (SWE)	11	8
12. Eva Katzová (CZE)	12	12

British Junior Men's Figure Skating Championships:

1. Dennis Silverthorne (GRB)
2. Adrian Pryce-Jones (GRB)
3. Peter J. Scholes (GRB)

British Junior Ladies Figure Skating Championships:

1. Elizabeth M. Whittington (GRB)
2. Winnie Silverthorne (GRB)
3. K. Everard (GRB)
4. J. Thompson (GRB)
5. Peggy Tomlins (GRB)
6. A. Trausel (GRB)

For the first time, skaters from one country (Great Britain) swept the podium in the ladies event at the European Figure Skating Championships. For the first time, commentary from the European Championships was broadcast on BBC Radio.

Sources: Evening Standard, January 24, 1939; BBC Programme Index; Protocol, Championship of Europe in Figure Skating for Ladies 1939; Seventy-five years of European and World's championships in figure skating, International Skating Union, 1970

1939 EUROPEAN FIGURE SKATING CHAMPIONSHIPS
(pairs)
Zakopane, Poland, February 4, 1939

European Pairs Skating Championships:

1. Maxi Herber/Ernst Baier (GER)
2. Ilse Pausin/Erich Pausin (GER)
3. Inge Koch/Günther Noack (GER)
4. Erika Bass/Béla Barcza-Rotter (HUN)
5. Stephanie Kalusz/Erwin Kalusz (POL)
6. Gisela Grätz/Otto Weiß (GER)
7. Silva Palme/Paul Schwab (YUG)
8. Trude Heuchert/Guber Heuchert (ROM)
9. Ileana Moldovan/Alfred Eisenbeisser (ROM)

For the first time, skaters from one country swept the podium in the pairs event at the European Figure Skating Championships. Siblings Ilse and Erich Pausin were actually Austrian, but their country had been annexed by Nazi Germany in The Anschluss on March 12, 1938.

Sources: Völkischer Beobachter, February 6, 1939; Seventy-five years of European and World's championships in figure skating, International Skating Union, 1970

1940-1946
EVENT NOT HELD*

*The European Championships were cancelled during World War II. Though the war finally ended in 1945, Europe was in a state of turmoil. There was insufficient time to arrange to find a country prepared to host the European Championships until 1947.

Source: Skating Around the World: International Skating Union, the One Hundredth Anniversary History 1892 -1992, Benjamin T. Wright

Jeannette Altwegg, European Champion 1951-1952. Prisma by Dukas Presseagentur GmbH / Alamy Stock Photo.

THE AGE OF AUSTERITY

1947 EUROPEAN FIGURE SKATING CHAMPIONSHIPS
Davos, Switzerland, January 31-February 2, 1947

European Men's Figure Skating Championships:

	CF	FS
1. Hans Gerschwiler (SUI)	1	1
2. Vladislav Čáp (CZE)	2	3
3. Fernand Leemans (BEL)	5	2
4. Arthur J. Apfel (GRB)	4	4
5. Zdeněk Fikar (CZE)	3	6
6. Fritz Dürst (SUI)	6	5
WD. Josef Dědič (CZE)	-	-
WD. Ivan Mauer (CZE)	-	-

European Ladies Figure Skating Championships:

	CF	FS
1. Barbara Ann Scott (CAN)	1	1
2. Gretchen Van Zandt Merrill (USA)	3	2
3. Daphne Walker (GRB)	2	3
4. Jeannette Altwegg (GRB)	4	6
5. Jiřina Nekolová (CZE)	6	5
6. Alena Vrzáňová (CZE)	7	4
7. Marion Davies (GRB)	5	10
8. Maja Hug (SUI)	8	8
9. Bridget Shirley Adams (GRB)	9	14
10. Jill Hood-Linzee (GRB)	11	11
11. Dagmar Lerchová (CZE)	10	15
12. Barbara Wyatt (GRB)	12	12
13. Roberta Scholdan (USA)	15	7
14. Ursula Arnold (SUI)	13	16
15. Simone Clinckers (BEL)	17	9
16. Patricia Molony (AUS)	14	18

17. Lotti Höner (SUI)	18	13
18. Gun Hammarin (SWE)	19	17
19. Anne-Marie Sjöberg (SWE)	20	19
WD. Gun Ericson (SWE)	16	-

European Pairs Skating Championships:

1. Micheline Lannoy/Pierre Baugniet (BEL)
2. Winnie Silverthorne/Dennis Silverthorne (GRB)
3. Suzanne Diskeuve/Edmond Verbustel (BEL)
4. Denise Fayolle/Guy Pigier (FRA)
5. Běla Zachova/Jaroslav Zach (CZE)
6. Jennifer Nicks/John Nicks (GRB)
7. Luny Unold/Hans Kuster (SUI)
8. Denise Favart/Jacques Favart (FRA)
9. Pamela Davis/Ernest H.C. Yates (GRB)
10. Eva Doušová/Jaroslav Sadílek (GRB)
11. Kerstin Wikman/Harry Berlin (SWE)

Barbara Ann Scott and Micheline Lannoy and Pierre Baugniet were the first Canadian and Belgian winners at the European Figure Skating Championships. Scott was also the first Canadian to compete in the event.

Sources: L'express, February 3, 1947; Neue Zürcher Nachrichten, February 3, 1947; Programme, 1947 European Figure Skating Championships; Seventy-five years of European and World's championships in figure skating, International Skating Union, 1970

1948 EUROPEAN FIGURE SKATING CHAMPIONSHIPS
Prague, Czechoslovakia, January 13-15, 1948

European Men's Figure Skating Championships:

	CF	FS
1. Dick Button (USA)	2	1
2. Hans Gerschwiler (SUI)	1	3
3. Edi Rada (AUT)	3	2
4. Ede Király (HUN)	4	5

5. Johnny Lettengarver (USA)	5	4
6. Zdeněk Fikar (CZE)	7	6
7. Hellmut Seibt (AUT)	8	7
8. Vladislav Čáp (CZE)	6	9
9. Josef Dědič (CZE)	9	8
WD. Dennis Silverthorne (GRB)	-	-
WD. Dr. Hellmut May (AUT)	-	-
WD. Fernand Leemans (BEL)	-	-
WD. Ivan Mauer (CZE)	-	-

European Ladies Figure Skating Championships:

	CF	FS
1. Barbara Ann Scott (CAN)	1	1
2. Eva Pawlik (AUT)	4	2
3. Alena Vrzáňová (CZE)	3	3
4. Jiřina Nekolová (CZE)	2	4
5. Jeannette Altwegg (GRB)	5	11
6. Dagmar Lerchová (CZE)	7	5
7. Andrea Kékesy (HUN)	8	8
8. Bridget Shirley Adams (GRB)	6	13
9. Marion Davies (GRB)	11	12
10. Barbara Wyatt (GRB)	10	15
11. Martha Musilek-Bachem (AUT)	15	6
12. Milena Tumová (CZE)	14	9
13. Ingeborg Solar (AUT)	16	10
14. Éva Lindner (HUN)	13	16
15. Hildegard Appeltauer (AUT)	9	19
16. Mária Saáry (HUN)	12	17
17. Beryl Bailey (GRB)	19	7
18. Roberta Scholdan (USA)	17	18
19. Věra Masáková (CZE)	18	14
WD. Györgi Botond Mohr (HUN)	-	-
WD. Jill Hood Linzee (GRB)	-	-

European Pairs Skating Championships:

1. Andrea Kékesy/Ede Király (HUN)
2. Blažena Knittlová/Karel Vosátka (CZE)

3. Herta Ratzenhofer/Emil Ratzenhofer (AUT)
4. Joan Thompson/Robert S. Ogilvie (GRB)
5. Jennifer Nicks/John Nicks (GRB)
6. Marianna Nagy/László Nagy (HUN)
7. Györgyi Botond Mohr/Ferenc Kertész (HUN)
8. Susi Giebisch/Hellmut Seibt (AUT)
9. Dagmar Hrubá/Jiří Očenášek (CZE)
10. Elly Stärck/Harry Gareis (AUT)
11. P. Přenosilová/František Landi (CZE)
WD. D. Hrubá/J. Očenášek (CZE)

Dick Button made history as the first and only American skater to win a gold medal at the European Figure Skating Championships and Barbara Ann Scott successfully defended her title, making it the first and last time a North American skater won two consecutive European titles.

Prior to the 1948 event, the ISU decided to only accept entries from skating federations in Continental Europe moving forward. They allowed North American skaters to compete in 1948 because "it would be anything but sporting to introduce that... rule the first year that a North American skater won."

Sources: Courrier de Genève, January 15, 1948; Barbara Ann Scott: Queen of the Ice, Ryan Stevens, 2024; Programme, 1948 European Figure Skating Championships; Seventy-five years of European and World's championships in figure skating, International Skating Union, 1970

1949 EUROPEAN FIGURE SKATING CHAMPIONSHIPS
Milan, Italy, January 28-30, 1949

European Men's Figure Skating Championships:

	CF	FS
1. Edi Rada (AUT)	1	1
2. Ede Király (HUN)	2	2
3. Hellmut Seibt (AUT)	3	3
4. Carlo Fassi (ITA)	5	4
5. Vladislav Čáp (CZE)	6	5

6. Zdeněk Fikar (CZE) 4 6

European Ladies Figure Skating Championships:

	CF	FS
1. Eva Pawlik (AUT)	1	2
2. Alena Vrzáňová (CZE)	3	1
3. Jeannette Altwegg (GRB)	2	3
4. Jiřina Nekolová (CZE)	4	6
5. Dagmar Lerchová (CZE)	7	4
6. Bridget Shirley Adams (GRB)	5	13
7. Jacqueline du Bief (FRA)	10	5
8. Barbara Wyatt (GRB)	8	9
9. Valda Osborn (GRB)	9	10
10. Andrea Kékesy (HUN)	12	7
11. Lilly Fuchs (AUT)	6	16
12. Beryl Bailey (GRB)	11	11
13. Joan Lister (GRB)	13	12
14. Susi Giebisch (AUT)	14	8
15. Helga Haid (AUT)	15	15
16. Grazia Barcellona (ITA)	16	14

European Pairs Skating Championships:

1. Andrea Kékesy/Ede Király (HUN)
2. Marianna Nagy/László Nagy (HUN)
3. Herta Ratzenhofer/Emil Ratzenhofer (AUT)
4. Běla Zachova/Jaroslav Zach (CZE)
5. Suzanne Gheldolf/Jacques Renard (BEL)
6. Jennifer Nicks/John Nicks (GRB)
7. Margot Walle/Allan Fjeldheim (NOR)
8. Elly Stärck/Harry Gareis (AUT)
9. Grazia Barcellona/Carlo Fassi (ITA)
10. Eliane Steinemann/André Calame (SUI)
11. Pamela Davis/Peter Scholes (GRB)
12. Silva Palme/Marko Lajović (YUG)

Sources: La tribune de Genève, January 29, 1949; Skating World magazine, February 1949; Programme, 1949 European Figure Skating Championships;

Seventy-five years of European and World's championships in figure skating, International Skating Union, 1970

1950 EUROPEAN FIGURE SKATING CHAMPIONSHIPS
Oslo, Norway, February 17-19, 1950

European Men's Figure Skating Championships:

	CF	FS
1. Ede Király (HUN)	1	1
2. Hellmut Seibt (AUT)	2	2
3. Carlo Fassi (ITA)	4	3
4. Zdeněk Fikar (CZE)	3	5
5. Kurt Sönning (SUI)	5	4
6. Kalle Tuulos (FIN)	7	6
7. Per Cock-Clausen (DEN)	6	7
WD. Edmond Verbustel (BEL)	-	-

European Ladies Figure Skating Championships:

	CF	FS
1. Alena Vrzáňová (CZE)	1	1
2. Jeannette Altwegg (GRB)	2	2
3. Jacqueline du Bief (FRA)	4	3
4. Barbara Wyatt (GRB)	3	6
5. Dagmar Lerchová (CZE)	5	5
6. Beryl Bailey (GRB)	7	4
7. Regula Arnold (SUI)	6	8
8. Alexandra Černá (CZE)	9	7
9. Miloslava Tumová (CZE)	10	9
10. Gun Ericson (SWE)	8	13
11. Susi Wirz (SUI)	12	11
12. Yolande Jobin (SUI)	11	14
13. Leena Pietilä (FIN)	13	10
14. Bjørg Løhner (NOR)	14	12
15. Ingeborg Nilsson (NOR)	15	15
WD. Klára Erdős (HUN)	-	-
WD. Marit Henie (NOR)	-	-
WD. Jiřina Nekolová (ISU)	-	-

European Pairs Skating Championships:

1. Marianna Nagy/László Nagy (HUN)
2. Eliane Steinemann/André Calame (SUI)
3. Jennifer Nicks/John Nicks (GRB)
4. Běla Zachova/Jaroslav Zach (CZE)
5. Elly Stärck/Harry Gareis (AUT)
6. Soňa Buriánová/Miloslav Balun (CZE)
WD. Suzanne Gheldolf/Jacques Renard (BEL)
WD. Denise Favart/Jacques Favart (FRA)

Alena Vrzáňová made history as the first Czechoslovakian woman to win a gold medal at the European Figure Skating Championships.

Jiřina Nekolová made history as one of the first of many skaters to defect from a Communist regime. She was listed as a competitor in Oslo, under the ISU flag, but she ultimately withdrew.

Sources: Border Morning Mail, December 19, 1949; Nationen, February 15, 1950; Neue Zürcher Nachrichten, February 20, 1950; Die Tat, February 20, 1950; Programme, 1950 European Figure Skating Championships; Seventy-five years of European and World's championships in figure skating, International Skating Union, 1970

1951 EUROPEAN FIGURE SKATING CHAMPIONSHIPS
Zürich, Switzerland, February 2-4, 1951

European Men's Figure Skating Championships:

	CF	FS
1. Hellmut Seibt (AUT)	1	1
2. Horst Faber (FRG)	2	2
3. Carlo Fassi (ITA)	3	3
4. Michael Carrington (GRB)	4	4
5. Freimut Stein (FRG)	5	5
6. François Pache (SUI)	6	6
7. Martin Felsenreich (AUT)	7	7
8. Fritz Loosli (SUI)	8	8

European Ladies Figure Skating Championships:

	CF	FS
1. Jeannette Altwegg (GRB)	1	2
2. Jacqueline du Bief (FRA)	2	1
3. Barbara Wyatt (GRB)	3	3
4. Valda Osborn (GRB)	4	6
5. Beryl Bailey (GRB)	5	4
6. Gundi Busch (FRG)	7	7
7. Helga Dudzinski (FRG)	11	5
8. Lotte Schwenk (AUT)	9	9
9. Susi Wirz (SUI)	8	10
10. Inge Jell (FRG)	12	8
11. Yolande Jobin (SUI)	6	13
12. Ghislaine Kopf (SUI)	10	11
13. Leena Pietilä (FIN)	13	12
14. Gun Ericson (SWE)	15	15
15. Lidy Stoppelman (NED)	16	16
16. Bjørg Løhner (NOR)	18	14
17. Rietje van Erkel (NED)	17	17
18. Yvonne Ruts (NED)	19	18
WD. Erika Kraft (FRG)	14	-

European Pairs Skating Championships:

1. Ria Baran/Paul Falk (FRG)
2. Eliane Steinemann/André Calame (SUI)
3. Jennifer Nicks/John Nicks (GRB)
4. Silvia Grandjean/Michel Grandjean (SUI)
5. Inge Minor/Hermann Braun (FRG)
6. Elly Stärck/Harry Gareis (AUT)
7. Marlies Schrör/Hans Schwarz (FRG)
8. Elizabeth Williams/John McCann (GRB)
9. Silva Palme/Marco Lajović (YUG)
10. Doris Clayden/Ronald Clayden (GRB)

Lidy Stoppelman made history as the first Dutch woman to compete at the European Figure Skating Championships.

Sources: *La tribune de Genève*, February 3, 1951; *Neue Zürcher Zeitung*, February 4, 1951; *Skating World magazine*, March 1951; *Skating magazine*, April 1951; *Seventy-five years of European and World's championships in figure skating*, International Skating Union, 1970

1952 EUROPEAN FIGURE SKATING CHAMPIONSHIPS
Vienna, Austria, February 4-6, 1952

European Men's Figure Skating Championships:

	CF	FS
1. Hellmut Seibt (AUT)	1	1
2. Carlo Fassi (ITA)	2	4
3. Michael Carrington (GRB)	3	2
4. Alain Giletti (FRA)	4	6
5. Martin Felsenreich (AUT)	5	3
6. Freimut Stein (FRG)	7	5
7. Zdeněk Fikar (CZE)	6	7
8. György Czakó (HUN)	9	8
9. Fritz Loosli (SUI)	8	10
10. Klaus Loichinger (FRG)	10	9

European Ladies Figure Skating Championships:

	CF	FS
1. Jeannette Altwegg (GRB)	1	3
2. Jacqueline du Bief (FRA)	2	1
3. Barbara Wyatt (GRB)	3	9
4. Erika Kraft (FRG)	5	4
5. Helga Dudzinski (FRG)	9	2
6. Valda Osborn (GRB)	4	7
7. Dagmar Lerchová (CZE)	8	6
8. Gundi Busch (FRG)	7	11
9. Eva Weidler (AUT)	11	8
10. Annelies Schilhan (AUT)	17	5
11. Erica Batchelor (GRB)	10	12
12. Miloslava Tumová (CZE)	12	10
13. Susi Wirz (SUI)	13	13
14. Yolande Jobin (SUI)	6	20
15. Ghislaine Kopf (SUI)	15	16

16. Patricia Devries (GRB)	14	14
17. Jarmila Königová (CZE)	16	19
18. Yvonne Sugden (GRB)	18	15
19. Relly Maydan (AUT)	21	18
20. Rosi Pettinger (FRG)	20	17
21. Lidy Stoppelman (NED)	19	22
22. Eszter Jurek (HUN)	23	21
WD. Leena Pietilä (FIN)	22	-
WD. Miroslava Náchodská (CZE)	-	-
WD. Doris Zerbe (SUI)	-	-

European Pairs Skating Championships:

1. Ria Baran/Paul Falk (FRG)
2. Jennifer Nicks/John Nicks (GRB)
3. Marianna Nagy/László Nagy (HUN)
4. Silvia Grandjean/Michel Grandjean (SUI)
5. Peri Horne/Raymond Lockwood (GRB)
6. Soňa Buriánová/Miloslav Balun (CZE)
7. Sissy Schwarz/Kurt Oppelt (AUT)
8. Éva Szöllősi/Gábor Vida (HUN)
9. Silva Palme/Marco Lajović (YUG)
WD. Inge Minor/Hermann Braun (FRG)

Sources: Wiener Montag, February 4, 1952; Skating World magazine, March 1952; Seventy-five years of European and World's championships in figure skating, International Skating Union, 1970

1953 EUROPEAN FIGURE SKATING CHAMPIONSHIPS
Dortmund, West Germany, January 23-25, 1953

European Men's Figure Skating Championships:

	CF	FS
1. Carlo Fassi (ITA)	1	2
2. Alain Giletti (FRA)	2	1
3. Freimut Stein (FRG)	4	3
4. Michael Booker (GRB)	3	4
5. Hubert Köpfler (SUI)	5	5

6. Martin Felsenreich (AUT)	6	6
7. Klaus Loichinger (FRG)	7	7
8. György Czakó (HUN)	9	8
WD. Kurt Oppelt (AUT)	8	-

European Ladies Figure Skating Championships:

	CF	FS
1. Valda Osborn (GRB)	1	2
2. Gundi Busch (FRG)	2	1
3. Erica Batchelor (GRB)	3	6
4. Helga Dudzinski (FRG)	5	3
5. Yvonne Sugden (GRB)	4	7
6. Annelies Schilhan (AUT)	7	5
7. Rosi Pettinger (FRG)	11	4
8. Elaine Skevington (GRB)	10	9
9. Lidy Stoppelman (NED)	6	11
10. Sissy Schwarz (AUT)	8	10
11. Nelly Maas (NED)	14	8
12. Doris Zerbe (SUI)	9	14
13. Fiorella Negro (ITA)	12	15
14. Joan Haanappel (NED)	16	13
15. Liliane de Becker (BEL)	13	17
16. Erika Rücker (FRG)	15	16
17. Eszter Jurek (HUN)	17	12

European Pairs Skating Championships:

1. Jennifer Nicks/John Nicks (GRB)
2. Marianna Nagy/László Nagy (HUN)
3. Sissy Schwarz/Kurt Oppelt (FRG)
4. Jean Higson/Robert S. Hudson (GRB)
5. Eva Neeb/Karl Probst (FRG)
6. Helga Krüger/Peter Voss (FRG)
7. Charlotte Michiels/Gaston van Ghelder (BEL)

Carlo Fassi made history as the first Italian skater to win a gold medal at the European Figure Skating Championships. Jennifer and John Nicks were the first British winners of the pairs event.

Sources: Die Weltpresse, January 26, 1953; Seventy-five years of European and World's championships in figure skating, International Skating Union, 1970

1954 EUROPEAN FIGURE SKATING CHAMPIONSHIPS
Bolzano, Italy, January 29-31, 1954

European Men's Figure Skating Championships:

	CF	FS
1. Carlo Fassi (ITA)	1	2
2. Alain Giletti (FRA)	2	1
3. Karol Divín (CZE)	4	3
4. Michael Booker (GRB)	3	4
5. Alain Calmat (FRA)	6	5
6. Norbert Felsinger (AUT)	5	6
7. Zdeněk Fikar (CZE)	7	9
8. Hanno Ströher (AUT)	8	11
9. François Pache (SUI)	9	10
10. Hans Müller (SUI)	10	12
11. Werner Kronemann (FRG)	11	7
12. Kurt Weilert (GDR)	12	8

European Ladies Figure Skating Championships:

	CF	FS
1. Gundi Busch (FRG)	1	1
2. Erica Batchelor (GRB)	2	2
3. Yvonne Sugden (GRB)	3	3
4. Annelies Schilhan (AUT)	4	5
5. Ingrid Wendl (AUT)	5	7
6. Hanna Eigel (AUT)	7	6
7. Clema C. Cowley (GRB)	6	9
8. Miloslava Tumová (CZE)	8	12
9. Hanna Walter (AUT)	11	8
10. Nelly Maas (NED)	15	4
11. Rosi Pettinger (FRG)	10	10
12. Dagmar Lerchová (CZE)	12	13
13. Lidy Stoppelman (NED)	9	19
14. Fiorella Negro (ITA)	13	17

15. Erika Rücker (FRG)	14	15
16. Lilo Kürzinger (FRG)	19	14
17. Alice Fischer (SUI)	17	16
18. Joan Haanappel (NED)	16	18
19. Sjoukje Dijkstra (NED)	21	11
20. Christianne Moreux (FRA)	18	21
21. Luisella Gaspari (ITA)	20	20
22. Manuela Angeli (ITA)	22	22

European Pairs Skating Championships:

1. Silvia Grandjean/Michel Grandjean (SUI)
2. Sissy Schwarz/Kurt Oppelt (AUT)
3. Soňa Balunová/Miloslav Balun (CZE)
4. Vera Kuhrüber/Horst Kuhrüber (GDR)
5. Alice Zettel/Klaus Loichinger (FRG)
6. Jean Higson/Robert S. Hudson (GRB)
7. Inge Minor/Hermann Braun (FRG)
8. Eva Neeb/Karl Probst (FRG)

European Ice Dancing Championships:

	CD	FD
1. Jean Westwood/Lawrence Demmy (GRB)	1	1
2. Nesta Davies/Paul Thomas (GRB)	2	2
3. Barbara Radford/Raymond Lockwood (GRB)	3	3
4. Bona Giammona/Giancarlo Sioli (ITA)	7	4
5. Edith Peikert/Hans Kutschera (AUT)	5	5
6. Fanny Besson/Jean Paul Guhel (FRA)	4	6
7. Helga Binder/Edwin Führich (AUT)	8	7
8. Catharina Odink/Jacobus Odink (NED)	6	10
9. Lucia Fischer/Rudolf Zorn (AUT)	9	8
10. C.G. Weinstein/C. Lambert (FRA)	10	9
11. A. Giuggiolini/G. Ceccattini (ITA)	11	11
12. Albertina Brown/Nigel Brown (SUI)	12	12

Jean Westwood and Lawrence Demmy made history as the first British ice dance team to win a gold medal at the European Figure Skating Championshps, leading the first British sweep of medals in the ice dancing event.

Silvia and Michel Grandjean made history as the first Swiss pair to win the title and Gundi Busch won Germany's first gold medal in the ladies event.

Sources: Skating World magazine, March 1954; Skating magazine, March 1954; Programme, 1954 European Figure Skating Championships; Seventy-five years of European and World's championships in figure skating, International Skating Union, 1970

1955 EUROPEAN FIGURE SKATING CHAMPIONSHIPS
Budapest, Hungary, January 27-29, 1955

European Men's Figure Skating Championships:

	CF	FS
1. Alain Giletti (FRA)	1	1
2. Michael Booker (GRB)	2	2
3. Karol Divín (CZE)	4	3
4. Norbert Felsinger (AUT)	3	7
5. Alain Calmat (FRA)	5	6
6. István Szenes (HUN)	6	4
7. Tilo Gutzeit (FRG)	8	5
8. Hans Müller (SUI)	7	9
9. György Czakó (HUN)	11	8
10. Manfred Schnelldorfer (FRG)	10	11
11. Ivan Mauer (CZE)	9	13
12. Miroslav Kutina (CZE)	12	10
13. Emanuel Koczyba (POL)	13	14
14. Leon Osadnik (POL)	14	12

European Ladies Figure Skating Championships:

	CF	FS
1. Hanna Eigel (AUT)	2	1
2. Yvonne Sugden (GRB)	1	3
3. Erica Batchelor (GRB)	3	2
4. Rosi Pettinger (FRG)	4	4
5. Hanna Walter (AUT)	6	5

6. Maryvonne Huet (FRA)	7	9
7. Fiorella Negro (ITA)	5	16
8. Miroslava Náchodská (CZE)	8	14
9. Erika Rücker (FRG)	11	11
10. Dagmar Řeháková (CZE)	17	7
11. Alice Fischer (SUI)	10	12
12. Michèle Allard (FRA)	16	10
13. Ilse Musyl (AUT)	13	15
14. Christianne Moreux (FRA)	9	19
15. Eszter Jurek (HUN)	18	8
16. Manuela Angeli (ITA)	12	21
17. Gilberte Naboudet (FRA)	15	20
18. Miloslava Tumová (CZE)	20	6
19. Luisella Gaspari (ITA)	14	22
20. Milena Kladrubská (CZE)	19	13
21. Hedvig Pálinkás (HUN)	21	17
22. Barbara Jankowska (POL)	22	18

European Pairs Skating Championships:

1. Marianna Nagy/László Nagy (HUN)
2. Věra Suchánková/Zdeněk Doležal (CZE)
3. Marika Kilius/Franz Ningel (GER)
4. Liesl Ellend/Konrad Lienert (AUT)
5. Alice Zettel/Klaus Loichinger (FRG)
6. Vivien Higson/Robert S. Hudson (GRB)
7. Soňa Buriánová/Miloslav Balun (CZE)
8. Éva Szöllősi/Gábor Vida (HUN)
9. Anna Bursche-Lindnerowa/Leon Osadnik (POL)

European Ice Dancing Championships:

	CD	FD
1. Jean Westwood/Lawrence Demmy (GRB)	1	1
2. Pamela Weight/Paul Thomas (GRB)	2	2
3. Barbara Radford/Raymond Lockwood (GRB)	3	3
4. Fanny Besson/Jean Paul Guhel (FRA)	5	4
5. Sigrid Knake/Günther Koch (FRG)	4	6
6. Bona Giammona/Giancarlo Sioli (ITA)	6	5

7. Lucia Fischer/Rudolf Zorn (AUT)	8	8
8. Edith Peikert/Hans Kutschera (AUT)	7	11
9. Rózsa Madarász/Gyula Madarász (HUN)	10	7
10. Catharina Odink/Jacobus Odink (NED)	9	12
11. Edit Parádi/József Parádi (HUN)	12	10
12. Luise Lehner/Georg Lenitz (AUT)	11	13
13. Aranka Tóth/Endre Tóth (HUN)	13	9
14. Maria Göth/Willi Wernz (FRG)	14	14

Alain Giletti made history as the first singles skater from France to win a gold medal at the European Figure Skating Championships.

Sources: Skating magazine, April 1955; Seventy-five years of European and World's championships in figure skating, International Skating Union, 1

1956 EUROPEAN FIGURE SKATING CHAMPIONSHIPS
Paris, France, January 19-21, 1956

European Men's Figure Skating Championships:

	CF	FS
1. Alain Giletti (FRA)	1	3
2. Michael Booker (GRB)	2	1
3. Karol Divín (CZE)	3	2
4. Alain Calmat (FRA)	4	4
5. Tilo Gutzeit (FRG)	7	7
6. Norbert Felsinger (AUT)	5	16
7. François Pache (SUI)	8	11
8. István Szenes (HUN)	9	5
9. Brian Tuck (GRB)	6	13
10. Manfred Schnelldorfer (FRG)	10	12
11. Hans Müller (SUI)	12	8
12. Igor Persiantsev (SOV)	13	6
13. Hanno Ströher (AUT)	11	15
14. Hans-Jürgen Bäumler (FRG)	15	9
15. Lev Mikhailov (SOV)	14	10
16. Valentin Zakharov (SOV)	16	14

European Ladies Figure Skating Championships:

	CF	FS
1. Ingrid Wendl (AUT)	1	2
2. Yvonne Sugden (GRB)	3	1
3. Erica Batchelor (GRB)	2	7
4. Rosi Pettinger (FRG)	4	6
5. Hanna Walter (AUT)	7	3
6. Dianne Peach (GRB)	6	9
7. Sjoukje Dijkstra (NED)	5	11
8. Joan Haanappel (NED)	9	10
9. Erika Rücker (FRG)	10	13
10. Ilse Musyl (AUT)	12	12
11. Emma Giardini (ITA)	8	19
12. Alice Fischer (SUI)	11	20
13. Ina Bauer (FRG)	19	5
14. Jindra Kramperová (CZE)	16	8
15. Carine Borner (SUI)	13	16
16. Jana Dočekalová (CZE)	22	4
17. Miloslava Tumová-Zahorská (CZE)	14	18
18. Gilberte Naboudet (FRA)	17	17
19. Corinne Altman (FRA)	20	15
20. Milena Kladrubská (CZE)	21	14
21. Michèle Allard (FRA)	15	21
22. Britt Turid Aronsen (NOR)	18	22

European Pairs Skating Championships:

1. Sissy Schwarz/Kurt Oppelt (AUT)
2. Marianna Nagy/László Nagy (HUN)
3. Marika Kilius/Franz Ningel (FRG)
4. Joyce Coates/Anthony Holles (GRB)
5. Věra Suchánková/Zdeněk Doležal (CZE)
6. Liesl Ellend/Konrad Lienert (AUT)
7. Éva Szöllősi/Gábor Vida (AUT)
8. Lidiya Gerasimova/Yuriy Kiselov
9. Carolyn Krau/Rodney Ward (GRB)
10. Eva Neeb/Karl Probst (FRG)
11. Maya Belenkaya/Igor Moskvin (SOV)

12. Susy Holstein/Willy Wahl (SUI)
13. Vera Kuhrüber/Horst Kuhrüber (GDR)
14. Colette Tarozzi/Jean Vives (FRA)

European Ice Dancing Championships:

	CD	FD
1. Pamela Weight/Paul Thomas (GRB)	1	1
2. June Markham/Courtney Jones (GRB)	2	2
3. Barbara Thompson/Gerard Rigby (GRB)	3	3
4. Fanny Besson/Jean Paul Guhel (FRA)	4	4
5. Sigrid Knake/Günther Koch (FRG)	5	5
6. Catharina Odink/Jacobus Odink (NED)	6	6
7. Edith Peikert/Hans Kutschera (AUT)	8	7
8. Lucia Fischer/Rudolf Zorn (AUT)	7	8
9. Gerda Wohlgemuth/Hannes Burkhardt (FRG)	10	10
10. A. Giuggiolini/G. Ceccattini (ITA)	9	9
11. Rita Paucka/Peter Kwiet (FRG)	12	12
12. M-G. Locatelli/V. Toncelli (ITA)	11	13
13. Olga Cilardini/Gianfranco Canepa (ITA)	13	11

Though Russian skaters had participated in the European Figure Skating Championships prior to The Great War, Igor Persiantsev, Lev Mikhailov and Valentin Zakharov and Maya Belenkaya and Igor Moskvin made history as the first skaters to represent the Soviet Union at the event.

Sources: Skating magazine, April 1956; Seventy-five years of European and World's championships in figure skating, International Skating Union, 1970

1957 EUROPEAN FIGURE SKATING CHAMPIONSHIPS
Vienna, Austria, February 14-17, 1957

European Men's Figure Skating Championships:

	CF	FS
1. Alain Giletti (FRA)	1	4
2. Karol Divín (CZE)	3	1
3. Michael Booker (GRB)	2	2
4. Alain Calmat (FRA)	5	3

5. Norbert Felsinger (AUT)	4	8
6. Hans-Jürgen Bäumler (FRG)	7	5
7. Manfred Schnelldorfer (FRG)	8	7
8. Lev Mikhailov (SOV)	10	6
9. Karl Böhringer (AUT)	6	13
10. Hanno Ströher (AUT)	9	15
11. Valentin Zakharov (SOV)	13	9
12. Oleg Simantovskiy (SOV)	12	11
13. Igor Persiantsev (SOV)	11	12
14. Peter Jonas (AUT)	14	10
15. Pavel Fohler (CZE)	15	14
16. Bogusław Hnatyszyn (POL)	16	16

European Ladies Figure Skating Championships:

	CF	FS
1. Hanna Eigel (AUT)	2	5
2. Ingrid Wendl (AUT)	1	6
3. Hanna Walter (AUT)	3	2
4. Dianne Peach (GRB)	4	7
5. Erica Batchelor (GRB)	5	10
6. Ilse Musyl (AUT)	6	13
7. Patricia Pauley (GRB)	7	11
8. Jindra Kramperová (CZE)	10	3
9. Emma Giardini (ITA)	8	14
10. Ina Bauer (FRG)	15	1
11. Eszter Jurek (HUN)	11	9
12. Jitka Hlaváčková (CZE)	12	8
13. Jana Dočekalová (CZE)	17	4
14. Věra Zajíčková (CZE)	13	12
15. Dany Rigoulot (FRA)	16	15
16. Carla Tichatschek (ITA)	14	18
17. Maryvonne Huet (FRA)	9	22
18. Helga Zöllner (HUN)	18	17
19. Anna Galmarini (ITA)	21	16
20. Gitta Hägler (FRG)	19	20
21. Gabriele Weisert (FRG)	22	19
22. Grete Borgen (NOR)	20	21
23. Karin Dehle (NOR)	23	23

24. Bjørg Olsen (NOR) 24 24

European Pairs Skating Championships:

1. Věra Suchánková/Zdeněk Doležal (CZE)
2. Marianna Nagy/László Nagy (HUN)
3. Marika Kilius/Franz Ningel (FRG)
4. Liesl Ellend/Konrad Lienert (AUT)
5. Joyce Coates/Anthony Holles (GRB)
6. Nina Bakusheva/Stanislav Zhuk (SOV)
7. Diana Hinko/Heinz Döpfl (AUT)
8. Eszter Jurek/Miklós Kucharovits (HUN)
9. Hana Dvořáková/Karel Vosátka (CZE)
10. Rita Paucka/Peter Kwiet (FRG)
11. Barbara Jankowska/Zygmunt Kaczmarczyk (POL)
12. Roswitha Mauerhofer/Günther Mauerhofer (GDR)
13. Colette Tarozzi/Jean Vives (FRA)

European Ice Dancing Championships:

	CD	FD
1. June Markham/Courtney Jones (GRB)	1	1
2. Barbara Thompson/Gerard Rigby (GRB)	2	2
3. Kay Morris/Michael Robinson (GRB)	3	4
4. Bona Giammona/Giancarlo Sioli (ITA)	6	3
5. Sigrid Knake/Günther Koch (FRG)	4	5
6. Christiane Elien/Claude Lambert (FRA)	5	7
7. Edith Peikert/Hans Kutschera (AUT)	7	6
8. Adriana Giuggiolini/Germano Ceccattini (ITA)	9	8
9. Lucia Zorn/Rudolf Zorn (AUT)	8	9
10. Karin Weber/Herbert Beyer (FRG)	11	10
11. Rita Paucka/Peter Kwiet (FRG)	10	11
12. Brigitte Gröger/Alois Mitterhuber (AUT)	12	12
13. Christine Paschoud/Charly Pichard (SUI)	13	13
14. Anna Bursche-Lindnerowa/Leon Osadnik (POL)	14	14

A judging system referred to as The Finnish System, named so after its inventor Walter Jakobsson, was tested in the men's, ladies and pairs events. Ordinals were not used in this system. Instead, in each segment of the competition, each skater/team's highest and lowest marks were thrown out and their marks were then added to form a total. As figures were still worth far more than free skating, Ina Bauer of West Germany won the ladies free skate and still finished tenth overall due to a low score in the figures.

Věra Suchánková and Zdeněk Doležal made history as the first Czechoslovakian pair to win a gold medal at the European Figure Skating Championships.

For the first time, footage from the event was broadcast on BBC television, with commentary by Max Robertson.

Sources: Skating magazine, May 1957; BBC Programme Index; Seventy-five years of European and World's championships in figure skating, International Skating Union, 1970

Marika Kilius and Hans-Jürgen Bäumler, European Champions 1959-1964.
Sueddeutsche Zeitung Photo / Alamy Stock Photo.

THE SPACE AGE

1958 EUROPEAN FIGURE SKATING CHAMPIONSHIPS
Bratislava, Czechoslovakia, January 30-February 2, 1958

European Men's Figure Skating Championships:

	CF	FS
1. Karol Divín (CZE)	1	3
2. Alain Giletti (FRA)	2	2
3. Alain Calmat (FRA)	5	1
4. Michael Booker (GRB)	3	4
5. Norbert Felsinger (AUT)	4	8
6. Tilo Gutzeit (FRG)	7	5
7. Manfred Schnelldorfer (FRG)	6	9
8. Hans-Jürgen Bäumler (FRG)	9	6
9. Peter Jonas (AUT)	8	11
10. Lev Mikhailov (SOV)	13	7
11. Valentin Zakharov (SOV)	12	13
12. Karl Böhringer (AUT)	10	14
13. François Pache (SUI)	11	15
14. Pavel Fohler (CZE)	15	12
15. Jaromír Holan (CZE)	17	10
16. Igor Persiantsev (SOV)	14	16
17. Henryk Hanzel (POL)	16	19
18. Wouter Toledo (NED)	18	17
19. Marian Czakon (POL)	19	18

European Ladies Figure Skating Championships:

	CF	FS
1. Ingrid Wendl (AUT)	1	1
2. Hanna Walter (AUT)	2	3
3. Joan Haanappel (NED)	3	6
4. Dianne Peach (GRB)	4	9
5. Jindra Kramperová (CZE)	6	7
6. Sjoukje Dijkstra (NED)	5	10
7. Karin Frohner (AUT)	7	4

8. Regine Heitzer (AUT)	8	5
9. Dany Rigoulot (FRA)	9	13
10. Anna Galmarini (ITA)	10	8
11. Jana Dočekalová (CZE)	16	2
12. Jitka Hlaváčková (CZE)	12	12
13. Julia Golonková (CZE)	15	11
14. Petra Damm (FRG)	13	14
15. Rita Müller (SUI)	11	17
16. Dorle Kirchhofer (FRG)	17	18
17. Nicole Erdos (FRA)	14	15
18. Gabriele Weidert (FRG)	19	21
19. Helga Zöllner (HUN)	18	20
20. Edina Jurek (HUN)	21	16
21. Krystyna Wąsik (POL)	22	22
22. Jeanine Ferir (NED)	23	19
WD. Eszter Jurek (HUN)	20	-
WD. Ina Bauer (FRG)	-	-
WD. Patricia Pauley (GRB)	-	-

European Pairs Skating Championships:

1. Věra Suchánková/Zdeněk Doležal (CZE)
2. Nina Zhuk/Stanislav Zhuk (SOV)
3. Joyce Coates/Anthony Holles (GRB)
4. Marianna Nagy/László Nagy (HUN)
5. Marika Kilius/Hans-Jürgen Bäumler (FRG)
6. Hana Dvořáková/Karel Vosátka (CZE)
7. Barbara Jankowska/Zygmunt Kaczmarczyk (POL)
8. Eszter Jurek/Miklós Kucharovits (HUN)
9. Liesl Ellend/Konrad Lienert (AUT)
10. Ludmila Belousova/Oleg Protopopov (SOV)
11. Roswitha Mauerhofer/Günther Mauerhofer (FRG)
12. Diana Hinko/Heinz Döpfl (AUT)
13. Carolyn Krau/Rodney Ward (GRB)
14. Marie Hezinová/Karel Janouch (CZE)
15. Rita Paucka/Peter Kwiet (FRG)

European Ice Dancing Championships:

	CD	FD
1. June Markham/Courtney Jones (GRB)	1	1
2. Kay Morris/Michael Robinson (GRB)	2	2
3. Barbara Thompson/Gerard Rigby (GRB)	3	4
4. Christiane Guhel/Jean Paul Guhel (FRA)	4	3
5. Lucia Zorn/Rudolf Zorn (AUT)	7	5
6. Catharina Odink/Jacobus Odink (NED)	6	7
7. Annick de Trentinian/Philippe Aumond (FRA)	5	8
8. Edith Peikert/Alois Miterhuber (AUT)	8	6
9. Rita Paucka/Peter Kwiet (FRG)	9	9
10. Helga Michlmayr/Gerald Felsinger (AUT)	10	10
11. Petra Steigerwald/Hannes Burkhardt (FRG)	11	11
12. Aranka Tóth/Endre Tóth (HUN)	12	12
13. Svetlana Smirnova/Leonid Gordon (SOV)	13	13

Karol Divín earned his place in the record books as the first Czechoslovakian man to win a gold medal at the European Figure Skating Championships. Josef Slíva had won a gold medal at the European Championships in Štrbské Pleso in 1930, but the results of that event had been been declared null and void by the International Skating Union.

Sources: Skating World magazine, March 1958; Skating magazine, April 1958; Seventy-five years of European and World's championships in figure skating, International Skating Union, 1970

1959 EUROPEAN FIGURE SKATING CHAMPIONSHIPS
Davos, Switzerland, February 1-8, 1959

European Men's Figure Skating Championships:

	CF	FS
1. Karol Divín (CZE)	1	2
2. Alain Giletti (FRA)	2	3
3. Norbert Felsinger (AUT)	3	4
4. Alain Calmat (FRA)	6	1
5. Manfred Schnelldorfer (FRG)	5	5
6. Tilo Gutzeit (FRG)	4	8

7. Peter Jonas (AUT)	8	9
8. David Clements (GRB)	10	7
9. Hubert Köpfler (SUI)	7	12
10. Lev Mikhailov (SOV)	15	6
11. François Pache (SUI)	9	11
12. Sergio Brosio (ITA)	11	15
13. Bodo Bockenauer (GDR)	13	10
14. Igor Persiantsev (SOV)	12	13
15. Karl Böhringer (AUT)	14	14
16. Henryk Hanzel (POL)	17	18
17. Wouter Toledo (NED)	16	17
18. Jochen Niemann (FRG)	18	16

European Ladies Figure Skating Championships:

	CF	FS1	FS2
1. Hanna Walter (AUT)	1	5	-
2. Sjoukje Dijkstra (NED)	3	2	-
3. Joan Haanappel (NED)	2	7	-
4. Ina Bauer (FRG)	4	1	-
5. Regine Heitzer (AUT)	6	4	-
6. Jindra Kramperová (CZE)	7	6	-
7. Jana Dočekalová (CZE)	8	3	-
8. Dany Rigoulot (FRA)	5	9	-
9. Diana Clifton-Peach (GRB)	9	10	-
10. Liliane Crosa (SUI)	10	11	-
11. Anna Galmarini (ITA)	14	8	-
12. Jitka Hlaváčková (CZE)	11	12	-
13. Carla Tichatschek (ITA)	12	14	-
14. Franziska Schmidt (SUI)	20	13	-
15. Carolyn Krau (GRB)	15	16	-
16. Nicole Hassler (FRA)	13	19	-
17. Bärbel Martin (FRG)	19	15	-
18. Roswitha Sodoma (AUT)	16	18	-
19. Corinne Altmann (FRA)	18	17	-
20. Helga Zöllner (HUN)	17	20	-
21. Ursel Barkey (FRG)	21	-	22
22. Edina Jurek (HUN)	23	-	24
23. Karin Dehle (NOR)	22	-	26

24. Tatiana Nemtsova (SOV) 27 - 21
25. Jeanine Ferir (NED) 26 - 25
26. Éva Csoma (HUN) 24 - 27
27. Irina Lyulyakova (SOV) 28 - 23
28. Krystyna Wąsik (POL) 25 - 28

European Pairs Skating Championships:

1. Marika Kilius/Hans-Jürgen Bäumler (FRG)
2. Nina Zhuk/Stanislav Zhuk (SOV)
3. Joyce Coates/Anthony Holles (GRB)
4. Margret Göbl/Franz Ningel (FRG)
5. Rita Blumenberg/Werner Mensching (FRG)
6. Hana Dvořáková/Karel Vosatka (CZE)
7. Lyudmila Belousova/Oleg Protopopov (SOV)
8. Diana Hinko/Heinz Dopfl (AUT)
9. Barbara Jankowska/Zygmunt Kaczmarczyk (POL)
10. Roswitha Mauerhofer/Günther Mauerhofer (GDR)
11. Gerda Johner/Rüdi Johner (SUI)
12. Eva Romanová/Pavel Roman (CZE)

European Ice Dancing Championships:

	CD	FD
1. Doreen Denny/Courtney Jones (GRB)	1	1
2. Kay Morris/Michael Robinson (GRB)	2	3
3. Christiane Guhel/Jean Paul Guhel (FRA)	3	2
4. Rita Paucka/Peter Kwiet (FRG)	4	7
5. Elly Thal/Hannes Burkhardt (FRG)	6	5
6. Lucia Zorn/Rudolf Zorn (AUT)	5	6
7. Eva Romanová/Pavel Roman (CZE)	8	4
8. Annick de Trentinian/Philippe Aumond (FRA)	9	9
9. Catharina Odink/Jacobus Odink (NED)	7	11
10. Adriana Giuggiolini/Germano Ceccattini (ITA)	10	8
11. Helga Michlmayr/Georg Felsinger (AUT)	11	10
12. Danielle Jaton/Charly Pichard (SUI)	12	13
13. Maria Toncelli/Vinicio Toncelli (ITA)	14	15
14. Ludovica Boccacci/Gianfranco Canepa (ITA)	13	12
15. Elżbieta Zdankiewicz/Emanuel Koczyba (POL)	15	14

For the first time, there were so many entries in the ladies event that the ISU decided to only allow the top 20 skaters to compete in the free skating final. The remaining skaters competed in a 2nd Group to determine their final result.

Sources: Protocol, 1959 European Figure Skating Championships; Skating magazine, April 1959; Seventy-five years of European and World's championships in figure skating, International Skating Union, 1970

1960 EUROPEAN FIGURE SKATING CHAMPIONSHIPS
Garmisch-Partenkirchen, West Germany, February 4-7, 1960

European Men's Figure Skating Championships:

	CF	FS
1. Alain Giletti (FRA)	1	1
2. Norbert Felsinger (AUT)	2	2
3. Manfred Schnelldorfer (FRG)	3	5
4. Alain Calmat (FRA)	4	3
5. Tilo Gutzeit (FRG)	5	4
6. Peter Jonas (AUT)	7	6
7. David Clements (GRB)	6	8
8. Lev Mikhailov (SOV)	10	7
9. Per Kjølberg (NOR)	8	10
10. Robin Jones (GRB)	9	9
11. Hubert Köpfler (SUI)	11	14
12. Heinrich Podhajsky (AUT)	13	11
13. François Pache (SUI)	14	17
14. Pavel Fohler (CZE)	15	16
15. Bodo Bockenauer (GDR)	16	15
16. Henryk Hanzel (POL)	17	12
17. Sergio Brosio (ITA)	12	19
18. Michael Flebbe (GDR)	19	13
19. Valeri Meshkov (SOV)	18	18
20. Raymond Wiklander (SWE)	20	20
WD. Karol Divín (CZE)	-	-

European Ladies Figure Skating Championships:

	CF	FS
1. Sjoukje Dijkstra (NED)	1	1
2. Regine Heitzer (AUT)	3	2
3. Joan Haanappel (NED)	2	7
4. Karin Frohner (AUT)	5	5
5. Jana Mrázková (CZE)	7	3
6. Anna Galmarini (ITA)	9	4
7. Patricia Pauley (GRB)	6	9
8. Jindra Kramperová (CZE)	14	6
9. Anne Reynolds (GRB)	11	10
10. Nicole Hassler (FRA)	8	15
11. Dany Rigoulot (FRA)	10	13
12. Carolyn Krau (GRB)	12	17
13. Jitka Hlaváčková (CZE)	15	12
14. Carla Tichatschek (ITA)	13	16
15. Bärbel Martin (FRG)	18	14
16. Hella Henneis (AUT)	17	18
17. Franziska Schmidt (SUI)	24	8
18. Helga Zöllner (HUN)	20	19
19. Ursel Barkey (FRG)	19	20
20. Liliane Crosa (SUI)	16	25
21. Ann-Margreth Frei (SWE)	25	11
22. Yvette Busieau (BEL)	21	23
23. Edina Jurek (HUN)	23	24
24. Tatiana Nemtsova (SOV)	26	21
25. Karin Dehle (NOR)	22	27
26. Heidemarie Steiner (GDR)	27	22
27. Tamara Bratus (SOV)	28	26
WD. Ina Bauer (FRG)	4	-

European Pairs Skating Championships:

1. Marika Kilius/Hans-Jürgen Bäumler (FRG)
2. Nina Zhuk/Stanislav Zhuk (SOV)
3. Margret Göbl/Franz Ningel (FRG)
4. Ludmila Belousova/Oleg Protopopov (SOV)
5. Hana Dvořáková/Karel Vosátka (CZE)

6. Marie Hezinová/Karel Janouch (CZE)
7. Diana Hinko/Heinz Döpfl (AUT)
8. Margit Senf/Peter Göbel (GDR)
9. Gerda Johner/Rüdi Johner (SUI)
10. Tatiana Zhuk/Aleksandr Gavrilov (SOV)
11. Rita Blumenberg/Werner Mensching (GDR)

European Ice Dancing Championships:

	CD	FD
1. Doreen Denny/Courtney Jones (GRB)	1	1
2. Christiane Guhel/Jean Guhel (FRA)	2	2
3. Mary Parry/Roy Mason (GRB)	3	5
4. Rita Paucka/Peter Kwiet (FRG)	5	3
5. Anne Cross/L. Francis Williams (GRB)	4	7
6. Elly Thal/Hannes Burkhardt (FRG)	6	6
7. Eva Romanová/Pavel Roman (CZE)	7	4
8. Armelle Flichy/Pierre Brun (FRA)	9	8
9. Margot Nissen/Gerhard Maier (FRG)	11	9
10. Olga Gilardi/Germano Ceccattini (ITA)	10	10
11. Annick de Trentinian/Jacques Mer (FRA)	8	13
12. Ludovica Boccacci/Gianfranco Canepa (ITA)	13	12
13. Györgyi Korda/Pál Vásárhelyi (HUN)	12	14
14. Helga Michlmayr/Georg Felsinger (AUT)	16	11
WD. Catharina Odink/Jacobus Odink (NED)	15	-
WD. Elżbieta Zdankiewicz/Emanuel Koczyba (POL)	14	-

Sjoukje Dijkstra made history as the first Dutch skater to win a gold medal at the European Figure Skating Championships.

Television shone a spotlight on controversial judging. When Margret Göbl and Franz Ningel delivered a sensational performance in the pairs event and finished only third, the crowd booed the judges for several minutes. Commentators from eleven different stations independently asserted that Göbl and Ningel deserved to win. The Olympia-Eisstadion was flooded with telegrams, and the volume of angry telephone calls from viewers was so high that it overwhelmed the lines.

Sources: *Skating magazine, April 1960; Triumpf auf dem Eis*, Heinz Maegerlein, 1964; *Seventy-five years of European and World's championships in figure skating*, International Skating Union, 1970

1961 EUROPEAN FIGURE SKATING CHAMPIONSHIPS
West Berlin, West Germany, January 26-29, 1961

European Men's Figure Skating Championships:

	CF	FS
1. Alain Giletti (FRA)	1	1
2. Alain Calmat (FRA)	3	2
3. Manfred Schnelldorfer (FRG)	2	3
4. Peter Jonas (AUT)	4	4
5. Emmerich Danzer (AUT)	5	5
6. Robin Jones (GRB)	6	6
7. Sepp Schönmetzler (FRG)	7	7
8. Bodo Bockenauer (GDR)	11	8
9. Heinrich Podhajsky (AUT)	8	9
10. Per Kjølberg (NOR)	9	11
11. Peter Krick (FRG)	10	10
12. Wouter Toledo (NED)	13	12
13. Michael Flebbe (GDR)	12	13
14. Giordano Abbondati (ITA)	14	14
15. Ragnar Wikström (FIN)	15	15

European Ladies Figure Skating Championships:

	CF	FS
1. Sjoukje Dijkstra (NED)	1	1
2. Regine Heitzer (AUT)	2	5
3. Jana Mrázková (CZE)	5	3
4. Karin Frohner (AUT)	3	9
5. Dany Rigoulot (FRA)	4	11
6. Helli Sengstschmid (AUT)	10	2
7. Eva Grožajová (CZE)	11	6
8. Nicole Hassler (FRA)	6	10
9. Diana Clifton-Peach (GRB)	7	13
10. Jitka Hlaváčková (CZE)	8	12
11. Anne Reynolds (GRB)	9	8

12. Karin Gude (FRG)	12	4
13. Franziska Schmidt (SUI)	13	7
14. Christa von Kuczkowski-Fassi (ITA)	15	17
15. Danièle Giraud (FRA)	16	18
16. Ursula Barkey (FRG)	22	14
17. Éva Csoma (HUN)	19	19
18. Helga Zöllner (HUN)	14	23
19. Dorette Bek (SUI)	18	21
20. Silvana Saccozzi (ITA)	17	22
21. Gaby Seyfert (GDR)	21	15
22. Sandra Brugnera (ITA)	20	20
23. Heidemarie Steiner (GDR)	24	16
24. Willie ten Hoopen (NED)	23	24

European Pairs Skating Championships:

1. Marika Kilius/Hans-Jürgen Bäumler (FRG)
2. Margret Göbl/Franz Ningel (FRG)
3. Margit Senf/Peter Göbel (GDR)
4. Rita Blumenberg/Werner Mensching (FRG)
5. Diana Hinko/Heinz Döpfl (AUT)
6. Hana Dvořáková/Karel Vosátka (CZE)
7. Valerie Hunt/Peter Burrows (GRB)
8. Gerda Johner/Rüdi Johner (SUI)
9. Irene Müller/Hans-Georg Dallmer (GDR)
10. Renate Rößler/Klaus Wasserfuhr (GDR)

European Ice Dancing Championships:

	CD	FD
1. Doreen Denny/Courtney Jones (GRB)	1	1
2. Christiane Guhel/Jean Paul Guhel (FRA)	2	3
3. Linda Shearman/Michael Phillips (GRB)	4	4
4. Mary Parry/Roy Mason (GRB)	3	5
5. Eva Romanová/Pavel Roman (CZE)	5	2
6. Rita Paucka/Peter Kwiet (FRG)	7	6
7. Olga Gilardi/Germano Ceccattini (ITA)	6	7
8. Ludovica Boccacci/Gianfranco Canepa (ITA)	8	10
9. Armelle Flichy/Pierre Brun (FRA)	9	14

10. Jitka Babická/Jaromír Holan (CZE)	11	8
11. Györgyi Korda/Pál Vásárhelyi (HUN)	10	11
12. Christel Trebesiner/Georg Felsinger (AUT)	13	9
13. Margot Nissen/Klaus Ebel (FRG)	12	12
14. Marlyse Fornachon/Charly Pichard (SUI)	14	13
15. M. Schamberger/H-J. Schamberger (FRG)	15	15

Sources: Skating magazine, May 1961; Seventy-five years of European and World's championships in figure skating, International Skating Union, 1970

1962 EUROPEAN FIGURE SKATING CHAMPIONSHIPS
Geneva, Switzerland, February 27-March 3, 1962

European Men's Figure Skating Championships:

	CF	FS
1. Alain Calmat (FRA)	2	1
2. Karol Divín (CZE)	1	3
3. Manfred Schnelldorfer (FRG)	3	4
4. Peter Jonas (AUT)	4	7
5. Emmerich Danzer (AUT)	5	6
6. Bodo Bockenauer (GDR)	8	2
7. Robin Jones (FRG)	7	8
8. Sepp Schönmetzler (FRG)	9	5
9. Per Kjølberg (NOR)	10	9
10. Valeri Meshkov (SOV)	11	10
11. Károly Újlaky (HUN)	6	12
12. Malcolm Cannon (GRB)	14	16
13. Giordano Abbondati (ITA)	18	11
14. Heinrich Podhajsky (AUT)	12	15
15. Ralph Borghard (GDR)	17	14
16. Robert Dureville (FRA)	13	19
17. Fritz Keszler (FRG)	15	17
18. Alain Trouillet (FRA)	16	18
19. Markus Germann (SUI)	20	13
20. Wouter Toledo (NED)	19	20
21. Ragnar Wikström (FIN)	21	21

European Ladies Figure Skating Championships:

	CF	FS
1. Sjoukje Dijkstra (NED)	1	1
2. Regine Heitzer (AUT)	2	3
3. Karin Frohner (AUT)	3	5
4. Helli Sengstschmid (AUT)	6	2
5. Diana Clifton-Peach (GRB)	4	10
6. Nicole Hassler (FRA)	5	9
7. Franziska Schmidt (SUI)	8	6
8. Jana Mrázková (CZE)	9	4
9. Jacqueline Harbord (GRB)	7	8
10. Eva Grožajová (CZE)	10	7
11. Sandra Brugnera (ITA)	14	12
12. Gaby Seyfert (GDR)	16	13
13. Helga Zöllner (HUN)	17	14
14. Karin Dehle (NOR)	13	17
15. Ann-Margreth Frei (SWE)	19	11
16. Danièle Giraud (FRA)	11	18
17. Alena Pokorná (CZE)	15	16
18. Inge Paul (FRG)	12	19
19. Tamara Bratus (SOV)	20	15
20. Christine van de Putte (BEL)	18	20

European Pairs Skating Championships:

	FS1	FS2
1. Marika Kilius/Hans-Jürgen Bäumler (FRG)	2	2
2. Ludmila Belousova/Oleg Protopopov (SOV)	3	1
3. Margret Göbl/Franz Ningel (FRG)	1	3
4. Gerda Johner/Rüdi Johner (SUI)	4	4
5. Irene Müller/Hans-Georg Dallmer (GDR)	5	5
6. Brigitte Wokoeck/Heinz-Ulrich Walther (GDR)	7	6
7. Milada Kubíková/Jaroslav Votruba (CZE)	8	8
8. Diana Hinko/Bernhard Henhappel (AUT)	9	7
9. Rita Blumenberg/Werner Mensching (FRG)	6	9
10. Liv Lunde/Erik Grünert (NOR)	11	10
11. J. Steiner/J-P. Külling (SUI)	10	11
12. Vera Jeffery/Peter Webb (GRB)	12	12

European Ice Dancing Championships:

	CD	FD
1. Christiane Guhel/Jean Paul Guhel (FRA)	1	3
2. Linda Shearman/Michael Phillips (GRB)	2	2
3. Eva Romanová/Pavel Roman (CZE)	4	1
4. Mary Parry/Roy Mason (GRB)	3	4
5. Anne Cross/L. Francis Williams (GRB)	5	6
6. Helga Burkhardt/Hannes Burkhardt (FRG)	7	5
7. Olga Gilardi/Germano Ceccattini (ITA)	6	7
8. Marlyse Fornachon/Charly Pichard (SUI)	9	9
9. Jitka Babická/Jaromír Holan (CZE)	10	8
10. Armelle Flichy/Pierre Brun (FRA)	8	12
11. Gabriele Rauch/Rudi Matysik (FRG)	11	13
12. Györgyi Korda/Pál Vásárhelyi (HUN)	12	10
13. Christel Trebesiner/Georg Felsinger (AUT)	13	11
14. Maria Toncelli/Vinicio Toncelli (ITA)	14	14

Christiane and Jean Paul Guhel made history as the first French ice dance team to win a gold medal at the European Figure Skating Championships.

For the first time, a two-program system was used in the pairs event at the European Championships. As a trial, pairs performed their free program twice on subsequent days and the marks from both programs were added together to give overall ordinals and point totals.

Source: Protocol, 1962 European Figure Skating Championships

1963 EUROPEAN FIGURE SKATING CHAMPIONSHIPS
Budapest, Hungary, February 5-10, 1963

European Men's Figure Skating Championships:

	CF	FS
1. Alain Calmat (FRA)	1	1
2. Manfred Schnelldorfer (FRG)	2	2
3. Emmerich Danzer (AUT)	3	4
4. Peter Jonas (AUT)	4	5

5. Sepp Schönmetzler (FRG)	7	3
6. Ralph Borghard (GDR)	5	7
7. Valeri Meshkov (SOV)	6	6
8. Jenő Ébert (HUN)	9	8
9. Hugo Dümmler (FRG)	8	9
10. Heinrich Podhajsky (AUT)	10	11
11. Robert Dureville (FRA)	11	10
12. Malcolm Cannon (GRB)	13	13
13. Václav Kotek (CZE)	18	12
14. Wouter Toledo (NED)	15	14
15. Giordano Abbondati (ITA)	12	16
16. Philippe Pélissier (FRA)	16	15
17. Markus Germann (SUI)	14	18
18. Hywel Evans (GRB)	17	17
19. Günter Zöller (GDR)	19	20
20. Franciszek Spitol (POL)	20	19
21. Marián Filc (CZE)	21	21

European Ladies Figure Skating Championships:

	CF	FS
1. Sjoukje Dijkstra (NED)	1	1
2. Nicole Hassler (FRA)	3	2
3. Regine Heitzer (AUT)	2	9
4. Jana Mrázková (CZE)	4	3
5. Sally-Anne Stapleford (GRB)	5	11
6. Diana Clifton-Peach (GRB)	6	10
7. Jacqueline Harbord (GRB)	10	5
8. Ingrid Ostler (AUT)	7	7
9. Franziska Schmidt (SUI)	9	6
10. Gaby Seyfert (GDR)	8	4
11. Karin Gude (FRG)	13	12
12. Ann-Margreth Frei (SWE)	17	13
13. Sandra Brugnera (ITA)	14	14
14. Astrid Czermak (AUT)	16	15
15. Hana Mašková (CZE)	20	8
16. Zsuzsa Szentmiklóssy (HUN)	15	18
17. Christine van de Putte (BEL)	12	21
18. Micheline Joubert (FRA)	19	17

19. Dorette Bek (SUI)	18	20
20. Tamara Bratus (SOV)	21	16
21. Elżbieta Kościk (POL)	22	19
WD. Karin Dehle (NOR)	11	-

European Pairs Skating Championships:

	FS1	FS2
1. Marika Kilius/Hans-Jürgen Bäumler (FRG)	1	1
2. Ludmila Belousova/Oleg Protopopov (SOV)	2	2
3. Tatiana Zhuk/Aleksandr Gavrilov (SOV)	3	3
4. Margit Senf/Peter Göbel (GDR)	4	4
5. Milada Kubíková/Jaroslav Votruba (CZE)	5	5
6. Gerda Johner/Rüdi Johner (SUI)	6	7
7. Agnesa Wlachovská/Peter Bartosiewicz (CZE)	7	6
8. Brigitte Wokoeck/Heinz-Ulrich Walther (GDR)	8	10
9. Sonja Pfersdorf/Günther Matzdorf (FRG)	11	9
10. Irene Müller/Hans-Georg Dallmer (GDR)	12	8
11. Sigrid Riechmann/Wolfgang Danne (FRG)	10	11
12. Galina Sedova/Georgi Proskurin (SOV)	9	12
13. Inge Strell/Ferry Dedovich (AUT)	13	13
14. Gerlinde Schönbauer/Willy Bietak (AUT)	14	15
15. Mária Csordás/László Kondi (HUN)	15	14

European Ice Dancing Championships:

	CD	FD
1. Linda Shearman/Michael Phillips (GRB)	1	2
2. Eva Romanová/Pavel Roman (CZE)	2	1
3. Janet Sawbridge/David Hickinbottom (GRB)	3	3
4. Györgyi Korda/Pál Vásárhelyi (HUN)	5	4
5. Mary Parry/Roy Mason (GRB)	4	5
6. Marlyse Fornachon/Charly Pichard (SUI)	6	6
7. Jitka Babická/Jaromír Holan (CZE)	7	7
8. Ghislaine Houdas/Francis Gamichon (FRA)	8	10
9. Helga Burkhardt/Hannes Burkhardt (FRG)	9	8
10. Armelle Flichy/Pierre Brun (FRA)	10	11
11. Christel Trebesiner/Georg Felsinger (AUT)	12	9
12. Rita Paucka/Peter Kwiet (FRG)	11	12
13. Eva Reuter/Bernd Egert (GDR)	13	13

For the final time, the European Figure Skating Championships were held on outdoor ice, at the open-air Kisstadion in Budapest. Weather conditions were very poor and skaters had to contend with snow, sleet, wind and heavy fog. The ice had to be swept between every performance in the pairs event. In his report in "Winter Sports" magazine, sportswriter Howard Bass noted, "Two years ago the International Skating Union ruled that future international championships must be held on mechanically frozen ice. Several ISU delegates expressed the view that, in addition, it should be stipulated that the ice henceforth be covered, not only for the comfort of the spectators and participants, but to ensure equal conditions for all competitors. There are now sufficient suitable indoor rinks in Europe to justify such an amendment, which would induce others desirous of nomination to erect appropriate protection from the elements." The last ISU Championships to be held on outdoor ice were the 1967 World Figure Skating Championships in Vienna.

Sources: Protocol, 1963 European Figure Skating Championships; Winter Sports magazine, March 1963; Skating magazine, April 1963

1964 EUROPEAN FIGURE SKATING CHAMPIONSHIPS
Grenoble, France, January 14-18, 1964

European Men's Figure Skating Championships:

	CF	FS
1. Alain Calmat (FRA)	1	1
2. Manfred Schnelldorfer (FRG)	2	3
3. Karol Divín (CZE)	3	6
4. Emmerich Danzer (AUT)	5	2
5. Peter Jonas (AUT)	4	5
6. Sepp Schönmetzler (FRG)	6	4
7. Wolfgang Schwarz (AUT)	7	7
8. Giordano Abbondati (ITA)	10	8
9. Robert Dureville (FRA)	8	9
10. Hugo Dümmler (FRG)	9	10
11. Philippe Pélissier (FRA)	14	12
12. Jenő Ébert (HUN)	16	11

13. Markus Germann (SUI)	12	13
14. Wouter Toledo (NED)	11	14
15. Hywel Evans (GRB)	13	16
16. Franciszek Spitol (POL)	17	15
WD. Valeri Meshkov (SOV)	15	-

European Ladies Figure Skating Championships:

	CF	FS
1. Sjoukje Dijkstra (NED)	1	1
2. Regine Heitzer (AUT)	2	4
3. Nicole Hassler (FRA)	3	2
4. Sally-Anne Stapleford (GRB)	5	8
5. Helli Sengstschmid (AUT)	8	3
6. Diana Clifton-Peach (GRB)	4	15
7. Inge Paul (FRG)	9	5
8. Carol-Ann Warner (GRB)	6	13
9. Ingrid Ostler (AUT)	7	9
10. Jana Mrázková (CZE)	11	6
11. Zsuzsa Almássy (HUN)	10	7
12. Franziska Schmidt (SUI)	12	10
13. Ann-Margreth Frei (SWE)	15	12
14. Sandra Brugnera (ITA)	16	11
15. Christine van de Putte (BEL)	14	18
16. Monika Zing (SUI)	13	20
17. Alena Augustová (CZE)	19	14
18. Geneviève Burdel (FRA)	20	16
19. Sylvaine Duban (FRA)	18	19
20. Elżbieta Kościk (POL)	21	17
WD. Karin Dehle (NOR)	17	-

European Pairs Skating Championships:

	CCP	FS
1. Marika Kilius/Hans-Jürgen Bäumler (FRG)	1	1
2. Ludmila Belousova/Oleg Protopopov (SOV)	2	2
3. Tatiana Zhuk/Aleksandr Gavrilov (SOV)	3	3
4. Sonja Pfersdorf/Günther Matzdorf (FRG)	5	4
5. Gerda Johner/Rüdi Johner (SUI)	4	5
6. Sigrid Riechmann/Wolfgang Danne (FRG)	6	6

7. Tatiana Sharanova/Aleksandr Gorelik (SOV)	9	8
8. Agnesa Wlachovská/Peter Bartosiewicz (CZE)	7	9
9. Gerlinde Schönbauer/Willy Bietak (AUT)	11	7
10. Mária Csordás/László Kondi (HUN)	10	11
11. Monique Mathys/Yves Ällig (SUI)	13	10
12. Milada Kubíková/Jaroslav Votruba (CZE)	8	12
13. Micheline Joubert/Alain Trouillet (FRA)	12	13

European Ice Dancing Championships:

	CD	FD
1. Eva Romanová/Pavel Roman (CZE)	1	1
2. Janet Sawbridge/David Hickinbottom (GRB)	2	2
3. Yvonne Suddick/Roger Kennerson (GRB)	3	4
4. Györgyi Korda/Pál Vásárhelyi (HUN)	4	3
5. Marjorie McCoy/Ian Phillips (GRB)	5	5
6. Jitka Babická/Jaromír Holan (CZE)	6	6
7. Gabriele Rauch/Rudi Matysik (FRG)	7	8
8. Brigitte Martin/Francis Gamichon (FRA)	8	7
9. Christel Trebesiner/Georg Felsinger (AUT)	10	9
10. Jopie Wolf/Nico Wolf (NED)	11	10
11. Jutta Peters/Wolfgang Kunz (FRG)	12	11
12. Ghislaine Houdas/Pierre Brun (FRA)	9	12
13. Monique Mathys/Yves Ällig (SUI)	13	13

Eva Romanová and Pavel Roman made history as the first Czechoslovakian ice dance team to win a gold medal at the European Figure Skating Championships. Following the two-year trial of a format where pairs performed their free skating twice in subsequent years, a compulsory connected program with required elements was introduced. In an early win for the women's liberation movement, female judges outnumbered the men for the first time in the ladies event. The pioneering members of the first five-female judging panel at the European Championships were Charlotte Benedict-Stieber of The Netherlands, Jeanine Donnier-Blanc of France, Miss E. Braarud of Norway, Mollie Phillips of Great Britain and Mrs. H. Dudová of Czechoslovakia.

Sources: Skating magazine, March 1964; Seventy-five years of European and

World's championships in figure skating, International Skating Union, 1970;
Skating Around the World: International Skating Union, the One Hundredth Anniversary History 1892-1992, Benjamin T. Wright

1965 EUROPEAN FIGURE SKATING CHAMPIONSHIPS
Moscow, Soviet Union, February 11-16, 1965

European Men's Figure Skating Championships:

	CF	FS
1. Emmerich Danzer (AUT)	1	2
2. Alain Calmat (FRA)	2	1
3. Peter Jonas (AUT)	3	4
4. Sepp Schönmetzler (FRG)	4	3
5. Wolfgang Schwarz (AUT)	5	5
6. Robert Dureville (FRA)	6	7
7. Peter Krick (FRG)	8	8
8. Ondrej Nepela (CZE)	10	6
9. Philippe Pélissier (FRA)	9	10
10. Sergei Chetverukhin (SOV)	7	14
11. Giordano Abbondati (ITA)	11	12
12. Günter Zöller (GDR)	12	11
13. Marian Filc (CZE)	13	9
14. Jenő Ébert (HUN)	14	13
15. Hywel Evans (GRB)	15	16
16. Hans-Jürg Studer (SUI)	16	15

European Ladies Figure Skating Championships:

	CF	FS
1. Regine Heitzer (AUT)	1	4
2. Sally-Anne Stapleford (GRB)	2	8
3. Nicole Hassler (FRA)	4	5
4. Helli Sengstschmid (AUT)	5	2
5. Gaby Seyfert (GDR)	6	1
6. Diana Clifton-Peach (GRB)	3	11
7. Hana Mašková (CZE)	10	3
8. Jana Mrázková (CZE)	9	7
9. Astrid Czermak (AUT)	7	9
10. Angelika Wagner (FRG)	8	10

11. Uschi Keszler (FRG)	13	6
12. Zsuzsa Szentmiklóssy (HUN)	11	12
13. Sandra Brugnera (ITA)	12	15
14. Tamara Bratus (SOV)	17	14
15. Pia Zürcher (SUI)	16	16
16. Karin Dehle (NOR)	15	17
17. Britt Elfving (SWE)	19	13
18. Denise Neanne (FRA)	14	18
19. Marianne Bæk (DEN)	18	19
20. Pia Vingisaar (FIN)	20	20

European Pairs Skating Championships:

	CCP	FS
1. Ludmila Belousova/Oleg Protopopov (SOV)	1	1
2. Gerda Johner/Rüdi Johner (SUI)	2	2
3. Tatiana Zhuk/Aleksandr Gorelik (SOV)	3	3
4. Sonja Pfersdorf/Günther Matzdorf (FRG)	4	4
5. Irene Müller/Hans-Georg Dallmer (GDR)	5	5
6. Tatiana Tarasova/Georgi Proskurin (SOV)	7	6
7. Margot Glockshuber/Wolfgang Danne (FRG)	8	7
8. Agnesa Wlachovská/Peter Bartosiewicz (CZE)	6	10
9. Gerlinde Schönbauer/Willy Bietak (AUT)	9	8
10. Mária Csordás/László Kondi (HUN)	12	9
11. Gudrun Hauss/Walter Häfner (FRG)	10	11
12. Monique Mathys/Yves Ällig (SUI)	11	12
13. Věra Stehlíková/Karel Fajfr (CZE)	15	13
14. Ingeborg Strell/Fery Dedovich (AUT)	13	15
15. Renate Rößler/Klaus Wasserfuhr (GDR)	14	14
16. Glenis Parry/John Bayman (GRB)	16	16
17. Anna-Maija Rissanen/Ilka Varhee (FIN)	17	17

European Ice Dancing Championships:

	CD	FD
1. Eva Romanová/Pavel Roman (CZE)	1	1
2. Janet Sawbridge/David Hickinbottom (GRB)	2	4
3. Yvonne Suddick/Roger Kennerson (GRB)	3	2
4. Diane Towler/Bernard Ford (GRB)	4	3
5. Györgyi Korda/Pál Vásárhelyi (HUN)	5	5

6. Gabriele Rauch/Rudi Matysik (FRG)	6	6
7. Jitka Babická/Jaromír Holan (CZE)	7	8
8. Brigitte Martin/Francis Gamichon (FRA)	8	7
9. Jutta Peters/Wolfgang Kunz (FRG)	9	9
10. Christel Trebesiner/Georg Felsinger (AUT)	10	10
11. Annerose Baier/Eberhard Rüger (GDR)	11	11
12. Edit Mató/Károly Csanádi (HUN)	12	13
13. Nadezhda Velle/Aleksandr Treschev (SOV)	14	12
14. Ludmila Kotkova/Václav Kotek (CZE)	13	14
15. Heide Mezger/Herbert Rothkappel (AUT)	15	15

Ludmila Belousova and Oleg Protopopov made history as the first Soviet skaters to win a gold medal at the European Figure Skating Championships.

Sources: Skating magazine, May 1965; Seventy-five years of European and World's championships in figure skating, International Skating Union, 1970

1966 EUROPEAN FIGURE SKATING CHAMPIONSHIPS
Bratislava, Czechoslovakia, February 1-5, 1966

European Men's Figure Skating Championships:

	CF	FS
1. Emmerich Danzer (AUT)	2	1
2. Wolfgang Schwarz (AUT)	1	2
3. Ondrej Nepela (CZE)	3	4
4. Patrick Péra (FRA)	5	5
5. Robert Dureville (FRA)	4	8
6. Ralph Borghard (GDR)	7	3
7. Giordano Abbondati (ITA)	8	7
8. Marian Filc (CZE)	12	6
9. Peter Krick (FRG)	6	14
10. Günter Anderl (AUT)	9	10
11. Valeri Meshkov (SOV)	10	11
12. Sergei Chetverukhin (SOV)	11	12
13. Jenő Ébert (HUN)	14	9
14. Reinhard Ketterer (FRG)	15	13
15. Malcolm Cannon (GRB)	13	18

16. Zdzisław Pieńkowski (POL)	16	16
17. Hans-Jürg Studer (SUI)	18	15
18. Jan Ullmark (SWE)	17	17

European Ladies Figure Skating Championships:

	CF	FS
1. Regine Heitzer (AUT)	1	3
2. Gaby Seyfert (GDR)	4	1
3. Nicole Hassler (FRA)	3	5
4. Hana Mašková (CZE)	7	2
5. Diana Clifton-Peach (GRB)	2	11
6. Zsuzsa Almássy (HUN)	6	4
7. Sally-Anne Stapleford (GRB)	5	15
8. Uschi Keszler (FRG)	10	6
9. Elisabeth Mikula (FRG)	9	8
10. Angelika Wagner (FRG)	8	10
11. Beate Richter (GDR)	13	7
12. Elisabeth Nestler (AUT)	11	9
13. Pia Zürcher (SUI)	14	16
14. Alena Augustová (CZE)	12	19
15. Martina Clausner (GDR)	16	14
16. Micheline Joubert (FRA)	15	18
17. Elena Shcheglova (SOV)	21	12
18. Rita Trapanese (ITA)	19	13
19. Britt Elfving (SWE)	20	17
20. Denise Neanne (FRA)	17	20
21. Sylvia Oundjian (GRB)	18	21
22. Elżbieta Kościk (POL)	22	22
23. Anna-Maija Rissanen (FIN)	23	23

European Pairs Skating Championships:

	CCP	FS
1. Ludmila Belousova/Oleg Protopopov (SOV)	1	1
2. Tatiana Zhuk/Aleksandr Gorelik (SOV)	2	2
3. Margot Glockshuber/Wolfgang Danne (FRG)	3	3
4. Tatiana Tarasova/Georgi Proskurin (SOV)	4	5
5. Irene Müller/Hans-Georg Dallmer (GDR)	5	7
6. Gudrun Hauss/Walter Häfner (FRG)	6	6

7. Sonja Pfersdorf/Günther Matzdorf (FRG)	9	4
8. H. Steiner/H-U. Walther (GDR)	8	8
9. Brigitte Weise/Michael Brychcy (GDR)	12	9
10. Monique Mathys/Yves Ällig (SUI)	10	10
11. Gerlinde Schönbauer/Willy Bietak (AUT)	13	11
12. Mónika Szabó/Péter Szabó (SUI)	14	12
13. Agnesa Wlachovská/Peter Bartosiewicz (CZE)	7	17
14. Mária Csordás/László Kondi (HUN)	11	15
15. Evelyne Schneider/Fery Dedovich (AUT)	15	13
16. Bohunka Šrámková/Jan Šrámek (CZE)	16	14
17. Michele Bargauan/Emanuele Gianoli (ITA)	17	18
18. Janina Poremska/Piotr Szczypa (POL)	18	16
19. Anci Dolenc/Mitja Sketa (YUG)	19	19

European Ice Dancing Championships:

	CD	FD
1. Diane Towler/Bernard Ford (GRB)	1	1
2. Yvonne Suddick/Malcolm Cannon (GRB)	2	2
3. Jitka Babická/Jaromír Holan (CZE)	4	3
4. Brigitte Martin/Francis Gamichon (FRA)	3	5
5. Gabriele Matysik/Rudi Matysik (FRG)	6	4
6. Janet Sawbridge/Jon Lane (GRB)	5	7
7. Lyudmila Pakhomova/Viktor Ryzhkin (SOV)	7	6
8. Edit Mató/Károly Csanádi (HUN)	8	8
9. Annerose Baier/Eberhard Rüger (GDR)	9	9
10. Sylva Draisaitlová/Miroslav Gřešek (CZE)	10	10
11. Heide Mezger/Georg Felsinger (AUT)	11	11
12. C. Trebesiner/H. Rothkappel (AUT)	12	14
13. Angelika Buck/Erich Buck (FRG)	13	13
14. Susanna Carpani/Sergio Pirelli (ITA)	14	12
15. Truusje Geradts/Roland du Burck (NED)	15	15
16. Ilona Berecz/István Sugár (HUN)	16	16

History was made on the technological front at the European Figure Skating Championships. Helmut Strohmayer's report of the event in "Skating World" magazine noted, "Results were issued from the computer centre of the Research Institute of Economics and Organization of Building Industry very promptly - the evaluation of each category was processed by the computer in less than one minute. This was the first time a computer had been used in connection with a sports event in Czechoslovakia. Printed and bound copies of the protocol were available less than fourteen hours after the completion of the competitions."

Sources: Protocol, 1966 European Figure Skating Championships; Skating World magazine, March 1966, Winter Sports magazine, March 1966; Skating magazine, April 1966

1967 EUROPEAN FIGURE SKATING CHAMPIONSHIPS
Ljubljana, Yugoslavia, January 31-February 5, 1967

European Men's Figure Skating Championships:

	CF	FS
1. Emmerich Danzer (AUT)	1	1
2. Wolfgang Schwarz (AUT)	2	2
3. Ondrej Nepela (CZE)	3	3
4. Patrick Péra (FRA)	4	4
5. Sergei Chetverukhin (SOV)	6	5
6. Robert Dureville (FRA)	5	7
7. Günter Zöller (GDR)	7	6
8. Peter Krick (FRG)	8	11
9. Philippe Pélissier (FRA)	10	9
10. Marian Filc (CZE)	11	8
11. Günter Anderl (AUT)	9	14
12. Jenő Ébert (HUN)	12	12
13. Michael Williams (GRB)	16	10
14. Jürgen Eberwein (FRG)	13	13
15. Josef Tůma (CZE)	14	15
16. Zdzisław Pieńkowski (POL)	15	17
17. Daniel Höner (SUI)	17	16
18. Reinhard Mirmseker (GDR)	18	18
19. Tony Berntler (SWE)	19	19
20. Arne Hoffmann (DEN)	20	20

European Ladies Figure Skating Championships:

	CF	FS
1. Gaby Seyfert (GDR)	1	2
2. Hana Mašková (CZE)	2	1
3. Zsuzsa Almássy (HUN)	3	5
4. Sally-Anne Stapleford (GRB)	4	8
5. Trixi Schuba (AUT)	5	4
6. Monika Feldmann (FRG)	6	7
7. Elisabeth Mikula (AUT)	8	12
8. Elena Shcheglova (SOV)	12	3
9. Petra Ruhrmann (FRG)	10	9
10. Beate Richter (GDR)	11	6
11. Zsuzsa Szentmiklóssy (HUN)	9	13
12. Sylvaine Duban (FRA)	7	19
13. Linda Teresa Davis (GRB)	13	15
14. Martina Clausner (GDR)	14	14
15. Rita Trapanese (ITA)	15	16
16. Marie Víchová (CZE)	19	10
17. Micheline Joubert (FRA)	16	17
18. Eva Gašparcová (CZE)	20	11
19. Britt Elfving (SWE)	18	18
20. Pia Zürcher (SUI)	17	20
21. Barbara Warmińska (POL)	22	22
22. Jette Vad (DEN)	21	24
23. Katjuša Derenda (YUG)	23	23
24. Elena Mois (ROM)	24	21

European Pairs Skating Championships:

	CCP	FS
1. Ludmila Belousova/Oleg Protopopov (SOV)	1	1
2. Margot Glockshuber/Wolfgang Danne (FRG)	2	2
3. H. Steiner/H-U. Walther (GDR)	3	4
4. Gudrun Hauss/Walter Häfner (FRG)	4	3
5. Tatiana Sharanova/Anatoli Yevdokimov (SOV)	6	5
6. Tamara Moskvina/Alexei Mishin (SOV)	5	6
7. Brigitte Weise/Michael Brychcy (GDR)	8	7
8. Janina Poremska/Piotr Szczypa (POL)	7	8
9. Bohunka Šrámková/Jan Šrámek (CZE)	9	9

10. Monique Mathys/Yves Ällig (SUI)	10	11
11. Marianne Streifler/Herbert Wiesinger (FRG)	13	10
12. Irene Müller/Hans-Georg Dallmer (GDR)	12	12
13. Evelyne Schneider/Willy Bietak (AUT)	15	13
14. Mónika Szabó/Péter Szabó (SUI)	11	14
15. Linda Bernard/Raymond Wilson (GRB)	14	16
16. Anci Dolenc/Mitja Sketa (YUG)	16	15
17. Anikken Støa/Erik Grünert (NOR)	17	17

European Ice Dancing Championships:

	CD	FD
1. Diane Towler/Bernard Ford (GRB)	1	1
2. Yvonne Suddick/Malcolm Cannon (GRB)	2	2
3. Brigitte Martin/Francis Gamichon (FRA)	4	3
4. Janet Sawbridge/Jon Lane (GRB)	3	4
5. Gabriele Matysik/Rudi Matysik (FRG)	5	7
6. Jitka Babická/Jaromír Holan (CZE)	6	6
7. Annerose Baier/Eberhard Rüger (GDR)	7	8
8. Irina Grishkova/Viktor Ryzhkin (SOV)	9	5
9. Edit Mató/Károly Csanádi (HUN)	8	9
10. Lyudmila Pakhomova/Aleksandr Gorshkov (SOV)	10	10
11. Dana Novotná/Jaroslav Hainz (CZE)	11	11
12. Milena Tůmová/Josef Pešek (CZE)	13	13
13. Heide Mezger/Herbert Rothkappel (AUT)	12	16
14. Susanna Carpani/Sergio Pirelli (ITA)	14	14
15. Ilona Berecz/István Sugár (HUN)	15	12
16. Norma Allwelt/Michael Schmidt (GDR)	17	17
17. Truusje Geradts/Roland du Burck (NED)	16	15
18. Angelika Trojahn/Joachim Metz (FRG)	18	18

Gaby Seyfert became the first East German skater to win a gold medal at the European Figure Skating Championships. Diane Towler and Bernard Ford earned the first perfect 6.0's awarded in the ice dance event at the European Championships.

Sources: Protocol, 1967 European Figure Skating Championships; Winter Sports magazine, March 1967; Skating magazine, April 1967

1968 EUROPEAN FIGURE SKATING CHAMPIONSHIPS
Västerås, Sweden, January 23-27, 1968

European Men's Figure Skating Championships:

	CF	FS
1. Emmerich Danzer (AUT)	1	1
2. Wolfgang Schwarz (AUT)	2	2
3. Ondrej Nepela (CZE)	4	3
4. Patrick Péra (FRA)	3	7
5. Sergei Chetverukhin (SOV)	5	6
6. Peter Krick (FRG)	6	8
7. Marián Filc (CZE)	10	4
8. Günter Zöller (GDR)	7	10
9. Philippe Pélissier (FRA)	11	5
10. Vladimir Kurenbin (SOV)	8	11
11. Giordano Abbondati (ITA)	9	13
12. Sergei Volkov (SOV)	12	9
13. Michael Williams (GRB)	14	12
14. Jürgen Eberwein (FRG)	16	14
15. Günter Anderl (AUT)	13	17
16. Jacques Mrozek (FRA)	15	15
17. Zdzisław Pieńkowski (POL)	19	18
18. Zoltán Horváth (HUN)	17	21
19. Daniel Höner (SUI)	18	20
20. Thomas Callerud (SWE)	20	19
21. Jan Hoffmann (GDR)	22	16
22. Arnoud Hendriks (NED)	21	23
23. Erik Skjold (NOR)	24	22
24. Arne Hoffmann (DEN)	23	24

European Ladies Figure Skating Championships:

	CF	FS
1. Hana Mašková (CZE)	1	2
2. Gaby Seyfert (GDR)	3	1
3. Trixi Schuba (AUT)	2	6
4. Zsuzsa Almássy (HUN)	5	3
5. Sally-Anne Stapleford (GRB)	4	13
6. Elena Shcheglova (SOV)	9	4

7. Elisabeth Nestler (AUT)	8	8
8. Monika Feldmann (FRG)	6	12
9. Patricia Dodd (GRB)	7	17
10. Petra Ruhrmann (FRG)	10	11
11. Elisabeth Mikula (AUT)	11	10
12. Galina Grzhibovskaya (SOV)	17	5
13. Marie Víchová (CZE)	12	7
14. Martina Clausner (GDR)	14	9
15. Charlotte Walter (SUI)	15	14
16. Frances Waghorn (GRB)	13	18
17. Sonja Morgenstern (GDR)	19	15
18. Rita Trapanese (ITA)	18	19
19. Sylvaine Duban (FRA)	16	20
20. Anneke Heijdt (NED)	20	23
21. Elena Mois (ROM)	24	16
22. Tone Øien (NOR)	23	22
23. Eva Hermansson (SWE)	22	21
24. Jette Vad (DEN)	21	24
25. Dunja Vujčić (YUG)	25	25

European Pairs Skating Championships:

	CCP	FS
1. Ludmila Belousova/Oleg Protopopov (SOV)	1	1
2. Tamara Moskvina/Alexei Mishin (SOV)	6	2
3. H. Steiner/H-U. Walther (GDR)	2	3
4. Margot Glockshuber/Wolfgang Danne (FRG)	5	4
5. Irina Rodnina/Alexei Ulanov (SOV)	3	5
6. Gudrun Hauss/Walter Häfner (FRG)	4	6
7. Irene Müller/Hans-Georg Dallmer (GDR)	7	7
8. Liana Drahová/Peter Bartosiewicz (CZE)	8	8
9. Marianne Streifler/Herbert Wiesinger (FRG)	10	9
10. Brigitte Weise/Michael Brychcy (GDR)	9	11
11. Bohunka Šrámková/Jan Šrámek (CZE)	12	10
12. Evelyne Schneider/Willy Bietak (AUT)	15	12
13. Linda Bernard/Raymond Wilson (GRB)	14	13
14. Mónika Szabó/Péter Szabó (SUI)	13	14
15. Janina Poremska/Piotr Szczypa (POL)	11	15
16. Edith Sperl/Heinz Wirz (SUI)	17	17

17. Barbka Senk/Mitja Sketa (YUG)	20	16
18. F. Etlensperger/J.-R. Racle (FRA)	18	18
19. Grażyna Osmańska/Adam Brodecki (POL)	16	20
20. Bjerke Magnussen/Erik Grünert (NOR)	19	19

European Ice Dancing Championships:

	CD	FD
1. Diane Towler/Bernard Ford (GRB)	1	1
2. Yvonne Suddick/Malcolm Cannon (GRB)	2	2
3. Janet Sawbridge/Jon Lane (GRB)	3	3
4. Irina Grishkova/Viktor Ryzhkin (SOV)	4	5
5. Lyudmila Pakhomova/Aleksandr Gorshkov (SOV)	5	4
6. Angelika Buck/Erich Buck (FRG)	6	6
7. Annerose Baier/Eberhard Rüger (GDR)	7	7
8. Edit Mató/Károly Csanádi (HUN)	8	9
9. Milena Tůmová/Josef Pešek (CZE)	9	8
10. Dana Novotná/Jaromír Holan (CZE)	11	10
11. Susanna Carpani/Sergio Pirelli (ITA)	10	11
12. Ilona Berecz/István Sugár (HUN)	12	13
13. Claude Couste/Jean-Pierre Noullet (FRA)	14	12
14. Pascale Aynes/Pascal Germe (FRA)	13	16
15. Steffi Böhme/Bernd Egert (GDR)	15	15
16. Teresa Weyna/Piotr Bojańczyk (POL)	16	14
17. Edeltraud Rotty/Joachim Iglowstein (FRG)	17	17

Source: 100th Anniversary 1892-1992 - International Skating Union: Results 1968-1991 Figure Skating Championships, Elemér Terták, Benjamin T. Wright, Deut Häsler, 1992, courtesy World Figure Skating Museum & Hall of Fame

1969 EUROPEAN FIGURE SKATING CHAMPIONSHIPS
Garmisch-Partenkirchen, West Germany, February 4-8, 1969

European Men's Figure Skating Championships:

	CF	FS
1. Ondrej Nepela (CZE)	1	1
2. Patrick Péra (FRA)	2	2
3. Sergei Chetverukhin (SOV)	3	3

4. Günter Zöller (GDR)	4	6
5. Philippe Pélissier (FRA)	6	8
6. Haig Oundjian (GRB)	7	5
7. Sergei Volkov (SOV)	5	9
8. Marián Filc (CZE)	8	7
9. Yuri Ovchinnikov (SOV)	11	4
10. Jacques Mrozek (FRA)	10	11
11. Günter Anderl (AUT)	9	10
12. Reinhard Ketterer (FRG)	12	12
13. Klaus Grimmelt (FRG)	14	13
14. Josef Schneider (AUT)	13	17
15. Daniel Höner (SUI)	15	16
16. Jan Hoffmann (GDR)	19	14
17. Zdzisław Pieńkowski (POL)	18	18
18. Petr Starec (CZE)	17	19
19. Zoltán Horváth (HUN)	21	15
20. Thomas Callerud (SWE)	16	21
21. Arnoud Hendriks (NED)	20	22
22. György Fazekas (ROM)	22	23
23. Ragnar Wikström (FIN)	23	20

European Ladies Figure Skating Championships:

	CF	FS
1. Gaby Seyfert (GDR)	2	1
2. Hana Mašková (CZE)	3	2
3. Trixi Schuba (AUT)	1	7
4. Zsuzsa Almássy (AUT)	4	3
5. Elisabeth Nestler (AUT)	5	5
6. Elena Shcheglova (SOV)	7	4
7. Elisabeth Mikula (AUT)	8	9
8. Rita Trapanese (ITA)	11	6
9. Patricia Dodd (GRB)	6	16
10. Eileen Zillmer (FRG)	9	15
11. Charlotte Walter (SUI)	10	14
12. Sonja Morgenstern (GDR)	13	8
13. Ľudmila Bezáková (CZE)	14	10
14. Galina Grzhibovskaya (SOV)	17	11
15. Eleonora Barická (CZE)	16	12

16. Renate Zehnpfennig (FRG)	15	19
17. Frances Waghorn (GRB)	12	20
18. Christine Errath (GDR)	22	13
19. Zsófia Wagner (HUN)	20	17
20. Britt Elfving (SWE)	19	18
21. Zsuzsa Homolya (HUN)	18	22
22. Mirosława Nowak (POL)	21	21
23. Elena Mois (ROM)	23	23

European Pairs Skating Championships:

	SP	FS
1. Irina Rodnina/Alexei Ulanov (SOV)	2	1
2. Ludmila Belousova/Oleg Protopopov (SOV)	1	2
3. Tamara Moskvina/Alexei Mishin (SOV)	3	3
4. H. Steiner/H-U. Walther (GDR)	4	4
5. Gudrun Hauss/Walter Häfner (FRG)	5	5
6. Marianne Streifler/Herbert Wiesinger (FRG)	6	6
7. Manuela Groß/Uwe Kagelmann (GDR)	9	7
8. Janina Poremska/Piotr Szczypa (POL)	7	8
9. Mona Szabo/Pierre Szabo (FRA)	8	9
10. Evelyne Schneider/Willy Bietak (AUT)	10	10
11. Linda Bernard/Raymond Wilson (GRB)	11	11
12. Dana Fialová/Josef Tůma (CZE)	12	12

European Ice Dancing Championships:

	C/OSP	FD
1. Diane Towler/Bernard Ford (GRB)	1	1
2. Janet Sawbridge/Jon Lane (GRB)	2	3
3. Lyudmila Pakhomova/Aleksandr Gorshkov (SOV)	3	2
4. Angelika Buck/Erich Buck (FRG)	4	4
5. Annerose Baier/Eberhard Rüger (GDR)	5	5
6. Susan Getty/Roy Bradshaw (GRB)	6	6
7. Dana Holanová/Jaromír Holan (CZE)	7	7
8. Ilona Berecz/István Sugár (HUN)	8	9
9. Milena Tůmová/Josef Pešek (CZE)	9	8
10. Tatiana Zoitiuk/Viacheslav Zhigalin (SOV)	10	11
11. Elena Zharkova/Gennadi Karponosov (SOV)	11	10
12. Edit Mató/Károly Csanádi (HUN)	12	12

13. Edeltraud Rotty/Joachim Iglowstein (FRG)   13   13
14. E. Vachon/J-P. Noullet (FRA)   14   14
15. Teresa Weyna/Piotr Bojańczyk (POL)   15   15
16. Elfriede Rupp/Walter Leschetizky (AUT)   16   16
17. Christiane Dällenbach/Léo Barblan (SUI)   17   17

Lyudmila Pakhomova and Aleksandr Gorshkov made history as the first Soviet couple to win a medal in ice dancing at the European Figure Skating Championships. The pairs compulsory connected program was rebranded as the short program and the OSP (original set pattern dance) was added to the ice dance competition.

Source: 100th Anniversary 1892-1992 - International Skating Union: Results 1968-1991 Figure Skating Championships, Elemér Terták, Benjamin T. Wright, Beat Häsler, 1992, courtesy World Figure Skating Museum & Hall of Fame

John Curry, European Champion 1976. PA Images / Alamy Stock Photo.

THE DECADE OF DISCO

1970 EUROPEAN FIGURE SKATING CHAMPIONSHIPS
Leningrad, Soviet Union, February 4-8, 1970

European Men's Figure Skating Championships:

	CF	FS
1. Ondrej Nepela (CZE)	1	1
2. Patrick Péra (FRA)	2	5
3. Günter Zöller (GDR)	3	6
4. Sergei Chetverukhin (SOV)	4	3
5. Sergei Volkov (SOV)	5	7
6. Haig Oundjian (GRB)	8	4
7. Yuri Ovchinnikov (SOV)	11	2
8. Günter Anderl (AUT)	6	13
9. Jan Hoffmann (GDR)	10	9
10. Daniel Höner (SUI)	7	14
11. Jacques Mrozek (FRA)	9	11
12. John Curry (GRB)	14	10
13. Ralf Richter (GDR)	16	8
14. Klaus Grimmelt (FRG)	12	12
15. Zdeněk Pazdírek (CZE)	13	16
16. Jozef Žídek (CZE)	17	15
17. László Vajda (HUN)	19	17
18. Stefano Bargauan (ITA)	15	19
19. Didier Gailhaguet (FRA)	18	18
20. Thomas Callerud (SWE)	20	20
21. Piotr Roszko (POL)	21	21
22. György Fazekas (ROM)	22	23
23. Zoran Matas (YUG)	23	22

European Ladies Figure Skating Championships:

	CF	FS
1. Gaby Seyfert (GDR)	2	1
2. Trixi Schuba (AUT)	1	5
3. Zsuzsa Almássy (HUN)	3	2

4. Rita Trapanese (ITA)	6	3
5. Elisabeth Nestler (AUT)	5	7
6. Patricia Dodd (GRB)	4	9
7. Yelena Aleksandrova (SOV)	8	6
8. Ľudmila Bezáková (CZE)	9	8
9. Sonja Morgenstern (GDR)	13	4
10. Eileen Zillmer (FRG)	7	14
11. Charlotte Walter (SUI)	10	17
12. Alla Korneva (SOV)	12	12
13. Frances Waghorn (GRB)	11	16
14. Liana Drahová (CZE)	16	11
15. Simone Gräfe (GDR)	20	10
16. Cinzia Frosio (ITA)	15	15
17. Lia Does (NED)	17	18
18. Marion von Cetto (FRG)	14	19
19. Zsófia Wagner (HUN)	21	17
20. Mirosława Nowak (POL)	19	22
21. Anita Johansson (SWE)	22	21
22. Beatrice Huştiu (ROM)	23	20
WD. Joëlle Cartaux (FRA)	18	-

European Pairs Skating Championships:

	SP	FS
1. Irina Rodnina/Alexei Ulanov (SOV)	1	1
2. Lyudmila Smirnova/Andrei Suraikin (SOV)	2	2
3. H. Walther/H-U. Walther (GDR)	3	3
4. Galina Karelina/Georgiy Proskurin (SOV)	4	4
5. Almut Lehmann/Herbert Wiesinger (FRG)	5	5
6. Annette Kansy/Axel Salzmann (GDR)	6	6
7. Manuela Groß/Uwe Kagelmann (GDR)	7	7
8. Brunhilde Baßler/Eberhard Rausch (FRG)	8	8
9. Janina Poremska/Piotr Szczypa (POL)	9	9
10. Dana Fialová/Josef Tůma (CZE)	10	10
11. Mona Szabo/Pierre Szabo (FRA)	11	11
12. Grażyna Osmańska/Adam Brodecki (POL)	12	12
13. Evelyne Schneider/Willy Bietak (AUT)	13	13
14. Karin Künzle/Christian Künzle (SUI)	14	14
15. Éva Farkas/Tamas Korpás (HUN)	15	15

European Ice Dancing Championships:

	C/OSP	FD
1. Lyudmila Pakhomova/Aleksandr Gorshkov (SOV)	1	1
2. Angelika Buck/Erich Buck (FRG)	2	2
3. Tatiana Zoitiuk/Viacheslav Zhigalin (SOV)	5	3
4. Annerose Baier/Eberhard Rüger (GDR)	4	4
5. Susan Getty/Roy Bradshaw (GRB)	3	5
6. Elena Zharkova/Gennadi Karponosov (SOV)	6	6
7. Hilary Green/Glyn Watts (GRB)	7	7
8. Ilona Berecz/István Sugár (HUN)	8	8
9. Teresa Weyna/Piotr Bojańczyk (POL)	10	9
10. Elisabeth Bugiel/Michel Bouttier (FRA)	9	11
11. Matilde Ciccia/Lamberto Ceserani (ITA)	11	10
12. Astrid Kopp/Axel Kopp (FRA)	12	12
13. Krisztina Regőczy/András Sallay (HUN)	13	13
14. Světlana Marinovová/Miloš Buršík (CZE)	14	14
15. Eva Sklenská/Jan Gřešek (CZE)	15	15
16. Tatiana Grossen/Alessandro Grossen (SUI)	16	16

Lyudmila Pakhomova and Aleksandr Gorshkov made history as the first Soviet ice dance team to win a gold medal at the European Figure Skating Championships.

Source: 100th Anniversary 1892-1992 - International Skating Union: Results 1968-1991 Figure Skating Championships, Elemér Terták, Benjamin T. Wright, Beat Häsler, 1992, courtesy World Figure Skating Museum & Hall of Fame

1971 EUROPEAN FIGURE SKATING CHAMPIONSHIPS
Zürich, Switzerland, February 2-7, 1971

European Men's Figure Skating Championships:

	CF	FS
1. Ondrej Nepela (CZE)	1	2
2. Sergei Chetverukhin (SOV)	2	4
3. Haig Oundjian (GRB)	6	1
4. Jan Hoffmann (GDR)	4	5
5. Yuri Ovchinnikov (SOV)	7	3

6. Sergei Volkov (SOV)	3	10
7. John Curry (GRB)	11	6
8. Günter Anderl (AUT)	5	12
9. Jacques Mrozek (FRA)	8	7
10. Didier Gailhaguet (FRA)	9	8
11. Daniel Höner (SUI)	10	13
12. Jozef Žídek (CZE)	12	9
13. Klaus Grimmelt (FRG)	16	11
14. Josef Schneider (AUT)	14	14
15. László Vajda (HUN)	17	15
16. Stefano Bargauan (ITA)	13	16
17. Thomas Callerud (SWE)	20	17
18. György Fazekas (ROM)	18	18
19. Pekka Leskinen (FIN)	21	19
20. Bernard Bauer (SUI)	19	20
21. Zoran Matas (YUG)	22	21
22. Zdeněk Pazdírek (CZE)	15	22

European Ladies Figure Skating Championships:

	CF	FS
1. Trixi Schuba (AUT)	1	5
2. Zsuzsa Almássy (HUN)	3	2
3. Rita Trapanese (ITA)	2	4
4. Sonja Morgenstern (GDR)	8	1
5. Charlotte Walter (SUI)	5	8
6. Patricia Dodd (GRB)	4	10
7. Christine Errath (GDR)	10	3
8. Yelena Aleksandrova (SOV)	9	6
9. Eileen Zillmer (FRG)	6	13
10. Ľudmila Bezáková (CZE)	7	12
11. Jean Scott (GRB)	11	7
12. Marina Titova (SOV)	12	9
13. Judith Bayer (FRG)	14	11
14. Liana Drahová (CZE)	13	15
15. Anita Johansson (SWE)	15	16
16. Cinzia Frosio (ITA)	16	17
17. Beatrice Huştiu (ROM)	20	14
18. Sonja Balun (AUT)	17	18

19. Dianne de Leeuw (NED)	18	19
20. Marie-Claude Bierre (FRA)	19	20
21. Kirsten Frikke (DEN)	21	22
22. Helena Gazvoda (YUG)	22	21

European Pairs Skating Championships:

	SP	FS
1. Irina Rodnina/Alexei Ulanov (SOV)	1	1
2. Lyudmila Smirnova/Andrei Suraikin (SOV)	2	2
3. Galina Karelina/Georgiy Proskurin (SOV)	3	3
4. Manuela Groß/Uwe Kagelmann (GDR)	4	4
5. Almut Lehmann/Herbert Wiesinger (FRG)	5	6
6. Marlies Radunsky/Rolf Österreich (GDR)	6	5
7. Brunhilde Baßler/Eberhard Rausch (FRG)	7	7
8. Grażyna Osmańska/Adam Brodecki (POL)	8	8
9. Linda Connolly/Colin Taylforth (FRA)	10	9
10. Florence Cahn/Jean-Roland Racle (FRA)	11	10
11. Dana Fialová/Josef Tůma (CZE)	9	11
12. Karin Künzle/Christian Künzle (SUI)	12	12
13. Teresa Skrzek/Piotr Szczypa (POL)	13	13
14. Evelyne Schneider/Willy Bietak (AUT)	14	14
15. Helena Gazvoda/Silvio Švajger (YUG)	15	15

European Ice Dancing Championships:

	C/OSP	FD
1. Lyudmila Pakhomova/Aleksandr Gorshkov (SOV)	1	1
2. Angelika Buck/Erich Buck (FRG)	2	2
3. Susan Getty/Roy Bradshaw (GRB)	3	3
4. Tatiana Zoitiuk/Viacheslav Zhigalin (SOV)	4	4
5. Janet Sawbridge/Peter Dalby (GRB)	5	5
6. Elena Zharkova/Gennadi Karpono3sov (SOV)	6	6
7. Hilary Green/Glyn Watts (GRB)	7	7
8. Diana Skotnická/Martin Skotnický (CZE)	8	8
9. Teresa Weyna/Piotr Bojańczyk (POL)	9	9
10. Ilona Berecz/István Sugár (HUN)	10	10
11. Anne-Claude Wolfers/Roland Mars (FRA)	11	12
12. Matilde Ciccia/Lamberto Ceserani (ITA)	12	11
13. Astrid Kopp/Axel Kopp (FRA)	13	13

14. Krisztina Regőczy/András Sallay (HUN)	14	14
15. Tatiana Grossen/Alessandro Grossen (SUI)	15	16
16. Sylvia Fuchs/Michael Fuchs (FRG)	16	17
17. Ewa Kołodziej/Tadeusz Góra (POL)	17	15
18. Brigitte Ydrault/Pascal Germe (FRA)	18	19
19. Agnes Arco/Adrian Perco (AUT)	19	18
20. Vivi Poulsen/Kurt Poulsen (DEN)	20	20

Source: 100th Anniversary 1892-1992 - International Skating Union: Results 1968-1991 Figure Skating Championships, Elemér Terták, Benjamin T. Wright, Beat Häsler, 1992, courtesy World Figure Skating Museum & Hall of Fame

1972 EUROPEAN FIGURE SKATING CHAMPIONSHIPS
Göteborg, Sweden, February 6-11, 1972

European Men's Figure Skating Championships:

	CF	FS
1. Ondrej Nepela (CZE)	1	1
2. Sergei Chetverukhin (SOV)	2	3
3. Patrick Péra (FRA)	3	7
4. Haig Oundjian (GRB)	6	4
5. John Curry (GRB)	5	5
6. Vladimir Kovalev (SOV)	4	6
7. Yuri Ovchinnikov (SOV)	7	2
8. Didier Gailhaguet (FRA)	9	8
9. Daniel Höner (SUI)	8	11
10. Zdeněk Pazdírek (CZE)	10	9
11. Bernd Wunderlich (GDR)	14	10
12. Josef Schneider (AUT)	11	12
13. Stefano Bargauan (ITA)	12	13
14. László Vajda (HUN)	13	14
15. Harald Kuhn (FRG)	15	15
16. Günther Hilgarth (AUT)	18	16
17. Gordon Andison (GRB)	16	17
18. György Fazekas (ROM)	17	19
19. Pekka Leskinen (FIN)	19	18
20. Peter Augustovič (CZE)	20	22

21. Thomas Öberg (SWE)	22	20
22. Zoran Matas (YUG)	21	21
23. John Ferdinandsen (DEN)	23	23
WD. Günter Zöller (GDR)	-	-

European Ladies Figure Skating Championships:

	CF	FS
1. Trixi Schuba (AUT)	1	5
2. Rita Trapanese (ITA)	3	3
3. Sonja Morgenstern (GDR)	6	1
4. Zsuzsa Almássy (HUN)	4	4
5. Christine Errath (GDR)	7	2
6. Charlotte Walter (SUI)	2	15
7. Jean Scott (GRB)	5	9
8. Maria McLean (GRB)	8	7
9. Dianne de Leeuw (NED)	10	6
10. Yelena Aleksandrova (SOV)	9	12
11. Isabel de Navarre (FRG)	11	11
12. Liana Drahová (CZE)	16	8
13. Gerti Schanderl (FRG)	18	10
14. Anita Johansson (SWE)	14	13
15. Karin Iten (SUI)	12	14
16. Cinzia Frosio (ITA)	13	17
17. Sonja Balun (AUT)	17	18
18. Urszula Zielińska (POL)	15	21
19. Hana Knapová (CZE)	20	20
20. Marie-Claude Bierre (FRA)	23	16
21. Steffi Knoll (GDR)	21	23
22. Iris Ebenwaldner (AUT)	22	22
23. Marina Sanaya (SOV)	28	19
24. Donna Walter (SUI)	19	25
25. Helena Gazvoda (YUG)	27	24
26. Manuela Bertelè (ITA)	24	26
27. Liv Egelund (NOR)	26	27
28. Kirsten Frikke (DEN)	25	28

European Pairs Skating Championships:

	SP	FS

1. Irina Rodnina/Alexei Ulanov (SOV)	1	1
2. Lyudmila Smirnova/Andrei Suraikin (SOV)	2	2
3. Manuela Groß/Uwe Kagelmann (GDR)	3	3
4. Almut Lehmann/Herbert Wiesinger (FRG)	4	4
5. Annette Kansy/Axel Salzmann (GDR)	6	5
6. Irina Chernyaeva/Vasili Blagov (SOV)	5	6
7. Marlies Radunsky/Rolf Österreich (GDR)	8	7
8. Grażyna Osmańska/Adam Brodecki (POL)	7	8
9. Corinna Halke/Eberhard Rausch (FRG)	9	9
10. Linda Connolly/Colin Taylforth (GRB)	10	10
11. Florence Cahn/Jean-Roland Racle (FRA)	11	11
12. Teresa Skrzek/Piotr Szczypa (POL)	12	12
13. Gabriele Cieplik/Reinhard Ketterer (FRG)	14	13
14. Karin Künzle/Christian Künzle (SUI)	13	14
15. Ursula Nemec/Michael Nemec (AUT)	15	15
16. Pascale Kovelmann/Jean-Pierre Rondel (FRA)	16	16
17. Miroslava Sáblíková/Pavel Komárek (CZE)	18	17
18. Jayne Torvill/Michael Hutchinson (GRB) 17	18	

European Ice Dancing Championships:

	C/OSP	FD
1. Angelika Buck/Erich Buck (FRG)	1	1
2. Lyudmila Pakhomova/Aleksandr Gorshkov (SOV)	2	2
3. Janet Sawbridge/Peter Dalby (GRB)	3	3
4. Hilary Green/Glyn Watts (SOV)	4	4
5. Tatiana Zoitiuk/Viacheslav Zhigalin (SOV)	5	5
6. Elena Zharkova/Gennadi Karponosov (RUS)	6	6
7. Diana Skotnická/Martin Skotnický (CZE)	7	7
8. Rosalind Druce/David Barker (GRB)	8	8
9. Teresa Weyna/Piotr Bojańczyk (POL)	9	9
10. Anne-Claude Wolfers/Roland Mars (FRA)	10	10
11. Krisztina Regőczy/András Sallay (HUN)	11	11
12. Matilde Ciccia/Lamberto Ceserani (ITA)	12	12
13. Sylvia Fuchs/Michael Fuchs (FRG)	13	13
14. Ewa Kołodziej/Tadeusz Góra (POL)	15	14
15. Brigitte Scheijbal/Walter Leschetizky (AUT)	14	15
16. Silvia Bodmer/Beat Steib (SUI)	16	16
17. Astrid Kopp/Axel Kopp (FRG)	17	17

18. Světlana Marinovová/Miloš Buršík (CZE)   18   18
19. Vivi Poulsen/Kurt Poulsen (DEN)   19   19

Angelika and Erich Buck made history as the first and only West German ice dance team to win a gold medal at the European Figure Skating Championships.

Source: 100th Anniversary 1892-1992 - International Skating Union: Results 1968-1991 Figure Skating Championships, Elemér Terták, Benjamin T. Wright, Beat Häsler, 1992, courtesy World Figure Skating Museum & Hall of Fame

1973 EUROPEAN FIGURE SKATING CHAMPIONSHIPS
Cologne, West Germany, February 6-11, 1973

European Men's Figure Skating Championships:

	CF	S/F
1. Ondrej Nepela (CZE)	1	4
2. Sergei Chetverukhin (SOV)	4	2
3. Jan Hoffmann (GDR)	3	3
4. John Curry (GRB)	5	5
5. Sergei Volkov (SOV)	2	8
6. Yuri Ovchinnikov (SOV)	10	1
7. László Vajda (HUN)	8	6
8. Jacques Mrozek (FRA)	7	7
9. Daniel Höner (SUI)	6	11
10. Zdeněk Pazdírek (CZE)	9	9
11. František Pechar (CZE)	12	10
12. Erich Reifschneider (FRG)	13	12
13. Günther Hilgarth (AUT)	14	13
14. Michael Fish (GRB)	11	15
15. Robin Cousins (GRB)	18	14
16. Jacek Tascher (POL)	16	16
17. Rolando Bragaglia (ITA)	15	17
18. György Fazekas (ROM)	17	18
19. Rob Ouwerkerk (NED)	19	19
20. Silvo Švejger (YUG)	20	20

European Ladies Figure Skating Championships:

	CF	S/F
1. Christine Errath (GDR)	4	1
2. Jean Scott (GRB)	2	5
3. Karin Iten (SUI)	1	8
4. Liana Drahová (CZE)	6	2
5. Gerti Schanderl (FRG)	9	3
6. Dianne de Leeuw (NED)	5	6
7. Maria McLean (GRB)	3	7
8. Anett Pötzsch (GDR)	12	4
9. Cinzia Frosio (ITA)	7	9
10. Sonja Balun (AUT)	10	11
11. Marina Sanaya (SOV)	16	10
12. Marie-Claude Bierre (FRA)	14	14
13. Susanne Altura (AUT)	13	16
14. Tatiana Oleneva (SOV)	15	13
15. Lise-Lotte Öberg (SWE)	17	15
16. Helena Gazvoda (YUG)	20	12
17. Manuela Bertelè (ITA)	11	19
18. Tarja Näsi (FIN)	23	17
19. Sophie Verlaan (NED)	19	20
20. Urszula Zielińska (POL)	18	21
21. Ágnes Erős (HUN)	21	18
22. Hanne Jensen (DEN)	22	22
WD. Donna Walter (SUI)	8	-

European Pairs Skating Championships:

	SP	FS
1. Irina Rodnina/Aleksandr Zaitsev (SOV)	1	1
2. Lyudmila Smirnova/Alexei Ulanov (SOV)	2	2
3. Almut Lehmann/Herbert Wiesinger (FRG)	3	3
4. Manuela Groß/Uwe Kagelmann (GDR)	5	4
5. Irina Chernyaeva/Vasili Blagov (SOV)	4	6
6. Romy Kermer/Rolf Österreich (GDR)	6	5
7. Karin Künzle/Christian Künzle (SUI)	10	7
8. Florence Cahn/Jean-Roland Racle (FRA)	7	11

9. Ursula Nemec/Michael Nemec (AUT)	8	9
10. Teresa Skrzek/Piotr Szczypa (POL)	9	10
11. Corinna Halke/Eberhard Rausch (FRG)	11	8
12. Ilona Urbanová/Aleš Zach (CZE)	12	12

European Ice Dancing Championships:

	C/OSP	FD
1. Lyudmila Pakhomova/Aleksandr Gorshkov (SOV)	1	1
2. Angelika Buck/Erich Buck (FRG)	2	2
3. Hilary Green/Glyn Watts (GRB)	3	3
4. Janet Sawbridge/Peter Dalby (GRB)	4	4
5. Tatiana Zoitiuk/Viacheslav Zhigalin (SOV)	5	5
6. Diana Skotnická/Martin Skotnický (CZE)	6	7
7. Irina Moiseeva/Andrei Minenkov (RUS)	7	6
8. Matilde Ciccia/Lamberto Ceserani (ITA)	8	8
9. Rosalind Druce/David Barker (GRB)	9	10
10. Krisztina Regőczy/András Sallay (HUN)	10	9
11. Anne-Claude Wolfers/Roland Mars (FRA)	11	12
12. Teresa Weyna/Piotr Bojańczyk (POL)	12	11
13. Sylvia Fuchs/Michael Fuchs (FRG)	13	13
14. Astrid Kopp/Axel Kopp (FRG)	15	15
15. Ewa Kołodziej/Tadeusz Góra (POL)	14	14
16. Gerda Bühler/Mathis Bächi (SUI)	16	16
17. Claude Couste/Eric Couste (FRA)	17	17

For the first time, short programs were skated in the singles events at the European Championships. As in the ice dance event, where the scores of the compulsories and original short program were grouped, the singles short program and free skating placements were combined in 1973. The winners of the short programs were Sergei Chetverukhin (SOV) and Christine Errath (GDR).

Irina Rodnina and Aleksandr Zaitsev set a new record for most perfect 6.0's (12) at the European Championships.

Sources: Bieler Tagblatt, February 10, 1973; Soviet Sport, February 10, 1973 (Issue #35); 100th Anniversary 1892-1992 - International Skating Union: Results 1968-1991 Figure Skating Championships, Elemér Terták,

Benjamin T. Wright, Beat Häsler, 1992, courtesy World Figure Skating Museum & Hall of Fame

1974 EUROPEAN FIGURE SKATING CHAMPIONSHIPS
Zagreb, Yugoslavia, January 29-February 3, 1974

European Men's Figure Skating Championships:

	CF	SP	FS
1. Jan Hoffmann (GDR)	2	1	1
2. Sergei Volkov (SOV)	1	5	6
3. John Curry (GRB)	4	4	2
4. Vladimir Kovalev (SOV)	3	3	5
5. Yuri Ovchinnikov (SOV)	8	2	3
6. László Vajda (HUN)	8	2	3
7. Didier Gailhaguet (FRA)	5	8	8
8. Zdeněk Pazdírek (CZE)	6	6	9
9. Bernd Wunderlich (GDR)	9	10	11
10. František Pechar (CZE)	10	7	10
11. Robin Cousins (GRB)	16	12	7
12. Erich Reifschneider (FRG)	12	11	13
13. Michael Glaubitz (GDR)	11	13	12
14. Ronald Koppelent (AUT)	14	15	12
15. Rolando Bragaglia (ITA)	13	14	17
16. Glyn Jones (GRB)	23	16	15
17. Pascal Delorme (FRA)	17	17	16
18. Thomas Öberg (SWE)	18	18	18
19. Pekka Leskinen (FIN)	15	24	19
20. Rob Ouwerkerk (NED)	20	19	20
21. Jacek Żylski (POL)	22	21	21
22. Silvo Švejger (YUG)	24	22	22
WD. György Fazekas (ROM)	19	20	-
WD. Paul Cechmanek (LUX)	21	23	-

European Ladies Figure Skating Championships:

	CF	SP	FS
1. Christine Errath (GDR)	4	1	1
2. Dianne de Leeuw (NED)	5	2	2
3. Liana Drahová (CZE)	2	7	4

4. Gerti Schanderl (FRG)	11	4	3
5. Karin Iten (SUI)	1	9	11
6. Maria McLean (GRB)	3	10	8
7. Anett Pötzsch (GDR)	6	6	7
8. Isabel de Navarre (FRG)	8	5	6
9. Marion Weber (GDR)	13	3	5
10. Sonja Balun (AUT)	9	8	9
11. Cinzia Frosio (ITA)	7	13	14
12. Hana Knapová (CZE)	16	12	12
13. Susanne Altura (AUT)	20	11	10
14. Marie-Claude Bierre (FRA)	12	16	17
15. Gail Keddie (GRB)	10	18	19
16. Lise-Lotte Öberg (SWE)	14	14	20
17. Helena Gazvoda (YUG)	23	22	13
18. Zdenka Fiurasková (CZE)	22	15	15
19. Sophie Verlaan (NED)	21	21	18
20. Evelyne Reusser (SUI)	19	19	22
21. Marina Sanaya (SOV)	26	23	16
22. Manuela Bertelè (ITA)	15	17	26
23. Petra Wagner (FRG)	18	28	23
24. Grażyna Dudek (POL)	24	20	21
25. Cathy Brunner (SUI)	17	24	28
26. Susan Broman (FIN)	28	25	24
27. Ágnes Erős (HUN)	25	26	25
28. Bente Tverran (NOR)	27	27	27

European Pairs Skating Championships:

	SP	FS
1. Irina Rodnina/Aleksandr Zaitsev (SOV)	1	1
2. Romy Kermer/Rolf Österreich (GDR)	3	2
3. Lyudmila Smirnova/Alexei Ulanov (SOV)	2	4
4. Manuela Groß/Uwe Kagelmann (GDR)	4	3
5. Nadezhda Gorshkova/Evgeni Shevalovski (SOV)	5	5
6. Karin Künzle/Christian Künzle (SUI)	6	6
7. Corinna Halke/Eberhard Rausch (FRG)	7	7
8. Ursula Nemec/Michael Nemec (AUT)	8	8
9. Katja Schubert/Knut Schubert (GDR)	10	9
10. Grażyna Kostrzewińska/Adam Brodecki (POL)	9	10

11. Teresa Skrzek/Piotr Sczypa (POL)	11	11
12. Florence Cahn/Jean-Roland Racle (FRA)	14	12
13. Rijana Hartmannová/Petr Starec (CZE)	13	13
14. Pascale Kovelmann/Jean-Pierre Rondel (FRA)	12	15
15. Linda McCafferty/Colin Taylforth (GRB)	15	14
16. Petra Schneider/Bogdan Pulcer (FRG)	16	16
17. Andrea Meier/Roland Meier (SUI)	17	17

European Ice Dancing Championships:

	C/OSP	FD
1. Lyudmila Pakhomova/Alexander Gorshkov (SOV)	1	1
2. Hilary Green/Glyn Watts (GRB)	2	2
3. Natalia Linichuk/Gennadi Karponosov (SOV)	3	3
4. Janet Sawbridge/Peter Dalby (GRB)	4	4
5. Irina Moiseeva/Andrei Minenkov (SOV)	5	5
6. Matilde Ciccia/Lamberto Ceserani (ITA)	6	6
7. Krisztina Regőczy/András Sallay (HUN)	7	7
8. Janet Thompson/Warren Maxwell (GRB)	8	8
9. Teresa Weyna/Piotr Bojańczyk (POL)	9	9
10. Diana Skotnická/Martin Skotnický (CZE)	10	10
11. Gerda Bühler/Mathis Bachi (SUI)	11	11
12. Sylvia Fuchs/Michael Fuchs (FRG)	12	12
13. Isabella Rizzi/Luigi Freroni (ITA)	13	13
14. Eva Peštová/Jiří Pokorný (CZE)	14	14
15. Brigitte Scheijbal/Walter Leschetizky (AUT)	15	15
16. Andrea Dohany/György Lenart (HUN)	16	16
17. Nicole Rinsant/Dirk Beyer (FRG)	17	17

Jan Hoffmann made history as the first East German man to win a gold medal at the European Figure Skating Championships. Paul Cechmanek was the first skater from Luxembourg to participate in the event.

Source: 100th Anniversary 1892-1992 - International Skating Union: Results 1968-1991 Figure Skating Championships, Elemér Terták, Benjamin T. Wright, Beat Häsler, 1992, courtesy World Figure Skating Museum & Hall of Fame

1975 EUROPEAN FIGURE SKATING CHAMPIONSHIPS
Copenhagen, Denmark, January 28-February 2, 1975

European Men's Figure Skating Championships:

	CF	SP	FS
1. Vladimir Kovalev (SOV)	2	1	1
2. John Curry (GRB)	3	3	3
3. Yuri Ovchinnikov (SOV)	7	2	2
4. Sergei Volkov (SOV)	1	4	6
5. László Vajda (HUN)	4	6	4
6. Zdeněk Pazdírek (CZE)	5	10	9
7. Bernd Wunderlich (GDR)	8	5	7
8. Hermann Schulz (GDR)	14	9	5
9. Didier Gailhaguet (FRA)	6	12	16
10. Ronald Koppelent (AUT)	9	7	11
11. Robin Cousins (GRB)	11	8	10
12. Pekka Leskinen (FIN)	10	13	8
13. Erich Reifschneider (FRG)	12	11	14
14. Miroslav Šoška (CZE)	13	15	12
15. Jacek Tascher (POL)	16	14	13
16. Jean-Christophe Simond (FRA)	18	16	15
17. Glyn Jones (GRB)	17	17	17
18. Thomas Öberg (SWE)	15	18	18
19. Paul Cechmanek (LUX)	20	19	19
20. Flemming Søderquist (DEN)	21	20	20
21. Rob Ouwerkerk (NED)	19	21	21

European Ladies Figure Skating Championships:

	CF	SP	FS
1. Christine Errath (GDR)	4	1	1
2. Dianne de Leeuw (NED)	2	2	2
3. Anett Pötzsch (GDR)	5	5	3
4. Liana Drahová (CZE)	6	4	5
5. Isabel de Navarre (FRG)	3	14	7
6. Susanna Driano (ITA)	8	3	6
7. Marion Weber (GDR)	7	7	4
8. Dagmar Lurz (FRG)	11	8	9
9. Evi Köpfli (SUI)	9	9	11

10. Karin Iten (SUI)	1	21	20
11. Gerti Schanderl (FRG)	13	6	12
12. Sonja Balun (AUT)	10	12	13
13. Hana Knapová (CZE)	12	11	10
14. Liudmila Bakonina (SOV)	19	10	8
15. Michelle Haider (SUI)	14	13	14
16. Grażyna Dudek (POL)	15	15	17
17. Marie-Claude Bierre (FRA)	20	16	15
18. Yvonne Kavanagh (GRB)	17	18	16
19. Gail Keddie (GRB)	16	19	19
20. Sophie Verlaan (NED)	21	17	18
21. Lise-Lotte Öberg (SWE)	18	22	22
22. Anne-Marie Verlaan (NED)	22	20	23
23. Sonja Stanek (AUT)	23	23	24
24. Susan Broman (FIN)	24	24	21
25. Helena Gazvoda (YUG)	25	25	25
26. Bente Larsen (NOR)	27	26	26
27. Carinne Henrotte (BEL)	26	27	27

European Pairs Skating Championships:

	SP	FS
1. Irina Rodnina/Aleksandr Zaitsev (SOV)	1	1
2. Romy Kermer/Rolf Österreich (GDR)	2	2
3. Manuela Groß/Uwe Kagelmann (GDR)	3	4
4. Marina Leonidova/Vladimir Bogolyubov (SOV)	5	3
5. Karin Künzle/Christian Künzle (SUI)	4	5
6. Nadezhda Gorshkova/Evgeni Shevalovski (SOV)	6	6
7. Kerstin Stolfig/Veit Kempe (GDR)	7	7
8. Corinna Halke/Eberhard Rausch (FRG)	8	8
9. Grażyna Kostrzewińska/Adam Brodecki (POL)	9	9
10. Ursula Nemec/Michael Nemec (AUT)	11	10
11. Teresa Skrzek/Piotr Sczypa (POL)	10	11
12. Ingrid Spieglová/Alan Spiegl (CZE)	12	12
13. Petra Schneider/Bogdan Pulcer (FRG)	13	13
WD. Gabriele Arco/Nikolaus Stephan (AUT)	14	-

European Ice Dancing Championships:

	C/OSP	FD
1. Lyudmila Pakhomova/Aleksandr Gorshkov (SOV)	1	1
2. Hilary Green/Glyn Watts (GRB)	2	3
3. Natalia Linichuk/Gennadi Karponosov (SOV)	3	4
4. Irina Moiseeva/Andrei Minenkov (SOV)	4	2
5. Matilde Ciccia/Lamberto Ceserani (ITA)	5	6
6. Krisztina Regőczy/András Sallay (HUN)	7	5
7. Janet Thompson/Warren Maxwell (GRB)	6	7
8. Teresa Weyna/Piotr Bojańczyk (POL)	8	8
9. Kay Barsdell/Kenneth Foster (GRB)	9	10
10. Eva Peštová/Jiří Pokorný (CZE)	10	9
11. Christina Henke/Udo Dönsdorf (FRG)	11	11
12. Stefania Bertele/Walter Cecconi (ITA)	12	12
13. Ewa Kołodziej/Tadeusz Góra (POL)	13	13
14. Isabella Rizzi/Luigi Freroni (ITA)	14	14
15. Gerda Bühler/Maxime Erlanger (SUI)	15	15
16. Susi Handschmann/Peter Handschmann (AUT)	16	16

Vladimir Kovalev made history as the first Soviet skater to win a gold medal in the men's event at the European Figure Skating Championships.

Source: 100th Anniversary 1892-1992 - International Skating Union: Results 1968-1991 Figure Skating Championships, Elemér Terták, Benjamin T. Wright, Beat Häsler, 1992, courtesy World Figure Skating Museum & Hall of Fame

1976 EUROPEAN FIGURE SKATING CHAMPIONSHIPS
Geneva, Switzerland, January 13-18, 1976

European Men's Figure Skating Championships:

	CF	SP	FS
1. John Curry (GRB)	3	3	1
2. Vladimir Kovalev (SOV)	1	1	4
3. Jan Hoffmann (GDR)	4	2	2
4. Yuri Ovchinnikov (SOV)	7	6	3
5. Sergei Volkov (SOV)	2	4	6

6. Robin Cousins (GRB)	13	7	5
7. Zdeněk Pazdírek (CZE)	6	8	7
8. László Vajda (HUN)	5	5	8
9. Pekka Leskinen (FIN)	8	9	9
10. Ronald Koppelent (AUT)	10	10	10
11. Mario Liebers (GDR)	12	14	11
12. Miroslav Šoška (CZE)	9	13	12
13. Jean-Christophe Simond (FRA)	11	12	13
14. Glyn Jones (GRB)	16	11	14
15. Grzegorz Głowania (POL)	19	16	15
16. Gilles Beyer (FRA)	15	15	16
17. Gerd-Walter Gräbner (FRG)	17	17	18
18. Gerhard Hubmann (AUT)	14	19	22
19. Rolando Bragaglia (ITA)	18	21	19
20. Paul Cechmanek (LUX)	21	18	17
21. Martin Sochor (SUI)	20	20	20
22. Matjaž Krušec (YUG)	23	22	21
23. Flemming Søderquist (DEN)	22	23	23

European Ladies Figure Skating Championships:

	CF	SP	FS
1. Dianne de Leeuw (HOL)	2	1	1
2. Anett Pötzsch (GDR)	3	3	2
3. Christine Errath (GDR)	4	2	3
4. Isabel de Navarre (FRG)	1	5	8
5. Susanna Driano (ITA)	6	4	4
6. Dagmar Lurz (FRG)	7	8	6
7. Danielle Rieder (SUI)	9	6	7
8. Elena Vodorezova (SOV)	16	7	5
9. Gerti Schanderl (FRG)	8	10	10
10. Karena Richardson (GRB)	15	9	11
11. Grażyna Dudek (POL)	12	12	9
12. Hana Knapová (CZE)	11	11	14
13. Claudia Kristofics-Binder (AUT)	13	13	12
14. Lotta Crispin (SWE)	20	14	13
15. Evi Köpfli (SUI)	10	16	17
16. Marie-Claude Bierre (FRA)	14	15	16
17. Niina Kyottinen (FIN)	22	18	15

18. Anne-Marie Verlaan (HOL)	18	17	18
19. Katja Seretti (ITA)	17	21	19
20. Sophie Verlaan (HOL)	19	23	20
21. Maja Župančić (YUG)	21	19	22
22. Bente Larsen (NOR)	23	20	21
WD. Marion Weber (GDR)	5	-	-

European Pairs Skating Championships:

	SP	FS
1. Irina Rodnina/Aleksandr Zaitsev (SOV)	1	1
2. Romy Kermer/Rolf Österreich (GDR)	2	2
3. Irina Vorobieva/Aleksandr Vlasov (SOV)	3	3
4. Manuela Groß/Uwe Kagelmann (GDR)	4	4
5. Karin Künzle/Christian Künzle (SUI)	5	5
6. Kerstin Stolfig/Veit Kempe (GDR)	7	6
7. Marina Leonidova/Vladimir Bogolyubov (SOV)	6	7
8. Corinna Halke/Eberhard Rausch (FRG)	8	8
9. Ursula Nemec/Michael Nemec (AUT)	9	9
10. Gabriele Beck/Jochen Stahl (FRG)	12	10
11. Erika Taylforth/Colin Taylforth (GRB)	10	12
12. Ingrid Spieglová/Alan Spiegl (CZE)	13	11
13. Gabriele Arco/Nikolaus Stephan (AUT)	11	13

European Ice Dancing Championships:

	C/OSP	FD
1. Lyudmila Pakhomova/Aleksandr Gorshkov (SOV)	1	1
2. Irina Moiseeva/Andrei Minenkov (SOV)	2	2
3. Natalia Linichuk/Gennadi Karponosov (SOV)	3	3
4. Krisztina Regőczy/András Sallay (HUN)	5	4
5. Hilary Green/Glyn Watts (GRB)	4	5
6. Matilde Ciccia/Lamberto Ceserani (ITA)	7	7
7. Teresa Weyna/Piotr Bojańczyk (POL)	8	8
8. Janet Thompson/Warren Maxwell (GRB)	6	6
9. Eva Peštová/Jiří Pokorný (CZE)	9	9
10. Kay Barsdell/Kenneth Foster (GRB)	10	10
11. Susi Handschmann/Peter Handschmann (SUI)	11	11
12. Stefania Bertele/Walter Cecconi (ITA)	12	12
13. Marie-Joelle Michel/Frédéric Gardin (FRA)	13	13

14. Isabella Rizzi/Luigi Freroni (ITA)	15	14
15. Ewa Kołodziej/Tadeusz Góra (POL)	14	15
16. Christina Henke/Udo Dönsdorf (FRG)	16	16
17. Gerda Bühler/Maxime Erlanger (SUI)	17	17

In their final trip to the European Figure Skating Championships, Lyudmila Pakhomova and Aleksandr Gorshkov set a record for the most ice dance titles won at the event (6).

In an era of notorious bloc judging, Czechoslovakian judge Jozef Lojkovič disobeyed instructions to place Vladimir Kovalev first, giving his deciding vote in the men's event to John Curry. Lojkovič was denied judging opportunities in major events for a decade because he broke ranks.

Sources: Le nouvelliste, January 14, 16 and 17, 1976; The Guardian, June 30, 1976; The Globe and Mail, Beverley Smith, December 14, 2004; 100th Anniversary 1892-1992 - International Skating Union: Results 1968-1991 Figure Skating Championships, Elemér Terták, Benjamin T. Wright, Beat Häsler, 1992, courtesy World Figure Skating Museum & Hall of Fame

1977 EUROPEAN FIGURE SKATING CHAMPIONSHIPS
Helsinki, Finland, January 25-29, 1977

European Men's Figure Skating Championships:

	CF	SP	FS
1. Jan Hoffmann (GDR)	2	1	1
2. Vladimir Kovalev (SOV)	1	3	3
3. Robin Cousins (GRB)	7	2	2
4. Yuri Ovchinnikov (SOV)	4	4	4
5. Pekka Leskinen (FIN)	3	5	7
6. Konstantin Kokora (SOV)	6	7	5
7. Ronald Koppelent (AUT)	9	6	6
8. Mario Liebers (GDR)	5	9	8
9. Miroslav Šoška (CZE)	8	8	9
10. Kurt Kürzinger (FRG)	11	11	11
11. Gerhard Hubmann (AUT)	12	15	10
12. Grzegorz Głowania (POL)	16	10	12

13. Glyn Jones (GRB)	14	14	13
14. Thomas Öberg (SWE)	13	12	14
15. Matjaž Krušec (YUG)	15	13	15
WD. Christophe Boyadjian (FRA)	10	16	-

European Ladies Figure Skating Championships:

	CF	SP	FS
1. Anett Pötzsch (GDR)	1	1	1
2. Dagmar Lurz (FRG)	2	4	5
3. Susanna Driano (ITA)	3	2	4
4. Marion Weber (GDR)	4	8	6
5. Elena Vodorezova (SOV)	9	4	3
6. Denise Biellmann (SUI)	15	3	2
7. Kristiina Wegelius (FIN)	8	7	7
8. Claudia Kristofics-Binder (AUT)	5	9	9
9. Karin Enke (GDR)	7	6	13
10. Danielle Rieder (SUI)	6	19	11
11. Zhanna Ilina (SOV)	19	11	8
12. Debbie Cottrill (GDR)	14	14	14
13. Karena Richardson (GRB)	17	12	10
14. Gerti Schanderl (FRG)	10	10	15
15. Grażyna Dudek (POL)	12	13	17
16. Sanda Dubravčić (YUG)	21	16	12
17. Eva Ďurišinová (CZE)	11	17	19
18. Franca Bianconi (ITA)	18	15	18
19. Lotta Crispin (SWE)	22	20	16
20. Anne-Marie Verlaan (NED)	16	18	21
21. Doina Mitricica (ROM)	23	24	20
22. Anne-Sophie de Kristoffy (FRA)	20	21	22
23. Katja Seretti (ITA)	13	22	24
24. Bente Larsen (NOR)	24	23	23
25. Gloria Mas (ESP)	25	25	25

European Pairs Skating Championships:

	SP	FS
1. Irina Rodnina/Aleksandr Zaitsev (SOV)	1	1
2. Irina Vorobieva/Aleksandr Vlasov (SOV)	2	2
3. Marina Cherkasova/Sergei Shakhrai (SOV)	3	3

4. Manuela Mager/Uwe Bewersdorf (GDR)	4	4
5. Sabine Baeß/Tassilo Thierbach (GDR)	5	6
6. Ingrid Spieglová/Alan Spiegl (CZE)	6	5
7. Elżbieta Łuczyńska/Marek Chrolenko (POL)	7	7
8. Susanne Scheibe/Andreas Nischwitz (FRG)	8	8
9. Sabine Fuchs/Xavier Videau (FRA)	9	9
10. Gabriele Beck/Jochen Stahl (FRG)	11	10
11. Chantal Zürcher/Paul Huber (SUI)	10	11

European Ice Dancing Championships:

	C/OSP	FD
1. Irina Moiseeva/Andrei Minenkov (SOV)	1	1
2. Krisztina Regőczy/András Sallay (HUN)	2	2
3. Natalia Linichuk/Gennadi Karponosov (SOV)	3	3
4. Janet Thompson/Warren Maxwell (GRB)	4	4
5. Marina Zoueva/Andrei Vitman (SOV)	5	5
6. Kay Barsdell/Kenneth Foster (GRB)	6	7
7. Liliana Řeháková/Stanislav Drastich (CZE)	7	6
8. Susi Handschmann/Peter Handschmann (SUI)	8	8
9. Isabella Rizzi/Luigi Freroni (ITA)	9	9
10. Halina Gordon-Półtorak/Tadeusz Góra (POL)	10	10
11. Anna Pisánská/Jiří Musil (CZE)	11	11
12. Stefania Bertele/Walter Cecconi (ITA)	12	12
13. Elżbieta Wegrzyk/Andrzej Alberciak (POL)	14	14
14. Muriel Boucher/Yves Malatier (FRA)	13	13

Gloria Mas made history as the first skater to represent Spain at the European Figure Skating Championships.

Source: The Globe and Mail, Beverley Smith, December 14, 2004; 100th Anniversary 1892-1992 - International Skating Union: Results 1968-1991 Figure Skating Championships, Elemér Terták, Benjamin T. Wright, Beat Häsler, 1992, courtesy World Figure Skating Museum & Hall of Fame

1978 EUROPEAN FIGURE SKATING CHAMPIONSHIPS
Strasbourg, France, January 31-February 5, 1978

European Men's Figure Skating Championships:

	CF	SP	FS
1. Jan Hoffmann (GDR)	2	2	2
2. Vladimir Kovalev (SOV)	1	4	4
3. Robin Cousins (GRB)	5	1	1
4. Igor Bobrin (SOV)	3	3	5
5. Yuri Ovchinnikov (SOV)	7	6	3
6. Mario Liebers (GDR)	4	5	6
7. Rudi Cerne (FRG)	10	8	7
8. Miroslav Šoška (CZE)	9	7	9
9. Gerd-Walter Gräbner (FRG)	6	9	12
10. Gilles Beyer (FRA)	14	11	8
11. Grzegorz Głowania (POL)	12	10	10
12. Andrew Bestwick (GRB)	13	12	11
13. Thomas Öberg (SWE)	11	13	13
14. Bruno Watschinger (AUT)	15	16	14
15. Matjaž Krušec (YUG)	18	15	15
16. Francis Demarteau (BEL)	16	14	16
17. Jan Glerup (DEN)	17	17	17
WD. Helmut Kristofics-Binder (AUT)	8	-	-

European Ladies Figure Skating Championships:

	CF	SP	FS
1. Anett Pötzsch (GDR)	1	6	2
2. Dagmar Lurz (FRG)	2	4	3
3. Elena Vodorezova (SOV)	8	1	4
4. Denise Biellmann (SUI)	12	3	1
5. Susanna Driano (ITA)	4	2	6
6. Kristiina Wegelius (FIN)	5	9	5
7. Carola Weißenberg (GDR)	10	5	7
8. Danielle Rieder (SUI)	6	8	13
9. Natalia Strelkova (SOV)	14	7	9
10. Karena Richardson (GRB)	11	13	10
11. Renata Baierová (CZE)	22	10	9
12. Karin Riediger (FRG)	15	12	12

13. Zhanna Iljina (SOV)	17	17	11
14. Garnet Ostermeier (FRG)	7	11	17
15. Susan Broman (FIN)	9	16	15
16. Sanda Dubravčić (YUG)	19	14	14
17. Astrid Jansen in de Wal (HOL)	21	18	16
18. Franca Bianconi (ITA)	18	19	19
19. Cécile Antonelli (FRA)	13	21	21
20. Christina Svensson (SWE)	24	20	18
21. Helena Chwila (POL)	23	22	20
22. Patricia Fiorucci (ITA)	20	23	22
WD. Anne-Sophie de Kristoffy (FRA)	16	15	-
WD. Claudia Kristofics-Binder (AUT)	3	-	-

European Pairs Skating Championships:

	SP	FS
1. Irina Rodnina/Aleksandr Zaitsev (SOV)	1	1
2. Marina Cherkasova/Sergei Shakhrai (SOV)	4	2
3. Manuela Mager/Uwe Bewersdorf (GDR)	2	3
4. Sabine Baeß/Tassilo Thierbach (GDR)	3	4
5. Ingrid Spieglová/Alan Spiegl (CZE)	5	5
6. Kerstin Stolfig/Veit Kempe (GDR)	6	6
7. Marina Pestova/Stanislav Leonovich (SOV)	7	8
8. Susanne Scheibe/Andreas Nischwitz (FRG)	8	7
9. Sabine Fuchs/Xavier Videau (FRA)	10	9
10. Elżbieta Łuczyńska/Marek Chrolenko (POL)	9	10
11. Gabriele Beck/Jochen Stahl (FRG)	12	11
12. Catherine Brunet/Philippe Brunet (FRA)	11	12
13. Ruth Lindsey/Alan Beckwith (GRB)	13	13

European Ice Dancing Championships.

	C/OSP	FD
1. Irina Moiseeva/Andrei Minenkov (SOV)	1	1
2. Natalia Linichuk/Gennadi Karponosov (SOV)	2	2
3. Krisztina Regőczy/András Sallay (HUN)	3	3
4. Janet Thompson/Warren Maxwell (GRB)	4	4
5. Liliana Řeháková/Stanislav Drastich (CZE)	5	5
6. Marina Zoueva/Andrei Vitman (SOV)	6	6
7. Kay Barsdell/Kenneth Foster (GRB)	7	7

8. Isabella Rizzi/Luigi Freroni (ITA)	8	8
9. Jayne Torvill/Christopher Dean (GRB)	9	9
10. Susi Handschmann/Peter Handschmann (AUT)	10	10
11. Henriette Fröschl/Christian Steiner (FRG)	11	11
12. Halina Gordon-Półtorak/Jacek Tascher (POL)	12	13
13. Muriel Boucher/Yves Malatier (FRA)	13	12
14. Elisabetta Parisi/Marco Gobbo (ITA)	14	14
15. Elisabeth Luksch/Peter Schubl (SUI)	16	15
16. Rita Karpat/Istvan Palasthy (HUN)	15	16
WD. Jolanta Wesołowska/Andrzej Alberciak (POL)	-	-

Following years of particularly egregious judging discrepancies, the ISU took the unprecedented step of banning all Soviet judges from ISU Championships during the 1978/1979 season. When Soviet judges were allowed to return the following year, the Soviet Federation sent 3 judges to the European Figure Skating Championships that had earned suspensions before the blanket ban came into effect.

Sources: Journal du Jura, February 3, 1978; Skating magazine, March 1978; The Globe and Mail, June 5, 1978; 100th Anniversary 1892-1992 - International Skating Union: Results 1968-1991 Figure Skating Championships, Elemér Terták, Benjamin T. Wright, Beat Häsler, 1992, courtesy World Figure Skating Museum & Hall of Fame; Cracked Ice: Figure Skating's Inner World, Sonia Bianchetti Garbato, 2004

1979 EUROPEAN FIGURE SKATING CHAMPIONSHIPS
Zagreb, Yugoslavia, January 30-February 4, 1979

European Men's Figure Skating Championships:

	CF	SP	FS
1. Jan Hoffmann (GDR)	2	3	4
2. Vladimir Kovalev (SOV)	1	2	3
3. Robin Cousins (GRB)	6	1	1
4. Jean-Christophe Simond (FRA)	5	4	2
5. Igor Bobrin (SOV)	3	5	7
6. Konstantin Kokora (SOV)	12	7	5
7. Hermann Schulz (GDR)	8	8	6

8. Mario Liebers (GDR)	4	6	11
9. Miroslav Šoška (CZE)	7	10	13
10. László Vajda (HUN)	11	11	12
11. Norbert Schramm (FRG)	13	9	8
12. Thomas Nieder (FRG)	16	14	9
13. Helmut Kristofics-Binder (AUT)	9	12	15
14. Grzegorz Głowania (POL)	14	15	10
15. Christopher Howarth (GRB)	18	13	14
16. Michel Lotz (FRA)	10	16	18
17. Jozef Sabovčík (CZE)	15	18	16
18. Thomas Öberg (SWE)	17	17	17
19. Matjaž Krušec (YUG)	20	19	19
20. Antti Kontiola (FIN)	19	20	20

European Ladies Figure Skating Championships:

	CF	SP	FS
1. Anett Pötzsch (GDR)	1	1	2
2. Dagmar Lurz (FRG)	2	2	5
3. Denise Biellmann (SUI)	8	3	1
4. Kristiina Wegelius (FIN)	3	6	8
5. Carola Weißenberg (GDR)	9	8	6
6. Karin Riediger (FRG)	11	11	4
7. Sanda Dubravčić (YUG)	15	5	3
8. Susanna Driano (ITA)	4	19	11
9. Debbie Cottrill (GRB)	7	7	13
10. Kira Ivanova (SOV)	13	9	12
11. Renata Baierová (CZE)	12	4	14
12. Karena Richardson (GRB)	6	16	15
13. Susan Broman (FIN)	5	13	18
14. Katarina Witt (GDR)	18	12	7
15. Petra Ernert (FRG)	16	10	10
16. Jeanne Chapman (NOR)	10	17	17
17. Natalia Strelkova (SOV)	17	18	9
18. Sonja Stanek (AUT)	14	15	19
19. Anita Siegfried (SUI)	21	14	16
20. Astrid Jansen in de Wal (NED)	22	20	21
21. Corinne Wyrsch (SUI)	20	23	20
22. Anne-Sophie de Kristoffy (FRA)	19	22	24

23. Franca Bianconi (ITA)	23	25	22
24. Christina Svensson (SWE)	24	21	25
25. Genevieve Schoumacker (BEL)	25	24	23
26. Helena Chwila (POL)	26	26	26
27. Heidi Bartelsen (DEN)	27	27	28
28. Margarita Dimitrova (BUL)	29	28	27
29. Gloria Mas (ESP)	28	29	29

European Pairs Skating Championships:

	SP	FS
1. Marina Cherkasova/Sergei Shakhrai (SOV)	1	1
2. Irina Vorobieva/Igor Lisovski (SOV)	3	2
3. Sabine Baeß/Tassilo Thierbach (GDR)	2	3
4. Marina Pestova/Stanislav Leonovich (SOV)	6	4
5. Kerstin Stolfig/Veit Kempe (GDR)	5	5
6. Ingrid Spieglová/Alan Spiegl (CZE)	4	6
7. Kornelia Haufe/Kersten Bellmann (GDR)	7	7
8. Christina Riegel/Andreas Nischwitz (FRG)	8	8
9. Maria Jeżak/Lech Matuszewski (POL)	9	9
10. Christine Eicher/Paul Huber (SUI)	10	10

European Ice Dancing Championships:

	C/OSP	FD
1. Natalia Linichuk/Gennadi Karponosov (SOV)	1	1
2. Irina Moiseeva/Andrei Minenkov (SOV)	2	2
3. Krisztina Regőczy/András Sallay (HUN)	3	3
4. Liliana Řeháková/Stanislav Drastich (CZE)	4	4
5. Natalia Karamysheva/Rostislav Sinitsyn (SOV)	5	5
6. Jayne Torvill/Christopher Dean (GRB)	6	7
7. Susi Handschmann/Peter Handschmannn (AUT)	7	6
8. Isabella Rizzi/Luigi Freroni (ITA)	8	8
9. Henriette Fröschl/Christian Steiner (FRG)	9	9
10. Anna Pisánská/Jiří Musil (CZE)	11	11
11. Karen Barber/Nicky Slater (GRB)	10	10
12. Halina Gordon-Półtorak/Tadeusz Góra (POL)	12	12
13. Martine Olivier/Yves Tarayre (FRA)	13	13
14. Jindra Holá/Karol Foltán (CZE)	15	14
15. Regula Lattmann/Hanspeter Müller (SUI)	14	15

16. Gabriella Remport/Sándor Nagy (HUN)		16	16
17. Claudia Koch/Peter Schubl (AUT)		17	17

Margarita Dimitrova made history as the first skater to represent Bulgaria at the European Figure Skating Championships.

Source: 100th Anniversary 1892-1992 - International Skating Union: Results 1968-1991 Figure Skating Championships, Elemér Terták, Benjamin T. Wright, Beat Häsler, 1992, courtesy World Figure Skating Museum & Hall of Fame

Jayne Torvill and Christopher Dean, European Champions 1981-1982, 1984 and 1994, with coach Betty Callaway. PA Images / Alamy Stock Photo.

THE DECADE OF DECADENCE

1980 EUROPEAN FIGURE SKATING CHAMPIONSHIPS
Göteborg, Sweden, January 22–27, 1980

European Men's Figure Skating Championships:

	CF	SP	FS
1. Robin Cousins (GRB)	3	3	1
2. Jan Hoffmann (GDR)	2	1	2
3. Vladimir Kovalev (SOV)	1	2	3
4. Igor Bobrin (SOV)	5	4	4
5. Hermann Schulz (GDR)	8	7	5
6. Jean-Christophe Simond (FRA)	6	8	7
7. Mario Liebers (GDR)	7	5	6
8. Konstantin Kokora (SOV)	4	6	9
9. Jozef Sabovčík (CZE)	11	9	8
10. Thomas Öberg (SWE)	13	14	10
11. Patrice Macrez (FRA)	10	15	11
12. Helmut Kristofics-Binder (AUT)	9	13	14
13. Gilles Beyer (FRA)	12	10	15
14. Ludwik Jankowski (POL)	18	12	12
15. Christopher Howarth (GRB)	15	16	13
16. Antti Kontiola (FIN)	17	17	17
17. Eric Krol (BEL)	19	19	16
18. Miljan Begović (YUG)	16	18	18
19. István Simon (HUN)	20	20	20
20. Boyko Aleksiev (BUL)	21	21	19
WD. Rudi Cerne (FRG)	14	11	-

European Ladies Figure Skating Championships:

	CF	SP	FS
1. Anett Pötzsch (GDR)	1	9	1
2. Dagmar Lurz (FRG)	2	1	3
3. Susanna Driano (ITA)	4	2	4

4. Kristiina Wegelius (FIN)	3	7	8
5. Sanda Dubravčić (YUG)	9	3	2
6. Debbie Cottrill (GRB)	5	6	6
7. Carola Weißenberg (GDR)	8	4	5
8. Danielle Rieder (SUI)	7	5	12
9. Karin Riediger (FRG)	13	8	9
10. Renata Baierová (CZE)	17	12	10
11. Kira Ivanova (SOV)	14	10	11
12. Karena Richardson (GRB)	10	14	13
13. Katarina Witt (GDR)	24	11	7
14. Susan Broman (FIN)	11	19	16
15. Editha Dotson (BEL)	19	17	14
16. Myriam Oberwiler (SUI)	20	16	15
17. Anne-Sophie de Kristoffy (FRA)	15	18	18
18. Astrid Jansen in de Wal (NED)	21	20	17
19. Pia Snellman (FIN)	25	21	19
20. Bodil Olsson (SWE)	23	22	20
21. Maristella Maderna (ITA)	18	24	22
22. Nevenka Lisak (YUG)	22	25	21
23. Hanne Gamborg (DEN)	26	23	23
24. Gloria Mas Gil (ESP)	27	26	24
WD. Claudia Kristofics-Binder (AUT)	6	13	-
WD. Denise Biellmann (SUI)	12	15	-
WD. Christina Riegel (FRG)	16	-	-

European Pairs Skating Championships:

	SP	FS
1. Irina Rodnina/Alexander Zaitsev (SOV)	1	1
2. Marina Cherkasova/Sergei Shakhrai (SOV)	2	2
3. Marina Pestova/Stanislav Leonovich (SOV)	4	3
4. Sabine Baeß/Tassilo Thierbach (GDR)	5	4
5. Manuela Mager/Uwe Bewersdorf (GDR)	3	5
6. Christina Riegel/Andreas Nischwitz (FRG)	7	6
7. Kerstin Stolfig/Veit Kempe (GDR)	6	7
8. Ingrid Spieglová/Alan Spiegl (CZE)	8	8
9. Gabriele Beck/Jochen Stahl (FRG)	9	11
10. Maria Jeżak/Lech Matuszewski (POL)	11	9
11. Susan Garland/Robert Daw (GRB)	10	10

European Ice Dancing Championships:

	C/OSP	FD
1. Natalia Linichuk/Gennadi Karponosov (SOV)	1	1
2. Krisztina Regőczy/András Sallay (HUN)	3	3
3. Irina Moiseeva/Andrei Minenkov (SOV)	2	2
4. Jayne Torvill/Christopher Dean (GRB)	4	4
5. Liliana Řeháková/Stanislav Drastich (CZE)	5	5
6. Natalia Bestemianova/Andrei Bukin (SOV)	6	6
7. Henriette Fröschl/Christian Steiner (FRG)	7	8
8. Karen Barber/Nicky Slater (GRB)	8	7
9. Susi Handschmann/Peter Handschmann (SUI)	9	9
10. Anna Pisánská/Jiří Musil (CZE)	10	10
11. Nathalie Hervé/Pierre Béchu (FRA)	11	12
12. Gabriella Remport/Sándor Nagy (HUN)	13	11
13. Elisabetta Parisi/Roberto Pelizzola (ITA)	12	13
14. Birgit Goller/Peter Klisch (FRG)	14	14
15. Regula Lattmann/Hanspeter Müller (SUI)	15	15

In her final trip to the European Figure Skating Championships, Irina Rodnina set a record for the most European pairs titles won by any one skater. Rodnina won a total of 11 European titles, 7 of them with Aleksandr Zaitsev.

Sources: Aftonbladet, January 23, 1980; Dagens Nyheter, January 24, 1980; Neue Zürcher Zeitung, January 25 and 26, 1980; Skating magazine, March 1980

1981 EUROPEAN FIGURE SKATING CHAMPIONSHIPS
Innsbruck, Austria, February 3-8, 1981

European Men's Figure Skating Championships:

	CF	SP	FS
1. Igor Bobrin (SOV)	2	4	1
2. Jean-Christophe Simond (FRA)	1	6	3
3. Norbert Schramm (FRG)	7	1	2
4. Hermann Schulz (GDR)	3	2	4
5. Jozef Sabovčík (CZE)	4	3	7
6. Vladimir Kotin (SOV)	8	5	5

7. Grzegorz Filipowski (POL)	6	9	8
8. Falko Kirsten (GDR)	10	10	6
9. Alexandr Fadeev (SOV)	9	7	9
10. Patrice Macrez (FRA)	5	14	11
11. Christopher Howarth (GRB)	15	13	10
12. Thomas Öberg (SWE)	11	12	13
13. Lars Åkesson (SWE)	14	8	15
14. Mark Pepperday (GRB)	19	11	12
15. Bruno Watschinger (AUT)	13	16	14
16. Richard Furrer (SUI)	12	15	17
17. Ivan Králik (CZE)	18	19	16
18. Bruno Delmaestro (ITA)	17	18	18
19. Miljan Begović (YUG)	16	17	19
20. Boyko Aleksiev (BUL)	20	20	20
21. José-Antonio Rodrigo (ESP)	21	21	21

European Ladies Figure Skating Championships:

	CF	SP	FS
1. Denise Biellmann (SUI)	4	1	1
2. Sanda Dubravčić (YUG)	5	2	2
3. Claudia Kristofics-Binder (AUT)	1	7	4
4. Kristiina Wegelius (FIN)	3	4	5
5. Katarina Witt (GDR)	8	6	3
6. Debbie Cottrill (GRB)	2	3	8
7. Kira Ivanova (SOV)	6	5	6
8. Karin Riediger (FRG)	7	8	7
9. Carola Paul (GDR)	9	9	10
10. Manuela Ruben (FRG)	11	13	9
11. Karen Wood (GRB)	10	16	11
12. Anita Siegfried (SUI)	13	10	13
13. Karin Telser (ITA)	14	11	14
14. Pairi Nieminen (FIN)	20	12	12
15. Rudina Pasveer (NED)	15	15	15
16. Catarina Lindgren (SWE)	19	14	16
17. Franca Bianconi (ITA)	18	17	17
18. Editha Dotson (BEL)	17	20	18
19. Petra Malivuk (YUG)	16	21	21
20. Beata Nachrzter (POL)	22	18	19

21. Nevenka Lisak (YUG)	21	19	20
22. Ysvetanka Stefanova (BUL)	23	24	22
23. Rosario Esteban (ESP)	24	23	23
WD. Béatrice Farinacci (FRA)	12	22	-

European Pairs Skating Championships:

	SP	FS
1. Irina Vorobieva/Igor Lisovski (SOV)	1	1
2. Christina Riegel/Andreas Nischwitz (FRG)	3	2
3. Marina Cherkasova/Sergei Shakhrai (SOV)	2	3
4. Birgit Lorenz/Knut Schubert (GDR)	5	4
5. Veronika Pershina/Marat Akbarov (SOV)	4	5
6. Susan Garland/Robert Daw (GRB)	6	6

European Ice Dancing Championships:

	C/OSP	FD
1. Jayne Torvill/Christopher Dean (GRB)	1	1
2. Irina Moiseeva/Andrei Minenkov (SOV)	2	2
3. Natalia Linichuk/Gennadi Karponosov (SOV)	3	3
4. Natalia Bestemianova/Andrei Bukin (SOV)	4	4
5. Karen Barber/Nicky Slater (GRB)	5	5
6. Nathalie Hervé/ Pierre Béchu (FRA)	6	6
7. Jana Beránková/Jan Barták (CZE)	7	7
8. Birgit Goller/Peter Klisch (FRG)	8	8
9. Wendy Sessions/Stephen Williams (GRB)	9	9
10. Judit Péterfy/Csaba Bálint (HUN)	10	10
11. Elisabetta Parisi/Roberto Pelizzola (ITA)	11	11
12. Gabriella Remport/Sándor Nagy (HUN)	12	12
13. Jindra Holá/Karol Foltán (CZE)	13	13
14. Maria Kniffer/Manfed Hübler (AUT)	14	14
15. Regula Lattmann/Hanspeter Müller (SUI)	15	15
16. Petra Born/Rainer Schönborn (FRG)	16	16
17. Marianne von Bommel/Wayne Deweyert (NED)	17	17
18. Iwona Bielas/Jacek Jasiaczek (POL)	18	18
19. Ulla Örnmarker/Thomas Svedberg (SWE)	19	19

Denise Biellmann made history as the first Swiss skater to win a gold medal in the ladies event at the European Figure Skating

Championships. Runner-up Sanda Dubravčić won Yugoslavia's first medal at the European Championships.

Sources: Skating magazine, May 1981; Canadian Skater magazine, July/August 1981

1982 EUROPEAN FIGURE SKATING CHAMPIONSHIPS
Lyon, France, February 2-7, 1982

European Men's Figure Skating Championships:

	CF	SP	FS
1. Norbert Schramm (FRG)	4	2	1
2. Jean-Christophe Simond (FRA)	1	6	2
3. Igor Bobrin (SOV)	2	5	3
4. Rudi Cerne (FRG)	8	3	5
5. Alexandr Fadeev (SOV)	10	4	4
6. Heiko Fischer (FRG)	3	7	7
7. Vladimir Kotin (SOV)	5	9	6
8. Jozef Sabovčík (CZE)	7	1	8
9. Grzegorz Filipowski (POL)	6	8	9
10. Didier Monge (FRA)	12	10	10
11. Philippe Paulet (FRA)	13	11	11
12. Thomas Hlavik (AUT)	15	12	12
13. Oliver Höner (SUI)	11	13	14
14. Bruno Delmaestro (ITA)	17	14	13
15. Miljan Begović (YUG)	16	16	16
16. Mark Pepperday (GRB)	19	15	15
17. Lars Åkesson (SWE)	14	21	17
18. Edward van Campen (NED)	22	18	18
19. Todd Sand (DEN)	18	19	20
20. Thierry Michels (LUX)	23	17	19
21. András Száraz (HUN)	21	20	21
22. Eric Krol (BEL)	20	22	22
23. Boyko Aleksiev (BUL)	25	24	23
24. Fernando Soria (ESP)	24	23	24
WD. Alexander König (GDR)	9	-	-

European Ladies Figure Skating Championships:

	CF	SP	FS
1. Claudia Kristofics-Binder (AUT)	1	3	3
2. Katarina Witt (GDR)	6	1	1
3. Elena Vodorezova (SOV)	4	2	4
4. Debbie Cottrill (GRB)	3	5	5
5. Claudia Leistner (FRG)	11	4	2
6. Kristiina Wegelius (FIN)	2	8	9
7. Carola Paul (GDR)	8	6	10
8. Karen Wood (GRB)	12	12	6
9. Janina Wirth (GDR)	10	18	7
10. Anna Antonova (SOV)	18	7	8
11. Myriam Oberwiler (SUI)	16	10	11
12. Hana Veselá (CZE)	15	9	12
13. Sandra Cariboni (SUI)	13	14	16
14. Manuela Ruben (FRG)	9	15	19
15. Sonja Stanek (AUT)	7	17	20
16. Parthena Sarafidis (AUT)	17	19	14
17. Pairi Nieminen (FIN)	21	16	13
18. Karin Telser (ITA)	14	11	21
19. Béatrice Farinacci (FRA)	22	13	18
20. Liisa Seitsonen (FIN)	24	20	15
21. Katrien Pauwels (BEL)	19	24	17
22. Catarina Lindgren (SWE)	20	21	22
23. Anette Nygaard (DEN)	26	23	23
24. Nevenka Lisak (YUG)	23	29	24
25. Rosario Esteban (ESP)	28	25	25
26. Nora Miklosi (HUN)	27	26	26
27. Ingrid Aalders (NED)	25	27	28
28. Tsvetanka Stefanova (BUL)	29	28	27
WD. Sanda Dubravčić (YUG)	5	22	-
WD. Petra Malivuk (YUG)	30	-	-

European Pairs Skating Championships:

	SP	FS
1. Sabine Baeß/Tassilo Thierbach (GDR)	2	1
2. Marina Pestova/Stanislav Leonovich (SOV)	3	2
3. Irina Vorobieva/Igor Lisovski (SOV)	1	3

4. Veronika Pershina/Marat Akbarov (SOV)	4	4
5. Birgit Lorenz/Knut Schubert (GDR)	5	5
6. Susan Garland/Robert Daw (GRB)	6	6
7. Bettina Hage/Stefan Zins (FRG)	8	7
8. Nathalie Tortel/Xavier Videau (FRA)	7	8
9. Gaby Galambos/Jürg Galambos (SUI)	9	9

European Ice Dancing Championships:

	C/OSP	FD
1. Jayne Torvill/Christopher Dean (GRB)	1	1
2. Natalia Bestemianova/Andrei Bukin (SOV)	2	2
3. Irina Moiseeva/Andrei Minenkov (SOV)	3	3
4. Olga Volozhinskaya/Aleksandr Svinin (SOV)	4	4
5. Karen Barber/Nicky Slater (GRB)	5	5
6. Nathalie Hervé/Pierre Béchu (FRA)	6	6
7. Jana Beránková/Jan Barták (CZE)	7	7
8. Judit Péterfy/Csaba Bálint (HUN)	10	8
9. Wendy Sessions/Stephen Williams (GRB)	9	9
10. Birgit Goller/Peter Klisch (FRG)	8	10
11. Petra Born/Rainer Schönborn (FRG)	11	11
12. Jindra Holá/Karol Foltán (CZE)	12	12
13. Isabella Micheli/Roberto Pelizzola (ITA)	14	13
14. Maria Kniffer/Manfred Hubler (AUT)	13	14
15. Marianne van Bommel/Wayne Deweyert (NED)	15	15
16. Martine Olivier/Philippe Boissier (FRA)	16	16
17. Esther Guiglia/Roland Mader (SUI)	17	17
18. Salia Saarinen/Kim Jacobson (FIN)	18	18
19. Ulla Ornamerker/Thomas Svedberg (SWE)	19	19

Norbert Schramm made history as the first West German winner of the men's event at the European Figure Skating Championships, while Sabine Baeß and Tassilo Thierbach won East Germany's first gold medal in the pairs event.

Jayne Torvill and Christopher Dean set a new record for most perfect 6.0's awarded in the ice dance event (11).

Sources: L'impartial, February 5, 1982; L'express, February 6, 1982;

Skating magazine, March 1982; *Canadian Skater magazine*, March/April 1982

1983 EUROPEAN FIGURE SKATING CHAMPIONSHIPS
Dortmund, West Germany, January 31-February 6, 1983

European Men's Figure Skating Championships:

	CF	SP	FS
1. Norbert Schramm (FRG)	4	1	1
2. Jozef Sabovčík (CZE)	2	2	5
3. Alexandr Fadeev (SOV)	9	3	2
4. Heiko Fischer (FRG)	3	4	6
5. Vladimir Kotin (SOV)	6	8	3
6. Jean-Christophe Simond (FRA)	1	6	7
7. Rudi Cerne (FRG)	7	5	4
8. Grzegorz Filipowski (POL)	5	7	8
9. Laurent Depouilly (FRA)	10	13	9
10. Fernand Fédronic (FRA)	8	14	11
11. Lars Åkesson (SWE)	12	10	12
12. Falko Kirsten (GDR)	13	9	13
13. Thomas Hlavik (AUT)	15	15	10
14. Miljan Begović (YUG)	14	11	15
15. Mark Pepperday (GRB)	17	16	14
16. Richard Furrer (SUI)	11	18	18
17. Bruno Delmaestro (ITA)	18	18	17
18. Petr Barna (CZE)	19	20	16
19. Todd Sand (DEN)	16	19	19
20. András Száraz (HUN)	20	12	20
21. Fernando Soria (ESP)	21	21	21

European Ladies Figure Skating Championships:

	CF	SP	FS1	FS2
1. Katarina Witt (GDR)	2	1	1	-
2. Elena Vodorezova (SOV)	1	3	5	-
3. Claudia Leistner (FRG)	9	2	2	-
4. Manuela Ruben (FRG)	6	6	3	-
5. Anna Kondrashova (SOV)	12	5	4	-
6. Kristiina Wegelius (FIN)	5	8	7	-

7. Anna Antonova (SOV)	11	7	6	-
8. Janina Wirth (GDR)	10	4	8	-
9. Sonja Stanek (AUT)	4	11	10	-
10. Sanda Dubravčić (YUG)	7	13	11	-
11. Karin Telser (ITA)	13	10	9	-
12. Parthena Sarafidis (AUT)	8	18	13	-
13. Sandra Cariboni (SUI)	3	19	16	-
14. Karin Hendschke (GDR)	19	9	12	-
15. Katrien Pauwels (BEL)	14	15	14	-
16. Hana Veselá (CZE)	17	12	15	-
17. Agnès Gosselin (FRA)	16	14	-	1
18. Li Scha Wang (NED)	18	17	-	4
19. Hanne Gamborg (DEN)	21	22	-	2
20. Susan Jackson (GRB)	23	20	-	3
21. Catarina Lindgren (SWE)	20	21	-	5
22. Elise Ahonen (FIN)	22	24	-	6
23. Nora Miklosi (HUN)	25	23	-	7
24. Rosario Esteban (ESP)	24	25	-	8
WD. Karen Wood (GRB)	15	16	-	-

European Pairs Skating Championships:

	SP	FS
1. Sabine Baeß/Tassilo Thierbach (GDR)	1	1
2. Elena Valova/Oleg Vasiliev (SOV)	4	2
3. Birgit Lorenz/Knut Schubert (GDR)	2	3
4. Veronika Pershina/Marat Akbarov (SOV)	3	4
5. Marina Avstriskaya/Yuri Kvashnin (SOV)	5	5
6. Babette Preußler/Torsten Ohlow (GDR)	8	6
7. Claudia Massari/Leonardo Azzola (FRG)	6	7
8. Susan Garland/Robert Daw (GRB)	7	8
9. Jana Havlova/René Novotný (CZE)	9	9
10. Nathalie Tortel/Xavier Douillard (FRA)	12	10
11. Birgit Kuß/Uwe Fischbeck (FRA)	11	11
12. Naija Pekkala/Pekka Pekkala (FIN)	10	12

European Ice Dancing Championships:

	CD	OSP	FD
1. N. Bestemianova/A. Bukin (SOV)	1	1	1

2. O. Volozhinskaya/A. Svinin (SOV)	4	2	2
3. K. Barber/N. Slater (GRB)	2	4	3
4. M. Klimova/S. Ponomarenko (SOV)	3	3	4
5. Nathalie Hervé/Pierre Béchu (FRA)	5	6	5
6. Petra Born/Rainer Schönborn (FRG)	6	5	6
7. Wendy Sessions/Stephen Williams (GRB)	7	7	7
8. Isabella Micheli/Roberto Pelizzola (ITA)	8	8	8
9. Jindra Holá/Karol Foltán (CZE)	9	9	9
10. Judit Péterfy/Csaba Bálint (HUN)	10	10	10
11. A. Becherer/Ferdinand Becherer (FRG)	12	11	11
12. M. van Bommel/W. Deweyert (NED)	11	12	12
13. Graziella Ferpozzi/Marco Ferpozzi (SUI)	13	14	13
14. Martine Olivier/Philippe Boissier (FRA)	14	13	14
15. Kathrin Beck/Christoff Beck (AUT)	15	15	15
16. B. Wierzchowska/R. Kazanowski (POL)	16	16	16
17. Hristina Boyanova/Yavor Ivanov (BUL)	17	17	17

Due to the large number of entries, a "B" group was introduced for skaters who did not finish in the top 16 after the combined results of the compulsory figures and short program were calculated. This system was largely criticized when Agnès Gosselin of France won the "B" Group, landing the only triple Lutz combination of the entire ladies event, but could finish no higher than 17th. Long-time British sportswriter and author Howard Bass remarked, "Somewhat comparable to the Wimbledon Plate in Tennis, [it is] a somewhat pointless exercise."

Source: Canadian Skater magazine, April/May 1983; Skating magazine, April 1983

1984 EUROPEAN FIGURE SKATING CHAMPIONSHIPS
Budapest, Hungary, January 27-29, 1984

European Men's Figure Skating Championships:

	CF	SP	FS
1. Alexandr Fadeev (SOV)	4	1	1
2. Rudi Cerne (FRG)	3	3	2
3. Norbert Schramm (FRG)	6	2	3

4. Jozef Sabovčík (FRG)	2	5	5
5. Heiko Fischer (FRG)	5	4	6
6. Vladimir Kotin (SOV)	7	7	4
7. Vitali Egorov (SOV)	9	12	7
8. Grzegorz Filipowski (POL)	8	9	9
9. Falko Kirsten (GDR)	13	8	8
10. Petr Barna (CZE)	12	10	10
11. Laurent Depouilly (FRA)	10	11	11
12. Thomas Hlavik (AUT)	16	13	12
13. Lars Åkesson (SWE)	11	17	14
14. Miljan Begović (YUG)	15	15	13
15. Paul Robinson (GRB)	17	14	15
16. Oliver Höner (SUI)	14	16	16
17. Wojciech Gwinner (POL)	19	19	17
18. András Száraz (HUN)	18	18	18
19. Lars Dresler (DEN)	20	21	19
20. Edward van Campen (NED)	21	20	20
21. Fernando Soria (ESP)	22	22	21
WD. Jean-Christophe Simond (FRA)	1	6	-

European Ladies Figure Skating Championships:

	CF	SP	FS
1. Katarina Witt (GDR)	2	1	1
2. Manuela Ruben (FRG)	4	4	2
3. Anna Kondrashova (SOV)	5	2	4
4. Kira Ivanova (SOV)	8	6	3
5. Sanda Dubravčić (YUG)	6	8	7
6. Sandra Cariboni (SUI)	3	11	10
7. Simone Koch (GDR)	16	5	6
8. Karin Telser (ITA)	10	10	8
9. Agnès Gosselin (FRA)	13	16	5
10. Cornelia Tesch (FRG)	8	7	13
11. Parthena Sarafidis (AUT)	7	14	11
12. Karin Hendschke (GDR)	14	9	9
13. Katrien Pauwels (BEL)	11	13	12
14. Susan Jackson (GRB)	19	12	14
15. Elise Ahonen (FIN)	17	15	15
16. Susanna Peltola (FIN)	12	19	18

17. Susanne Gschwend (AUT)	18	17	17
18. Tamara Téglássy (HUN)	20	18	16
19. Nevenka Lisak (YUG)	15	20	19
20. Anette Nygaard (DEN)	21	21	20
21. Marta Cierco (ESP)	22	22	21
WD. Elena Vodorezova (SOV)	1	3	-

European Pairs Skating Championships:

	SP	FS
1. Elena Valova/Oleg Vasiliev (SOV)	1	1
2. Sabine Baeß/Tassilo Thierbach (GDR)	2	2
3. Birgit Lorenz/Knut Schubert (GDR)	3	3
4. Larisa Selezneva/Oleg Makarov (SOV)	4	4
5. Marina Avstriskaya/Yuri Kvashnin (SOV)	5	5
6. Babette Preußler/Tobias Schröter (GDR)	6	6
7. Dagmar Kovarova/Jozef Komar (CZE)	8	7
8. Claudia Massari/Leonardo Azzola (FRG)	7	8
9. Susan Garland/Ian Jenkins (GRB)	9	9
10. Gaby Galambos/Jürg Galambos (SUI)	10	10
11. Sylvie Vacquero/Didier Manaud (FRA)	11	11

European Ice Dancing Championships:

	CD	OSP	FD
1. Jayne Torvill/Christopher Dean (GRB)	1	1	1
2. N. Bestemianova/A. Bukin (SOV)	2	2	2
3. M. Klimova/S. Ponomarenko (SOV)	3	3	3
4. Karen Barber/Nicky Slater (GRB)	4	4	4
5. O. Volozhinskaya/A.Svinin (SOV)	5	5	5
6. Petra Born/Rainer Schönborn (FRG)	6	6	6
7. Wendy Sessions/Stephen Williams (GRB)	7	7	7
8. Nathalie Hervé/Pierre Béchu (FRA)	8	8	8
9. Jindra Holá/Karol Foltán (CZE)	9	9	9
10. Isabella Micheli/Roberto Pelizzola (ITA)	10	12	10
11. M. van Bommel/W. Deweyert (NED)	11	10	11
12. A. Becherer/F. Becherer (FRG)	12	11	12
13. Graziella Ferpozzi/Marco Ferpozzi (SUI)	13	13	13
14. Viera Mináríková/Ivan Havránek (CZE)	14	14	14
15. Gabriella Remport/Sándor Nagy (HUN)	15	16	15

16. Kathrin Beck/Christoff Beck (AUT)	16	15	16
17. Klára Engi/Attila Tóth (HUN)	17	17	17
18. B. Wierzchowska/R.Kazanowski (POL)	19	18	18
19. Sophie Merigot/Philippe Berthe (FRA)	18	19	19
20. Brunhilde Bianchi/Walter Rizzo (ITA)	20	20	20
21. Hristina Boyanova/Yavor Ivanov (BUL)	21	21	21

Jayne Torvill and Christopher Dean received a perfect 6.0 for their Rhumba – the first perfect mark awarded for a compulsory dance at the European Figure Skating Championships. They earned another six 6.0's in the OSP and 11 in the free dance, making them the first ice dance team to earn perfect marks in all three phases of the competition at any ISU Championship. They duplicated this feat at the 1984 World Figure Skating Championships in Ottawa.

Sources: Skating magazine, February 1984; Poster, 1984 European Figure Skating Championships

1985 EUROPEAN FIGURE SKATING CHAMPIONSHIPS
Göteborg, Sweden, February 4-10, 1985

European Men's Figure Skating Championships:

	CF	SP	SF	FS
1. Jozef Sabovčík (CZE)	2	1	-	2
2. Vladimir Kotin (SOV)	4	2	-	1
3. Grzegorz Filipowski (POL)	5	4	-	3
4. Heiko Fischer (FRG)	3	8	-	4
5. Falko Kirsten (GDR)	9	5	-	5
6. Viktor Petrenko (SOV)	8	3	-	8
7. Fernand Fédronic (FRA)	1	7	-	11
8. Richard Zander (FRG)	7	9	-	7
9. Lars Åkesson (SWE)	6	6	-	9
10. Petr Barna (CZE)	10	10	-	6
11. Alessandro Riccitelli (ITA)	15	11	-	10
12. Nils Köpp (GDR)	13	13	-	12
13. Ralph Burghart (AUT)	12	12	-	15
14. Lars Dresler (DEN)	14	17	-	13
15. Stephen Pickavance (GRB)	16	14	-	14

16. Oula Jääskeläinen (FIN)	20	16	-	16
17. Wojciech Gwinner (POL)	19	19	1	17
18. Imre Raábe (HUN)	18	20	2	18
19. Edward van Campen (NED)	17	21	3	19
20. Fernando Soria (ESP)	21	18	4	-
WD. Oliver Höner (SUI)		11	15	-

European Ladies Figure Skating Championships:

	CF	SP	SF	FS
1. Katarina Witt (GDR)	1	4	-	1
2. Kira Ivanova (SOV)	2	1	-	2
3. Claudia Leistner (FRG)	4	2	-	3
4. Simone Koch (GDR)	9	3	-	4
5. Anna Kondrashova (SOV)	3	7	-	6
6. Natalia Lebedeva (SOV)	11	6	-	5
7. Claudia Villiger (SUI)	7	8	-	8
8. Patricia Neske (FRG)	6	13	-	7
9. Agnès Gosselin (FRA)	8	10	-	9
10. Susan Jackson (GRB)	12	11	-	11
11. Sandra Cariboni (SUI)	5	17	-	14
12. Constanze Gensel (GDR)	20	5	-	10
13. Lotta Falkenbäck (SWE)	14	15	-	12
14. Elise Ahonen (FIN)	13	12	-	15
15. Tamara Téglássy (HUN)	19	9	-	13
16. Katrien Pauwels (BEL)	10	14	-	17
17. Florence Copp (FRA)	17	18	-	16
18. Sabine Paal (AUT)	16	16	-	19
19. Beatrice Gelmini (ITA)	15	19	2	20
20. Paola Tosi (UTA)	23	21	1	18
21. C. Sjoholm-Jorgensem (DEN)	21	17	3	-
22. Nevenka Lisak (YUG)	18	20	5	-
23. Vibeke Sørensen (NOR)	22	22	4	-
24. Gabriela Ballová (CZE)	25	24	7	-
25. Tjin Li Wang (NED)	24	23	8	-
26. Marta Olozagarre (ESP)	26	26	9	-

European Pairs Skating Championships:

	SP	FS
1. Elena Valova/Oleg Vasiliev (SOV)	1	1
2. Larisa Selezneva/Oleg Makarov (SOV)	2	2
3. Veronika Pershina/Marat Akbarov (SOV)	4	3
4. Birgit Lorenz/Knut Schubert (GDR)	3	4
5. Manuela Landgraf/Ingo Steuer (GDR)	6	5
6. Claudia Massari/Daniele Caprano (FRG)	5	6
7. Lenka Knapová/René Novotný (CZE)	7	7
WD. Dagmar Kovarova/Jozef Komar (CZE)	8	-

European Ice Dancing Championships:

	CD	OSP	FD
1. N. Bestemianova/A. Bukin (SOV)	1	1	1
2. M. Klimova/S. Ponomarenko (SOV)	2	2	2
3. Petra Born/Rainer Schönborn (FRG)	4	3	3
4. Karen Barber/Nicky Slater (GRB)	3	4	4
5. N. Annenko/G. Sretenski (SOV)	5	5	5
6. Kathrin Beck/Christoff Beck (AUT)	7	6	6
7. Isabella Micheli/Roberto Pelizzola (ITA)	6	7	7
8. Jindra Holá/Karol Foltán (CZE)	8	8	8
9. Klára Engi/Attila Tóth (HUN)	9	9	9
10. A. Becherer/F. Becherer (FRG)	10	10	10
11. Sharon Jones/Paul Askham (GRB)	11	11	11
12. Martine Olivier/Philippe Boissier (FRA)	12	12	12
13. Brunhilde Bianchi/Walter Rizzo (ITA)	14	14	13
14. Isabelle Cousin/Martial Mette (FRA)	13	13	14
15. Gaby Schuppli/Markus Merz (SUI)	15	15	15
16. Asa Agblad/Christer Thornell (SWE)	16	16	16

After the singles short programs, the 18 skaters with the highest combined ranking qualified for the final. The remaining skaters competed in a semi-final, with the top 2 skaters earning the right to qualify for the free skating final.

Fernand Fédronic of France made history as the first and only skater of colour to win the figures at the European Figure Skating Championships.

Sources: *Het Parool*, February 5, 1985; *Journal du Jura*, February 7, 1985; *Het vrije volk: democratisch-socialistisch dagblad*, February 7, 1985; *Skating magazine*, March 1985; *Skating Around the World: International Skating Union, the One Hundredth Anniversary History 1892 -1992*, Benjamin T. Wright

1986 EUROPEAN FIGURE SKATING CHAMPIONSHIPS
Copenhagen, Denmark, January 27-February 2, 1986

European Men's Figure Skating Championships:

	CF	SP	SF	FS
1. Jozef Sabovčík (CZE)	1	1	-	1
2. Vladimir Kotin (SOV)	4	2	-	2
3. Alexandr Fadeev (SOV)	2	3	-	3
4. Viktor Petrenko (SOV)	5	7	-	4
5. Grzegorz Filipowski (POL)	6	6	-	6
6. Falko Kirsten (GDR)	10	9	-	5
7. Petr Barna (CZE)	8	5	-	8
8. Laurent Depouilly (FRA)	9	10	-	7
9. Richard Zander (FRG)	7	12	-	9
10. Lars Akesson (SWE)	11	8	-	11
11. Philippe Roncoli (FRA)	13	14	-	10
12. Lars Dresler (DEN)	19	13	-	12
13. Nils Köpp (GDR)	14	18	-	13
14. Oliver Höner (SUI)	12	19	-	15
15. Thomas Hlavik (AUT)	17	17	-	14
16. Alessandro Riccitelli (ITA)	15	11	1	19
17. András Száraz (HUN)	20	15	-	16
18. Stephen Pickavance (GRB)	16	20	4	17
19. Oula Jääskeläinen (FIN)	18	21	2	18
20. Peter Johansson (SWE)	22	16	3	-
21. Tomislav Čižmešija (YUG)	21	24	5	-
22. Boyko Aleksiev (BUL)	24	23	6	-
23. Fernando Soria (ESP)	23	33	7	-
WD. Heiko Fischer (FRG)	3	4	-	-

European Ladies Figure Skating Championships:

	CF	SP	SF	FS
1. Katarina Witt (GDR)	2	3	-	1
2. Kira Ivanova (SOV)	1	2	-	3
3. Anna Kondrashova (SOV)	4	1	-	2
4. Natalia Lebedeva (SOV)	5	6	-	4
5. Claudia Leistner (FRG)	3	4	-	7
6. Claudia Villiger (SUI)	9	8	-	6
7. Susan Jackson (GRB)	10	7	-	8
8. Constanze Gensel (GDR)	17	5	-	5
9. Agnès Gosselin (FRA)	7	10	-	9
10. Susanne Becher (FRG)	8	9	-	10
11. Joanne Conway (GRB)	11	11	-	11
12. Cornelia Tesch (FRG)	6	13	-	14
13. Lotta Falkenbäck (SWE)	15	15	-	12
14. Tamara Téglássy (HUN)	16	12	-	13
15. Elise Ahonen (FIN)	13	18	-	15
16. Željka Čižmešija (YUG)	12	19	2	18
17. Li Scha Wang (NED)	20	14	-	16
18. Manuela Tschupp (SUI)	14	17	3	19
19. Beatrice Gelmini (ITA)	19	16	-	17
20. Sandra Escoda (ESP)	22	23	4	-
21. Anita Thorenfeldt (NOR)	21	21	6	-
22. Petya Gavazova (BUL)	23	22	5	-
WD. Florence Copp (FRA)	18	20	1	-

European Pairs Skating Championships:

	SP	FS
1. Elena Valova/Oleg Vasiliev (SOV)	1	1
2. Ekaterina Gordeeva/Sergei Grinkov (SOV)	2	2
3. Elena Bechke/Valeri Kornienko (SOV)	4	3
4. Katrin Kanitz/Tobias Schröter (GDR)	3	4
5. Manuela Landgraf/Ingo Steuer (GDR)	5	5
6. Lenka Knapová/René Novotný (CZE)	7	6
7. Marianne Ocvirek/Holger Maletz (FRG)	6	7
8. Sylvie Vacquero/Didier Manaud (FRA)	9	8
9. Kerstin Kimminus/Stefan Pfrengle (FRG)	8	9
10. Cheryl Peake/Andrew Naylor (GRB)	10	10

WD. Larisa Selezneva/Oleg Makarov (SOV) - -
WD. Veronika Pershina/Marat Akbarov (SOV) - -

European Ice Dancing Championships:

	CD	OSP	FD
1. N. Bestemianova/A. Bukin (SOV)	1	2	1
2. M. Klimova/S. Ponomarenko (SOV)	2	1	2
3. N. Annenko/G. Sretenski (SOV)	3	3	3
4. Kathrin Beck/Christoff Beck (AUT)	4	4	4
5. A. Becherer/F. Becherer (FRG)	5	5	5
6. Klára Engi/Attila Tóth (HUN)	7	6	6
7. I. Micheli/R. Pelizzola (ITA)	6	7	8
8. I. Duchesnay/P. Duchesnay (FRA)	8	8	7
9. Sharon Jones/Paul Askham (GRB)	9	10	9
10. Viera Reháková/Ivan Havránek (CZE)	10	9	10
11. Elizabeth Coates/Alan Abretti (GRB)	12	12	11
12. S. Calegari/P. Camerlengo (ITA)	11	11	12
13. Kinga Wertan/Janos Demeter (HUN)	13	13	13
14. C. Schmidlin/D. Schmidlin (SUI)	14	14	14
15. A. Weppelmann/H. Schamberger (FRG)	15	15	15
16. Hristina Boyanova/Yavor Ivanov (BUL)	17	17	16
17. B. Kawełczyk/T. Politański (POL)	16	16	17
18. Susanna Rahkamo/Petri Kokko (FIN)	18	18	18

For the first time, Soviet couples swept the podium in the ice dance event at the European Figure Skating Championships.

Larisa Selezneva and Oleg Makarov and Veronika Pershina and Marat Akbarov were listed as the Soviet Union's 2nd and 3rd entries. ISU officials were surprised when 2 other teams arrived in Copenhagen in their place, as there had been no prior notification of any change.

Sources: Skate magazine yearbook, 1986; Skating magazine, March 1986

1987 EUROPEAN FIGURE SKATING CHAMPIONSHIPS
Sarajevo, Yugoslavia, February 3-8, 1987

European Men's Figure Skating Championships:

	CF	SP	FS
1. Alexandr Fadeev (SOV)	1	1	1
2. Vladimir Kotin (SOV)	2	3	2
3. Viktor Petrenko (SOV)	3	2	3
4. Grzegorz Filipowski (POL)	5	11	4
5. Falko Kirsten (GDR)	7	4	7
6. Richard Zander (FRG)	4	12	6
7. Philippe Roncoli (FRA)	13	6	5
8. Petr Barna (CZE)	9	5	8
9. Oliver Höner (SUI)	8	8	9
10. Frédéric Harpagès (FRA)	6	7	11
11. Paul Robinson (GRB)	11	9	10
12. Oula Jääskeläinen (FIN)	16	10	13
13. Thomas Hlavik (AUT)	12	15	14
14. Peter Johansson (SWE)	18	13	12
15. Alessandro Riccitelli (ITA)	15	14	16
16. Tomislav Čižmešija (YUG)	14	18	17
17. Ralph Burghart (AUT)	10	19	19
18. Lars Dresler (DEN)	20	16	15
19. András Száraz (HUN)	17	22	18
20. Przemysław Noworyta (POL)	19	17	20
21. Jaroslav Suchý (CZE)	21	20	21
22. Boyko Aleksiev (BUL)	22	21	22
23. Fernando Soria (ESP)	23	23	23

European Ladies Figure Skating Championships:

	CF	SP	FS
1. Katarina Witt (GDR)	4	1	1
2. Kira Ivanova (SOV)	1	3	2
3. Anna Kondrashova (SOV)	3	2	3
4. Claudia Leistner (FRG)	2	4	4
5. Susanne Becher (FRG)	5	5	5
6. Claudia Villiger (SUI)	6	7	8
7. Tamara Téglássy (HUN)	11	9	6

8. Natalia Skrabnevskaya (SOV)	7	14	7
9. Iveta Voralová (CZE)	10	6	10
10. Agnès Gosselin (FRA)	12	11	9
11. Željka Čižmešija (YUG)	8	12	12
12. Gina Fulton (GRB)	9	15	11
13. Hélène Persson (SWE)	14	8	16
14. Yvonne Pokorny (AUT)	16	13	13
15. Stéfanie Schmid (SUI)	18	10	14
16. Beatrice Gelmini (ITA)	15	16	15
17. Tiia-Riikka Pietikainen (FIN)	17	19	18
18. Mirela Gawłowska (POL)	13	18	21
19. Anita Thorenfeldt (NOR)	21	17	17
20. Sandra Escoda (ESP)	19	20	19
21. Petya Gavazova (BUL)	20	21	20

European Pairs Skating Championships:

	SP	FS
1. Larisa Selezneva/Oleg Makarov (SOV)	2	1
2. Elena Valova/Oleg Vasiliev (SOV)	1	2
3. Katrin Kanitz/Tobias Schröter (GDR)	4	3
4. Lenka Knapová/René Novotný (CZE)	5	4
5. Cheryl Peake/Andrew Naylor (GRB)	6	5
6. Sonja Adalbert/Daniele Caprano (FRG)	8	6
7. Lisa Cushley/Neil Cushley (GRB)	7	7
8. Charline Mauger/Benoît Vandenberghe (FRA)	9	8
WD. Ekaterina Gordeeva/Sergei Grinkov (SOV)	3	-

European Ice Dancing Championships:

	CD	OSP	FD
1. N. Bestemianova/A. Bukin (SOV)	1	1	1
2. M. Klimova/S. Ponomarenko (SOV)	2	2	2
3. N. Annenko/G. Sretenski (SOV)	3	3	3
4. Kathrin Beck/Christoff Beck (AUT)	4	4	4
5. I. Duchesnay/P. Duchesnay (FRA)	7	6	5
6. Klára Engi/Attila Tóth (HUN)	6	5	6
7. A. Becherer/F. Becherer (FRG)	5	7	7
8. Sharon Jones/Paul Askham (GRB)	8	8	8
9. Lia Trovati/Roberto Pelizzola (ITA)	9	9	9

10. Viera Řeháková/Ivan Havránek (CZE)	10	10	10
11. Corinne Paliard/Didier Courtois (FRA)	11(t)	11	11
12. Elizabeth Coates/Alan Abretti (GRB)	11(t)	12	12
13. S. Calegari/P. Camerlengo (ITA)	13	13	13
14. H. Górna/A. Dostatni (POL)	15	15	15
15. A. Weppelmann/H. Schamberger (FRG)	14	14	15
16. Andrea Juklova/Martin Šimeček (CZE)	17	16	16
17. Kinga Wertan/Janos Demeter (HUN)	16	17	17
18. Susanna Rahkamo/Petri Kokko (FIN)	18	19	18
19. Hristina Boyanova/Yavor Ivanov (BUL)	19	18	19
20. Désirée Schlegel/Patrick Brecht (SUI)	20	20	20
21. Ursula Holik/Herbert Holik (AUT)	21	21	21

Source: Skating magazine, April 1987

1988 EUROPEAN FIGURE SKATING CHAMPIONSHIPS
Prague, Czechoslovakia, January 12-16, 1988

European Men's Figure Skating Championships:

	CF	SP	FS
1. Alexandr Fadeev (SOV)	1	1	1
2. Vladimir Kotin (SOV)	2	3	3
3. Viktor Petrenko (SOV)	5	2	2
4. Grzegorz Filipowski (POL)	4	5	4
5. Richard Zander (FRG)	6	4	6
6. Heiko Fischer (FRG)	3	6	7
7. Petr Barna (CZE)	8	7	5
8. Oliver Höner (SUI)	7	8	8
9. Paul Robinson (GRB)	13	10	9
10. Axel Médéric (FRA)	12	9	13
11. Frédéric Lipka (FRA)	10	20	10
12. Alessandro Riccitelli (ITA)	11	17	14
13. András Száraz (HUN)	15	19	11
14. Ralph Burghart (AUT)	9	13	17
15. Peter Johansson (SWE)	20	12	12
16. Oula Jääskeläinen (FIN)	17	11	16
17. Michael Huth (GDR)	21	16	15
18. Rico Krahnert (GDR)	19	14	18

19. Henrik Walentin (DEN)	18	15	19
20. Jaroslav Suchý (CZE)	16	21	21
21. Tomislav Čižmešija (YUG)	14	23	22
22. Cornel Gheorghe (ROM)	23	18	20
23. Przemysław Noworyta (POL)	22	22	23
24. Fernando Soria (ESP)	24	24	24

European Ladies Figure Skating Championships:

	CF	SP	FS
1. Katarina Witt (GDR)	2	1	1
2. Kira Ivanova (SOV)	1	2	3
3. Anna Kondrashova (SOV)	3	3	2
4. Claudia Leistner (FRG)	4	6	5
5. Simone Koch (GDR)	11	4	4
6. Natalia Gorbenko (SOV)	6	13	7
7. Agnès Gosselin (FRA)	8	7	9
8. Tamara Téglássy (HUN)	9	11	8
9. Marina Kielmann (FRG)	17	5	6
10. Joanne Conway (GRB)	5	14	12
11. Iveta Voralová (CZE)	13	18	11
12. Stéfanie Schmid (SUI)	16	9	13
13. Beatrice Gelmini (ITA)	15	19	10
14. Katrien Pauwels (BEL)	7	17	16
15. Mirela Gawłowska (POL)	12	8	18
16. Claude Péri (FRA)	20	10	14
17. Željka Čižmešija (YUG)	10	12	20
18. Lotta Falkenbäck (SWE)	14	15	17
19. Petra Vonmoos (SUI)	23	16	15
20. Yvonne Pokorny (AUT)	18	22	19
21. Anisette Torp-Lind (DEN)	22	20	21
22. Kateřina Nováková (CZE)	19	21	23
23. Elina Hänninen (FIN)	21	23	22
24. Eva Plaszko (HUN)	25	24	24
25. Marta Olozagarre (ESP)	24	26	-
26. Anita Thorenfeldt (NOR)	26	25	-
27. Asia Alexieva (BUL)	27	27	-

European Pairs Skating Championships:

	SP	FS
1. Ekaterina Gordeeva/Sergei Grinkov (SOV)	1	1
2. Larisa Selezneva/Oleg Makarov (SOV)	2	2
3. Peggy Schwarz/Alexander König (GDR)	3	3
4. Natalia Mishkutenok/Artur Dmitriev (SOV)	4	4
5. Mandy Wötzel/Axel Rauschenbach (GDR)	6	5
6. Lenka Knapová/René Novotný (CZE)	5	6
7. Brigitte Groh/Holger Maletz (FRG)	7	7
8. Cheryl Peake/Andrew Naylor (GRB)	8	8
9. Anuschka Gläser/Stefan Pfrengle (FRG)	9	9
10. Lisa Cushley/Neil Cushley (GRB)	10	10
11. Dagmar Kovářová/Karel Kovář (CZE)	11	11

European Ice Dancing Championships:

	CD	OSP	FD
1. N. Bestemianova/A. Bukin (SOV)	1	1	1
2. N. Annenko/G. Sretenski (SOV)	2	2	2
3. I. Duchesnay/P. Duchesnay (FRA)	5	4	3
4. Maya Usova/Alexandr Zhulin (SOV)	4	3	4
5. Kathrin Beck/Christoff Beck (AUT)	3	4	5
6. Klára Engi/Attila Tóth (HUN)	6	6	6
7. Lia Trovati/Roberto Pelizzola (ITA)	7	7	7
8. Sharon Jones/Paul Askham (GRB)	9	8	8
9. Viera Řeháková/Ivan Havránek (CZE)	10	9	9
10. Corinne Paliard/Didier Courtois (FRA)	11	10	10
11. S. Calegari/P. Camerlengo (ITA)	12	11	11
12. H. Górna/A. Dostatni (POL)	13	12	12
13. Andrea Juklova/Martin Šimeček (CZE)	14	13	13
14. A. Weppelmann/H. Schamberger (FRG)	15	15	14
15. Susanna Rahkamo/Petri Kokko (FIN)	16	14	15
16. Désirée Schlegel/Patrick Brecht (SUI)	17	16	16
17. Annalisa Meyers/Justin Green (GRB)	18	17	17
WD. A. Becherer/F. Becherer (FRG)	8	-	-

After the discontinuation of the semi-final, the results of the compulsory figures and short program were combined and only the top 24 skaters advanced to the free skate.

Over a decade before the IJS Judging System was introduced, Katarina Witt earned the final perfect 6.0's ever awarded in the ladies event at the European Figure Skating Championships. Witt received five 6.0's in the short program and two in the free skating.

Source: Skating magazine, February 1988; Video footage, 1988 European Figure Skating Championships

1989 EUROPEAN FIGURE SKATING CHAMPIONSHIPS
Birmingham, England, January 17-21, 1989

European Men's Figure Skating Championships:

	CF	OP	FS
1. Alexandr Fadeev (SOV)	2	1	1
2. Grzegorz Filipowski (POL)	3	2	2
3. Petr Barna (CZE)	4	3	3
4. Dmitri Gromov (SOV)	11	4	4
5. Daniel Weiss (FRG)	5	5	7
6. Viacheslav Zagorodniuk (SOV)	8	8	5
7. Axel Médéric (FRA)	7	6	13
8. Peter Johansson (SWE)	16	12	6
9. Lars Dresler (DEN)	12	7	12
10. Alessandro Riccitelli (ITA)	9	13	10
11. András Száraz (HUN)	13	9	11
12. Ronny Winkler (GDR)	18	11	8
13. Éric Millot (FRA)	15	14	9
14. Ralph Burghart (AUT)	6	16	14
15. Christian Newberry (GRB)	10	15	15
16. Oula Jääskeläinen (FIN)	19	18	16
17. Tomislav Čižmešija (YUG)	14	19	18
18. Jan Erik Digernes (NOR)	21	17	17
19. John Martin (GRB)	17	21	19
20 Boyko Aleksiev (BUL)	20	20	-
WD. Richard Zander (FRG)	1	10	-
WD. Viktor Petrenko (SOV)	-	-	-
WD. Oliver Höner (SUI)	-	-	-
WD. Mark Bachofen (SUI)	-	-	-

European Ladies Figure Skating Championships:

	CF	OP	FS
1. Claudia Leistner (FRG)	1	1	1
2. Natalia Lebedeva (SOV)	4	3	2
3. Patricia Neske (FRG)	8	5	3
4. Simone Lang (GDR)	6	2	6
5. Natalia Gorbenko (SOV)	3	7	7
6. Joanne Conway (GRB)	2	4	10
7. Evelyn Großmann (GDR)	12	6	5
8. Surya Bonaly (FRA)	17	8	4
9. Tamara Téglássy (HUN)	10	11	8
10. Yvonne Gómez (ESP)	13	10	9
11. Željka Čižmešija (YUG)	5	12	12
12. Yvonne Pokorny (AUT)	7	13	11
13. Sabine Contini (ITA)	14	9	15
14. Hélène Persson (SWE)	11	15	16
15. Anisette Torp-Lind (DEN)	21	14	13
16. Stefanie Schmid (SUI)	15	17	14
17. Claude Péri (FRA)	9	16	17
18. Jacqueline Soames (GRB)	18	19	18
19. Jeltje Schulten (NED)	19	20	19
20. Iveta Voralová (CZE)	20	21	-
21. Sandrine Goes (BEL)	25	18	-
22. Elina Hänninen (FIN)	22	22	-
23. Anita Thorenfeldt (NOR)	24	24	-
24. Asia Aleksieva (BUL)	23	25	-
25. Andrea Gránitz (HUN)	26	26	-
WD. Mirela Gawłowska (POL)	16	23	-

European Pairs Skating Championships:

	OP	FS
1. Larisa Selezneva/Oleg Makarov (SOV)	1	1
2. Mandy Wötzel/Axel Rauschenbach (GDR)	2	2
3. Natalia Mishkutenok/Artur Dmitriev (SOV)	3	3
4. Elena Kvitchenko/Rashid Kadyrkaev (SOV)	4	4
5. Cheryl Peake/Andrew Naylor (GRB)	5	5
6. Anuschka Gläser/Stefan Pfrengle (FRG)	6	6
7. Lisa Cushley/Neil Cushley (GRB)	7	7

8. Sonja Adalbert/Daniele Caprano (FRG)	8	8
9. Anna Górecka/Arkadiusz Górecki (POL)	9	9
WD. Ekaterina Gordeeva/Sergei Grinkov (SOV)	-	-
WD. Angela Caspary/Marno Kreft (GDR)	-	-
WD. Karina Steizer/Piotr Szczerbowski (POL)	-	-

European Ice Dancing Championships:

	CD	OSP	FD
1. M. Klimova/S. Ponomarenko (SOV)	1	1	1
2. Maya Usova/Alexandr Zhulin (SOV)	2	2	2
3. N. Annenko/G. Sretenski (SOV)	3	3	3
4. Klára Engi/Attila Tóth (HUN)	4	4	4
5. S. Calegari/P. Camerlengo (ITA)	6	6	5
6. Sharon Jones/Paul Askham (GRB)	5	5	6
7. Andrea Juklova/Martin Šimeček (CZE)	8	7	7
8. Dominique Yvon/Frédéric Palluel (FRA)	7	8	8
9. M. Grajcar/A. Dostatni (POL)	9	9	9
10. A. Weppelmann/H. Schamberger (FRG)	11	10	10
11. Sophie Moniotte/Pascal Lavanchy (FRA)	10	11	11
12. Susanna Rahkamo/Petri Kokko (FIN)	12	12	12
13. Anna Croci/Luca Mantovani (ITA)	13	13	13
14. Karen Quinn/Alan Abretti (GRB)	15	15	14
15. K. Kerekes/C. Szentpéteri (HUN)	14	14	15
16. D. Gerencser/B. Columberg (SUI)	16	16	16
17. Ursula Holik/Herbert Holik (AUT)	17	17	17

Claudia Leistner made history as the first and only West German skater to win a gold medal in the ladies event at the European Figure Skating Championships.

Sources: Programme, 1989 European Figure Skating Championships; Skating magazine, March 1989

Susanna Rahkamo and Petri Kokko, European Champions 1995. Allstar Picture Library Ltd / Alamy Stock Photo

THE AGE OF GLOBALIZATION

1990 EUROPEAN FIGURE SKATING CHAMPIONSHIPS
Leningrad, Soviet Union, January 30-February 4, 1990

European Men's Figure Skating Championships:

	CF	OP	FS
1. Viktor Petrenko (SOV)	2	3	1
2. Petr Barna (CZE)	4	1	2
3. Viacheslav Zagorodniuk (SOV)	6	2	3
4. Grzegorz Filipowski (POL)	3	4	4
5. Richard Zander (FRG)	1	9	5
6. Oliver Höner (SUI)	8	5	7
7. Daniel Weiss (FRG)	5	6	8
8. Philippe Candeloro (FRA)	17	7	6
9. Ralph Burghart (AUT)	7	10	9
10. Peter Johansson (SWE)	11	8	12
11. Ronny Winkler (GDR)	16	12	10
12. Cornel Gheorghe (ROM)	21	13	11
13. Alessandro Riccitelli (ITA)	10	14	15
14. Henrik Walentin (DEN)	22	11	13
15. Steven Cousins (GRB)	15	15	14
16. Lars Dresler (DEN)	9	18	16
17. Oula Jääskeläinen (FIN)	20	16	17
18. Alcuin Schulten (NED)	12	19	19
19. Éric Millot (FRA)	18	17	18
20. Tomislav Čižmešija (YUG)	13	22	20
21. Pavel Vančo (CZE)	14	23	-
22. András Száraz (HUN)	19	20	-
23. Massimo Salvade (ITA)	24	21	-
24. Emanuele Ancorini (SWE)	25	24	-
25. Alexandre Geers (BEL)	23	26	-
26. Jan Erik Digernes (NOR)	26	25	-
27. Alexander Mladenov (BUL)	27	27	-

WD. Dmitri Gromov (SOV) - - -
WD. Axel Médéric (FRA) - - -
WD. John Martin (GRB) - - -
WD. Christian Newberry (GRB) - - -

European Ladies Figure Skating Championships:

	CF	OP	FS
1. Evelyn Großmann (GDR)	5	2	1
2. Natalia Lebedeva (SOV)	1	1	4
3. Marina Kielmann (FRG)	8	5	2
4. Surya Bonaly (FRA)	11	3	3
5. Patricia Neske (FRG)	2	6	5
6. Tanja Krienke (GDR)	12	4	6
7. Natalia Skrabnevskaya (SOV)	3	7	9
8. Tamara Téglássy (HUN)	9	9	7
9. Carola Wolff (FRG)	7	11	10
10. Larisa Zamotina (SOV)	19	8	8
11. Hélène Persson (SWE)	10	10	12
12. Beatrice Gelmini (ITA)	6	16	11
13. Željka Čižmešija (YUG)	4	12	18
14. Laëtitia Hubert (FRA)	20	13	13
15. Emma Murdoch (GRB)	13	14	17
16. Yvonne Pokorny (AUT)	15	18	14
17. Lenka Kulovaná (CZE)	17	19	15
18. Maria Fuglsang (DEN)	14	15	19
19. Michèle Claret (SUI)	16	20	16
20. Astrid Winklemann (NED)	18	21	20
21. Meri Karvosenoja (FIN)	28	17	-
22. Sandrine Goes (BEL)	22	22	-
23. Andrea Law (GRB)	21	25	-
24. Anita Thorenfeldt (NOR)	25	23	-
25. Milena Marinovich (BUL)	26	24	-
26. Beata Zielińska (POL)	23	26	-
27. Cristina Perez (ESP)	27	27	-
WD. Laia Papell (ESP)	24	-	-
WD. Claudia Leistner (FRG)	-	-	-
WD. Simone Lang (FRG)	-	-	-
WD. Yvonne Gómez (ESP)	-	-	-

WD. Anisette Torp-Lind (DEN) - - -
WD. Claude Péri (FRA) - - -
WD. Stéfanie Schmid (SUI) - - -
WD. Sabine Contini (ITA) - - -
WD. Jeltje Schulten (NED) - - -

European Pairs Skating Championships:

	OP	FS
1. Ekaterina Gordeeva/Sergei Grinkov (SOV)	3	1
2. Larisa Selezneva/Oleg Makarov (SOV)	2	2
3. Natalia Mishkutenok/Artur Dmitriev (SOV)	1	3
4. Peggy Schwarz/Alexander König (GDR)	4	5
5. Anuschka Gläser/Stefan Pfrengle (FRG)	7	4
6. Radka Kovaříková/René Novotný (CZE)	5	6
7. Ines Müller/Ingo Steuer (GDR)	6	7
8. Cheryl Peake/Andrew Naylor (GRB)	8	8
9. Catherine Barker/Michael Aldred (GRB)	9	9
10. Henriette Worner/Andreas Sigurdsson (FRG)	10	10
11. Katarzyna Głowacka/Krzysztof Korcarz (POL)	11	11
12. Saskia Bourgeois/Guy Bourgeois (SUI)	13	12
13. Svetlana Dragaeva/Karel Kovář (ISU)	12	13
WD. Mandy Wötzel/Axel Rauschenbach (GDR)	-	-
WD. Elena Kvitchenko/Rashid Kadyrkaev (SOV)	-	-
WD. Sonja Adalbert/Daniele Caprano (FRG)	-	-
WD. Anna Górecka/Arkadiusz Górecki (POL)	-	-

European Ice Dancing Championships:

	CD	OSP	FD
1. M. Klimova/S. Ponomarenko (SOV)	1	1	1
2. Maya Usova/Alexandr Zhulin (SOV)	2	2	2
3. I. Duchesnay/P. Duchesnay (FRA)	4	3	3
4. Klára Engi/Attila Tóth (HUN)	3	4	4
5. Oksana Grishuk/Evgeni Platov (SOV)	5	5	5
6. Dominique Yvon/Frédéric Palluel (FRA)	7	7	6
7. Susanna Rahkamo/Petri Kokko (FIN)	6	6	7
8. Anna Croci/Luca Mantovani (ITA)	8	8	8
9. Ivana Střondalová/Milan Brzý (CZE)	9	9	9
10. M. Grajcar/A. Dostatni (POL)	10	10	10

11. Monika Mandikova/Oliver Pekar (CZE)	11	11	11
12. Lynn Burton/Andrew Place (GRB)	12	12	12
13. K. Kerekes/C. Szentpéteri (HUN)	13	13	14
14. Ann Hall/Jason Blomfield (GRB)	15	15	13
15. P. Zietemann/F. Ladd-Oshiro (FRG)	14	14	15
16. Saskia Stahler/Sven Authorsen (FRG)	16	16	17
17. D. Gerencser/B. Columberg (SUI)	17	18	16
18. Michela Cesaro/Carlo Soave (ITA)	18	17	18
19. Petia Gavazova/Nikolai Tonev (BUL)	20	19	19
20. K. Długoszewska/A. Szaszor (POL)	19	21	20
21. Monika Müksch/Bernhard Hatzl (AUT)	21	20	-
22. J. van Leeuwen/E. van Luuewen (NED)	22	22	-
WD. N. Annenko/G. Sretenski (SOV)	-	-	-
WD. S. Calegari/P. Camerlengo (ITA)	-	-	-
WD. S. Jones/P. Askham (GRB)	-	-	-
WD. Andrea Juklova/Martin Šimeček (CZE)	-	-	-
WD. Weppelmann/Schamberger (FRG)	-	-	-
WD. Ursula Holik/Herbert Holik (AUT)	-	-	-

Though the Berlin Wall fell in November of 1989, representatives of both the East and West German federations participated in the 1990 European Figure Skating Championships, during a period of restructuring in the German reunification process.

Compulsory figures were skated for the final time in the men's and ladies events at the European Championships. Richard Zander of West Germany and Natalia Lebedeva of the Soviet Union made history as the final skater to win the figures.

Svetlana Dragaeva and Karel Kovář made history as the first pairs team to compete as representatives of the ISU at the European Championships. Dragaeva hailed from the Soviet Union; Kovář from Czechoslovakia.

Sources: Programme, 1990 European Figure Skating Championships; Rudé právo, February 1, 1990; Skating magazine, February 1990

1991 EUROPEAN FIGURE SKATING CHAMPIONSHIPS
Sofia, Bulgaria, January 22-27, 1991

European Men's Figure Skating Championships:

	OP	FS
1. Viktor Petrenko (SOV)	1	1
2. Petr Barna (CZE)	2	2
3. Viacheslav Zagorodniuk (SOV)	3	3
4. Éric Millot (FRA)	5	4
5. Philippe Candeloro (FRA)	4	5
6. Alexei Urmanov (SOV)	6	6
7. Mirko Eichhorn (GER)	10	7
8. Steven Cousins (GRB)	11	8
9. Oliver Höner (SUI)	7	10
10. Daniel Weiss (GER)	12	9
11. Ronny Winkler (GER)	9	11
12. Oula Jääskeläinen (FIN)	8	12
13. Alessandro Riccitelli (ITA)	15	13
14. Cornel Gheorghe (ROM)	13	14
15. Henrik Walentin (DEN)	16	15
16. Jan Erik Digernes (NOR)	17	16
17. Tomislav Čižmešija (YUG)	14	18
18. Niclas Karlsson (SWE)	18	17
19. Nikolai Tonev (BUL)	19	19
20. Maarten van Mechelen (LUX)	20	20
21. Emanuele Ancorini (SWE)	21	-
22. Alexandre Geers (BEL)	22	-
WD. Ralph Burghart (AUT)	-	-

European Ladies Figure Skating Championships:

	OP	FS
1. Surya Bonaly (FRA)	2	1
2. Evelyn Großmann (GER)	1	3
3. Marina Kielmann (GER)	6	2
4. Joanne Conway (GRB)	3	4
5. Patricia Neske (GER)	5	5
6. Lenka Kulovaná (CZE)	4	6
7. Yulia Vorobieva (SOV)	7	7

8. Natalia Gorbenko (SOV)	9	8
9. Simone Lang (GER)	8	10
10. Laëtitia Hubert (FRA)	13	9
11. Larisa Zamotina (SOV)	11	11
12. Sabine Contini (ITA)	14	12
13. Anisette Torp-Lind (DEN)	10	15
14. Hélène Persson (SWE)	12	16
15. Nathalie Krieg (SUI)	19	13
16. Zuzanna Szwed (POL)	17	14
17. Marion Krijgsman (NED)	16	17
18. Željka Čižmešija (YUG)	15	18
19. Anita Markoczy (HUN)	18	19
20. Codruţa Moiseanu (ROM)	21	-
21. Milena Marinovich (BUL)	22	-
22. Kaisa Kella (FIN)	23	-
23. Anita Thorenfeldt (NOR)	24	-
24. Marta Andrade Vidal (ESP)	25	-
25. Sandrine Goes (BEL)	26	-
WD. Tamara Téglássy (HUN)	20	-

European Pairs Skating Championships:

	OP	FS
1. Natalia Mishkutenok/Artur Dmitriev (SOV)	2	1
2. Elena Bechke/Denis Petrov (SOV)	1	2
3. Evgenia Shishkova/Vadim Naumov (SOV)	3	3
4. Radka Kovaříková/René Novotný (CZE)	6	4
5. Mandy Wötzel/Axel Rauschenbach (GER)	5	5
6. Anuschka Gläser/Stefan Pfengle (GER)	4	6
7. Ines Müller/Ingo Steuer (GER)	7	7
8. Cheryl Peake/Andrew Naylor (GRB)	10	8
9. Katarzyna Głowacka/Krzysztof Korcarz (POL)	8	9
10. Saskia Bourgeois/Guy Bourgeois (SUI)	9	10
11. Catherine Barker/Michael Aldred (GRB)	11	11
12. Anna Tabacchi/Massimo Salvade (ITA)	12	12

European Ice Dancing Championships:

	CD	OD	FD
1. M. Klimova/S. Ponomarenko (SOV)	1(t)	2	1
2. I. Duchesnay/P. Duchesnay (FRA)	3	1	2
3. Maya Usova/Alexandr Zhulin (SOV)	1(t)	3	3
4. Klára Engi/Attila Tóth (HUN)	4	4	4
5. Oksana Grishuk/Evgeni Platov (SOV)	5	5	5
6. S. Calegari/P. Camerlengo (ITA)	6	6	6
7. Dominique Yvon/Frédéric Palluel (FRA)	7	7	7
8. Susanna Rahkamo/Petri Kokko (FIN)	8	8	8
9. Sophie Moniotte/Pascal Lavanchy (FRA)	9	9	9
10. K. Mrázová/M. Šimeček (CZE)	10	10	10
11. J. Goolsbee/H. Schamberger (GER)	12	11	11
12. Monika Mandiková/Oliver Pekár (CZE)	11	12	12
13. Saskia Stahler/Sven Authorsen (GER)	13	13	14
14. R. Woodward/C. Szentpéteri (HUN)	14	14	13
15. D. Gerencser/B. Columberg (SUI)	16	16	15
16. Ann Hall/Jason Blomfield (GRB)	15	15	16
17. Kati Uski/Juha Sasi (FIN)	17	18	17
18. J. van Leeuwen/E. van Leeuwen (NED)	19	19	18
WD. Maria Hadjiiska/Hristo Nikolov (BUL)	18	17	-

Surya Bonaly made history as the first woman of colour to win a gold medal at the European Figure Skating Championships. She was also the first French skater to win a gold medal in the ladies event.

Sources: La liberté, January 25, 1991; Skating magazine, May 1991

1992 EUROPEAN FIGURE SKATING CHAMPIONSHIPS
Lausanne, Switzerland, January 21-26, 1992

European Men's Figure Skating Championships:

	OP	FS
1. Petr Barna (CZE)	1	2
2. Viktor Petrenko (CIS)	4	1
3. Alexei Urmanov (CIS)	3	3
4. Viacheslav Zagorodniuk (CIS)	2	4
5. Grzegorz Filipowski (POL)	6	5

6. Nicolas Pétorin (FRA)	5	6
7. Steven Cousins (GRB)	8	8
8. Éric Millot (FRA)	11	7
9. Konstantin Kostin (LAT)	12	9
10. Henrik Walentin (DEN)	10	11
11. Ralph Burghart (AUT)	13	10
12. Ronny Winkler (GER)	9	12
13. Mirko Eichhorn (GER)	7	13
14. Oula Jääskeläinen (FIN)	14	14
15. Marius Cristian Negrea (ROM)	15	15
16. John Martin (GRB)	18	16
17. Gilberto Viadana (ITA)	16	17
18. Jan Erik Digernes (NOR)	17	18
19. Patrick Meier (SUI)	21	19
20. Jaroslav Suchý (CZE)	20	21
21. Emanuele Ancorini (SWE)	23	20
22. Alcuin Schulten (NED)	19	23
23. Jordi Lafarga (ESP)	24	22
24. Rastislav Vnučko (CZE)	22	24
25. Ivan Dinev (BUL)	25	-
26. Balázs Grenczer (HUN)	26	-

European Ladies Figure Skating Championships:

	OP	FS
1. Surya Bonaly (FRA)	1	1
2. Marina Kielmann (GER)	5	2
3. Patricia Neske (GER)	4	3
4. Simone Lang (GER)	2	4
5. Lenka Kulovaná (CZE)	3	6
6. Laëtitia Hubert (FRA)	8	5
7. Marie-Pierre Leray (FRA)	7	7
8. Yulia Vorobieva (CIS)	13	8
9. Joanne Conway (GRB)	9	10
10. Zuzanna Szwed (POL)	12	9
11. Alice Sue Claeys (BEL)	10	11
12. Charlene von Saher (GRB)	15	12
13. Nathalie Krieg (SUI)	11	14
14. Tatiana Rachkova (CIS)	6	17

15. Irena Zemanová (CZE)	17	13
16. Krisztina Czakó (HUN)	14	15
17. Anisette Torp-Lind (DEN)	18	16
18. Hélène Persson (SWE)	19	18
19. Viktoria Dimitrova (BUL)	21	19
20. Alma Lepina (LAT)	16	22
21. Mila Kajas (FIN)	22	20
22. Marion Krijgsman (NED)	23	21
23. Mojca Kopač (SLO)	20	24
24. Olga Vassiljeva (EST)	24	23
25. Marta Andrade Vidal (ESP)	25	-
26. Anita Thorenfeldt (NOR)	26	-
27. Yvonne Pokorny (AUT)	27	-
28. Edita Katkauskaite (LIT)	28	-
29. Sabine Contini (ITA)	29	-
30. Codruța Moiseanu (ROM)	30	-

European Pairs Skating Championships:

	OP	FS
1. Natalia Mishkutenok/Artur Dmitriev (CIS)	2	1
2. Elena Bechke/Denis Petrov (CIS)	1	2
3. Evgenia Shishkova/Vadim Naumov (CIS)	4	3
4. Radka Kovaříková/René Novotný (CZE)	3	4
5. Peggy Schwarz/Alexander König (GER)	6	5
6. Mandy Wötzel/Axel Rauschenbach (GER)	5	6
7. Anuschka Gläser/Stefan Pfengle (GER)	7	7
8. Leslie Monod/Cédric Monod (SUI)	9	8
9. Cheryl Peake/Andrew Naylor (GRB)	8	9
10. Beata Zielińska/Mariusz Siudek (POL)	10	10
11. Anna Tabacchi/Massimo Salvade (ITA)	11	11
12. Line Haddad/Sylvain Privé (FRA)	12	12
13. Kathryn Pritchard/Jason Briggs (GRB)	13	13

European Ice Dancing Championships:

	CD	OD	FD
1. M. Klimova/S. Ponomarenko (CIS)	1	1	1
2. Maya Usova/Alexandr Zhulin (CIS)	2	2	2
3. Oksana Grishuk/Evgeni Platov (CIS)	3	3	3

4. S. Calegari/P. Camerlengo (ITA)	4(t)	4	4
5. Klára Engi/Attila Tóth (HUN)	4(t)	5	5
6. Susanna Rahkamo/Petri Kokko (FIN)	6	6	6
7. D. Yvon/F. Palluel (FRA)	7	7	7
8. S. Moniotte/P. Lavanchy (FRA)	8	8	8
9. K. Mrázová/M. Šimeček (CZE)	9	9	9
10. J. Goolsbee/H. Schamberger (GER)	10(t)	10	10
11. Anna Croci/Luca Mantovani (ITA)	10(t)	11	11
12. Marina Morel/Gwendal Peizerat (FRA)	10(t)	12	12
13. R. Woodward/C. Szentpétery (HUN)	13	13	13
14. Radmila Chroboková/Milan Brzy (CZE)	16	14	14
15. M. Drobiazko/P. Vanagas (LIT)	14	16	15
16. V. Le Tensorer/J. Kienzle (SUI)	17	15	16
17. Melanie Bruce/Andrew Place (GRB)	15	17	17
18. Albena Denkova/Hristo Nikolov (BUL)	18	18	18
19. A. Domańska/M. Głowacki (POL)	20(t)	20	19
20. D-L. Maritczak/I-A. Maritczak (AUT)	19	19	20
21. Katri Uski/Juha Sasi (FIN)	20(t)	21	21

The ISU celebrated its 100th Anniversary by holding the European Figure Skating Championships in Switzerland, where its Headquarters were located.

After the breakup of the Soviet Union, many former Soviet skaters skated as representatives of the the Commonwealth of Independent States (CIS), while others represented newly-formed countries.

Olga Vassiljeva made history as the first skater to represent Estonia at the European Figure Skating Championships. Edita Katkauskaite and Margarita Drobiazko and Povilas Vanagas were the first Lithuanians to participate. Mojca Kopač was the first Slovenian to participate.

Source: Skating magazine, May 1992

1993 EUROPEAN FIGURE SKATING CHAMPIONSHIPS
Helsinki, Finland, January 12-17, 1993

European Men's Figure Skating Championships:

	TP	FS
1. Dmitri Dmitrenko (UKR)	1	3
2. Philippe Candeloro (FRA)	6	1
3. Éric Millot (FRA)	7	2
4. Konstantin Kostin (LAT)	5	4
5. Alexei Urmanov (RUS)	4	6
6. Michael Tyllesen (DEN)	8	5
7. Oleg Tataurov (RUS)	3	8
8. Oula Jääskeläinen (FIN)	2	9
9. Steven Cousins (GRB)	9	7
10. Ronny Winkler (GER)	10	10
11. Henrik Walentin (DEN)	14	11
12. Roman Ekimov (RUS)	12	13
13. Jaroslav Suchý (CZE)	15	12
14. John Martin (GRB)	11	14
15. Gilberto Viadana (ITA)	19	15
16. Besarion Tsintsadze (GEO)	18	16
17. Robert Grzegorczyk (POL)	13	19
18. Daniel Peinado (ESP)	16	18
19. Jan Erik Digernes (NOR)	20	17
20. Szabolcs Vidrai (HUN)	17	21
21. Rastislav Vnučko (SVK)	22	20
22. Alexander Murashko (BLS)	23	22
23. Tomislav Čižmešija (CRO)	21	23
24. Marek Sząszor (POL)	25	-
25. Ivan Dinev (BUL)	26	-
26. Florian Tuma (AUT)	27	-
27. Nicolas Binz (SUI)	28	-
28. Raimo Reinsalu (EST)	29	-
WD. Cornel Gheorghe (ROM)	24	-

European Ladies Figure Skating Championships:

	QRA	QRB	TP	FS
1. Surya Bonaly (FRA)	1	-	1	1
2. Oksana Baiul (UKR)	-	2	3	2
3. Marina Kielmann (GER)	-	3	2	3
4. Tanja Szewczenko (GER)	2	-	4	4
5. Maria Butyrskaya (RUS)	-	7	5	5
6. Krisztina Czakó (HUN)	-	5	6	6
7. Zuzanna Szwed (POL)	4	-	8	7
8. Alice Sue Claeys (BEL)	-	1	7	9
9. Marie-Pierre Leray (FRA)	-	4	13	8
10. Simone Lang (GER)	3	-	9	10
11. Lenka Kulovaná (CZE)	-	6	12	12
12. Olga Markova (RUS)	-	8	10	14
13. Alma Lepina (LAT)	5	-	11	15
14. Nathalie Krieg (SUI)	-	9	20	11
15. Anna Rechnio (POL)	-	10	18	13
16. Irena Zemanová (CZE)	9	-	14	18
17. Viktoria Dimitrova (BUL)	-	12	19	16
18. Mojca Kopač (SLO)	8	-	17	17
19. Charlene von Saher (GRB)	6	-	15	19
20. Cristina Mauri (ITA)	-	11	23	20
21. Kaisa Kella (FIN)	-	14	24	21
22. Marion Krijgsman (NED)	7	-	22	22
23. Olga Vassiljeva (EST)	12	-	25	23
24. Andrea Kus (AUT)	13	-	-	-
24. Marta Andrade Vidal (ESP)	13	-	-	-
26. Emma Warmington (GRB)	14	-	-	-
27. Marianne Aarnes (NOR)	15	-	-	-
27. Ann-Marie Söderholm (SWE)	-	15	-	-
29. Ivana Jakupčević (CRO)	16	-	-	-
29. Inna Ovsiannikova (BLS)	-	16	-	-
31. Edita Katkauskaitė (LIT)	17	-	-	-
WD. Laëtitia Hubert (FRA)	10	-	16	-
WD. Anisette Torp-Lind (DEN)	11	-	21	-

European Pairs Skating Championships:

	TP	FS
1. Marina Eltsova/Andrei Bushkov (RUS)	2	1
2. Mandy Wötzel/Ingo Steuer (GER)	3	2
3. Evgenia Shishkova/Vadim Naumov (RUS)	1	4
4. Radka Kovaříková/René Novotný (CZE)	5	3
5. Peggy Schwarz/Alexander König (GER)	4	5
6. Leslie Monod/Cédric Monod (SUI)	6	6
7. Elena Tobiash/Sergei Smirnov (RUS)	7	7
8. Elena Berezhnaya/Oleg Shliakhov (LAT)	8	8
9. Beata Zielińska/Mariusz Siudek (POL)	10	9
10. S. Pristav/V. Tkachenko (UKR)	9	10
11. Jekaterina Silnitzkaja/Marno Kreft (GER)	11	11
12. Jacqueline Soames/John Jenkins (GRB)	12	12
13. Vicky Pearce/Clive Shorten (GRB)	15	13
14. Sarah Abitbol/Stéphane Bernadis (FRA)	13	14
15. Elena Grigoreva/Serghei Sheiko (BLS)	14	15

European Ice Dancing Championships:

	CD	OD	FD
1. Maya Usova/Alexandr Zhulin (RUS)	1	1	1
2. Oksana Grishuk/Evgeni Platov (RUS)	2	2	2
3. Susanna Rahkamo/Petri Kokko (FIN)	3	3	3
4. Anjelika Krylova/Vladimir Fedorov (RUS)	5	4	4
5. S. Calegari/P. Camerlengo (ITA)	4	5	6
6. Sophie Moniotte/Pascal Lavanchy (FRA)	6	6	5
7. Irina Romanova/Igor Yaroshenko (UKR)	7	7	7
8. Kateřina Mrázová/Martin Šimeček (CZE)	9	8	8
9. Tatiana Navka/Samvel Gezalian (BLS)	8	9	9
10. J. Goolsbee/H. Schamberger (GER)	10	10	10
11. M. Drobiazko/P. Vanagas (LIT)	11	11	11
12. M. Humphreys/J. Lanning (GRB)	12	12	12
13. Irina Le Bed/Alexandre Piton (FRA)	13	13	14
14. A. Domańska/M. Głowacki (POL)	17	15	13
15. Radmila Chroboková/Milan Brzý (CZE)	14	14	15
16. Kati Winkler/René Lohse (GER)	15(t)	16	16
17. Barbara Minorini/Andrea Gilardi (ITA)	15(t)	17	17
18. Angelika Führing/Peter Wilczek (AUT)	18(t)	18	18

19. D. Gerencser/A. Stanislavov (SUI)	18(t)	19	19
20. Enikő Berkes/Szilárd Tóth (HUN)	20(t)	20	21
21. Noémi Vedres/Endre Szentirmai (HUN)	20(t)	22	20
22. Albena Denkova/Hristo Nikolov (BUL)	20(t)	21	22
23. Jelena Trocenko/Erik Samovich (LAT)	23	23	23

For the first time, qualifying rounds were held at the European Figure Skating Championships. Kaisa Kella of Finland failed to place high enough in her group to qualify, but earned the right to compete in the short program because of the ISU's rule that the host country automatically qualified one skater.

Dmitri Dmitrenko won Ukraine's first gold medal at the European Championships. Oksana Baiul made history the first skater from Ukraine to win a medal in the ladies event.

Alexander Mourashko, Inna Ovsiannikova, Elena Grigoreva and Serghei Sheiko and Tatiana Navka and Samvel Gezalian made history as the first skaters to represent Belarus at the event. Tomislav Čižmešija and Ivana Jakupčević made history as the first skaters to represent Croatia. Besarion Tsintsadze and Rastislav Vnučko became the first skaters to represent Georgia and Slovakia.

Sources: Etelä-Suomen Sanomat, January 11, 13 and 14, 1993; Skating magazine, April 1993; Taitoluistelu-magazine archives, The National Library of Finland

1994 EUROPEAN FIGURE SKATING CHAMPIONSHIPS
Copenhagen, Denmark, January 17-23, 1994

European Men's Figure Skating Championships:

	QRA	QRB	TP	FS
1. Viktor Petrenko (UKR)	-	2	1	1
2. Viacheslav Zagorodniuk (UKR)	1	-	3	2
3. Alexei Urmanov (RUS)	-	3	6	3
4. Éric Millot (FRA)	4	-	2	5
5. Philippe Candeloro (FRA)	-	1	7	4
6. Dmitri Dmitrenko (UKR)	2	-	4	6

7. Oleg Tataurov (RUS)	-	4	5	7
8. Michael Tyllesen (DEN)	3	-	11	8
9. Andrejs Vlascenko (LAT)	7	-	10	9
10. Ronny Winkler (GER)	5	-	9	11
11. Steven Cousins (GRB)	-	6	13	10
12. Cornel Gheorghe (ROM)	-	5	12	12
13. Zsolt Kerekes (HUN)	6	-	8	16
14. Thierry Cerez (FRA)	-	9	19	13
15. Besarion Tsintsadze (GEO)	-	10	15	15
16. Mirko Eichhorn (GER)	-	8	18	14
17. Ivan Dinev (BUL)	-	12	14	17
18. Zbigniew Komorowski (POL)	12	-	17	20
19. Markus Leminen (FIN)	8	-	23	18
20. Igor Lioutikov (AZE)	11	-	21	19
21. Rastislav Vnučko (SVK)	10	-	16	23
22. Daniel Peinado (ESP)	9	-	22	21
23. Jan Erik Digernes (NOR)	-	11	20	22
24. Oula Jääskeläinen (FIN)	13	-	-	-
24. Patrick Meier (SUI)	-	13	-	-
26. Tobias Karlsson (SWE)	14	-	-	-
26. John Martin (GRB)	-	14	-	-
28. Fabrizio Garattoni (ITA)	15	-	-	-
28. Floria Tuma (AUT)	-	15	-	-
30. Jaroslav Suchý (CZE)	16	-	-	-
30. Emrah Polatoglu (TUR)	-	16	-	-
32. Patrick Schmit (LUX)	17	-	-	-
32. Tomislav Čižmešija (CRO)	-	17	-	-
34. Jan Čejvan (SLO)	18	-	-	-
34. Vaidotas Juraitis (LIT)	-	18	-	-
36. Raimo Reinsalu (EST)	19	-	-	-
WD. Henrik Walentin (DEN)	7	-	-	-

European Ladies Figure Skating Championships:

	QRA	QRB	TP	FS
1. Surya Bonaly (FRA)	1	-	1	1
2. Oksana Baiul (UKR)	-	1	2	2
3. Olga Markova (RUS)	-	2	3	3
4. Maria Butyrskaya (RUS)	3	-	6	4

5. Tanja Szewczenko (GER)	-	6	5	5
6. Krisztina Czakó (HUN)	-	4	4	6
7. Anna Rechnio (POL)	9	-	7	7
8. Katarina Witt (GER)	-	3	9	8
9. Marina Kielmann (GER)	6	-	14	9
10. Nathalie Krieg (SUI)	-	5	12	10
11. Laëtitia Hubert (FRA)	4	-	10	12
12. Marie-Pierre Leray (FRA)	7	-	15	11
13. Irena Zemanová (CZE)	11	-	13	14
14. Zuzanna Szwed (POL)	8	-	16	13
15. Lyudmila Ivanova (UKR)	2	-	8	17
16. Alice Sue Claeys (BEL)	-	8	17	15
17. Mila Kajas (FIN)	5	-	11	19
18. Yulia Vorobieva (AZE)	-	7	20	16
19. Elena Liashenko (UKR)	10	-	19	18
20. Mojca Kopač (SLO)	-	11	23	20
21. Marta Andrade Vidal (ESP)	12	-	24	21
22. Silvia Fontana (ITA)	-	10	22	22
23. Stephanie Main (GRB)	-	12	18	24
24. Anisette Torp-Lind (DEN)	-	9	21	23
25. Helena Grundberg (SWE)	13	-	-	-
25. Tamara Panjkret (CRO)	-	13	-	-
27. Alma Lepina (LAT)	14	-	-	-
27. Zaneta Stefanikova (SVK)	-	14	-	-
29. Ingrida Zenkeviciute (LIT)	15	-	-	-
29. Tsvetelina Abrasheva (BUL)	-	15	-	-
31. Emilia Nagy (HUN)	16	-	-	-
31. Hege Gronnhaug (NOR)	-	16	-	-
33. Olga Vassilieva (EST)	17	-	-	-
33. Inna Ovsiannikova (BLS)	-	17	-	-
34. Christelle Damman (BEL)	18	-	-	-
35. Monique van der Velden (NED)	19	-	-	-
WD. Sandra Brajdic (SCG)	-	-	-	-

European Pairs Skating Championships:

	TP	FS
1. Ekaterina Gordeeva/Sergei Grinkov (RUS)	1	1
2. Evgenia Shishkova/Vadim Naumov (RUS)	2	3

3. Natalia Mishkutenok/Artur Dmitriev (RUS)	5	2
4. Radka Kovaříková/René Novotný (CZE)	3	4
5. Mandy Wötzel/Ingo Steuer (GER)	4	5
6. N. Krestianinova/A. Torchinski (AZE)	9	6
7. Peggy Schwarz/Alexander König (GER)	7	7
8. Elena Berezhnaya/Oleg Shliakhov (LAT)	6	9
9. Elena Beloussovskaya/Igor Maliar (UKR)	12	8
10. Anuschka Gläser/Axel Rauschenbach (GER)	8	11
11. Leslie Monod/Cédric Monod (SUI)	11	10
12. Marta Głuchowska/Mariusz Siudek (POL)	13	12
13. Marta Andrella/Dmitri Kaploun (ITA)	14	13
14. S. Pristav/V. Tkachenko (UKR)	10	17
15. Sarah Abitbol/Stéphane Bernadis (FRA)	17	14
16. Elena Grigoreva/Serghei Sheiko (BLS)	15	16
17. Dana Mednick/Jason Briggs (GRB)	19	15
18. Dorota Zagórska/Janusz Komendera (POL)	16	18
19. Ulrike Gerstl/Björn Lobenwein (AUT)	18	19

European Ice Dancing Championships:

	CD	OD	FD
1. Jayne Torvill/Christopher Dean (GRB)	2(t)	1	2
2. Oksana Grishuk/Evgeni Platov (RUS)	2(t)	3	1
3. Maya Usova/Alexandr Zhulin (RUS)	1	2	3
4. Susanna Rahkamo/Petri Kokko (FIN)	4(t)	4	5
5. Sophie Moniotte/Pascal Lavanchy (FRA)	6	5	4
6. Anjelika Krylova/Vladimir Fedorov (RUS)	4(t)	6	6
7. Irina Romanova/Igor Yaroshenko (UKR)	7	7	7
8. Kateřina Mrázová/Martin Šimeček (CZE)	8	8	8
9. J. Goolsbee/H. Schamberger (GER)	9	9	9
10. Tatiana Navka/Samvel Gezalian (BLS)	10(t)	10	10
11. M. Drobiazko/P. Vanagas (LIT)	10(t)	11	11
12. Marina Anissina/Gwendal Peizerat (FRA)	12	12	12
13. Y. Nechaeva/Y. Chesnichenko (LAT)	14	13	13
14. Radmila Chroboková/Milan Brzý (CZE)	13	14	14
15. A. Domańska/A. Głowacki (POL)	15	15	15
16. D. Gerencser/A. Stanislavov (SUI)	17	17	16
17. Barbara Fusar-Poli/Alberto Reani (ITA)	16	16	18
18. Angelika Führing/Peter Wilczek (AUT)	19	18	17

19. Yvonne Schulz/Sven Authorsen (GER)	20	19	19
20. Laura Bonardi/Alessandro Reani (ITA)	18	20	20
21. O. Pershankova/N. Morozov (AZE)	23	21	21
22. S. Chernikova/A. Sosnenko (UKR)	21	22	22
23. Viera Poráčová/Pavol Poráč (SVK)	22	23	24
24. Enikő Berkes/Szilárd Tóth (HUN)	24	24	23
25. Katri Kuusniemi/Juha Sasi (FIN)	26	25	-
26. Albena Denkova/Hristo Nikolov (BUL)	25	26	-
27. Anita Chaudhurti/Hans T'Hart (NED)	28	27	-
28. Tuire Haahti/Toni Mattila (FIN)	27	28	-
29. Anna Mosenkova/Dmitri Kurakin (EST)	29	29	-

For the first time, professional skaters were permitted to reinstate and compete in the European Figure Skating Championships. Reinstated professionals won three out of four disciplines in Copenhagen.

Igor Lioutikov, Yulia Vorobieva, Natalia Krestianinova and Alexei Torchinski and Olga Pershankova and Nikolai Morozov made history as the first skaters to represent Azerbaijan at the European Figure Skating Championships. Emrah Polatoglu was the first Turkish skater to participate.

Source: Eissport magazine, February 1994

1995 EUROPEAN FIGURE SKATING CHAMPIONSHIPS
Dortmund, Germany, January 29-February 5, 1995

European Men's Figure Skating Championships:

	QRA	QRB	SP	FS
1. Ilia Kulik (RUS)	1	-	1	2
2. Alexei Urmanov (RUS)	-	-	6	1
3. Viacheslav Zagorodniuk (UKR)	-	-	2	3
4. Philippe Candeloro (FRA)	-	-	3	5
5. Éric Millot (FRA)	-	-	9	4
6. Oleg Tataurov (RUS)	-	-	5	7
7. Dmitri Dmitrenko (UKR)	-	-	4	8
8. Steven Cousins (GRB)	-	2	10	6

9. Vasili Eremenko (UKR)	-	1	7	9
10. Cornel Gheorghe (ROM)	3	-	8	10
11. Ronny Winkler (GER)	-	-	12	11
12. Michael Tyllesen (DEN)	-	-	11	13
13. Fabrizio Garattoni (ITA)	2	-	15	12
14. Szabolcs Vidrai (HUN)	-	6	14	14
15. Markus Leminen (FIN)	-	3	16	16
16. Besarion Tsintsadze (GEO)	5	-	17	17
17. Alexander Murashko (BLS)	-	9	13	20
18. Patrick Meier (SUI)	4	-	24	15
19. Mirko Eichhorn (GER)	6	-	18	18
20. Johnny Rønne Jensen (DEN)	-	7	19	19
21. Ivan Dinev (BUL)	-	8	20	22
22. Patrick Schmit (LUX)	-	5	23	21
23. Jan Erik Digernes (NOR)	8	-	22	23
24. Daniel Peinado (ESP)	7	-	21	24
25. Florian Tuma (AUT)	-	4	25	-
26. Veli-Pekka Riihinen (SWE)	10	-	26	-
27. Rastislav Vnučko (SVK)	-	10	27	-
28. Roman Martõnenko (EST)	9	-	28	-
29. Zbigniew Komorowski (POL)	11	-	29	-
30. Marcus Deen (NED)	-	11	30	-
31. Emrah Polatoglu (TUR)	-	12	-	-
32. Radek Horák (CZE)	13	-	-	-
32. Vaidotas Juraitis (LIT)	-	13	-	-
34. Jan Čejvan (SLO)	14	-	-	-

European Ladies Figure Skating Championships:

	QRA	QRB	SP	FS
1. Surya Bonaly (FRA)	-	-	2	1
2. Olga Markova (RUS)	-	-	1	2
3. Elena Liashenko (UKR)	1	-	5	5
4. Tanja Szewczenko (GER)	-	-	4	6
5. Irina Slutskaya (RUS)	-	1	11	3
6. Marina Kielmann (GER)	-	-	13	4
7. Maria Butyrskaya (RUS)	-	-	3	10
8. Krisztina Czakó (HUN)	-	-	9	8
9. Anna Rechnio (POL)	-	-	12	7

10. Kateřina Beránková (CZE)	2	-	8	9
11. Yulia Lavrenchuk (UKR)	-	4	6	12
12. Laëtitia Hubert (FRA)	-	3	10	11
13. Zuzanna Szwed (POL)	-	2	7	13
14. Júlia Sebestyén (HUN)	5	-	15	15
15. T.S. Bombardieri (ITA)	4	-	18	14
16. Janine Bur (SUI)	-	8	16	17
17. Marta Andrade Vidal (ESP)	8	-	14	18
18. Alma Lepina (LAT)	7	-	19	16
19. Nathalie Krieg (SUI)	-	-	21	20
20. Mojca Kopač (SLO)	-	9	17	22
21. Julia Lautowa (AUT)	9	-	24	19
22. M. van der Velden (NED)	-	7	22	21
23. Malika Tahir (FRA)	6	-	20	23
24. Ivana Jakupčević (CRO)	-	10	25	-
25. Kaisa Kella (FIN)	-	5	26	-
26. Jenna Arrowsmith (GRB)	-	6	27	-
27. Helena Grundberg (SWE)	10	-	28	-
28. Kaja Hanevold (NOR)	11	-	29	-
29. Sofia Penkova (BUL)	-	11	30	-
30. Christelle Damman (BEL)	12	-	-	-
30. Olga Vassiljeva (EST)	-	12	-	-
32. Maria Fuglsang (DEN)	13	-	-	-
32. Anna Hatziathanassiou (GRE)	-	13	-	-
34. Ingrida Zenkeviciute (LIT)	14	-	-	-
WD. Lyudmila Ivanova (UKR)	3	-	20	-

European Pairs Skating Championships:

	SP	FS
1. Mandy Wötzel/Ingo Steuer (GER)	2	1
2. Radka Kovaříková/René Novotný (CZE)	1	2
3. Evgenia Shishkova/Vadim Naumov (RUS)	3	3
4. Marina Eltsova/Andrei Bushkov (RUS)	4	4
5. Elena Berezhnaya/Oleg Shliakhov (LAT)	5	5
6. Maria Petrova/Anton Sikharulidze (RUS)	6	6
7. Sarah Abitbol/Stéphane Bernadis (FRA)	8	7
8. Elena Beloussovskaya/Igor Maliar (UKR)	7	8
9. Dorota Zagórska/Mariusz Siudek (POL)	9	9

10. Jekaterina Silnitzkaja/Mirko Müller (GER)	11	10
11. Silvia Dimitrov/Rico Rex (GER)	10	11
12. Lesley Rogers/Michael Aldred (GRB)	12	12
12. Lilia Mashkovskaya/Igor Maliar (UKR)	15	13
14. Marta Andrella/Dmitri Kaploun (ITA)	13	14
15. Veronika Joukalová/Otto Dlabola (CZE)	14	15
16. Jeltje Schulten/Alcuin Schulten (NED)	16	16

European Ice Dancing Championships:

	CD	OD	FD
1. Susanna Rahkamo/Petri Kokko (FIN)	2	1	1
2. Sophie Moniotte/Pascal Lavanchy (FRA)	1	2	2
3. A. Krylova/O. Ovsiannikov (RUS)	3	3	3
4. Tatiana Navka/Samvel Gezalian (BLS)	4	4	4
5. Marina Anissina/Gwendal Peizerat (FRA)	5(t)	5	5
6. Kateřina Mrázová/Martin Šimeček (CZE)	7	6	6
7. Irina Romanova/Igor Yaroshenko (UKR)	5(t)	8	7
8. J. Goolsbee/H. Schamberger (GER)	8	7	8
9. Irina Lobacheva/Ilia Averbukh (RUS)	9	9	9
10. B. Fusar-Poli/M. Margaglio (ITA)	11	10	10
11. M. Drobiazko/P. Vanagas (LIT)	10	11	11
12. S. Nowak/S. Kolasiński (POL)	13	13	12
13. D. Gerencser/A. Stanislavov (SUI)	12	12	13
14. E. Grushina/R. Goncharov (UKR)	14	14	14
15. Kati Winkler/René Lohse (GER)	17	15	15
16. Allison McLean/Konrad Schaub (AUT)	19	17	16
17. Elena Kustarova/Vazgen Azroyan (RUS)	15	18	17
18. Michelle Fitzgerald/Vincent Kyle (GRB)	16	16	18
19. Claire Wileman/Andrew Place (GRB)	18	19	19
20. Lynn Burton/Duncan Lenard (GRB)	20	20	20
21. Kaho Koinuma/Tigran Arakelian (ARM)	21	21	21
22. Albena Denkova/Hristo Nikolov (BUL)	23	24	21
23. Enikő Berkes/Szilárd Tóth (HUN)	22	23	23
24. Anna Mosenkova/Dmitri Kurakin (EST)	24	22	24
25. Anita Chaudhurti/Hans T'Hart (NED)	25	25	-

The qualifying rounds were reworked. "Seeded" skaters weren't required to participate, based on a classification sheet published by the ISU. The classification sheet took into account the results of several competitions, including the previous year's World Championships.

Susanna Rahkamo and Petri Kokko made history as the first Finnish skaters to win a gold medal at the European Figure Skating Championships. Ilia Kulik became the first Russian singles skater to win a gold medal at the event.

Kaho Koinuma and Tigran Arakelian made history as the first skaters to represent Armenia at the event. Anna Hatziathanassiou made history as the first Greek skater to compete.

Source: Eissport magazine, February 1995

1996 EUROPEAN FIGURE SKATING CHAMPIONSHIPS
Sofia, Bulgaria, January 22-28, 1996

European Men's Figure Skating Championships:

	QRA	QRB	SP	FS
1. Viacheslav Zagorodniuk (UKR)	-	-	1	1
2. Igor Pashkevich (RUS)	-	1	4	2
3. Ilia Kulik (RUS)	-	-	2	3
4. Steven Cousins (GRB)	-	-	7	4
5. Philippe Candeloro (FRA)	-	-	7	4
6. Alexei Yagudin (RUS)	-	2	5	5
7. Dmitri Dmitrenko (UKR)	-	-	6	7
8. Éric Millot (FRA)	-	-	9	8
9. Cornel Gheorghe (ROM)	-	-	8	10
10. Szabolcs Vidrai (HUN)	-	4	12	9
11. Ivan Dinev (BUL)	3	-	10	11
12. Evgeni Pliuta (UKR)	4	-	13	12
13. Patrick Meier (SUI)	-	5	15	13
14. Markus Leminen (FIN)	-	6	11	16
15. Fabrizio Garattoni (ITA)	7	-	18	14
16. Neil Wilson (GRB)	-	3	17	15
17. Michael Tyllesen (DEN)	2	-	16	17
18. Robert Grzegorczyk (POL)	-	8	14	19

19. Patrick Schmit (LUX)	5	-	20	18
20. Florian Tuma (AUT)	-	7	19	20
21. Alexander Murashko (BLS)	6	-	24	21
22. Margus Hernits (EST)	8	-	23	22
23. Jordi Pedro Roya (ESP)	-	9	22	23
24. Jan Čejvan (SLO)	-	10	21	24
25. Róbert Kažimír (SVK)	9	-	25	-
26. Vakhtang Murvanidze (GEO)	-	12	26	-
27. Jaroslav Suchý (CZE)	11	-	27	-
28. Luiz Taifas (ROM)	10	-	28	-
29. Marcus Deen (NED)	-	11	29	-
30. Aramayis Grigoryan (ARM)	12	-	-	-
31. Yeler Tekelioğlu (TUR)	13	-	-	-
WD. Andrejs Vlascenko (GER)	1	-	-	-

European Ladies Figure Skating Championships:

	QRA	QRB	SP	FS
1. Irina Slutskaya (RUS)	-	-	2	1
2. Surya Bonaly (FRA)	-	-	1	2
3. Maria Butyrskaya (RUS)	-	-	4	3
4. Elena Liashenko (UKR)	-	-	5	4
5. Tanja Szewczenko (GER)	-	-	3	5
6. Krisztina Czakó (HUN)	-	-	8	7
7. Zuzanna Szwed (POL)	1	-	7	8
8. Vanessa Gusmeroli (FRA)	-	1	6	10
9. Yulia Vorobieva (AZE)	3	-	9	9
10. Mila Kajas (FIN)	2	-	16	6
11. Olga Markova (RUS)	-	-	11	11
12. Anna Rechnio (POL)	-	-	14	12
13. Lenka Kulovaná (CZE)	-	3	12	13
14. Kateřina Beránková (CZE)	-	-	13	14
15. Mojca Kopač (SLO)	-	6	17	16
16. Astrid Hochstetter (GER)	-	5	15	17
17. Véronique Fleury (FRA)	4	-	24	15
18. Yulia Lavrenchuk (UKR)	-	2	10	22
19. Diána Póth (HUN)	5	-	20	18
20. Silvia Fontana (ITA)	-	4	22	19
21. Denise Jaschek (AUT)	8	-	21	20

22. Alma Lepina (LAT)	-	10	18	23
23. Lucinda Ruh (SUI)	-	7	23	21
24. Lyudmila Ivanova (UKR)	-	8	19	25
25. Sofia Penkova (BUL)	-	9	28	24
26. Christelle Damman (BEL)	7	-	25	-
27. Stephanie Main (GRB)	6	-	26	-
28. Ivana Jakupčević (CRO)	9	-	27	-
29. Klara Bramfeldt (SWE)	10	-	29	-
30. Kaja Hanevold (NOR)	11	-	30	-
31. Zuzana Paurová (SVK)	11	-	-	-
32. Ece Aksüyek (TUR)	12	-	-	-
32. Jekaterina Golovatenko (EST)	-	12	-	-
34. Marta Senra (ESP)	13	-	-	-
34. Georgina de Wit (NED)	-	13	-	-
36. Roxana Luca (ROM)	14	-	-	-
36. Ellen Ambartsoumian (ARM)	-	14	-	-

European Pairs Skating Championships:

	SP	FS
1. Oksana Kazakova/Artur Dmitriev (RUS)	2	1
2. Mandy Wötzel/Ingo Steuer (GER)	1	2
3. Sarah Abitbol/Stéphane Bernadis (FRA)	5	3
4. Marina Eltsova/Andrei Bushkov (RUS)	3	4
5. Maria Petrova/Anton Sikharulidze (RUS)	4	5
6. Dorota Zagórska/Mariusz Siudek (POL)	6	6
7. Elena Beloussovskaya/Sergei Potalov (UKR)	7	7
8. Silvia Dimitrov/Rico Rex (GER)	8	8
9. Line Haddad/Sylvain Privé (FRA)	9	9
10. Lesley Rogers/Michael Aldred (GRB)	11	10
11. Evgenia Filonenko/Igor Marchenko (UKR)	10	11
12. Elaine Asanakis/Joel McKeever (GRE)	13	12
13. Veronika Joukalová/Otto Dlabola (CZE)	12	13
14. M. Sroczyńska/S. Borowiecki (POL)	14	14
15. Jeltje Schulten/Alcuin Schulten (NED)	16	15
16. Olga Bogouslavska/Juri Salmonov (LAT)	15	16
17. Ekaterina Nekrassova/Valdis Mintals (EST)	17	17

European Ice Dancing Championships:

	CD	OD	FD
1. Oksana Grishuk/Evgeni Platov (RUS)	1	1	1
2. A. Krylova/O. Ovsiannikov (RUS)	2	2	2
3. Irina Romanova/Igor Yaroshenko (UKR)	4	3	3
4. Marina Anissina/Gwendal Peizerat (FRA)	3	4	4
5. Irina Lobacheva/Ilia Averbukh (RUS)	5	5	5
6. M. Drobiazko/P. Vanagas (LIT)	6	6	6
7. Kateřina Mrázová/Martin Šimeček (CZE)	9	7	7
8. B. Fusar-Poli/M. Margaglio (ITA)	7(t)	8	8
9(t). Kati Winkler/René Lohse (GER)	7(t)	10	9
9(t). S. Nowak/S. Kolasiński (POL)	10	9	9
11. Marika Humphreys/Philip Askew (GRB)	11	11	11
12. Barbara Piton/Alexandre Piton (FRA)	12(t)	12	12
13. E. Grushina/R. Goncharov (UKR)	12(t)	13	13
14. Agnes Jacquemard/Alexis Gayet (FRA)	14(t)	14	14
15. Šárka Vondrková/Lukáš Král (CZE)	14(t)	15	15
16. Cornelia Diener/Alexei Pospelov (SUI)	16	16	17
17. Francesca Fermi/Andrea Baldi (ITA)	17(t)	17	16
18. Enikő Berkes/Endre Szentirmai (HUN)	17(t)	18	18
19. Barbara Hanley/Vasily Serkov (LIT)	19(t)	20	19
20. Anna Mosenkova/Dmitri Kurakin (EST)	22	19	21
21. Kaho Koinuma/Tigran Arakelian (ARM)	21	23	20
22. Katri Kuusniemi/Jamie Walker (FIN)	19(t)	21	22
23. Maikki Uotila/Toni Mattila (FIN)	23	22	24
24. Z. Babušíková/M. Mesároš (SVK)	24	24	23

Irina Slutskaya made history as the first Russian skater to win a gold medal in the ladies event at the European Figure Skating Championships.

Source: Eissport magazine, February 1996

1997 EUROPEAN FIGURE SKATING CHAMPIONSHIPS
Paris, France, January 21-25, 1997

European Men's Figure Skating Championships:

	QRA	QRB	SP	FS
1. Alexei Urmanov (RUS)	-	1	6	1
2. Philippe Candeloro (FRA)	2	-	4	2
3. Viacheslav Zagorodniuk (UKR)	6	-	2	3
4. Ilia Kulik (RUS)	4	-	1	5
5. Alexei Yagudin (RUS)	-	3	5	4
6. Andrejs Vlascenko (GER)	-	4	3	6
7. Igor Pashkevich (AZE)	-	2	9	7
8. Dmitri Dmitrenko (UKR)	3	-	8	8
9. Ivan Dinev (BUL)	-	8	11	10
10. Michael Tyllesen (DEN)	8	-	14	9
11. Steven Cousins (GRB)	-	5	10	11
12. Evgeni Pliuta (UKR)	1	-	7	13
13. Markus Leminen (FIN)	12	-	15	12
14. Michael Shmerkin (ISR)	5	-	12	15
15. Neil Wilson (GRB)	-	10	16	14
16. Cornel Gheorghe (ROM)	-	6	13	17
17. Patrick Meier (SUI)	-	11	18	16
18. Gilberto Viadana (ITA)	-	9	17	18
19. Thierry Cerez (FRA)	-	7	19	20
20. Vakhtang Murvanidze (GEO)	11	-	24	19
21. Patrick Schmit (LUX)	9	-	20	21
22. Roman Martõnenko (EST)	13	-	23	22
23. Jordi Pedro Roya (ESP) -	14	21	23	
24. Róbert Kažimír (SVK)	-	15	22	24
25. Robert Grzegorczyk (POL)	-	12	26	-
26. Alexander Murashko (BLS)	10	-	28	-
27. Jan Čejvan (SLV)	15	-	25	-
28. Marius Cristian Negrea (ROM)	14	-	27	-
29. Karel Nekola (CZE)	-	16	-	-
30. Matthew van den Broeck (BEL)	16	-	-	-
31. Edgar Grigoryan (ARM)	-	17	-	-
WD. Florian Tuma (AUT)	-	13	-	-
WD. Szabolcs Vidrai (HUN)	7	-	-	-

European Ladies Figure Skating Championships:

	QRA	QRB	SP	FS
1. Irina Slutskaya (RUS)	2	-	1	1
2. Krisztina Czakó (HUN)	6	-	2	4
3. Yulia Lavrenchuk (UKR)	8	-	5	3
4. Maria Butyrskaya (RUS)	1	-	9	2
5. Elena Liashenko (UKR)	-	1	7	7
6. Vanessa Gusmeroli (FRA)	3	-	3	9
7. Eva-Maria Fitze (GER)	-	2	12	6
8. Olga Markova (RUS)	4	-	10	8
9. Surya Bonaly (FRA)	-	6	6	10
10. Zuzanna Szwed (POL)	-	8	18	5
11. Lenka Kulovaná (CZE)	7	-	4	12
12. Laëtitia Hubert (FRA)	-	5	11	11
13. Anna Rechnio (POL)	-	7	8	14
14. Yulia Vorobieva (AZE)	-	3	17	13
15. Anina Fivian (SUI)	14	-	15	15
16. Julia Lautowa (AUT)	-	4	14	16
17. Veronika Dytrt (GER)	5	-	13	17
18. Alisa Drei (FIN)	-	9	16	19
19. Mojca Kopač (SLO)	-	11	21	18
20. Diána Póth (HUN)	-	10	20	20
21. Marta Andrade Vidal (ESP)	10	-	19	22
22. T.S. Bombardieri (ITA)	12	-	22	21
23. Anna Dimova (BUL)	11	-	24	23
24. Zuzana Paurová (SVK)	-	12	23	24
25. Sanna-Maija Wiksten (FIN)	9		25	-
26. Klara Bramfeldt (SWE)	-	13	26	-
27. Ivana Jakupčević (CRO)	-	14	27	-
28. Jenna Arrowsmith (GRB)	13		29	-
29. Jekaterina Golovatenko (EST)	15		28	-
30. Kaja Hanevold (NOR)	-	15	30	-
31. Anastasia Efimova (AZE)	16	-	-	-
31. Valeria Trifancova (LAT)	-	16	-	-
33. Selma Duijn (NED)	17	-	-	-
33. Patricia Ferriot (BEL)	-	17	-	-
35. Noemi Bedo (ROM)	18	-	-	-
35. Ece Aksüyek (TUR)	-	18	-	-

37. Merine Tadevosyan (ARM)   19   -   -   -
37. Valentina Gazeleridou (GRE)   -   19   -   -

European Pairs Skating Championships:

	SP	FS
1. Marina Eltsova/Andrei Bushkov (RUS)	1	1
2. Mandy Wötzel/Ingo Steuer (GER)	2	2
3. Elena Berezhnaya/Anton Sikharulidze (RUS)	4	3
4. Sarah Abitbol/Stéphane Bernadis (FRA)	3	4
5. Evgenia Shishkova/Vadim Naumov (RUS)	5	5
6. Peggy Schwarz/Mirko Müller (GER)	8	6
7. Dorota Zagórska/Mariusz Siudek (POL)	6	7
8. Elena Beloussovskaya/Stanislav Morozov (UKR)	10	8
9. Lesley Rogers/Michael Aldred (GRB)	9	9
10. Elaine Asanakis/Joel McKeever (GRE)	11	10
11. Evgenia Filonenko/Igor Marchenko (UKR)	7	12
12. Sabrina Lefrançois/Nicolas Osseland (FRA)	12	11
13. Inga Rodionova/Aleksandr Anichenko (AZE)	13	13
14. Svetlana Plachonina/Dmitri Kaploun (BLS)	14	14
15. Ekaterina Nekrassova/Valdis Mintals (EST)	16	15
16. Maria Krasiltseva/Alexander Chestnikh (ARM)	15	16
17. Oľga Beständigová/Jozef Beständig (SVK)	17	17

European Ice Dancing Championships:

	CD	OD	FD
1. Oksana Grishuk/Evgeni Platov (RUS)	1	1	1
2. A. Krylova/O. Ovsiannikov (RUS)	2	2	2
3. Sophie Moniotte/Pascal Lavanchy (FRA)	4	3	3
4. Marina Anissina/Gwendal Peizerat (FRA)	3	4	4
5. Irina Lobacheva/Ilia Averbukh (RUS)	5	5	5
6. Irina Romanova/Igor Yaroshenko (UKR)	6	6	6
7. B. Fusar-Poli/M. Margaglio (ITA)	7	8	7
8. M.Drobiazko/Povilas Vanagas (LIT)	8(t)	7	8
9. Sylwia Nowak/Sebastian Kolasiński (POL)	10	9	9
10. K. Mrázová/M. Šimeček (CZE)	8(t)	10	10
11. D. Gerencser/P. Camerlengo (ITA)	11(t)	11	11
12. Tatiana Navka/Nikolai Morozov (BLS)	11(t)	12	12
13. E. Grushina/R. Goncharov (UKR)	13(t)	13	13

14. Galit Chait/Sergei Sakhnovski (ISR)	16	14	14
15. Marika Humphreys/Philip Askew (GRB)	13(t)	15	15
16. Iwona Filipowicz/Michał Szumski (POL)	15	16	16
17. Albena Denkova/Maxim Staviski (BUL)	17(t)	17	17
18. Natalia Gudina/Vitali Kurkudym (UKR)	20(t)	18	18
19. Stephanie Rauer/Thomas Rauer (GER)	20(t)	19	19
20. Šárka Vondrková/Lukáš Král (CZE)	17(t)	22	20
21. Angelika Führing/Bruno Ellinger (AUT)	22(t)	20	21
22. Jenny Dahlen/Juris Razgulajevs (LAT)	19	21	23
23. Melissa Mohler/Michael Usthoff (GER)	22(t)	23	22
24. Bianca Szijgyarto/Szilárd Tóth (HUN)	24	25	24
25. Kaho Koinuma/Tigran Arakelian (ARM)	27	24	-
26. Maikki Uotila/Toni Mattila (FIN)	25	26	-
27. Anna Mosenkova/Dmitri Kurakin (EST)	26	27	-
28. B. Poliačková/M. Mesároš (SVK)	28(t)	28	-
29. L. Chakmakjian/C.Lapaige (BEL)	28(t)	29	-

In the days of dial-up, the Fédération française des sports de glace (FSG) made history as the first skating federation in the world to develop a website for the European Figure Skating Championships.

The qualifying rounds were reworked once again. All skaters were required to participate, with qualifying results factored in with short program and free skate scores to determine the overall result.

For the first time, skaters from Israel were invited to participate in the European Championships. Michael Shmerkin and Galit Chait and Sergei Sakhnovski made history as the first Israeli entrants.

Source: Eissport magazine, February 1997; Website, Fédération française des sports de glace

1998 EUROPEAN FIGURE SKATING CHAMPIONSHIPS
Milan, Italy, January 11-18, 1998

European Men's Figure Skating Championships:

	SP	FS
1. Alexei Yagudin (RUS)	1	1
2. Evgeni Plushenko (RUS)	3	2
3. Alexandr Abt (RUS)	2	4
4. Andrejs Vlascenko (GER)	4	5
5. Philippe Candeloro (FRA)	9	3
6. Steven Cousins (GRB)	7	6
7. Viacheslav Zagorodniuk (UKR)	6	7
8. Dmitri Dmitrenko (UKR)	5	8
9. Michael Tyllesen (DEN)	8	9
10. Ivan Dinev (BUL)	12	10
11. Gilberto Viadana (ITA)	11	12
12. Patrick Meier (SUI)	14	11
13. Michael Shmerkin (ISR)	10	14
14. Thierry Cerez (FRA)	16	13
15. Robert Grzegorczyk (POL)	15	15
16. Margus Hernits (EST)	21	16
17. Szabolcs Vidrai (HUN)	19	17
18. Cornel Gheorghe (ROM)	13	20
19. Sven Meyer (GER)	18	18
20. Patrick Schmit (LUX)	23	19
21. Róbert Kažimír (SVK)	22	21
22. Johnny Rønne Jensen (DEN)	17	24
23. Markus Leminen (FIN)	20	23
24. Radek Horák (CZE)	24	22
25. Hristo Turlakov (BUL)	25	-
26. Vakhtang Murvanidze (GEO)	26	-
27. Sergejs Telenkov (LAT)	27	-
28. Jan Čejvan (SLO)	28	-
29. Daniel Peinado (ESP)	29	-
30. Matthew van den Broeck (BEL)	30	-
WD. Igor Pashkevich (AZE)	-	-

European Ladies Figure Skating Championships:

	SP	FS
1. Maria Butyrskaya (RUS)	5	1
2. Irina Slutskaya (RUS)	3	2
3. Tanja Szewczenko (GER)	1	3
4. Elena Liashenko (UKR)	7	4
5. Krisztina Czakó (HUN)	4	6
6. Surya Bonaly (FRA)	2	7
7. Julia Soldatova (RUS)	11	5
8. Julia Lautowa (AUT)	12	8
9. Yulia Vorobieva (AZE)	10	9
10. Alisa Drei (FIN)	9	10
11. Vanessa Gusmeroli (FRA)	8	11
12. Yulia Lavrenchuk (UKR)	6	12
13. Mojca Kopač (SLV)	15	13
14. Zuzana Paurová (SVK)	13	15
15. Tony Sabrina Bombardieri (ITA)	14	17
16. Sabina Wojtala (POL)	17	16
17. Júlia Sebestyén (HUN)	22	14
18. Helena Grundberg (SWE)	18	18
19. Ivana Jakupčević (CRO)	16	21
20. Sofia Penkova (BUL)	19	20
21. Jekaterina Golovatenko (EST)	23	19
22. Marion Krijgsman (NED)	21	23
23. Kateřina Blohonová (CZE)	24	22
24. Valeria Trifancova (LAT)	20	24
25. Anina Fivian (SUI)	25	-
26. Kaja Hanevold (NOR)	26	-
27. Salome Chigogidze (GEO)	27	-
28. Marta Senra (ESP)	28	-
29. Noemi Bedo (ROM)	29	-
30. Ellen Mareels (BEL)	30	-

European Pairs Skating Championships:

	SP	FS
1. Elena Berezhnaya/Anton Sikharulidze (RUS)	1	1
2. Oksana Kazakova/Artur Dmitriev (RUS)	3	2
3. Sarah Abitbol/Stéphane Bernadis (FRA)	2	3

4. Dorota Zagórska/Mariusz Siudek (POL)	4	4
5. Peggy Schwarz/Mirko Müller (GER)	6	5
6. Evgenia Filonenko/Igor Marchenko (UKR)	5	6
7. Julia Obertas/Dmitri Palamarchuk (UKR)	8	7
8. Kateřina Beránková/Otto Dlabola (CZE)	7	8
9. Inga Rodionova/Aleksandr Anichenko (AZE)	9	9
10. Marsha Poluiashenko/Andrew Seabrook (GRB)	10	10
11. Elaine Asanakis/Joel McKeever (GRE)	11	11
12. Oľga Beständigová/Jozef Beständig (SVK)	12	12
13. Ekaterina Nekrassova/Valdis Mintals (LAT)	14	13
14. Maria Krasiltseva/Alexander Chestnikh (ARM)	13	14
WD. Marina Eltsova/Andrei Bushkov (RUS)	-	-

European Ice Dancing Championships:

	CD	OD	FD
1. Oksana Grishuk/Evgeni Platov (RUS)	1	2	1
2. A. Krylova/O. Ovsiannikov (RUS)	2	1	2
3. Marina Anissina/Gwendal Peizerat (FRA)	3	3	3
4. Irina Lobacheva/Ilia Averbukh (RUS)	4	4	4
5. B. Fusar-Poli/M. Margaglio (ITA)	5	5	5
6. M. Drobiazko/P. Vanagas (LIT)	7	6	6
7. Sophie Moniotte/Pascal Lavanchy (FRA)	6	7	7
8. Irina Romanova/Igor Yaroshenko (UKR)	8	8	8
9. Kati Winkler/René Lohse (GER)	11	9	9
10. Tatiana Navka/Nikolai Morozov (BLS)	9	11	10
11. S. Nowak/S. Kolasiński (POL)	10	10	11
12. Galit Chait/Sergei Sakhnovski (ISR)	14	12	12
13. D. Gerencser/P. Camerlengo (ITA)	12(t)	13	13
14. K. Mrázová/M. Šimeček (CZE)	12(t)	14	14
15. I. Delobel/O. Schoenfelder (FRA)	15(t)	15	15
16. Albena Denkova/Maxim Staviski (BUL)	15(t)	16	16
17. Z. Merzová/T. Morbacher (SVK)	18	17	17
18. C. Clements/G. Shortland (GRB)	19(t)	18	18
19. Angelika Führing/Bruno Ellinger (AUT)	19(t)	19	19
20. X. Smetanenko/S. Gezalian (ARM)	17	21	21
21. Kornélia Bárány/András Rosnik (HUN)	23	20	20
22. E. Hugentobler/D. Hugentobler (SUI)	21	22	22
23. K. Kalesnik/A. Terentjev (EST)	22	23	23

Qualifying rounds for men and ladies were not held, due to a lower than usual number of entries.

Sources: Eissport magazine, February 1998; Skating magazine, March 1998

1999 EUROPEAN FIGURE SKATING CHAMPIONSHIPS
Prague, Czech Republic, January 24-31, 1999

European Men's Figure Skating Championships:

	QRA	QRB	SP	FS
1. Alexei Yagudin (RUS)	3	-	2	1
2. Evgeni Plushenko (RUS)	-	1	3	2
3. Alexei Urmanov (RUS)	-	2	1	3
4. Andrejs Vlascenko (GER)	2	-	6	4
5. Laurent Tobel (FRA)	1	-	9	5
6. Ivan Dinev (BUL)	4	-	4	7
7. Evgeni Pliuta (UKR)	-	3	7	6
8. Vincent Restencourt (FRA)	-	5	5	8
9. Vitali Danilchenko (UKR)	-	4	11	10
10. Patrick Meier (SUI)	-	8	12	9
11. Robert Grzegorczyk (POL)	7	-	10	11
12. Sergei Rylov (AZE)	-	6	15	12
13. Neil Wilson (GRB)	8	-	13	13
14. Szabolcs Vidrai (HUN)	5	-	8	18
15. Róbert Kažimír (SVK)	9	-	17	14
16. Margus Hernits (EST)	-	10	18	15
17. Stefan Lindemann (GER)	6	-	14	19
18. Michael Tyllesen (DEN)	-	12	16	16
19. Johnny Rønne Jensen (DEN)	-	9	21	17
20. Gheorghe Chiper (ROM)	13	-	19	21
21. Vakhtang Murvanidze (GEO)	-	7	22	22
22. Jan Čejvan (SLV)	12	-	23	20
23. Lukáš Rakowski (CZE)	10	-	20	24
24. Clive Shorten (GRB)	-	14	24	23
25. Patrick Schmit (LUX)	-	13	25	-
26. Sergejs Telenkov (LAT)	-	11	28	-
27. Hristo Turlakov (BUL)	-	15	26	-
28. Angelo Dolfini (ITA)	14	-	27	-

29. Markus Leminen (FIN)	11	-	29	-
30. Filip Stiller (SWE)	15	-	30	-
31. Clemens Jonas (AUT)	16	-	-	-
31. Miguel Alegre (ESP)	-	16	-	-
33. Matthew van den Broeck (BEL)	17	-	-	-
33. Edgar Grigoryan (ARM)	-	17	-	-
35. Panagiotis Markouizos (GRE)	-	18	-	-

European Ladies Figure Skating Championships:

	QRA	QRB	SP	FS
1. Maria Butyrskaya (RUS)	1	-	1	1
2. Julia Soldatova (RUS)	-	1	3	3
3. Viktoria Volchkova (RUS)	2	-	2	5
4. Diána Póth (HUN)	3	-	6	4
5. Vanessa Gusmeroli (FRA)	-	2	5	6
6. Júlia Sebestyén (HUN)	7	-	11	2
7. Elena Liashenko (UKR)	6	-	4	9
8. Yulia Lavrenchuk (UKR)	5	-	7	8
9. Alisa Drei (FIN)	8	-	9	7
10. Sabina Wojtala (POL)	-	3	12	10
11. Julia Lautowa (AUT)	4	-	8	12
12. Eva-Maria Fitze (GER)	-	4(t)	10	13
13. Silvia Fontana (ITA)	-	8	15	11
14. Zuzana Paurová (SVK)	9	-	14	14
15. Yulia Vorobieva (AZE)	-	7	17	15
16. Kaja Hanevold (NOR)	-	11	13	17
17. Marion Krijgsman (NED)	-	9	18	16
18. Valeria Trifancova (LAT)	12	-	16	19
19. Olga Vassiljeva (EST)	-	10	24	18
20. Veronika Dytrtová (CZE)	10	-	18	22
21. Idora Hegel (CRO)	-	14	20	21
22. Klara Bramfeldt (SWE)	14	-	22	20
23. Sanna-Maija Wiksten (FIN)	11	-	21	24
24. Anna Dimova (BUL)	13	-	23	23
25. Christel Borghi (SUI)	-	13	25	-
26. Ingrida Snieskiene (LIT)	15	-	26	-
27. Dorothee Derroitte (BEL)	-	12	28	-
28. Helena Pajović (YUG)	-	15	27	-

29. Salome Chigogidze (GEO)	16	-	-	-
29. Marta Senra (ESP)	-	16	-	-
31. Anna Chatziathanassiou (GRE)	-	17	-	-
WD. Tanja Szewczenko (GER)	-	4(t)	-	-
WD. Laëtitia Hubert (FRA)	-	6	-	-
WD. Mojca Kopač (SLO)	-	-	-	-
WD. Stephanie Main Lees (GRB)	-	-	-	-

European Pairs Skating Championships:

	SP	FS
1. Maria Petrova/Alexei Tikhonov (RUS)	5	1
2. Dorota Zagórska/Mariusz Siudek (POL)	4	2
3. Sarah Abitbol/Stéphane Bernadis (FRA)	2	3
4. Peggy Schwarz/Mirko Müller (GER)	3	5
5. Tatiana Totmianina/Maxim Marinin (RUS)	7	4
6. Yulia Obertas/Dmitri Palamarchuk (UKR)	6	6
7. Kateřina Beránková/Otto Dlabola (CZE)	8	7
8. Tatiana Chuvaeva/Viacheslav Chiliy (UKR)	10	8
9. Evgenia Filonenko/Igor Marchenko (UKR)	9	9
10. Oľga Beständigová/Jozef Beständig (SVK)	13	10
11. Ekaterina Danko/Gennadi Emeljenenko (BLS)	12	11
12. Inga Rodionova/Aleksandr Anichenko (AZE)	11	12
13. Mariana Kautz/Norman Jeschke (GER)	14	13
14. Maria Krasiltseva/Artem Znachkov (ARM)	16	14
15. Milena Marinovitch/Stoyan Kazakov (BUL)	15	15
WD. Elena Berezhnaya/Anton Sikharulidze (RUS)	1	-
WD. Michaela Krutská/Marek Sedlmajer (CZE)	-	-

European Ice Dancing Championships:

	CD	OSP	FD
1. A. Krylova/O. Ovsiannikov (RUS)	1	1	1
2. Marina Anissina/Gwendal Peizerat (FRA)	2	2	2
3. Irina Lobacheva/Ilia Averbukh (RUS)	3	3	3
4. B. Fusar-Poli/M. Margaglio (ITA)	4	4	4
5. M. Drobiazko/P. Vanagas (LIT)	5	5	5
6. Kati Winkler/René Lohse (GER)	6	6	6
7. E. Grushina/R. Goncharov (UKR)	7	7	7
8. S. Nowak/S. Kolasiński (POL)	8	8	9

9. Albena Denkova/Maxim Staviski (BUL)	9(t)	9	8
10. Galit Chait/Sergei Sakhnovski (ISR)	9(t)	10	10
11. T. Navka/R. Kostomarov (RUS)	11	11	11
12. I. Delobel/O. Schoenfelder (FRA)	12	12	12
13. D. Deniaud/M. Jaffredo (FRA)	13	13	13
14. C. Clements/G. Shortland (GRB)	14	14	14
15. E. Hugentobler/D. Hugentobler (SUI)	15	15	15
16. Stephanie Rauer/Thomas Rauer (GER)	16(t)	16	16
17. Z. Merzová/T. Morbacher (SVK)	16(t)	18	17
18. Francesca Fermi/Diego Rinaldi (ITA)	18	17	18
19. Angelika Führing/Bruno Ellinger (AUT)	19	19	19
20. Gabriela Hrazska/Jiří Prochazká (CZE)	21	20	20
21. Kristina Kobaladze/Oleg Voiko (UKR)	22	21	21
22. Jenny Dahlen/Igor Lukanin (AZE)	20	22	22
23. Bianca Szíjgyártó/Tamas Sári (HUN)	23	23	23
24. K. Kalesnik/A. Terentjev (EST)	24	24	24
25. P-M. Gustafsson/A. Grönlund (FIN)	25	-	-
26. A-M. Poulsen/D. Blazek (DEN)	26	-	-

For the first time, the qualifying rounds for both the men's and ladies events contributed to the overall score, with qualifying making up 20%, the short program 30%, and free skating 50%.

Sources: Protocol, 1999 European Figure Skating Championships; Eissport magazine, March 1999

2000 EUROPEAN FIGURE SKATING CHAMPIONSHIPS
Vienna, Austria, February 6-13, 2000

European Men's Figure Skating Championships:

	QRA	QRB	SP	FS
1. Evgeni Plushenko (RUS)	-	1	2	1
2. Alexei Yagudin (RUS)	1	-	1	2
3. Dmitri Dmitrenko (UKR)	-	2	3	3
4. Alexandr Abt (RUS)	2	-	6	4
5. Ivan Dinev (BUL)	-	3	4	6
6. Vitali Danilchenko (UKR)	-	5	5	7
7. Andrejs Vlascenko (GER)	9	-	9	5

8. Stefan Lindemann (GER)	-	6	7	9
9. Stanick Jeannette (FRA)	-	4	12	8
10. Vincent Restencourt (FRA)	3	-	8	11
11. Szabolcs Vidrai (HUN)	-	8	11	10
12. Michael Tyllesen (DEN)	4	-	10	13
13. Margus Hernits (EST)	6	-	14	12
14. Robert Grzegorczyk (POL)	-	7	13	14
15. Gabriel Monnier (FRA)	8	-	15	15
16. Vakhtang Murvanidze (GEO)	5	-	16	16
17. Sergei Rylov (AZE)	10	-	18	18
18. Matthew Davies (GRB)	-	9	17	19
19. Michael Shmerkin (ISR)	-	11	20	17
20. Angelo Dolfini (ITA)	12	-	19	20
21. Kristoffer Berntsson (SWE)	-	14	22	21
22. Patrick Schmit (LUX)	13	-	23	22
23. Hristo Turlakov (BUL)	-	10	25	23
24. Juraj Sviatko (SVK)	-	15	21	24
25. Christian Horvath (AUT)	-	16	29	25
26. Lukáš Rakowski (CZE)	15	-	24	-
27. Jan Čejvan (SLO)	-	12	26	-
28. Kevin van der Perren (BEL)	11	-	27	-
29. Gheorghe Chiper (ROM)	-	13	28	-
30. Oscar Peter (SUI)	14	-	30	-
31. Markus Leminen (FIN)	16	-	-	-
32. Yon Garcia (ESP)	17	-	-	-
32. Maurice Lim (NED)	-	17	-	-
34. Panagiotis Markouizos (GRE)	18	-	-	-
34. Aidas Reklys (LIT)	-	18	-	-
WD. Patrick Meier (SUI)	7	-	-	-

European Ladies Figure Skating Championships:

	QRA	QRB	SP	FS
1. Irina Slutskaya (RUS)	-	1	1	1
2. Maria Butyrskaya (RUS)	1	-	4	2
3. Viktoria Volchkova (RUS)	-	2	2	4
4. Vanessa Gusmeroli (FRA)	-	4	3	3
5. Elena Liashenko (UKR)	-	3	6	6
6. Júlia Sebestyén (HUN)	2	-	13	5

7. Mikkeline Kierkgaard (DEN)	5	-	9	8
8. Silvia Fontana (ITA)	-	6	5	10
9. Tamara Dorofejev (HUN)	9	-	11	7
10. Alisa Drei (FIN)	3	-	7	12
11. Diána Póth (HUN)	4	-	16	9
12. Julia Lautowa (AUT)	6	-	10	13
13. Anna Rechnio (POL)	-	5	17	11
14. Mojca Kopač (SLO)	-	9	8	15
15. Galina Maniachenko (UKR)	-	7	15	14
16. Sarah Meier (SUI)	7	-	14	16
17. Sanna-Maija Wiksten (FIN)	8	-	12	18
18. Zoya Douchine (GER)	-	8	20	19
19. Olga Vassiljeva (EST)	14	-	21	17
20. Anna Lundström (SWE)	-	10	19	20
21. Karen Venhuizen (NED)	10	-	23	21
22. Yulia Lebedeva (ARM)	-	12	18	24
23. Tamsin Sear (GRB)	12	-	22	23
24. Kaja Hanevold (NOR)	13	-	24	22
25. Sara Falotico (BEL)	11	-	26	-
26. Sabina Wojtala (POL)	-	14	25	-
27. Idora Hegel (CRO)	-	11	29	-
28. Valeria Trifancova (LAT)	-	13	28	-
29. Eva Chudá (CZE)	-	15	27	-
30. Roxana Luca (ROM)	15	-	30	-
31. Silvia Končoková (SVK)	16	-	-	-
31. Dominyka Valiukevičiūtė (LIT)	-	16	-	-
33. Melania Albea (ESP)	17	-	-	-
33. Helena Pajović (YUG)	-	17	-	-
35. Liza Menagia (GRE)	-	18	-	-
WD. Yulia Vorobieva (AZE)	-	-	-	-

European Pairs Skating Championships:

	SP	FS
1. Maria Petrova/Alexei Tikhonov (RUS)	1	2
2. Dorota Zagórska/Mariusz Siudek (POL)	3	3
3. Sarah Abitbol/Stéphane Bernadis (FRA)	5	4
4. Peggy Schwarz/Mirko Müller (GER)	4	5
5. Tatiana Totmianina/Maxim Marinin (RUS)	6	6

6. Yulia Obertas/Dmitri Palamarchuk (UKR)	7	7
7. Aliona Savchenko/Stanislav Morozov (UKR)	11	8
8. Kateřina Beránková/Otto Dlabola (CZE)	10	9
9. Mariana Kautz/Norman Jeschke (GER)	8	11
10. Viktorya Shklover/Valdis Mintals (EST)	12	10
11. Inga Rodionova/Andrei Kroukov (AZE) 9	12	
12. Oľga Beständigová/Jozef Beständig (SVK)	13	13
13. Ekaterina Danko/Gennadi Emeljenenko (BEL)	14	15
14. Catherine Huc/Vivien Rolland (FRA)	17	14
15. Maria Krasiltseva/Artem Znachkov (ARM)	16	17
16. E. Filonenko/A. Chestnikh (GEO)	15	18
17. Sarah Kemp/Daniel Thomas (GRB)	20	16
18. Line Haddad/Vitali Lycenko (ISR)	18	19
19. Tatjana Zaharjeva/Jurijs Salmanovs (LAT)	19	20
WD. Olga Semkina/Alexey Minin (BUL)	-	-
DQ. Elena Berezhnaya/Anton Sikharulidze (RUS)	2	1

European Ice Dancing Championships:

	CD	OD	FD
1. Marina Anissina/Gwendal Peizerat (FRA)	1	1	1
2. B. Fusar-Poli/M. Margaglio (ITA)	2	2	2
3. M. Drobiazko/P. Vanagas (LIT)	3(t)	4	3
4. Irina Lobacheva/Ilia Averbukh (RUS)	3(t)	4	3
5. Kati Winkler/René Lohse (GER)	5(t)	5	5
6. Galit Chait/Sergei Sakhnovski (ISR)	5(t)	6	6
7. S. Nowak/S. Kolasiński (POL)	8	7	7
8. E. Grushina/R. Goncharov (UKR)	7	8	8
9. I. Delobel/O. Schoenfelder (FRA)	9	10	9
10. A. Semenovich/R. Kostomarov (RUS)	10	9	10
11. Federica Faiella/Luciano Milo (ITA)	13	12	11
12. O. Potdykova/D. Petukhov (RUS)	11(t)	11	13
13. E. Hugentobler/D. Hugentobler (SUI)	11(t)	13	12
14. A. Błażowska/M. Kozubek (POL)	14	14	14
15. Stephanie Rauer/Thomas Rauer (GER)	15	15	15
16. Julie Keeble/Łukasz Zalewski (GRB)	16	16	16
17. K. Kovalová/D. Szurman (CZE)	18(t)	17	17
18. Kristina Kobaladze/Oleg Voiko (UKR)	17	18	18
19. Zita Gebora/András Visontai (HUN)	18(t)	19	19

20. Z. Ďurkovská/M. Mesároš (SVK)	20	20	20
21. Anna Mosenkova/Sergey Sychov (EST)	21	21	21
22. A. de Carbonnel/A. Malkov (BLS)	23	22	22
23. Tiffany Hyden/Vazgen Azroyan (ARM)	22	23	24
24. Ana Galitch/Andrej Griazev (BIH)	24	24	23
WD. B. Hanley/A. Kirsanov (LAT)	-	-	-

Margarita Drobiazko and Povilas Vanagas made history as the first Lithuanian skaters to win a medal at the European Figure Skating Championships. Ana Galitch and Andrej Griazev made history as the first skaters to represent Bosnia and Herzegovina at the event.

Elena Berezhnaya and Anton Sikharulidze were stripped of their gold medals, following a positive doping test. Berezhnaya was found to have pseudoephedrine in her system. At the time, she was suffering from bronchitis and had been prescribed medication containing the prohibited substance by a physician in New Jersey.

Sources: Protocol, 2000 European Figure Skating Championships; Entry List, 2000 European Figure Skating Championships

2001 EUROPEAN FIGURE SKATING CHAMPIONSHIPS
Bratislava, Slovakia, January 21-28, 2001

European Men's Figure Skating Championships:

	QRA	QRB	SP	FS
1. Evgeni Plushenko (RUS)	-	1	1	1
2. Alexei Yagudin (RUS)	1	-	2	2
3. Stanick Jeannette (FRA)	3	-	5	3
4. Alexandr Abt (RUS)	2	-	3	5
5. Sergei Davydov (BLS)	-	4	6	7
6. Andrejs Vlascenko (GER)	-	6	4	8
7. Ivan Dinev (BUL)	-	3	13	4
8. Frédéric Dambier (FRA)	7	-	9	6
9. Stéphane Lambiel (SUI)	-	5	7	9
10. Róbert Kažimír (SVK)	5	-	11	10
11. Vakhtang Murvanidze (GEO)	8	-	8	11
12. Markus Leminen (FIN)	-	7	10	12

13. Vitali Danilchenko (UKR)	4	-	17	13
14. Konstantin Kostin (LAT)	-	9	12	16
15. Gheorghe Chiper (ROM)	-	2	15	17
16. Silvio Smalun (GER)	-	12	16	14
17. Sergei Rylov (AZE)	-	8	14	18
18. Alexei Kozlov (EST)	6	-	21	15
19. Robert Grzegorczyk (POL)	-	14	18	19
20. Michael Shmerkin (ISR)	10	-	20	20
21. Kristoffer Berntsson (SWE)	9	-	24	21
22. Konstantin Tupikov (UKR)	12	-	19	23
23. Kevin van der Perren (BEL)	15	-	22	22
24. Zoltán Tóth (HUN)	11	-	25	-
25. Angelo Dolfini (ITA)	-	11	27	-
26. Gregor Urbas (SLO)	-	13	26	-
27. Alan Street (GRB)	13	-	28	-
28. Hristo Turlakov (BUL)	-	15	29	-
29. Daniel Peinado (ESP)	14	-	30	-
30. Clemens Jonas (AUT)	16	-	-	-
30. Lukáš Rakowski (CZE)	-	16	-	-
32. Aidas Reklys (LIT)	-	17	-	-
32. Panagiotis Markouizos (GRE)	17	-	-	-
34. Miloš Milanović (YUG)	18	-	-	-
WD. Dmitri Dmitrenko (UKR)	-	10	23	-
WD. Konstantin Beljev (BLS)	-	-	-	-
WD. Maurice Lim (NED)	-	-	-	-

European Ladies Figure Skating Championships:

	QRA	QRB	SP	FS
1. Irina Slutskaya (RUS)	1	-	1	1
2. Maria Butyrskaya (RUS)	-	1	3	2
3. Viktoria Volchkova (RUS)	5	-	2	5
4. Elena Liashenko (UKR)	2	-	6	4
5. Sarah Meier (SUI)	3	-	5	6
6. Júlia Sebestyén (HUN)	-	4	11	3
7. Elina Kettunen (FIN)	4	-	10	7
8. Galina Maniachenko (UKR)	-	5	7	10
9. Vanessa Gusmeroli (FRA)	-	6	4	14
10. Vanessa Giunchi (ITA)	-	8	13	8

11. Silvia Fontana (ITA)	6	-	9	13
12. Susanne Stadlmüller (GER)	-	9	12	12
13. Z. Babiaková-Paurová (SVK)	-	11	14	11
14. Tamara Dorofejev (HUN)	-	7	22	9
15. Sabina Wojtala (POL)	-	3	15	18
16. Hristina Vassileva (BUL)	-	12	18	15
17. Zoe Jones (GRB)	7	-	17	19
18. Anna Wenzel (AUT)	-	13	21	16
19. Alisa Drei (FIN)	9	-	23	17
20. Lenka Šeniglová (CZE)	-	10	19	20
21. Karen Venhuizen (NED)	12	-	16	21
22. Idora Hegel (CRO)	8	-	20	23
23. Yulia Vorobieva (AZE)	10	-	25	22
24. Klara Bramfeldt (SWE)	-	14	24	-
25. Roxana Luca (ROM)	11	-	27	-
26. Anja Bratec (SLO)	14	-	26	-
27. Daria Zuravicky (ISR)	13	-	28	-
28. Olga Vassiljeva (EST)	-	15	29	-
29. Ellen Mareels (BEL)	16	-	-	-
29. Melania Albea (ESP)	-	16	-	-
31. Julija Selepen (LIT)	17	-	-	-
31. Yulia Lebedeva (ARM)	-	17	-	-
33. Anna Chatziathanassiou (GRE)	-	18	-	-
WD. Julia Soldatova (BLS)	-	2	8	-
WD. Kaja Hanevold (NOR)	15	-	-	-
WD. Laëtitia Hubert (FRA)	-	-	-	-
WD. Valeria Trifancova (LAT)	-	-	-	-
WD. Claudia di Costanzo (ITA)	-	-	-	-

European Pairs Skating Championships:

	SP	FS
1. Elena Berezhnaya/Anton Sikharulidze (RUS)	1	1
2. Tatiana Totmianina/Maxim Marinin (RUS)	3	2
3. Sarah Abitbol/Stéphane Bernadis (FRA)	2	3
4. Maria Petrova/Alexei Tikhonov (RUS)	4	4
5. Sabrina Lefrançois/Jérôme Blanchard (FRA)	6	5
6. Aliona Savchenko/Stanislav Morozov (UKR)	7	6
7. Oľga Beständigová/Jozef Beständig (SVK)	8	7

8. Inga Rodionova/Andrei Kroukov (AZE)	9	9
9. Mariana Kautz/Norman Jeschke (GER)	12	8
10. Viktoria Shklover/Valdis Mintals (EST)	10	10
11. Michaela Krutská/Marek Sedlmajer (CZE)	14	11
12. Maria Krasiltseva/Artem Znachkov (ARM)	13	12
13. Ivana Djurin/Andrei Maximov (YUG)	15	13
WD. Dorota Zagórska/Mariusz Siudek (POL)	5	-
WD. Tatiana Chuvaeva/Dmitri Palamarchuk (UKR)	11	-
WD. Kateřina Beránková/Otto Dlabola (CZE)	-	-

European Ice Dancing Championships:

	CD	OD	FD
1. B. Fusar-Poli/M. Margaglio (ITA)	1(t)	1	1
2. Marina Anissina/Gwendal Peizerat (FRA)	1(t)	2	3
3. Irina Lobacheva/Ilia Averbukh (RUS)	3	3	2
4. M. Drobiazko/P. Vanagas (LIT)	4	4	4
5. Galit Chait/Sergei Sakhnovski (ISR)	5	5	5
6. Kati Winkler/René Lohse (GER)	6	6	6
7. E. Grushina/R. Goncharov (UKR)	7(t)	7	7
8. Albena Denkova/Maxim Staviski (BUL)	7(t)	8	9
9. T. Navka/R. Kostomarov (RUS)	9	9	8
10. I. Delobel/O. Schoenfelder (FRA)	10	10	10
11. S. Nowak/S. Kolasiński (POL)	11	11	11
12. M. Humphreys/V. Baranov (GRB)	13	13	12
13. E. Hugentobler/D. Hugentobler (SUI)	12	12	13
14. A. Ouabdelsselam/B. Delmas (FRA)	14	14	14
15. Gloria Agogliati/Luciano Milo (ITA)	15	15	15
16. Kristin Freizer/Igor Lukanin (AZE)	17(t)	16	17
17. N. Gudina/A. Beletsky (ISR)	17(t)	18	16
18. Zita Gebora/András Visontai (HUN)	16	17	18
19. K. Kovalová/D. Szurman (CZE)	19	19	19
20. V. Anselmi/F. Pedrazzini (ITA)	21(t)	20	20
21. Stephanie Rauer/Thomas Rauer (GER)	20	21	21
22. A. Kauc/F. Bernadowski (POL)	21(t)	22	24
23. A. Beknazarova/Y. Kocherzhenko (UKR)	24	24	22
24. Z. Ďurkovská/M. Mesároš (SVK)	23	23	23
25. Anna Mosenkova/Sergey Sychov (EST)	25(t)	25	-
26. Tiffany Hyden/Vazgen Azroyan (ARM)	25(t)	26	-

27. A. de Carbonnel/A. Malkov (BLS)	27	27	-
28. Kamilla Szolnoki/Dejan Illes (CRO)	28	28	-
29. T. Siniaver/T. Tukvadze (GEO)	29	29	-
30. Ana Galitch/Andrei Shishkov (BIH)	30(t)	30	-
31. D. Valiukeviciute/A. Radisauskas (LIT)	30(t)	31	-

Barbara Fusar-Poli and Maurizio Margaglio won Italy's first gold medal in the ice dance event at the European Figure Skating Championships. Elena Berezhnaya and Anton Sikharulidze earned the final perfect 6.0 awarded at the European Championships in the pairs event.

Sources: Protocol, 2001 European Figure Skating Championships; Entries, 2001 European Figure Skating Championships

2002 EUROPEAN FIGURE SKATING CHAMPIONSHIPS
Lausanne, Switzerland, January 14-20, 2002

European Men's Figure Skating Championships:

	QRA	QRB	SP	FS
1. Alexei Yagudin (RUS)	1	-	1	1
2. Alexandr Abt (RUS)	-	1	2	2
3. Brian Joubert (FRA)	-	2	3	6
4. Stéphane Lambiel (SUI)	4	-	6	4
5. Frédéric Dambier (FRA)	-	4	10	3
6. Ilia Klimkin (RUS)	2	-	4	8
7. Ivan Dinev (BUL)	3	-	9	5
8. Andrejs Vlascenko (GER)	-	5	5	7
9. Sergei Davydov (BLS)	6	-	7	10
10. Gabriel Monnier (FRA)	5	-	11	9
11. Dmitri Dmitrenko (UKR)	-	3	8	12
12. Stefan Lindemann (GER)	-	7	12	11
13. Kevin van der Perren (BEL)	-	6	13	13
14. Tomáš Verner (CZE)	-	8	17	14
15. Margus Hernits (EST)	8	-	14	16
16. Vakhtang Murvanidze (GEO)	-	9	18	15
17. Juraj Sviatko (SVK)	9	-	16	17
18. Gheorghe Chiper (ROM)	-	10	15	19

19. Gregor Urbas (SLO)	-	11	19	18
20. Sergei Rylov (AZE)	11	-	24	20
21. Kristoffer Berntsson (SWE)	7	-	26	21
22. Angelo Dolfini (ITA)	-	12	22	22
23. Matthew Davies (GRB)	12	-	21	23
24. Patrick Meier (SUI)	-	15	20	24
25. Michael Shmerkin (ISR)	-	13	23	-
26. Markus Leminen (FIN)	13	-	25	-
27. Hristo Turlakov (BUL)	10	-	29	-
28. Bertalan Zákány (HUN)	14	-	27	-
29. Daniel Peinado (ESP)	15	-	28	-
30. Clemens Jonas (AUT)	-	14	30	-
31. Aidas Reklys (LIT)	16	-	-	-
31. Bartosz Domański (POL)	-	16	-	-
33. Tayfun Anar (TUR)	17	-	-	-
33. Ivan Kinčík (SVK)	-	17	-	-
35. Aramayis Grigoryan (ARM)	18	-	-	-
35. Miloš Milanović (YUG)	-	18	-	-
WD. Panagiotis Markouizos (GRE)	-	-	-	-

European Ladies Figure Skating Championships:

	QRA	QRB	SP	FS
1. Maria Butyrskaya (RUS)	-	1	1	2
2. Irina Slutskaya (RUS)	1	-	3	1
3. Viktoria Volchkova (RUS)	2	-	2	3
4. Galina Maniachenko (UKR)	-	2	4	4
5. Elina Kettunen (FIN)	5	-	7	5
6. Susanna Pöykiö (FIN)	-	3	6	7
7. Silvia Fontana (ITA)	3	-	5	8
8. Laëtitia Hubert (FRA)	7	-	10	6
9. Elena Liashenko (UKR)	-	5	8	9
10. Júlia Sebestyén (HUN)	-	4	11	10
11. Vanessa Gusmeroli (FRA)	4	-	9	12
12. Julia Lautowa (AUT)	-	7	12	11
13. Sarah Meier (SUI)	6	-	13	13
14. Mojca Kopač (SLO)	8	-	14	14
15. Z. Babiaková-Paurová (SVK)	-	6	15	15
16. Marta Andrade Vidal (ESP)	-	10	16	16

17. Lucie Krausová (CZE)	-	9	18	17
18. Idora Hegel (CRO)	-	8	21	19
19. Vanessa Giunchi (ITA)	-	12	17	20
20. Svetlana Pilipenko (UKR)	14	-	23	18
21. Roxana Luca (ROM)	-	11	20	22
22. Yulia Lebedeva (ARM)	9	-	19	24
23. Tamara Dorofejev (HUN)	11	-	24	21
24. Sara Falotico (BEL)	13	-	22	23
25. Sabina Wojtala (POL)	-	13	25	-
26. Åsa Persson (SWE)	10	-	27	-
27. Tuğba Karademir (TUR)	-	15	26	-
28. Karen Venhuizen (NED)	12	-	28	-
29. Daria Zuravicky (ISR)	-	14	29	-
30. Georgina Papavasiliou (GRE)	15	-	30	-
31. Olga Vassiljeva (EST)	16	-	-	-
31. Andrea Diewald (GER)	-	16	-	-
33. Gintarė Vostrecovaitė (LIT)	17	-	-	-
33. Ksenia Jastsenjski (YUG)	-	17	-	-
WD. Julia Soldatova (BLS)	-	-	-	-

European Pairs Skating Championships:

	SP	FS
1. Tatiana Totmianina/Maxim Marinin (RUS)	1	1
2. Sarah Abitbol/Stéphane Bernadis (FRA)	3	2
3. Maria Petrova/Alexei Tikhonov (RUS)	2	3
4. Dorota Zagórska/Mariusz Siudek (POL)	4	4
5. Kateřina Beránková/Otto Dlabola (CZE)	5	5
6. Tatiana Chuvaeva/Dmitri Palamarchuk (UKR)	6	7
7. Viktoria Borzenkova/Andrei Chuvilyaev (RUS)	11	6
8. Mariana Kautz/Norman Jeschke (GER)	9	8
9. Marie-Pierre Leray/Nicolas Osseland (FRA)	7(t)	9
10. Tiffany Ann Sfikas/Andrew Seabrook (GRB)	7(t)	10
11. Viktoria Shklover/Valdis Mintals (EST)	12	11
12. Michela Cobisi/Ruben De Pra (ITA)	13	12
13. Oľga Beständigová/Jozef Beständig (SVK)	14	13
14. Maria Guerassimenko/Vladimir Futas (SVK)	15	14
15. Maria Krasiltseva/Artem Znachkov (ARM)	17	15
16. Jelena Sirokhvatova/Jurijs Salmanovs (LAT)	16	16

17. Diana Rennik/Aleksei Saks (EST) 18 17
WD. Sarah Jentgens/Mirko Müller (GER) 10 -

European Ice Dancing Championships:

	CD	OD	FD
1. Marina Anissina/Gwendal Peizerat (FRA)	1(t)	1	1
2. B. Fusar-Poli/M. Margaglio (ITA)	1(t)	2	2
3. Irina Lobacheva/Ilia Averbukh (RUS)	3	3	3
4. M. Drobiazko/P. Vanagas (LIT)	4	4	4
5. Galit Chait/Sergei Sakhnovski (ISR)	5	5	5
6. Albena Denkova/Maxim Staviski (BUL)	6	6	6
7. T. Navka/R. Kostomarov (RUS)	7	7	7
8. E. Grushina/R. Goncharov (UKR)	8	8	8
9. E. Hugentobler/D. Hugentobler (SUI)	9(t)	9	9
10. S. Nowak/S. Kolasiński (POL)	9(t)	10	10
11. M. Humphreys/V. Baranov (GRB)	11(t)	12	11
12. Federica Faiella/Massimo Scali (ITA)	14(t)	13	12
13. A. Ouabdelsselam/B. Delmas (FRA)	13	14	13
14. Kristin Fraser/Igor Lukanin (AZE)	14(t)	15	14
15. Natalia Gudina/Alexei Beletski (ISR)	16	16	15
16. V. Morávková/J. Procházka (CZE)	17	17	16
17. Stephanie Rauer/Thomas Rauer (GER)	18	18	17
18. Julia Golovina/Oleg Voiko (UKR)	22	19	18
19. Roxane Petetin/Mathieu Jost (FRA)	20	21	19
20. Zita Gebora/András Visontai (HUN)	21	22	20
21. Jessica Huot/Juha Valkama (FIN)	23	23	21
22. Anna Mosenkova/Sergey Sychov (EST)	24	24	22
23. T. Siniaver/T. Tukvadze (GEO)	25	25	-
WD. N. Romaniuta/D. Barantsev (RUS)	11(t)	11	-
WD. Jill Vernekohl/Dmitri Kurakin (GER)	19	19	-

Sources: Protocol, 2002 European Figure Skating Championships; Entries, 2002 European Figure Skating Championships

2003 EUROPEAN FIGURE SKATING CHAMPIONSHIPS
Malmö, Sweden, January 20-26, 2003

European Men's Figure Skating Championships:

	SP	FS
1. Evgeni Plushenko (RUS)	1	1
2. Brian Joubert (FRA)	2	2
3. Stanick Jeannette (FRA)	4	3
4. Ilia Klimkin (RUS)	3	4
5. Stéphane Lambiel (SUI)	6	5
6. Stanislav Timchenko (RUS)	5	7
7. Vakhtang Murvanidze (GEO)	8	8
8. Frédéric Dambier (FRA)	13	6
9. Gheorge Chiper (ROM)	10	9
10. Kevin van der Perren (BEL)	11	11
11. Silvio Smalun (GER)	9	12
12. Stefan Lindemann (GER)	7	13
13. Sergei Davydov (BLS)	15	10
14. Neil Wilson (GRB)	12	15
15. Kristoffer Berntsson (SWE)	16	14
16. Ivan Dinev (BUL)	14	18
17. Zoltán Tóth (HUN)	19	16
18. Gregor Urbas (SLO)	20	17
19. Karel Zelenka (ITA)	17	20
20. Konstantin Tupikov (UKR)	24	19
21. Hristo Turlakov (BUL)	21	21
22. Clemens Jonas (AUT)	18	23
23. Sergei Kotov (ISR)	23	22
24. Sergei Shiliaev (BLS)	22	24
25. Alexei Kozlov (EST)	25	-
26. Bartosz Domański (POL)	26	-
27. Ari-Pekka Nurmenkari (FIN)	27	-
28. Aidas Reklys (LIT)	28	-
29. Lukaš Kuzmiak (SVK)	29	-
30. Aramayis Grigoryan (ARM)	30	-
WD. Tomáš Verner (CZE)	-	-

European Ladies Figure Skating Championships:

	QRA	QRB	SP	FS
1. Irina Slutskaya (RUS)	-	2	2	1
2. Elena Sokolova (RUS)	-	1	1	2
3. Júlia Sebestyén (HUN)	-	4	3	3
4. Carolina Kostner (ITA)	-	3	7	4
5. Elena Liashenko (UKR)	3	-	4	6
6. Galina Maniachenko (UKR)	-	6	5	7
7. Alisa Drei (FIN)	-	5	10	5
8. Viktoria Volchkova (RUS)	1	-	6	9
9. Susanna Pöykiö (FIN)	-	7	8	8
10. Elina Kettunen (FIN)	2	-	9	11
11. Anne-Sophie Calvez (FRA)	4	-	11	10
12. Daria Timoshenko (AZE)	9	-	12	13
13. Lucie Krausová (CZE)	-	8	16	12
14. Idora Hegel (CRO)	8	-	15	14
15. Olga Vassiljeva (EST)	7	-	14	16
16. Z. Babiaková-Paurová (SVK)	6	-	13	19
17. Diána Póth (HUN)	5	-	17	18
18. Sabina Wojtala (POL)	12	-	18	15
19. Jenna McCorkell (GRB)	10	-	24	17
20. Vanessa Giunchi (ITA)	-	9	21	20
21. Annette Dytrt (GER)	-	11	20	22
22. Kimena Brog-Meier (SUI)	-	12	23	21
23. Mojca Kopač (SLO)	-	10	19	25
24. Sara Falotico (BEL)	-	13	22	24
25. Åsa Persson (SWE)	14	-	28	23
26. Julia Lautowa (AUT)	11	-	25	-
27. Tuğba Karademir (TUR)	13	-	26	-
28. Hristina Vassileva (BUL)	-	14	27	-
29. Karen Venhuizen (NED)	-	15	29	-
30. Roxana Luca (ROM)	15	-	30	-
31. Anna Bernauer (LUX)	16	-	-	-
31. Gintarė Vostrecovaitė (LIT)	-	16	-	-
33. Aleksandra Petushko (LAT)	17	-	-	-
33. Georgina Papavasiliou (GRE)	-	17	-	-

European Pairs Skating Championships:

	SP	FS
1. Tatiana Totmianina/Maxim Marinin (RUS)	2	1
2. Sarah Abitbol/Stéphane Bernadis (FRA)	3	2
3. Maria Petrova/Alexei Tikhonov (RUS)	1	3
4. Dorota Zagórska/Mariusz Siudek (POL)	5	4
5. Julia Obertas/Alexei Sokolov (RUS)	4	5
6. Kateřina Beránková/Otto Dlabola (CZE)	6	6
7. Tatiana Volosozhar/Petro Kharchenko (UKR)	8	7
8. Nicole Nönnig/Matthias Bleyer (GER)	9	8
9. Eva-Maria Fitze/Rico Rex (GER)	7	9
10. Tatiana Chuvaeva/Dmitri Palamarchuk (UKR)	10	10
11. Maria Guerassimenko/Vladimir Futas (SVK)	11	11
12. Olga Boguslavska/Andrei Brovenko (LAT)	13	12
13. Diana Rennik/Aleksei Saks (EST)	12	13

European Ice Dancing Championships:

	CD	OD	FD
1. Irina Lobacheva/Ilia Averbukh (RUS)	1	1	1
2. Albena Denkova/Maxim Staviski (BUL)	2	2	2
3. T. Navka/R. Kostomarov (RUS)	3	3	3
4. E. Grushina/R. Goncharov (UKR)	4	4	4
5. Kati Winkler/René Lohse (GER)	5	5	5
6. Galit Chait/Sergei Sakhnovski (ISR)	6	6	6
7. I. Delobel/O. Schoenfelder (FRA)	7	7	7
8. Federica Faiella/Massimo Scali (ITA)	8	8	8
9. S. Nowak/S. Kolasiński (POL)	9	9	9
10. Kristin Fraser/Igor Lukanin (AZE)	10	10	10
11. Natalia Gudina/Alexei Beletski (ISR)	11	11	11
12. O. Domnina/M. Shabalin (RUS)	12	13	12
13. V. Morávková/J. Procházka (CZE)	13	12	13
14. Nóra Hoffmann/Attila Elek (HUN)	14	14	14
15. Julia Golovina/Oleg Voiko (UKR)	15	15	15
16. P. O'Connor/J. O'Dougherty (GRB)	16	17	16
17. Roxane Petetin/Mathieu Jost (FRA)	17	16	17
18. M. Paoletti/F. Pedrazzini (ITA)	18	18	18
19. T. Siniaver/T. Tukvadze (GEO)	19	19	19
20. Jessica Huot/Juha Valkama (FIN)	20	20	20

21. A. Dulej/S. Janicki (POL)	22	22	21
22. M. Timofeieva/E. Striganov (EST)	21	21	22

For the first time, only one compulsory dance was skated at the European Championships, accounting for 20% of the total score. When the first official European Ice Dancing Championships were held in 1954, 4 compulsory dances were skated, accounting for 60% of the total score.

Albena Denkova and Maxim Staviski made history as the first Bulgarian skaters to win a medal at the European Championships. Irina Lobacheva and Ilya Averbukh were the final ice dancers to receive perfect 6.0s at the event, earning perfect marks for presentation in both the original and free dances.

Source: Figure Skating History: The Evolution of Dance on Ice, Lynn Copley-Graves, 1992; Protocol, 2003 European Figure Skating Championships

Javier Fernández, European Champion 2013-2019. Album / Archivo ABC / Maya Balanya / Alamy Stock Photo.

THE DIGITAL REVOLUTION

2004 EUROPEAN FIGURE SKATING CHAMPIONSHIPS
Budapest, Hungary, February 2-8, 2004

European Men's Figure Skating Championships:

	QRA	QRB	SP	FS
1. Brian Joubert (FRA)	1	-	2	1
2. Evgeni Plushenko (RUS)	-	1	1	2
3. Ilia Klimkin (RUS)	-	2	3	3
4. Frédéric Dambier (FRA)	2	-	4	4
5. Stefan Lindemann (GER)	-	3	8	6
6. Stéphane Lambiel (SUI)	4	-	12	5
7. Andrejs Vlascenko (GER)	-	5	6	9
8. Andrei Griazev (RUS)	3	-	15	7
9. Gheorge Chiper (ROM)	-	4	17	8
10. Tomáš Verner (CZE)	10	-	10	10
11. Kevin van der Perren (BEL)	6	-	13	11
12. Sergei Davydov (BLS)	8	-	7	14
13. Kristoffer Berntsson (SWE)	-	6	5	17
14. Gregor Urbas (SLO)	11	-	11	12
15. Vitali Danilchenko (UKR)	5	-	16	15
16. Karel Zelenka (ITA)	-	9	19	13
17. Vakhtang Murvanidze (GEO)	-	8	9	20
18. Ivan Dinev (BUL)	9	-	18	16
19. Damien Djordjevic (FRA)	12	-	14	18
20. Patrick Meier (SUI)	7	-	19	19
21. Trifun Živanović (SCG)	-	7	21(t)	21
22. Ari-Pekka Nurmenkari (FIN)	-	11	21(t)	22
23. Matthew Davies (GRB)	14	-	23	23
24. Sergei Kotov (ISR)	-	12	24	24
25. Zoltán Tóth (HUN)	-	10	26	25
26. Juraj Sviatko (SVK)	13	-	25	-
27. Yon Garcia (ESP)	-	13	28	-

28. Andrei Dobrokhodov (AZE)	15	-	27	-
29. Aidas Reklys (LIT)	-	14	29	-
30. Adrian Matei (ROM)	-	15	30	-
31. Clemens Jonas (AUT)	16	-	-	-
31. Wim Hermans (BEL)	-	16	-	-
33. Przemysław Domański (POL)	17	-	-	-

European Ladies Figure Skating Championships:

	SP	FS
1. Júlia Sebestyén (HUN)	1	1
2. Elena Liashenko (UKR)	2	3
3. Elena Sokolova (RUS)	6	2
4. Viktória Pavuk (HUN)	3	4
5. Carolina Kostner (ITA)	5	5
6. Susanna Pöykiö (FIN)	4	6
7. Alisa Drei (FIN)	10	7
8. Julia Lautowa (AUT)	8	9
9. Z. Babiaková-Paurová (SVK)	9	10
10. Sarah Meier (SUI)	14	8
11. Annette Dytrt (GER)	12	12
12. Daria Timoshenko (AZE)	13	13
13. Galina Maniachenko (UKR)	7	17
14. Jenna McCorkell (GRB)	20	11
15. Valentina Marchei (ITA)	17	14
16. Kristina Oblasova (RUS)	15	15
17. Mojca Kopač (SLO)	11	18
18. Tatiana Basova (RUS)	16	16
19. Petra Lukáčíková (CZE)	19	19
20. Anna Bernauer (LUX)	21	21
21. Sara Falotico (BEL)	24	20
22. Karen Venhuizen (NED)	18	23
23. Tuğba Karademir (TUR)	23	22
24. Gintarė Vostrecovaitė (LIT)	22	24
25. Candice Didier (FRA)	25	-
26. Olga Orlova (UKR)	26	-
27. Sonia Radeva (BUL)	27	-
28. Olga Vassiljeva (EST)	28	-
29. Krystsina Mikhailava (BEL)	29	-

30. Simona Punga (ROM) 30 -
WD. Kristel Popovic (SCG) - -

European Pairs Skating Championships:

	SP	FS
1. Tatiana Totmianina/Maxim Marinin (RUS)	1	1
2. Maria Petrova/Alexei Tikhonov (RUS)	2	2
3. Dorota Zagórska/Mariusz Siudek (POL)	3	3
4. Julia Obertas/Sergei Slavnov (RUS)	4	4
5. Kateřina Beránková/Otto Dlabola (CZE)	5	5
6. Sabrina Lefrançois/Jérôme Blanchard (FRA)	7	6
7. Eva-Maria Fitze/Rico Rex (GER)	6	7
8. Marylin Pla/Yannick Bonheur (FRA)	8	8
9. Julia Beloglazova/Andrei Bekh (UKR)	9	9
10. Rebecca Handke/Daniel Wende (GER)	10	10
11. Veronika Havlíčková/Karel Štefl (CZE)	11	11
12. Diana Rennik/Aleksei Saks (EST)	12	12
13. Olga Boguslavska/Andrei Brovenko (LAT)	13	13
14. Milica Brozovic/Vladimir Futas (SVK)	15	14
15. Julia Shapiro/Vadim Akolzin (ISR)	14	15
WD. Tatiana Volosozhar/Petr Kharchenko (UKR)	-	-

European Ice Dancing Championships:

	CD	OD	FD
1. T. Navka/R. Kostomarov (RUS)	1	1	1
2. Albena Denkova/Maxim Staviski (BUL)	2	3	2
3. E. Grushina/R. Goncharov (UKR)	3	2	3
4. I. Delobel/O. Schoenfelder (FRA)	4	4	4
5. Galit Chait/Sergei Sakhnovski (ISR)	5	5	5
6. Federica Faiella/Massimo Scali (ITA)	6	6	6
7. Oksana Domnina/Maxim Shabalin (RUS)	7	7	7
8. S. Kulikova/V. Novikov (RUS)	10	8	8
9. Natalia Gudina/Alexei Beletski (ISR)	9	9	9
10. Sinead Kerr/John Kerr (GRB)	12	10	10
11. Nóra Hoffmann/Attila Elek (HUN)	8	11	11
12. Roxane Petetin/Mathieu Jost (FRA)	11	12	12
13. A. Grebenkina/V. Azroyan (ARM)	16	14	13
14. Alexandra Kauc/Michał Zych (POL)	14	13	15

15. Yulia Golovina/Oleg Voiko (UKR)	13	16	14
16. Christina Beier/William Beier (GER)	15	15	16
17. Barbara Herzog/Dmitri Matsyuk (AUT)	17	19	17
18. Jessica Huot/Juha Valkama (FIN)	18	17	18
19. Petra Pachlová/Petr Knoth (CZE)	19	20	19
20. Alessia Aureli/Andrea Vaturi (ITA)	20	18	21
21. A. Dulej/S. Janicki (POL)	21	21	20
22. C-M. Zatzman/A. Radisauskas (LIT)	22	22	22

For over a century, the 6.0 Judging System was used at the European Figure Skating Championships. 2004 marked the final time the system was used. Belarusian judge Aleksey Shirshov made history as the final judge to award at perfect 6.0 at the European Championships. Shirshov awarded a 6.0 to Evgeni Plushenko in the men's short program. Júlia Sebestyén made history as the first Hungarian skater to win a gold medal in the ladies event at the European Figure Skating Championships.

Sources: Entries, 2004 European Figure Skating Championships; Protocol, 2004 European Figure Skating Championships

2005 EUROPEAN FIGURE SKATING CHAMPIONSHIPS
Turin, Italy, January 25-30, 2005

European Men's Figure Skating Championships:

	SP	FS
1. Evgeni Plushenko (RUS)	2	1
2. Brian Joubert (FRA)	1	2
3. Stefan Lindemann (GER)	5	3
4. Stéphane Lambiel (SUI)	3	7
5. Andrei Griazev (RUS)	4	5
6. Kevin van der Perren (BEL)	6	6
7. Frédéric Dambier (FRA)	12	4
8. Gheorghe Chiper (ROM)	7	8
9. Samuel Contesti (FRA)	8	9
10. Kristoffer Berntsson (SWE)	10	12
11. Jamal Othman (SUI)	13	11
12. Sergei Davydov (BLS)	9	14

13. Roman Serov (ISR)	15	10
14. Andrei Lezin (RUS)	18	13
15. Vakhtang Murvanidze (GEO)	14	15
16. Silvio Smalun (GER)	11	18
17. Trifun Zivanovic (SCG)	16	16
18. Viktor Pfeifer (AUT)	17	17
19. John Hamer (GRB)	20	19
20. Martin Liebers (GER)	22	20
21. Lukáš Rakowski (CZE)	19	22
22. Vitali Danilchenko (UKR)	23	21
23. Juraj Sviatko (SVK)	24	23
24. Ari-Pekka Nurmenkari (FIN)	21	24
25. Paolo Bacchini (ITA)	32	25
26. Andrei Dobrokhodov (AZE)	25	-
27. Gregor Urbas (SLO)	26	-
28. Maciej Kuś (POL)	27	-
29. Michal Matloch (CZE)	28	-
30. Zoltán Tóth (HUN)	29	-
31. Aidas Reklys (LIT)	30	-
32. Juan Legaz (ESP)	31	-
33. Alper Uçar (TUR)	33	-

European Ladies Figure Skating Championships:

	SP	FS
1. Irina Slutskaya (RUS)	1	1
2. Susanna Pöykiö (FIN)	3	3
3. Elena Liashenko (UKR)	4	2
4. Júlia Sebestyén (HUN)	2	6
5. Elena Sokolova (RUS)	5	4
6. Galina Maniachenko (UKR)	6	5
7. Carolina Kostner (ITA)	7	7
8. Daria Timoshenko (AZE)	8	11
9. Idora Hegel (CRO)	13	8
10. Sarah Meier (SUI)	14	9
11. Elina Kettunen (FIN)	11	10
12. Annette Dytrt (GER)	9	13
13. Kiira Korpi (FIN)	12	12
14. Fleur Maxwell (LUX)	10	16

15. Roxana Luca (ROM)	16	15
16. Jenna McCorkell (GRB)	17	14
17. Lina Johansson (SWE)	18	18
18. Diána Póth (HUN)	15	19
19. Tuğba Karademir (TUR)	21	17
20. Karen Venhuizen (NED)	19	21
21. Candice Didier (FRA)	20	22
22. Sonia Radeva (BUL)	24	20
23. Andrea Kreuzer (AUT)	23	23
24. Bianka Pádár (HUN)	22	24
25. Petra Lukáčíková (CZE)	25	-
26. Elena Glebova (EST)	26	-
27. Jacqueline Belenyesiová (SVK)	27	-
28. Laura Fernandez (ESP)	28	-
29. Gintarė Vostrecovaitė (LIT)	29	-
30. Teodora Poštič (SLO)	30	-
31. Valentina Marchei (ITA)	31	-
32. Evgenia Melnik (BLS)	32	-
33. Cindy Carquillat (SUI)	33	-
34. Melissandre Fuentes (AND)	34	-
35. Karin Brandstätter (AUT)	35	-
36. Isabelle Pieman (BEL)	36	-
37. Nina Bates (BIH)	37	-

European Pairs Skating Championships:

	SP	FS
1. Tatiana Totmianina/Maxim Marinin (RUS)	1	1
2. Julia Obertas/Sergei Slavnov (RUS)	2	2
3. Maria Petrova/Alexei Tikhonov (RUS)	3	3
4. Aliona Savchenko/Robin Szolkowy (GER)	4	4
5. Tatiana Volosozhar/Stanislav Morozov (UKR)	5	5
6. Rebecca Handke/Daniel Wende (GER)	6	6
7. Marylin Pla/Yannick Bonheur (FRA)	8	9
8. Oľga Beständigová/Jozef Beständig (SVK)	9	7
9. Julia Beloglazova/Andrei Bekh (UKR)	11	8
10. Julia Shapiro/Vadim Akolzin (ISR)	7	10
11. Diana Rennik/Aleksei Saks (EST)	10	12
12. Rumiana Spassova/Stanimir Todorov (BUL)	13	11

13. Olga Boguslavska/Andrei Brovenko (LAT) 12 13

European Ice Dancing Championships:

	CD	OD	FD
1. T. Navka/R. Kostomarov (RUS)	1	1	1
2. E. Grushina/R. Goncharov (UKR)	2	2	3
3. I. Delobel/O. Schoenfelder (FRA)	4	4	2
4. Galit Chait/Sergei Sakhnovski (ISR)	5	3	4
5. Federica Faiella/Massimo Scali (ITA)	6	6	5
6. Oksana Domnina/Maxim Shabalin (RUS)	7	7	6
7. S. Kulikova/V. Novikov (RUS)	10	8	7
8. Sinead Kerr/John Kerr (GRB)	8	9	8
9. Kristin Fraser/Igor Lukanin (AZE)	9	10	9
10. Nóra Hoffmann/Attila Elek (HUN)	11	11	10
11. A. Grebenkina/V. Azroyan (ARM)	13	12	11
12. N. Péchalat/F. Bourzat (FRA)	14	13	13
13. Natalia Gudina/Alexei Beletski (ISR)	12	17	12
14. P. O'Connor/J. O'Dougherty (GRB)	16	14	14
15. Christina Beier/William Beier (GER)	17	16	16
16. Julia Golovina/Oleg Voiko (UKR)	18	18	15
17. Alexandra Kauc/Michał Zych (POL)	15	15	18
18. Alessia Aureli/Andrea Vaturi (ITA)	19	19	17
19. D. Janošťáková/J. Procházka (CZE)	21	20	19
20. Daniela Keller/Fabian Keller (SUI)	20	21	20
21. Anna Galcheniuk/Oleg Krupen (BLS)	22	22	21
WD. A. Denkova/M. Staviski (BUL)	3	5	-

The IJS Judging System made its debut at the European Figure Skating Championships, to less than glowing reviews. The qualifying rounds were discontinued.

Melissandre Fuentes made history as the first skater to represent Andorra at the European Championships.

Source: Eissport magazine, February 2005; Protocol, 2005 European Figure Skating Championships; Cracked Ice blog, Sonia Bianchetti Garbato, February 2005

2006 EUROPEAN FIGURE SKATING CHAMPIONSHIPS
Lyon, France, January 17-22, 2006

European Men's Figure Skating Championships:

	SP	FS
1. Evgeni Plushenko (RUS)	1	1
2. Stéphane Lambiel (SUI)	3	2
3. Brian Joubert (FRA)	2	3
4. Frédéric Dambier (FRA)	4	5
5. Ilia Klimkin (RUS)	8	4
6. Alban Préaubert (FRA)	5	8
7. Kevin van der Perren (BEL)	11	7
8. Silvio Smalun (GER)	9	9
9. Gheorghe Chiper (ROM)	6	11
10. Tomáš Verner (CZE)	7	14
11. Ivan Dinev (BUL)	16	6
12. Stefan Lindemann (GER)	10	10
13. Sergei Davydov (BLS)	15	13
14. Kristoffer Berntsson (SWE)	13	16
15. Sergei Dobrin (RUS)	14	17
16. Anton Kovalevski (UKR)	22	12
17. Gregor Urbas (SLO)	18	15
18. Viktor Pfeifer (AUT)	12	19
19. Karel Zelenka (ITA)	19	18
20. Adrian Schultheiss (SWE)	17	22
21. Jamal Othman (SUI)	23	20
22. Roman Serov (ISR)	21	21
23. Ari-Pekka Nurmenkari (FIN)	20	23
24. Aidas Reklys (LIT)	24	24
25. John Hamer (GRB)	25	-
26. Zoltán Tóth (HUN)	26	-
27. Michael Chrolenko (NOR)	27	-
28. Przemysław Domański (POL)	28	-
29. Trifun Živanović (SCG)	29	-
30. Igor Macypura (SVK)	30	-
31. Zeus Issariotis (GRE)	31	-
32. Alper Uçar (TUR)	32	-
33. Boris Martinec (CRO)	33	-

34. Adrian Matei (ROM) 34 -
35. Yediel Cantón (ESP) 35 -

European Ladies Figure Skating Championships:

	SP	FS
1. Irina Slutskaya (RUS)	1	1
2. Elena Sokolova (RUS)	2	2
3. Carolina Kostner (ITA)	5	3
4. Sarah Meier (SUI)	3	4
5. Elene Gedevanishvili (GEO)	4	6
6. Kiira Korpi (FIN)	11	5
7. Susanna Pöykiö (FIN)	7	8
8. Alisa Drei (FIN)	9	7
9. Viktoria Volchkova (RUS)	6	15
10. Annette Dytrt (GER)	12	9
11. Idora Hegel (CRO)	10	11
12. Viktória Pavuk (HUN)	8	12
13. Tuğba Karademir (TUR)	17	10
14. Júlia Sebestyén (HUN)	13	13
15. Elena Glebova (EST)	14	16
16. Sonia Radeva (BUL)	21	14
17. Nadège Bobillier-Chaumont (FRA)	15	19
18. Andrea Kreuzer (AUT)	20	17
19. Valentina Marchei (ITA)	19	18
20. Teodora Poštič (SLO)	18	20
21. Martine Zuiderwijk (NED)	16	21
22. Ekaterina Proyda (UKR)	24	22
23. Jacqueline Belenyesiová (SVK)	23	23
24. Lina Johansson (SUI)	22	24
25. Fleur Maxwell (LUX)	25	-
26. Ivana Hudziecová (CZE)	26	-
27. Cindy Carquillat (SUI)	27	-
28. Željka Krizmanić (CRO)	28	-
29. Olga Zadvornova (LAT)	29	-
30. Kirsten Verbist (BEL)	30	-
31. Ksenia Jastsenjski (SCG)	31	-
32. Rūta Gajauskaitė (LIT)	32	-
WD. Roxana Luca (ROM)	-	-

European Pairs Skating Championships:

	SP	FS
1. Tatiana Totmianina/Maxim Marinin (RUS)	1	1
2. Aliona Savchenko/Robin Szolkowy (GER)	3	2
3. Maria Petrova/Alexei Tikhonov (RUS)	2	3
4. Julia Obertas/Sergei Slavnov (RUS)	4	4
5. Dorota Zagórska/Mariusz Siudek (POL)	5	5
6. Marylin Pla/Yannick Bonheur (FRA)	7	6
7. Eva-Maria Fitze/Rico Rex (GER)	8	7
8. Rebecca Handke/Daniel Wende (GER)	6	8
9. Rumiana Spassova/Stanimir Todorov (BUL)	9	9
10. Julia Beloglazova/Andrei Bekh (UKR)	11	10
11. Stacey Kemp/David King (GRB)	13	11
12. Diana Rennik/Aleksei Saks (EST)	14	12
13. Alina Dikhtiar/Filip Zalevski (UKR)	12	13
WD. Olga Prokuronova/Karel Štefl (CZE)	10	-

European Ice Dancing Championships:

	CD	OD	FD
1. T. Navka/R. Kostomarov (RUS)	3	1	1
2. E. Grushina/R. Goncharov (UKR)	1	3	4
3. M. Drobiazko/P. Vanagas (LIT)	2	5	2
4. I. Delobel/O. Schoenfelder (FRA)	4	2	3
5. Galit Chait/Sergei Sakhnovski (ISR)	5	4	5
6. Oksana Domnina/Maxim Shabalin (RUS)	7	6	6
7. Federica Faiella/Massimo Scali (ITA)	6	7	10
8. Sinead Kerr/John Kerr (GRB)	8	9	7
9. Kristin Fraser/Igor Lukanin (AZE)	9	8	9
10. Jana Khokhlova/Sergei Novitski (RUS)	10	10	8
11. Nathalie Péchalat/Fabian Bourzat (FRA)	11	11	11
12. Nóra Hoffmann/Attila Elek (HUN)	13	12	12
13. Christina Beier/William Beier (GER)	12	13	13
14. A. Grebenkina/V. Azroyan (ARM)	14	14	14
15. A. Zaretski/R. Zaretski (ISR)	17	15	15
16. Alexandra Kauc/Michał Zych (POL)	16	17	16
17. Julia Golovina/Oleg Voiko (UKR)	15	16	17
18. Alessia Aureli/Andrea Vaturi (ITA)	19	18	18
19. Kamila Hájková/David Vincour (CZE)	18	20	19

20. P. Towler-Green/P. Poole (GRB)	20	19	21
21. Zsuzsanna Nagy/György Elek (HUN)	21	21	20
22. Leonie Krail/Oscar Peter (SUI)	22	22	22

In her final trip to the European Figure Skating Championships, Irina Slutskaya set a record for the most gold medals in the ladies event (7).

Source: Protocol, 2006 European Figure Skating Championships

2007 EUROPEAN FIGURE SKATING CHAMPIONSHIPS
Warsaw, Poland, January 22-28, 2007

European Men's Figure Skating Championships:

	SP	FS
1. Brian Joubert (FRA)	2	1
2. Tomáš Verner (CZE)	1	3
3. Kevin van der Perren (BEL)	4	2
4. Sergei Davydov (BLS)	3	4
5. Andrei Lutai (RUS)	5	6
6. Alban Préaubert (FRA)	6	5
7. Karel Zelenka (ITA)	8	7
8. Jamal Othman (SUI)	11	10
9. Gregor Urbas (SLO)	12	9
10. Kristoffer Berntsson (SWE)	7	11
11. Stefan Lindemann (GER)	17	8
12. Yannick Ponsero (FRA)	10	13
13. Anton Kovalevski (UKR)	9	15
14. Moris Pfeifhofer (SUI)	14	16
15. Philipp Tischendorf (GER)	16	14
16. Andrei Griazev (RUS)	13	17
17. Igor Macypura (SVK)	20	12
18. Sergei Dobrin (RUS)	15	19
19. Pavel Kaška (CZE)	21	18
20. Przemysław Domański (POL)	24	20
21. John Hamer (GRB)	18	21
22. Boris Martinec (CRO)	19	22
23. Ari-Pekka Nurmenkari (FIN)	22	23

24. Sergei Kotov (ISR)	23	24
25. Alper Uçar (TUR)	25	-
26. Michael Chrolenko (NOR)	26	-
27. Manuel Koll (AUT)	27	-
28. Javier Fernández (ESP)	28	-
29. Adrian Matei (ROM)	29	-
30. Naiden Borichev (BUL)	30	-
31. Ivan Blagov (AZE)	31	-
32. Zoltán Kelemen (ROM)	32	-
WD. Stéphane Lambiel (SUI)	33	-
WD. Zeus Issariotis (GRE)	34	-

European Ladies Figure Skating Championships:

	SP	FS
1. Carolina Kostner (ITA)	2	1
2. Sarah Meier (SUI)	1	2
3. Kiira Korpi (FIN)	5	4
4. Susanna Pöykiö (FIN)	7	5
5. Valentina Marchei (ITA)	12	3
6. Alisa Drei (FIN)	9	6
7. Elena Sokolova (RUS)	8	7
8. Elene Gedevanishvili (GEO)	3	9
9. Júlia Sebestyén (HUN)	4	10
10. Tuğba Karademir (TUR)	13	8
11. Alexandra Ievleva (RUS)	6	14
12. Elena Glebova (EST)	10	12
13. Tamar Katz (ISR)	11	13
14. Lina Johansson (SWE)	15	15
15. Jenna McCorkell (GRB)	20	11
16. Idora Hegel (CRO)	14	16
17. Anne-Sophie Calvez (FRA)	16	17
18. Viktória Pavuk (HUN)	21	18
19. Kristin Wieczorek (GER)	23	19
20. Christiane Berger (GER)	17	22
21. Roxana Luca (ROM)	22	21
22. Anna Jurkiewicz (POL)	24	20
23. Radka Bártová (SVK)	19	23
24. Irina Movchan (UKR)	18	24

25. Kathrin Freudelsperger (AUT)	25	-
26. Karen Venhuizen (NED)	26	-
27. Sonia Radeva (BUL)	27	-
28. Ksenia Doronina (RUS)	28	-
29. Julia Sheremet (BLS)	29	-
30. Mérovée Ephrem (MON)	30	-
31. Maria-Elena Papasotiriou (GRE)	31	-
32. Isabelle Pieman (BEL)	32	-
33. Ivana Hudziecová (CZE)	33	-
34. Melissandre Fuentes (AND)	34	-
35. Ksenia Jastsenjski (SRB)	35	-
36. Julia Teplih (LAT)	36	-
37. Rūta Gajauskaitė (LIT)	37	-
38. Kristina Shlobina (AZE)	38	-

European Pairs Skating Championships:

	SP	FS
1. Aliona Savchenko/Robin Szolkowy (GER)	1	1
2. Maria Petrova/Alexei Tikhonov (RUS)	2	2
3. Dorota Siudek/Mariusz Siudek (POL)	3	3
4. Julia Obertas/Sergei Slavnov (RUS)	4	5
5. Tatiana Volosozhar/Stanislav Morozov (UKR)	5	4
6. Elena Efaieva/Alexei Menshikov (RUS)	7	6
7. Mari Vartmann/Florian Just (GER)	6	9
8. Marylin Pla/Yannick Bonheur (FRA)	12	7
9. Laura Magitteri/Ondřej Hotárek (ITA)	9	8
10. Dominika Piątkowska/Dmitri Khromin (POL)	8	11
11. Stacey Kemp/David King (GRB)	13	10
12. Rebecca Handke/Daniel Wende (GER)	10	13
13. Adeline Canac/Maximin Coia (FRA)	11	12
14. Diana Rennik/Aleksei Saks (EST)	14	14
WD. Ekaterina Sosinova/Fedor Sokolov (AZE)	-	-
WD. Angelika Pylkina/Niklas Hogner (SWE)	-	-
WD. Julia Beloglazova/Andrei Bekh (UKR)	-	-

European Ice Dancing Championships:

	CD	OD	FD
1. I. Delobel/O. Schoenfelder (FRA)	1	1	2

2. Oksana Domnina/Maxim Shabalin (RUS)	2	2	1
3. A. Denkova/M. Staviski (RUS)	3	3	3
4. J. Khokhlova/S. Novitski (RUS)	5	4	4
5. Sinead Kerr/John Kerr (GRB)	6	6	5
6. Federica Faiella/Massimo Scali (ITA)	4	5	6
7. Kristin Fraser/Igor Lukanin (AZE)	8	9	7
8. Anna Cappellini/Luca Lanotte (ITA)	9	8	7
9. Pernelle Carron/Mathieu Jost (FRA)	14	10	8
10. A. Zadorozhniuk/S. Verbillo (UKR)	10	12	9
11. A. Zaretski/R. Zaretski (ISR)	12	11	12
12. Ekaterina Rubleva/Ivan Shefer (RUS)	11	13	10
13. Alla Beknazarova/Vladimir Zuev (UKR)	13	14	15
14. A. Grebenkina/V. Azrojan (ARM)	15	17	14
15. Grethe Grünberg/Kristjan Rand (EST)	20	15	13
16. N. Zhiganshina/A. Gazsi (GER)	16	16	16
17. Kamila Hájková/David Vincour (CZE)	19	19	17
18. K. Copely/D. Stagniūnas (LIT)	21	20	18
19. Barbora Silná/Dmitri Matsyuk (AUT)	17	18	23
20. Zsuzsanna Nagy/György Elek (HUN)	23	21	20
21. Joanna Budner/Jan Mościcki (POL)	22	22	21
22. Nora von Bergen/David DeFazio (SUI)	24	23	19
23. P. Towler-Green/P. Poole (GRB)	18	24	22
24. N-A. House/A. Reklys (LIT)	25	25	-
25. Goulakos/Neumann-Aubichon (GRE)	26	26	-
26. Evgenia Melnik/Oleg Krupen (BLS)	27	27	-
WD. Nóra Hoffmann/Attila Elek (HUN)	7	7	-

Carolina Kostner made history as the first Italian skater to win a gold medal in the ladies event at the European Figure Skating Championships. Mérovée Ephrem was the first skater from Monaco to participate.

Sources: Entries, 2007 European Figure Skating Championships; Protocol, 2007 European Figure Skating Championships

2008 EUROPEAN FIGURE SKATING CHAMPIONSHIPS
Zagreb, Croatia, January 21-27, 2008

European Men's Figure Skating Championships:

	SP	FS
1. Tomáš Verner (CZE)	1	1
2. Stéphane Lambiel (SUI)	3	2
3. Brian Joubert (FRA)	2	4
4. Sergei Voronov (RUS)	6	3
5. Kevin van der Perren (BEL)	4	5
6. Adrian Schultheiss (SWE)	8	6
7. Kristoffer Berntsson (SWE)	5	10
8. Andrei Lutai (RUS)	9	9
9. Sergei Davydov (BLS)	12	7
10. Alban Préaubert (FRA)	10	8
11. Gregor Urbas (SLO)	7	13
12. Yannick Ponsero (FRA)	11	12
13. Peter Liebers (GER)	21	11
14. Clemens Brummer (GER)	17	14
15. Karel Zelenka (ITA)	13	16
16. Michal Březina (CZE)	14	15
17. Javier Fernández (ESP)	16	17
18. Alexandr Kazakov (BLS)	18	18
19. Paolo Bacchini (ITA)	20	19
20. Vitali Sazonets (UKR)	22	20
21. Konstantin Tupikov (POL)	15	21
22. Moris Pfeifhofer (SUI)	23	22
23. Manuel Koll (AUT)	19	23
24. Josip Gluhak (CRO)	28	24
25. Ruben Blommaert (BEL)	24	25
26. Elliot Hilton (GRB)	25	-
27. Danil Privalov (AZE)	26	-
28. Mikko Minkkinen (FIN)	27	-
29. Alper Uçar (TUR)	29	-
30. Maxim Shipov (ISR)	30	-
31. Naiden Borichev (BUL)	31	-
32. Luka Čadež (SLO)	32	-
33. Igor Macypura (SVK)	33	-

34. Tigran Vardanjan (HUN)	34	-
35. Zoltán Kelemen (ROM)	35	-

European Ladies Figure Skating Championships:

	SP	FS
1. Carolina Kostner (ITA)	1	2
2. Sarah Meier (SUI)	4	1
3. Laura Lepistö (FIN)	3	3
4. Júlia Sebestyén (HUN)	5	4
5. Kiira Korpi (FIN)	2	5
6. Valentina Marchei (ITA)	6	6
7. Elene Gedevanishvili (GEO)	8	8
8. Jenna McCorkell (GRB)	7	10
9. Ksenia Doronina (RUS)	10	9
10. Jenni Vähämaa (FIN)	12	7
11. Tuğba Karademir (TUR)	11	11
12. Annette Dytrt (GER)	9	13
13. Stefania Berton (ITA)	13	12
14. Karen Venhuizen (NED)	15	14
15. Nella Simaová (CZE)	14	17
16. Tamar Katz (ISR)	17	16
17. Nina Petushkova (RUS)	19	15
18. Viktoria Helgesson (SWE)	16	19
19. Anna Jurkiewicz (POL)	20	18
20. Sonia Lafuente (ESP)	18	21
21. Katherine Hadford (HUN)	22	20
22. Roxana Luca (ROM)	23	22
23. Viviane Käser (SUI)	24	23
24. Olga Ikonnikova (EST)	21	24
25. Maria Dikanović (CRO)	40	25
26. Gwendoline Didier (FRA)	25	-
27. Julia Sheremet (BLS)	26	-
28. Bettina Heim (SUI)	27	-
29. Ekaterina Proyda (UKR)	28	-
30. Jacqueline Belenyesiová (SVK)	29	-
31. Erle Harstad (NOR)	30	-
32. Barbara Klerk (BEL)	31	-
33. Denise Koegl (AUT)	32	-

34. Sonia Radeva (BUL) 33 -
35. Stasia Rage (LAT) 34 -
36. Teodora Poštič (SLO) 35 -
37. Ksenia Jastsenjski (SRB) 36 -
38. Mérovée Ephrem (MON) 37 -
39. Maria-Elena Papasotiriou (GRE) 38 -
40. Beatričė Rožinskaitė (LIT) 39 -

European Pairs Skating Championships:

	SP	FS
1. Aliona Savchenko/Robin Szolkowy (GER)	1	1
2. Maria Mukhortova/Maxim Trankov (RUS)	2	2
3. Yuko Kawaguchi/Alexander Smirnov (RUS)	4	3
4. Tatiana Volosozhar/Stanislav Morozov (UKR)	3	4
5. Arina Ushakova/Sergei Karev (RUS)	5	6
6. Stacey Kemp/David King (GRB)	7	5
7. Mari Vartmann/Florian Just (GER)	6	8
8. Mélodie Chataigner/Medhi Bouzzine (FRA)	8	79.
Dominika Piątkowska/Dmitri Khromin (POL)	9	10
10. M. Zanforlin/F. Degli Esposti (ITA)	10	9
11. Laura Magitteri/Ondřej Hotárek (ITA)	11	11
12. Ekaterina Sosinova/Fedor Sokolov (ISR)	12	13
13. Ekaterina Kostenko/Roman Talan (UKR)	13	12
14. Amy Ireland/Michael Bahoric (CRO)	14	15
15. Ariel Fay Gagnon/Chad Tsagris (GRE)	15	14

European Ice Dancing Championships:

	CD	OD	FD
1. Oksana Domnina/Maxim Shabalin (RUS)	2	2	1
2. I. Delobel/O. Schoenfelder (FRA)	1	1	2
3. J. Khokhlova/S. Novitski (RUS)	3	3	3
4. Federica Faiella/Massimo Scali (ITA)	4	4	4
5. N. Péchalat/F. Bourzat (FRA)	5	6	5
6. Sinead Kerr/John Kerr (GRB)	6	5	6
7. Anna Cappellini/Luca Lanotte (ITA)	10	7	7
8. A. Zaretski/R. Zaretski (ISR)	7	9	9
9. Pernelle Carron/Mathieu Jost (FRA)	11	8	8
10. Kristin Fraser/Igor Lukanin (AZE)	8	10	10

11. A. Zadorozhniuk/S. Verbillo (UKR)	9	12	11
12. K. Copely/D. Stagniūnas (LIT)	14	11	12
13. Ekaterina Rubleva/Ivan Shefer (RUS)	12	13	13
14. A. Beknazarova/V. Zuev (UKR)	13	14	15
15. Christina Beier/William Beier (GER)	16	15	14
16. Barbora Silná/Dmitri Matsyuk (AUT)	15	17	16
17. Kamila Hájková/David Vincour (CZE)	18	16	17
18. P. Towler-Green/P. Poole (GRB)	19	18	18
19. Joanna Budner/Jan Mościcki (POL)	20	19	19
20. Leonie Krail/Oscar Peter (SUI)	21	21	20
21. Krisztina Barta/Ádám Tóth (HUN)	22	20	21
22. Ksenia Shmirina/Egor Maistrov (BLS)	23	22	22
23. K. Kiudmaa/A. Trohlev (EST)	25	24	23
24. Nadine Ahmed/Bruce Porter (AZE)	26	25	-
WD. Ina Demireva/Juri Kurakin (BUL)	24	23	-
WD. A. Grebenkina/V. Azroyan (ARM)	17	-	-

Sources: Protocol, 2008 European Figure Skating Championships

2009 EUROPEAN FIGURE SKATING CHAMPIONSHIPS
Helsinki, Finland, January 20-25-2009

European Men's Figure Skating Championships:

	SP	FS
1. Brian Joubert (FRA)	1	2
2. Samuel Contesti (ITA)	3	3
3. Kevin van der Perren (BEL)	4	4
4. Yannick Ponsero (FRA)	9	1
5. Alban Préaubert (FRA)	5	5
6. Tomáš Verner (CZE)	2	7
7. Andrei Lutai (RUS)	8	6
8. Kristoffer Berntsson (SWE)	7	10
9. Sergei Voronov (RUS)	6	13
10. Michal Březina (CZE)	17	8
11. Javier Fernández (ESP)	12	11
12. Jamal Othman (SUI)	20	9
13. Artem Borodulin (RUS)	15	12
14. Ari-Pekka Nurmenkari (FIN)	10	19

15. Peter Liebers (GER)	14	16
16. Igor Macypura (SVK)	19	14
17. Przemysław Domański (POL)	16	18
18. Adrian Schultheiss (SWE)	11	21
19. Anton Kovalevski (UKR)	13	20
20. Clemens Brummer (GER)	22	17
21. Gregor Urbas (SLO)	24	15
22. Alexander Majorov (SWE)	18	23
23. Boris Martinec (CRO)	21	22
24. Elliot Hilton (GRB)	23	24
25. Ruben Blommaert (BEL)	25	-
26. Maxim Shipov (ISR)	26	-
27. Kutay Eryoldaş (TUR)	27	-
28. Damjan Ostojič (BIH)	28	-
29. Viktor Pfeifer (AUT)	29	-
30. Georgi Kenchadze (BUL)	30	-
31. Alexandr Kazakov (BLS)	31	-
32. Dmitri Kagirov (BLS)	32	-
33. Tomi Pulkkinen (SUI)	33	-
34. Zoltán Kelemen (ROM)	34	-
35. Tigran Vardanjan (HUN)	35	-
36. Boyito Mulder (NED)	36	-
37. Saulius Ambrulevičius (LIT)	37	-
38. Beka Shankulashvili (GEO)	38	-
39. Gegham Vardanyan (ARM)	39	-
WD. Alper Uçar (TUR)	-	-

European Ladies Figure Skating Championships·

	SP	FS
1. Laura Lepistö (FIN)	1	2
2. Carolina Kostner (ITA)	3	1
3. Susanna Pöykiö (FIN)	2	3
4. Alena Leonova (RUS)	11	4
5. Kiira Korpi (FIN)	7	6
6. Katarina Gerboldt (RUS)	5	8
7. Annette Dytrt (GER)	12	5
8. Júlia Sebestyén (HUN)	14	7
9. Jenna McCorkell (GRB)	4	12

10. Tuğba Karademir (TUR)	9	10
11. Ivana Reitmayerová (SVK)	6	11
12. Elena Glebova (EST)	13	9
13. Candice Didier (FRA)	16	13
14. Nella Simaová (CZE)	10	17
15. Francesca Rio (ITA)	17	15
16. Stefania Berton (ITA)	18	16
17. Viktoria Helgesson (SWE)	24	14
18. Teodora Poštič (SLO)	15	18
19. Irina Movchan (UKR)	8	20
20. Kerstin Frank (AUT)	22	19
21. Karly Robertson (GRB)	21	21
22. Manouk Gijsman (NED)	19	22
23. Sonia Lafuente (ESP)	20	23
24. Isabelle Pieman (BEL)	23	24
25. Elene Gedevanishvili (GEO)	25	-
26. Nicole Graf (SUI)	26	-
27. Roxana Luca (ROM)	27	-
28. Noémie Silberer (SUI)	28	-
29. Erle Harstad (NOR)	29	-
30. Emma Hagieva (AZE)	30	-
31. Katherine Hadford (HUN)	31	-
32. Zanna Pugaca (LAT)	32	-
33. Sonia Radeva (BUL)	33	-
34. Mirna Libric (CRO)	34	-
35. Karina Sinding Johnson (DEN)	35	-
36. Beatričė Rožinskaitė (LIT)	36	-
37. Julia Sheremet (BLS)	37	-
38. Clara Peters (IRL)	38	-
39. Maria Papasotiriou (GRE)	39	-
40. Ani Vardanyan (ARM)	40	-
WD. Jenna Syken (ISR)	-	-
WD. Bianka Pádár (HUN)	-	-

European Pairs Skating Championships:

	SP	FS
1. Aliona Savchenko/Robin Szolkowy (GER)	2	1
2. Yuko Kawaguchi/Alexander Smirnov (RUS)	3	2

3. Maria Mukhortova/Maxim Trankov (RUS)	1	4
4. Tatiana Volosozhar/Stanislav Morozov (UKR)	4	3
5. Lubov Ilyushechkina/Nodari Maisuradze (RUS)	5	5
6. Nicole Della Monica/Yannick Kocon (ITA)	8	6
7. Erica Risseeuw/Robert Paxton (GRB)	10	7
8. Maylin Hausch/Daniel Wende (GER)	9	8
9. Adeline Canac/Maximin Coia (FRA)	7	10
10. Vanessa James/Yannick Bonheur (FRA)	12	9
11. Stacey Kemp/David King (GRB)	6	11
12. Anaïs Morand/Antoine Dorsaz (SUI)	11	13
13. M. Zanforlin/F. Degli Esposti (ITA)	15	12
14. Maria Sergejeva/Ilja Glebov (EST)	13	14
15. Joanna Sulej/Mateusz Chruściński (POL)	14	15
16. Krystyna Klimczak/Janusz Karweta (POL)	16	16
17. Jessica Crenshaw/Chad Tsagris (GRE)	18	17
18. Ekaterina Kostenko/Roman Talan (UKR)	17	18
19. Gabriela Čermanová/Martin Hanulák (SVK)	19	19
20. Nina Ivanova/Filip Zalevski (BUL)	21	-
WD. Ekaterina Sokolova/Fedor Sokolov (ISR)	20	-

European Ice Dancing Championships:

	CD	OD	FD
1. Jana Khokhlova/Sergei Novitski (RUS)	1	1	1
2. Federica Faiella/Massimo Scali (ITA)	2	2	4
3. Sinead Kerr/John Kerr (GRB)	3	3	3
4. Nathalie Péchalat/Fabian Bourzat (FRA)	4	4	2
5. Anna Cappellini/Luca Lanotte (ITA)	7	6	5
6. Pernelle Carron/Matthieu Jost (FRA)	6	5	7
7. A. Zadorozhniuk/S. Verbillo (UKR)	9	9	6
8. Ekaterina Rubleva/Ivan Shefer (RUS)	12	10	9
9. Kristin Fraser/Igor Lukanin (AZE)	11	11	10
10. K. Copely/D. Stagniūnas (LIT)	15	8	8
11. A. Zaretski/R. Zaretski (ISR)	10	7	11
12. C. Hermann/D. Hermann (GER)	14	15	12
13. Alla Beknazarova/Vladimir Zuev (UKR)	13	13	13
14. Caitlin Mallory/Kristjan Rand (EST)	19	16	14
15. Barbora Silná/Dmitri Matsyuk (AUT)	17	14	19
16. Isabella Pajardi/Stefano Caruso (ITA)	18	17	15

17. Kamila Hájková/David Vincour (CZE)	16	19	16
18. C. Chitwood/M. Hanretty (GRB)	20	18	17
19. Terra Findlay/Benoît Richaud (FRA)	21	20	20
20. Joanna Budner/Jan Mościcki (POL)	22	22	18
21. Leonie Krail/Oscar Peter (SUI)	23	23	21
22. Oksana Klimova/Sasha Palomäki (FIN)	24	21	22
23. Ksenia Shmirina/Egor Maistrov (BLS)	25	24	23
24. Ina Demireva/Juri Kurakin (BUL)	26	25	-
26. Christa Goulakos/Bradley Yaeger (GRE)	27	26	-
27. Nadine Ahmed/Bruce Porter (AZE)	28	27	-
WD. N. Hoffmann/M. Zavozin (HUN)	8	12	-
WD. O. Domnina/M. Shabalin (RUS)	5	-	-

Clara Peters made history as the first skater to represent Ireland at the European Figure Skating Championships.

Source: Protocol, 2009 European Figure Skating Championships

2010 EUROPEAN FIGURE SKATING CHAMPIONSHIPS
Tallinn, Estonia, January 18-24, 2010

European Men's Figure Skating Championships:

	SP	FS
1. Evgeni Plushenko (RUS)	1	1
2. Stéphane Lambiel (SUI)	5	2
3. Brian Joubert (FRA)	2	3
4. Michal Březina (CZE)	4	5
5. Samuel Contesti (ITA)	7	4
6. Yannick Ponsero (FRA)	3	7
7. Alban Préaubert (FRA)	6	9
8. Javier Fernández (ESP)	13	6
9. Stefan Lindemann (GER)	9	8
10. Tomáš Verner (CZE)	8	10
11. Kevin van der Perren (BEL)	11	11
12. Adrian Schultheiss (SWE)	12	13
13. Anton Kovalevski (UKR)	14	14
14. Sergei Voronov (RUS)	17	12
15. Kristoffer Berntsson (SWE)	10	17

16. Paolo Bacchini (ITA)	16	15
17. Viktor Pfeifer (AUT)	15	16
18. Gregor Urbas (SLO)	20	18
19. Zoltán Kelemen (ROM)	18	20
20. Jorik Hendrickx (BEL)	19	19
21. Maciej Cieplucha (POL)	21	-
22. Ari-Pekka Nurmenkari (FIN)	22	-
23. Karel Zelenka (ITA)	23	-
24. Peter Reitmayer (SVK)	24	-
25. Maxim Shipov (ISR)	25	-
26. Boris Martinec (CRO)	26	-
27. Matthew Parr (GRB)	27	-
28. Damjan Ostojič (BIH)	28	-
29. Viktor Romanenkov (EST)	29	-
30. Alexandr Kazakov (BLS)	30	-
31. Kutay Eryoldaş (TUR)	31	-
32. Boyito Mulder (NED)	32	-
33. Marton Marko (HUN)	33	-
34. Saulius Ambrulevičius (LIT)	34	-
35. Girts Jekabsons (LAT)	35	-
36. Georgi Kenchadze (BUL)	36	-
37. Pierre Balian (ARM)	37	-
WD. Joffrey Bourdon (MNE)	-	-

European Ladies Figure Skating Championships:

	SP	FS
1. Carolina Kostner (ITA)	1	1
2. Laura Lepistö (FIN)	3	3
3. Elene Gedevanishvili (GEO)	4	2
4. Kiira Korpi (FIN)	2	5
5. Sarah Meier (SUI)	8	4
6. Júlia Sebestyén (HUN)	6	6
7. Alena Leonova (RUS)	5	7
8. Valentina Marchei (ITA)	7	8
9. Ksenia Makarova (RUS)	9	9
10. Elena Glebova (EST)	13	10
11. Viktoria Helgesson (SWE)	12	12
12. Tuğba Karademir (TUR)	10	13

13. Oksana Gozeva (RUS)	14	11
14. Jenna McCorkell (GRB)	11	17
15. Ivana Reitmayerová (SVK)	15	14
16. Sarah Hecken (GER)	16	16
17. Sonia Lafuente (ESP)	17	15
18. Natalia Popova (UKR)	20	18
19. Teodora Poštič (SLO)	19	19
20. Tamar Katz (ISR)	21	-
21. Katsiaryna Pakhamovich (BLS)	22	-
22. Karly Robertson (GRB)	23	-
23. Shira Willner (GER)	24	-
24. Miriam Ziegler (AUT)	25	-
25. Mirna Libric (CRO)	26	-
26. Martina Bocek (CZE)	27	-
27. Manouk Gijsman (NED)	28	-
28. Erle Harstad (NOR)	29	-
29. Birce Atabey (TUR)	30	-
30. Katherine Hadford (HUN)	31	-
31. Karina Sinding Johnson (DEN)	32	-
32. Isabelle Pieman (BEL)	33	-
33. Fleur Maxwell (LUX)	34	-
34. Beatričė Rožinskaitė (LIT)	35	-
35. Clara Peters (IRL)	36	-
36. Sabina Paquier (ROM)	37	-
37. Marina Seeh (SRB)	38	-
38. Zanna Pugaca (LAT)	39	-
39. Sonia Radeva (BUL)	40	-
40. Maria Papasotiriou (GRE)	41	-
WD. Susanna Pöykiö (FIN)	18	-
WD. Joelle Forte (AZE)	-	-
WD. Sonja Mugoša (MNE)	-	-

European Pairs Skating Championships:

	SP	FS
1. Yuko Kavaguti/Alexander Smirnov (RUS)	2	1
2. Aliona Savchenko/Robin Szolkowy (GER)	1	2
3. Maria Mukhortova/Maxim Trankov (RUS)	3	3
4. Tatiana Volosozhar/Stanislav Morozov (UKR)	4	4

5. Vera Bazarova/Yuri Larionov (RUS)	5	6
6. Nicole Della Monica/Yannick Kocon (ITA)	6	5
7. Vanessa James/Yannick Bonheur (FRA)	7	7
8. Anaïs Morand/Antoine Dorsaz (SUI)	11	8
9. Maylin Hausch/Daniel Wende (GER)	9	9
10. Adeline Canac/Maximin Coia (FRA)	8	11
11. Stacey Kemp/David King (GRB)	13	10
12. Erica Risseeuw/Robert Paxton (GRB)	14	12
13. Maria Sergejeva/Ilja Glebov (EST)	12	13
14. Joanna Sulej/Mateusz Chruściński (POL)	10	15
15. Jessica Crenshaw/Chad Tsagris (GRE)	16	14
16. Nina Ivanova/Filip Zalevski (BUL)	15	16
17. Lubov Bakirova/Mikalai Kamianchuk (BLS)	17	-
18. D. Montalbano/E. Krasnopolski (ISR)	18	-
19. Gabriela Čermanová/Martin Hanulák (SVK)	19	-
20. Viktória Hacht/Kristóf Trefil (HUN)	20	-
WD. M. Zanforlin/F. Degli Esposti (ITA)	-	-

European Ice Dancing Championships:

	CD	OD	FD
1. Oksana Domnina/Maxim Shabalin (RUS)	1	2	2
2. Federica Faiella/Massimo Scali (ITA)	3	1	1
3. Jana Khokhlova/Sergei Novitski (RUS)	2	4	3
4. Nathalie Péchalat/Fabian Bourzat (FRA)	5	3	4
5. Sinead Kerr/John Kerr (GRB)	4	5	5
6. Anna Cappellini/Luca Lanotte (ITA)	6	9	6
7. A. Zaretski/R. Zaretski (ISR)	7	6	9
8. A. Zadorozhniuk/S. Verbillo (UKR)	9	7	8
9. E. Bobrova/D. Soloviev (RUS)	8	8	7
10. N. Hoffmann/M. Zavozin (HUN)	11	11	10
11. Alla Beknazarova/Vladimir Zuev (UKR)	10	10	12
12. Pernelle Carron/Lloyd Jones (FRA)	12	12	11
13. Caitlin Mallory/Kristjan Rand (EST)	15	15	13
14. Zoé Blanc/Pierre-Loup Bouquet (FRA)	17	13	14
15. Christina Beier/William Beier (GER)	13	14	16
16. P. Coomes/N. Buckland (GRB)	16	16	15
17. Kira Geil/Dmitri Matsjuk (AUT)	14	19	-
18. Kamila Hájková/David Vincour (CZE)	18	17	-

19. Allison Reed/Otar Japaridze (GEO)	22	18	-
20. Nikola Višňová/Lukáš Csolley (SVK)	21	20	-
21. Katelyn Good/Nikolaj Sørensen (DEN)	20	21	-
22. Federica Testa/Christopher Mior (ITA)	19	24	-
23. N. Georgiadis/G. Hockley (GRE)	24	23	-
24. Oksana Klimova/Sasha Palomäki (FIN)	25	22	-
25. Ramona Elsener/Florian Roost (SUI)	23	25	-
26. L. Valadzenkava/V. Vakunov (BLS)	26	26	-
WD. V. Hoptman/P. Filchenkov (AZE)	-	-	-

Yuko Kavaguti made history as the first Japanese-born skater to win a gold medal at the European Figure Skating Championships. Elene Gedevanishvili made history as the first skater from Georgia to win a medal at the event.

Source: Protocol, m European Figure Skating Championships; Entries, 2010 European Figure Skating Championships

2011 EUROPEAN FIGURE SKATING CHAMPIONSHIPS
Bern, Switzerland, January 24-30, 2011

European Men's Figure Skating Championships:

	QR	SP	FS
1. Florent Amodio (FRA)	-	1	3
2. Brian Joubert (FRA)	-	7	1
3. Tomáš Verner (CZE)	-	5	2
4. Kevin van der Perren (BEL)	-	4	5
5. Artur Gachinski (RUS)	-	3	6
6. Samuel Contesti (ITA)	-	6	9
7. Konstantin Menshov (RUS)	-	14	4
8. Michal Březina (CZE)	-	2	10
9. Javier Fernández (ESP)	-	11	7
10. Alban Préaubert (FRA)	-	10	8
11. Peter Liebers (GER)	-	9	11
12. Paolo Bacchini (ITA)	-	12	13
13. Adrian Schultheiss (SWE)	-	15	12
14. Kristoffer Berntsson (SWE)	-	8	21
15. Anton Kovalevski (UKR)	-	19	14

16. Jorik Hendrickx (BEL)	1	13	19
17. Kim Lucine (MON)	2	20	15
18. Viktor Pfeifer (AUT)	-	17	20
19. Javier Raya (ESP)	5	21	17
20. Denis Wieczorek (GER)	3	22	16
21. Zoltán Kelemen (ROM)	4	23	18
22. Laurent Alvarez (SUI)	-	16	23
23. Maxim Shipov (ISR)	8	18	22
24. Stéphane Walker (SUI)	10	24	24
25. Maciej Cieplucha (POL)	9	25	-
26. Moris Pfeifhofer (SUI)	6	26	-
27. Ali Demirboğa (TUR)	11	27	-
28. Justus Strid (DEN)	7	28	-
29. David Richardson (GRB)	12	-	-
30. Tigran Vardanjan (HUN)	13	-	-
31. Damjan Ostojič (BIH)	14	-	-
32. Jakub Strobl (SVK)	15	-	-
33. Valtter Virtanen (FIN)	16	-	-
34. Saulius Ambrulevičius (LIT)	17	-	-
35. Mikhail Karaliuk (BLS)	18	-	-
36. Boyito Mulder (NED)	19	-	-
37. Georgi Kenchadze (BUL)	20	-	-
WD. Viktor Romanenkov (EST)	-	-	-

European Ladies Figure Skating Championships:

	QR	SP	FS
1. Sarah Meier (SUI)	-	3	2
2. Carolina Kostner (ITA)	-	6	1
3. Kiira Korpi (FIN)	-	1	4
4. Ksenia Makarova (RUS)	-	2	5
5. Alena Leonova (RUS)	-	13	3
6. Viktoria Helgesson (SWE)	-	4	7
7. Ira Vannut (BEL)	1	10	6
8. Elene Gedevanishvili (GEO)	-	5	8
9. Maé-Bérénice Méité (FRA)	2	7	10
10. Valentina Marchei (ITA)	-	8	14
11. Sarah Hecken (GER)	-	9	12
12. Sonia Lafuente (ESP)	-	11	11

13. Gerli Liinamäe (EST)	-	16	9
14. Jenna McCorkell (GRB)	-	12	15
15. Juulia Turkkila (FIN)	-	14	13
16. Romy Bühler (SUI)	4	15	17
17. Karina Sinding Johnson (DEN)	6	24	16
18. Svetlana Issakova (EST)	5	18	18
19. Viktória Pavuk (HUN)	-	19	21
20. Daša Grm (SLO)	-	21	20
21. Alice Garlisi (ITA)	3	22	19
22. Fleur Maxwell (LUX)	9	17	24
23. Hristina Vassileva (BUL)	10	20	22
24. Alexandra Kunova (SVK)	-	23	23
25. Anne Line Gjersem (NOR)	7	25	-
26. Irina Movchan (UKR)	-	26	-
27. Clara Peters (IRL)	8	27	-
28. Birce Atabey (TUR)	-	28	-
29. Belinda Schönberger (AUT)	11	-	-
30. Nastassia Hrybko (BLS)	12	-	-
31. Martina Boček (CZE)	13	-	-
32. Cecilia Törn (FIN)	14	-	-
33. Marina Seeh (SRB)	15	-	-
34. Katherine Hadford (HUN)	16	-	-
35. Georgia Glastris (GRE)	17	-	-
36. Sabina Măriuţă (ROM)	18	-	-
37. Mirna Libric (CRO)	19	-	-
WD. Manouk Gijsman (NED)	-	-	-

European Pairs Skating Championships:

	SP	FS
1. Aliona Savchenko/Robin Szolkowy (GER)	1	2
2. Yuko Kavaguti/Alexander Smirnov (RUS)	2	1
3. Vera Bazarova/Yuri Larionov (RUS)	3	3
4. Katarina Gerboldt/Alexander Enbert (RUS)	5	4
5. Stefania Berton/Ondřej Hotárek (ITA)	4	5
6. Maylin Hausch/Daniel Wende (GER)	6	6
7. Klára Kadlecová/Petr Bidař (CZE)	8	7
8. Stacey Kemp/David King (GRB)	7	9
9. Adeline Canac/Yannick Bonheur (FRA)	9	8

10. Lubov Bakirova/Mikalai Kamianchuk (BLS)	10	10
11. Katharina Gierok/Florian Just (GER)	11	11
12. Carolina Gillespie/Luca Demattè (ITA)	12	12
13. Natalia Zabiiako/Sergei Kulbach (EST)	14	13
14. Sally Hoolin/Jakub Šafránek (GRB)	13	14
15. Stina Martini/Severin Kiefer (AUT)	15	15
WD. D. Montalbano/E. Krasnapolski (ISR)	-	-

European Ice Dancing Championships:

	QR	SP	FS
1. Nathalie Péchalat/Fabian Bourzat (FRA)	-	1	1
2. E. Bobrova/D. Soloviev (RUS)	-	2	2
3. Sinead Kerr/John Kerr (GRB)	-	3	3
4. Elena Ilinykh/Nikita Katsalapov (RUS)	-	4	4
5. Federica Faiella/Massimo Scali (ITA)	-	9	5
6. E. Riazanova/I. Tkachenko (RUS)	-	5	6
7. N. Zhiganshina/A. Gazsi (GER)	2	7	7
8. Nóra Hoffmann/Maxim Zavozin (HUN)	-	6	8
9. Pernelle Carron/Lloyd Jones (FRA)	-	8	10
10. Lucie Myslivečková/Matěj Novák (CZE)	1	10	9
11. S. Heekin-Canedy/A. Shakalov (UKR)	-	11	11
12. I. Tobias/D. Stagniūnas (LIT)	8	12	13
13. N. Frolenkova/M. Kasalo (UKR)	-	13	12
14. P. Coomes/N. Buckland (GRB)	3	18	14
15. S. Hurtado/A. Díaz Bronchud (ESP)	5	17	15
16. L. Alessandrini/S. Vaturi (ITA) -	14	18	
17. Allison Reed/Otar Japaridze (GEO)	7	16	17
18. Federica Testa/Christopher Mior (ITA)	4	15	19
19. Ramona Elsener/Florian Roost (SUI)	12	19	16
20. Brooke Frieling/Lionel Rumi (ISR)	-	20	20
21. Irina Shtork/Taavi Rand (EST)	6	21	-
22. Nikola Višňová/Lukáš Csolley (SVK)	9	-	-
23. Kira Geil/Tobias Eisenbauer (AUT)	10	-	-
24. Zsuzsanna Nagy/Máté Fejes (HUN)	11	-	-
25. L. Valadzenkava/V. Vakunov (BLS)	13	-	-
26. Henna Lindholm/Ossi Kanervo (FIN)	14	-	-
27. K. Tremasova/D. Lichev (BUL)	15	-	-

After a six-year absence, a qualifying "preliminary" round for singles skaters and ice dance teams was reintroduced, in an attempt to manage the high number of entries. Skaters earned a bye to the short program based on their country's placements in the previous year's European Championships. For the first time ever, skaters also needed to achieve a minimum Technical Elements Score (TES) at an international event prior to participating in the competition. The latter change ultimately had a lasting impact on all disciplines, greatly limiting opportunities for development and growth for skaters from smaller skating federations throughout Europe.

In ice dancing, the original dance was replaced with the short dance.

For the first time, a dedicated Facebook page was created for the European Championships.

Sources: Protocol, 2011 European Figure Skating Championships; Website, 2011 European Figure Skating Championships; ISU Communication 1619, June 2010; ISU Communication 1609, Agenda of the 53rd Ordinary Congress, April 2010

2012 EUROPEAN FIGURE SKATING CHAMPIONSHIPS
Sheffield, England, January 23-29, 2012

European Men's Figure Skating Championships:

	PR	SP	FS
1. Evgeni Plushenko (RUS)	1	2	1
2. Artur Gachinski (RUS)	-	1	2
3. Florent Amodio (FRA)	-	5	3
4. Michal Březina (CZE)	-	6	4
5. Tomáš Verner (CZE)	-	3	6
6. Javier Fernández (ESP)	-	4	7
7. Samuel Contesti (ITA)	-	11	5
8. Brian Joubert (FRA)	-	10	8
9. Jorik Hendrickx (BEL)	-	8	9
10. Sergei Voronov (RUS)	-	14	10
11. Alexander Majorov (SWE)	-	9	11
12. Chafik Besseghier (FRA)	-	12	13

13. Kim Lucine (MON)	-	16	12
14. Zoltán Kelemen (ROM)	2	15	14
15. Peter Liebers (GER)	-	13	16
16. Paolo Bacchini (ITA)	-	17	18
17. Paul Fentz (GER)	4	23	15
18. Viktor Pfeifer (AUT)	-	21	17
19. Maciej Cieplucha (POL)	3	20	19
20. Justus Strid (DEN)	6	18	21
21. Dmitri Ignatenko (UKR)	-	24	20
22. Alexei Bychenko (ISR)	5	19	22
23. Viktor Romanenkov (EST)	8	22	23
24. Jason Thompson (GRB)	13	25	-
25. Pavel Kaška (CZE)	11	26	-
26. Vitali Luchanok (BLS)	7	27	-
27. Slavik Hayrapetyan (ARM)	10	28	-
28. Ali Demirboğa (TUR)	9	29	-
29. Laurent Alvarez (SUI)	12	-	-
30. Márton Markó (HUN)	14	-	-
31. Manol Atanassov (BUL)	15	-	-
WD. Kevin van der Perren (BEL)	-	7	-
WD. Ari-Pekka Nurmenkari (FIN)	-	-	-
WD. Saulius Ambrulevičius (LIT)	-	-	-
WD. Javier Raya (ESP)	-	-	-
WD. Stanislav Pertsov (UKR)	-	-	-

European Ladies Figure Skating Championships:

	PR	SP	FS
1. Carolina Kostner (ITA)	-	1	1
2. Kiira Korpi (FIN)	-	2	4
3. Elene Gedevanishvili (GEO)	-	4	3
4. Polina Korobeynikova (RUS)	1	12	2
5. Viktoria Helgesson (SWE)	-	5	5
6. Ksenia Makarova (RUS)	-	3	7
7. Alena Leonova (RUS)	-	6	6
8. Valentina Marchei (ITA)	-	7	9
9. Yrétha Silété (FRA)	4	8	11
10. Joshi Helgesson (SWE)	2	9	10
11. Elena Glebova (EST)	-	10	13

12. Natalia Popova (UKR)	5	19	8
13. Maé-Bérénice Méité (FRA)	-	11	15
14. Monika Simančíková (SVK)	3	14	12
15. Sonia Lafuente (ESP)	-	13	16
16. Alina Fjodorova (LAT)	6	18	14
17. Juulia Turkkila (FIN)	-	15	17
18. Jenna McCorkell (GRB)	-	16	19
19. Isabelle Pieman (BEL)	-	17	20
20. Romy Bühler (SUI)	-	24	18
21. Myriam Leuenberger (SUI)	-	21	21
22. Nathalie Weinzierl (GER)	-	20	22
23. Francesca Rio (ITA)	7	22	23
24. Karina Sinding Johnson (DEN)	-	23	24
25. Fleur Maxwell (LUX)	9	25	-
26. Kaat Van Daele (BEL)	10	26	-
27. Chelsea Rose Chiappa (HUN)	-	27	-
28. Clara Peters (IRL)	8	28	-
29. Birce Atabey (TUR)	11	-	-
30. Kerstin Frank (AUT)	12	-	-
31. Rimgailė Meškaitė (LIT)	13	-	-
32. Manouk Gijsman (NED)	14	-	-
33. Patricia Gleščič (SLO)	15	-	-
34. Camilla Gjersem (NOR)	16	-	-
35. Ksenia Bakusheva (BLS)	17	-	-
36. Eliška Březinová (CZE)	18	-	-
37. Daniela Stoeva (BUL)	19	-	-
38. Georgia Glastris (GRE)	20	-	-
39. Sabina Măriuță (ROM)	21	-	-
40. Marina Seeh (SRB)	22	-	-
41. Mirna Libric (CRO)	23	-	-
WD. Viktória Pavuk (HUN)	-	-	-

European Pairs Skating Championships:

	SP	FS
1. Tatiana Volosozhar/Maxim Trankov (RUS)	1	1
2. Vera Bazarova/Yuri Larionov (RUS)	2	2
3. Ksenia Stolbova/Fedor Klimov (RUS)	3	3
4. Stefania Berton/Ondřej Hotárek (ITA)	4	4

5. Mari Vartmann/Aaron Van Cleave (GER)	7	5
6. Vanessa James/Morgan Ciprès (FRA)	8	6
7. Maylin Hausch/Daniel Wende (GER)	5	7
8. Daria Popova/Bruno Massot (FRA)	6	9
9. Stacey Kemp/David King (GRB)	9	8
10. Lubov Bakirova/Mikalai Kamianchuk (BLS)	14	10
11. D. Montalbano/E. Krasnopolski (ISR)	12	11
12. Carolina Gillespie/Luca Demattè (ITA)	11	12
13. Alexandra Herbríková/Rudy Halmaert (CZE)	10	14
14. Anaïs Morand/Timothy Leemann (SUI)	13	15
15. Stina Martini/Severin Kiefer (AUT)	15	13
16. Sally Hoolin/James Hunt (GRB)	16	16
17. Elizabeta Makarova/Leri Kenchadze (BUL)	17	-
18. Maria Paliakova/Mikhail Fomichev (BLS)	18	-
WD. Aliona Savchenko/Robin Szolkowy (GER)	-	-

European Ice Dancing Championships:

	PR	SD	FD
1. N. Péchalat/F. Bourzat (FRA)	-	2	1
2. E. Bobrova/D. Soloviev (RUS)	-	1	2
3. Elena Ilinykh/Nikita Katsalapov (RUS)	-	7	3
4. Anna Cappellini/Luca Lanotte (ITA)	-	6	4
5. E. Riazanova/I. Tkachenko (RUS)	-	3	5
6. P. Coomes/N. Buckland (GRB)	-	4	6
7. Pernelle Carron/Lloyd Jones (FRA)	-	8	7
8. N. Zhiganshina/A. Gazsi (GER)	-	9	8
9. I. Tobias/D. Stagniūnas (LIT)	-	5	10
10. Julia Zlobina/Alexei Sitnikov (AZE)	1	11	9
11. Charlène Guignard/Marco Fabbri (ITA)	2	10	11
12. Tanja Kolbe/Stefano Caruso (GER)	6	13	13
13. Louise Walden/Owen Edwards (GRB)	4	14	14
14. Irina Shtork/Taavi Rand (EST)	7	19	12
15. S. Heekin-Canedy/D. Dun (UKR)	3	16	15
16. S. Hurtado/A. Díaz Bronchud (ESP)	5	12	17
17. Zsuzsanna Nagy/Máté Fejes (HUN)	-	18	16
18. Gabriela Kubová/Dmitri Kiselev (CZE)	-	17	18
19. Lucie Myslivečková/Neil Brown (CZE)	8	15	19
20. N. Frolenkova/M. Kasalo (UKR)	-	20	20

21. Tiffany Zahorski/Alexis Miart (FRA)	9	-	-
22. Ramona Elsener/Florian Roost (SUI)	10	-	-
23. Dóra Turóczi/Balázs Major (HUN)	11	-	-
24. Barbora Silná/Juri Kurakin (AUT)	12	-	-
25. Henna Lindholm/Ossi Kanervo (FIN)	13	-	-
26. Alisa Agafonova/Alper Uçar (TUR)	14	-	-
27. A. Zvorygina/M. Bernadowski (POL)	15	-	-
28. L. Valadzenkava/V. Vakunov (BLS)	16	-	-
29. Ekaterina Bugrov/Vasili Rogov (ISR)	17	-	-
30. K. Pecherkina/A. Jakushin (LAT)	18	-	-
31. A. Chistiakova/D. Lichev (BUL)	19	-	-

Sources: Protocol, 2012 European Figure Skating Championships; Entries, 2012 European Figure Skating Championships

2013 EUROPEAN FIGURE SKATING CHAMPIONSHIPS
Zagreb, Croatia, January 23-27, 2013

European Men's Figure Skating Championships:

	SP	FS
1. Javier Fernández (ESP)	2	1
2. Florent Amodio (FRA)	1	3
3. Michal Březina (CZE)	4	2
4. Brian Joubert (FRA)	3	5
5. Maxim Kovtun (RUS)	7	4
6. Alexander Majorov (SWE)	8	6
7. Sergei Voronov (RUS)	5	7
8. Viktor Pfeifer (AUT)	10	9
9. Chafik Besseghier (FRA)	11	10
10. Peter Liebers (GER)	17	8
11. Tomáš Verner (CZE)	9	19
12. Kim Lucine (MON)	12	16
13. Pavel Ignatenko (BLS)	14	15
14. Alexei Bychenko (ISR)	18	12
15. Yakov Godorozha (UKR)	15	14
16. Javier Raya (ESP)	19	11
17. Viktor Romanenkov (EST)	13	20
18. Zoltan Kelemen (ROM)	16	18

19. Maciej Cieplucha (POL)	23	13
20. Stéphane Walker (SUI)	24	17
21. Justus Strid (DEN)	22	21
22. Manol Atanassov (BUL)	21	22
23. Paolo Bacchini (ITA)	25	-
24. Valtter Virtanen (FIN)	26	-
25. Harry Mattick (GRB)	27	-
26. Saulius Ambrulevičius (LIT)	28	-
27. Ali Demirboga (TUR)	29	-
28. Paul Bonifacio Parkinson (ITA)	30	-
WD. Evgeni Plushenko (RUS)	6	-
WD. Pavel Kaška (CZE)	20	-

European Ladies Figure Skating Championships:

	SP	FS
1. Carolina Kostner (ITA)	2	2
2. Adelina Sotnikova (RUS)	1	3
3. Elizaveta Tuktamysheva (RUS)	4	1
4. Valentina Marchei (ITA)	3	4
5. Viktoria Helgesson (SWE)	6	7
6. Nikol Gosviani (RUS)	12	5
7. Sonia Lafuente (ESP)	11	6
8. Joshi Helgesson (SWE)	5	9
9. Nathalie Weinzierl (GER)	8	10
10. Maé-Bérénice Méité (FRA)	13	8
11. Lénaëlle Gilleron-Gorry (FRA)	7	14
12. Kerstin Frank (AUT)	15	12
13. Elena Glebova (EST)	9	13
14. Elene Gedevanishvili (GEO)	16	11
15. Monika Simančíková (SVK)	14	15
16. Anita Madsen (DEN)	17	16
17. Juulia Turkkila (FIN)	10	21
18. Kaat Van Daele (BEL)	18	18
19. Natalia Popova (UKR)	24	17
20. Tina Stuerzinger (SUI)	22	19
21. Jenna McCorkell (GRB)	19	20
22. Anne Line Gjersem (NOR)	23	22
23. Sıla Saygı (TUR)	21	23

24. Fleur Maxwell (LIT)	20	24
25. Anna Afonkina (BUL)	25	-
26. Alina Fjodorova (LAT)	26	-
27. Roberta Rodeghiero (ITA)	27	-
28. Patricia Gleščič (SLO)	28	-
29. Alisa Mikonsaari (FIN)	29	-
30. Eliška Březinová (CZE)	30	-
31. Inga Janulevičiūtė (LIT)	31	-
32. Michelle Couwenberg (NED)	32	-
33. Isabella Schuster-Velissariou (GRE)	33	-
34. Sabina Mariuta (ROM)	34	-
35. Mirna Libric (CRO)	35	-
36. Kristina Zakharanka (BLS)	36	-
WD. Kiira Korpi (FIN)	-	-
WD. Laura Raszyková (CZE)	-	-

European Pairs Skating Championships:

	SP	FS
1. Tatiana Volosozhar/Maxim Trankov (RUS)	1	1
2. Aliona Savchenko/Robin Szolkowy (GER)	2	2
3. Stefania Berton/Ondřej Hotárek (ITA)	3	3
4. Vanessa James/Morgan Ciprès (FRA)	4	4
5. Yuko Kavaguti/Alexander Smirnov (RUS)	5	5
6. Ksenia Stolbova/Fedor Klimov (RUS)	8	6
7. Daria Popova/Bruno Massot (FRA)	7	7
8. Mari Vartmann/Aaron Van Cleave (GER)	6	10
9. Nicole Della Monica/Matteo Guarise (ITA)	9	8
10. Stacey Kemp/David King (GRB)	10	11
11. Julia Lavrentieva/Yuri Rudyk (UKR)	11	9
12. Elizaveta Makarova/Leri Kenchadze (BUL)	13	12
13. Stina Martini/Severin Kiefer (AUT)	12	13
14. Maria Paliakova/Nikita Bochkov (BLS)	14	14
15. M. Klatka/R. Chruściński (POL)	15	15
WD. Vera Bazarova/Yuri Larionov (RUS)	-	-
WD. Maylin Hausch/Daniel Wende (GER)	-	-

European Ice Dancing Championships:

	SD	FD
1. Ekaterina Bobrova/Dmitri Soloviev (RUS)	1	2
2. Elena Ilinykh/Nikita Katsalapov (RUS)	2	1
3. Anna Cappellini/Luca Lanotte (ITA)	3	3
4. Ekaterina Riazanova/Ilia Tkachenko (RUS)	4	4
5. Penny Coomes/Nicholas Buckland (GRB)	6	5
6. Nelli Zhiganshina/Alexander Gazsi (GER)	7	6
7. Julia Zlobina/Alexei Sitnikov (AZE)	5	10
8. Tanja Kolbe/Stefano Caruso (GER)	9	7
9. Charlene Guignard/Marco Fabbri (ITA)	8	8
10. Pernelle Carron/Lloyd Jones (FRA)	10	9
11. Irina Shtork/Taavi Rand (EST)	14	11
12. Siobhan Heekin-Canedy/Dmitri Dun (UKR)	11	13
13. Alisa Agafanova/Alper Uçar (TUR)	12	12
14. Lucie Myslivečková/Neil Brown (CZE)	13	15
15. S. Hurtado Martin/A. Díaz Bronchud (ESP)	15	14
16. Zsuzsanna Nagy/Máté Fejes (HUN)	16	17
17. Federica Testa/Lukáš Csölley (SVK)	19	16
18. Ramona Elsener/Florian Roost (SUI)	17	18
19. Olesia Karmi/Max Lindholm (FIN)	20	19
20. Angelina Telegina/Otar Japaridze (GEO)	18	20
21. A. Zvorigina/M. Bernadowski (POL)	21	-
22. Charlotte Aiken/Josh Whidborne (GRB)	22	-
23. Kira Geil/Tobias Eisenbauer (AUT)	23	-
24. Lesia Valadzenkava/Vitali Vakunov (BLS)	24	-
25. Sarah Coward/Georgi Kenchadze (BUL)	25	-
WD. Nathalie Péchalat/Fabian Bourzat (FRA)	-	-
WD. Allison Reed/Vasili Rogov (ISR)	-	-

The qualifying rounds were again discontinued. The minimum Technical Element Scores (TES) for both the men's and ladies free skate increased by at least ten points. Javier Fernández made history as the first Spanish skater to win a gold medal at the European Figure Skating Championships.

Sources: Protocol, 2012 European Figure Skating Championships; Entries, 2012 European Figure Skating Championships

2014 EUROPEAN FIGURE SKATING CHAMPIONSHIPS
Budapest, Hungary, January 13-19, 2014

European Men's Figure Skating Championships:

	SP	FS
1. Javier Fernández (ESP)	1	1
2. Sergei Voronov (RUS)	2	2
3. Konstantin Menshov (RUS)	11	3
4. Michal Březina (CZE)	5	4
5. Maxim Kovtun (RUS)	4	5
6. Peter Liebers (GER)	8	7
7. Tomáš Verner (CZE)	3	8
8. Brian Joubert (FRA)	9	6
9. Jorik Hendrickx (BEL)	10	10
10. Alexei Bychenko (ISR)	13	9
11. Alexander Majorov (SWE)	6	13
12. Chafik Besseghier (FRA)	12	12
13. Florent Amodio (FRA)	7	20
14. Viktor Pfeifer (AUT)	16	11
15. Franz Streubel (GER)	19	14
16. Kim Lucine (MON)	18	16
17. Stéphane Walker (SUI)	17	17
18. Javier Raya (ESP)	20	15
19. Maciej Cieplucha (POL)	15	19
20. Pavel Ignatenko (BLS)	22	18
21. Zoltán Kelemen (ROM)	14	22
22. Yakov Godorozha (UKR)	21	23
23. Paul Bonifacio Parkinson (ITA)	24	21
24. Viktor Romanenkov (EST)	23	24
25. Sondre Oddvoll Bøe (NOR)	25	-
26. Marco Klepoch (SVK)	26	-
27. Matthew Parr (GRB)	27	-
28. Manol Atanassov (BUL)	28	-
29. Valtter Virtanen (FIN)	29	-
30. Kristóf Forgó (HUN)	30	-
31. Justus Strid (DEN)	31	-
32. Ali Demirboğa (TUR)	32	-
33. Manuel Koll (AUT)	33	-

34. Illya Solomin (SWE)	34	-
35. Sarkis Hayrapetyan (ARM)	35	-
WD. Matthias Versluis (FIN)	-	-
WD. Slavik Hayrapetyan (ARM)	-	-

European Ladies Figure Skating Championships:

	SP	FS
1. Yulia Lipnitskaya (RUS)	2	1
2. Adelina Sotnikova (RUS)	1	2
3. Carolina Kostner (ITA)	3	3
4. Alena Leonova (RUS)	4	5
5. Maé-Bérénice Méité (FRA)	5	4
6. Valentina Marchei (ITA)	6	6
7. Elena Glebova (EST)	8	7
8. Nathalie Weinzierl (GER)	10	8
9. Joshi Helgesson (SWE)	9	10
10. Elene Gedevanishvili (GEO)	7	13
11. Roberta Rodeghiero (ITA)	15	9
12. Juulia Turkkila (FIN)	12	12
13. Laurine Lecavelier (FRA)	13	11
14. Viktoria Helgesson (SWE)	11	14
15. Eliška Březinová (CZE)	16	16
16. Isabelle Olsson (SWE)	22	15
17. Nicole Rajičová (SVK)	14	18
18. Inga Janulevičiūtė (LIT)	21	17
19. Anne Line Gjersem (NOR)	18	19
20. Kaat Van Daele (BEL)	19	20
21. Agata Kryger (POL)	23	21
22. Marta García (ESP)	20	22
23. Natalia Popova (UKR)	17	24
24. Jenna McCorkell (GRB)	24	23
25. Janina Makeenka (BEL)	25	-
26. Tanja Odermatt (SUI)	26	-
27. Daša Grm (SLO)	27	-
28. Sonia Lafuente (ESP)	28	-
29. Anita Madsen (DEN)	29	-
30. Ieva Gaile (LAT)	30	-
31. Kerstin Frank (AUT)	31	-

32. Michelle Couwenberg (NED) 32 -
33. Fleur Maxwell (LUX) 33 -
34. Sarah Hecken (GER) 34 -
35. Danielle Montalbano (ISR) 35 -
36. Anna Afonkina (BUL) 36 -
37. Sıla Saygı (TUR) 37 -
WD. Clara Peters (IRL) - -
WD. Isabella Schuster-Velissariou (GRE) - -
WD. Bernadett Szakács (HUN) - -
WD. Alina Fjodorova (LAT) - -

European Pairs Skating Championships:

	SP	FS
1. Tatiana Volosozhar/Maxim Trankov (RUS)	1	2
2. Ksenia Stolbova/Fedor Klimov (RUS)	4	1
3. Vera Bazarova/Yuri Larionov (RUS)	3	3
4. Stefania Berton/Ondřej Hotárek (ITA)	5	4
5. Vanessa James/Morgan Ciprès (FRA)	6	5
6. Maylin Wende/Daniel Wende (GER)	8	6
7. Andrea Davidovich/Evgeni Krasnopolski (ISR)	7	7
8. Nicole Della Monica/Matteo Guarise (ITA)	9	8
9. Mari Vartmann/Aaron Van Cleave (GER)	10	9
10. Natalia Zabiiako/Alexandr Zaboev (EST)	12	10
11. Daria Popova/Bruno Massot (FRA)	11	11
12. Miriam Ziegler/Severin Kiefer (AUT)	15	12
13. Stacey Kemp/David King (GRB)	16	13
14. Maria Paliakova/Nikita Bochkov (BLS)	13	14
15. Amani Fancy/Christopher Boyadji (GRB)	14	15
16. A. Cernuschi/F. Ambrosini (ITA)	17	-
17. Elizaveta Makarova/Leri Kenchadze (BUL)	18	-
18. Julia Lavrentieva/Yuri Rudyk (UKR)	19	-
19. Veronica Grigorieva/Aritz Maestu Babarro (ESP)	20	-
WD. Aliona Savchenko/Robin Szolkowy (GER)	2	-
WD. M. Klatka/R. Chruściński (POL)	-	-

European Ice Dancing Championships:

	SD	FD
1. Anna Cappellini/Luca Lanotte (ITA)	1	1
2. Elena Ilinykh/Nikita Katsalapov (RUS)	2	2
3. Penny Coomes/Nicholas Buckland (GRB)	3	3
4. Victoria Sinitsina/Ruslan Zhiganshin (RUS)	4	4
5. Ekaterina Riazanova/Ilia Tkachenko (RUS)	5	5
6. Julia Zlobina/Alexei Sitnikov (AZE)	6	6
7. Nelli Zhiganshina/Alexander Gazsi (GER)	7	8
8. Charlène Guignard/Marco Fabbri (ITA)	8	7
9. Isabella Tobias/Deividas Stagniūnas (LIT)	9	9
10. S. Hurtado Martín/A. Díaz Bronchud (ESP)	11	11
11. Tanja Kolbe/Stefano Caruso (GER)	13	10
12. Federica Testa/Lukáš Csölley (SVK)	12	12
13. Pernelle Carron/Lloyd Jones (FRA)	10	13
14. Irina Shtork/Taavi Rand (EST)	14	15
15. Gabriella Papadakis/Guillaume Cizeron (FRA)	15	14
16. Justyna Plutowska/Peter Gerber (POL)	17	16
17. Alisa Agafonova/Alper Uçar (TUR)	16	18
18. L. Fournier Beaudry/N. Sørensen (DEN)	18	17
19. Lorenza Alessandrini/Simone Vaturi (ITA)	19	20
20. Henna Lindholm/Ossi Kanervo (FIN)	20	19
21. Dóra Turóczi/Balázs Major (HUN)	21	-
22. Ramona Elsener/Florian Roost (SUI)	22	-
23. Siobhan Heekin-Canedy/Dmitri Dun (UKR)	23	-
24. Allison Reed/Vasili Rogov (ISR)	24	-
25. Barbora Silná/Juri Kurakin (AUT)	25	-
26. Lucie Myslivečková/Neil Brown (CZE)	26	-
27. Angelina Telegina/Otar Japaridze (GEO)	27	-
28. Viktoria Kavaliova/Yurii Bieliaiev (BLS)	28	-
29. Carter Marie Jones/Richard Sharpe (GRB)	29	-
WD. Nathalie Péchalat/Fabian Bourzat (FRA)	-	-

Sources: Protocol, 2014 European Figure Skating Championships; Entries, 2014 European Figure Skating Championships

2015 EUROPEAN FIGURE SKATING CHAMPIONSHIPS
Stockholm, Sweden, January 26-February 1, 2015

European Men's Figure Skating Championships:

	SP	FS
1. Javier Fernández (ESP)	1	1
2. Maxim Kovtun (RUS)	4	2
3. Sergei Voronov (RUS)	2	3
4. Alexei Bychenko (ISR)	7	4
5. Michal Březina (CZE)	3	7
6. Peter Liebers (GER)	5	8
7. Adian Pitkeev (RUS)	9	6
8. Ivan Righini (ITA)	11	5
9. Florent Amodio (FRA)	6	10
10. Daniel Samohin (ISR)	8	9
11. Alexander Majorov (SWE)	10	11
12. Petr Coufal (CZE)	16	12
13. Franz Streubel (GER)	13	13
14. Javier Raya (ESP)	21	14
15. Phillip Harris (GRB)	12	17
16. Yaroslav Paniot (UKR)	14	18
17. Pavel Kaška (CZE)	17	15
18. Valtter Virtanen (FIN)	15	19
19. Justus Strid (DEN)	22	16
20. Patrick Myzyk (POL)	18	20
21. Pavel Ignatenko (BLS)	19	21
22. Sondre Oddvoll Bøe (NOR)	20	22
23. Larry Loupolover (AZE)	23	23
24. Slavik Hayrapetyan (ARM)	25	-
25. Stéphane Walker (SUI)	26	-
26. Engin Ali Artan (TUR)	27	-
27. Samuel Koppel (EST)	28	-
28. Marco Klepoch (SVK)	29	-
29. Manuel Koll (AUT)	30	-
WD. Chafik Besseghier (FRA)	24	-

European Ladies Figure Skating Championships:

	SP	FS
1. Elizaveta Tuktamysheva (RUS)	2	1
2. Elena Radionova (RUS)	1	2
3. Anna Pogorilaya (RUS)	3	3
4. Joshi Helgesson (SWE)	6	4
5. Viktoria Helgesson (SWE)	5	6
6. Maé-Bérénice Méité (FRA)	7	9
7. Angelina Kučvaļska (LAT)	17	5
8. Roberta Rodeghiero (ITA)	11	7
9. Nicole Schott (GER)	9	8
10. Laurine Lecavelier (FRA)	13	10
11. Nicole Rajičová (SVK)	8	12
12. Nathalie Weinzierl (GER)	15	11
13. Anastasia Galustyan (ARM)	12	14
14. Eveline Brunner (SUI)	10	15
15. Eliška Březinová (CZE)	21	13
16. Natalia Popova (UKR)	18	16
17. Kerstin Frank (AUT)	16	19
18. Sonia Lafuente (ESP)	20	18
19. Aleksandra Golovkina (LIT)	23	17
20. Fleur Maxwell (LUX)	14	22
21. Camilla Gjersem (NOR)	22	20
22. Gerli Liinamäe (EST)	24	21
23. Elene Gedevanishvili (GEO)	19	23
24. Birce Atabey (TUR)	25	-
25. Karly Robertson (GRB)	26	-
26. Pernille Sørensen (DEN)	27	-
27. Giada Russo (ITA)	28	-
28. Daša Grm (SLO)	29	-
29. Helery Halvin (EST)	30	-
30. Niki Wories (NED)	31	-
31. Netta Schreiber (ISR)	32	-
32. Ivett Tóth (HUN)	33	-
33. Micol Cristini (ITA)	34	-
34. Julia Sauter (ROM)	35	-
35. Daniela Stoeva (BUL)	36	-
36. Janina Makeenka (BLS)	37	-

37. Agata Kryger (POL) 38 -
WD. Kiira Korpi (FIN) 4 -

European Pairs Skating Championships:

	SP	FS
1. Yuko Kavaguti/Alexander Smirnov (RUS)	2	1
2. Ksenia Stolbova/Fedor Klimov (RUS)	1	2
3. Evgenia Tarasova/Vladimir Morozov (RUS)	5	3
4. Valentina Marchei/Ondřej Hotárek (ITA)	4	4
5. Vanessa James/Morgan Ciprès (FRA)	3	6
6. Nicole Della Monica/Matteo Guarise (ITA)	8	5
7. Mari Vartmann/Aaron Van Cleave (GER)	6	7
8. Miriam Ziegler/Severin Kiefer (AUT)	9	8
9. Caitlin Yankowskas/Hamish Gaman (GRB)	7	14
10. A. Cernuschi/F. Ambrosini (ITA)	13	9
11. Minerva Fabienne Hase/Nolan Seegert (GER)	11	10
12. Amani Fancy/Christopher Boyadji (GRB)	12	12
13. Elizaveta Makarova/Leri Kenchadze (BUL)	14	11
14. Maria Paliakova/Nikita Bochkov (BLS)	10	13

European Ice Dancing Championships:

	SD	FD
1. Gabriella Papadakis/Guillaume Cizeron (FRA)	1	1
2. Anna Cappellini/Luca Lanotte (ITA)	3	2
3. Alexandra Stepanova/Ivan Bukin (RUS)	4	3
4. Elena Ilinykh/Ruslan Zhiganshin (RUS)	2	8
5. S. Hurtado Martín/A. Díaz Bronchud (ESP)	6	4
6. Charlène Guignard/Marco Fabbri (ITA)	7	5
7. Nelli Zhiganshina/Alexander Gazsi (GER)	8	7
8. Federica Testa/Lukáš Csölley (SVK)	5	10
9. L. Fournier Beaudry/N. Sørensen (DEN)	9	9
10. Ksenia Monko/Kirill Khaliavin (RUS)	11	6
11. Alexandra Nazarova/Maxim Nikitin (UKR)	12	11
12. Alisa Agafonova/Alper Uçar (TUR)	13	12
13. Irina Shtork/Taavi Rand (EST)	14	13
14. Natalia Kaliszek/Maksym Spodyriev (POL)	15	14
15. Carolina Moscheni/Ádám Lukács (HUN)	16	16
16. Allison Reed/Vasili Rogov (ISR)	17	17

17. Cortney Mansour/Michal Češka (CZE)	19	15
18. Barbora Silná/Juri Kurakin (AUT)	18	18
19. Olesia Karmi/Max Lindholm (FIN)	20	19
20. Jennifer Urban/Sevan Lerche (GER)	21	-
21. Celia Robledo/Luis Fenero (ESP)	22	-
22. Misato Komatsubara/Andrea Fabbri (ITA)	23	-
23. Taylor Tran/Saulius Ambrulevičius (LIT)	24	-
24. Viktoria Kavaliova/Yurii Bieliaiev (BLS)	25	-
25. Olga Jakushina/Andrey Nevskiy (LAT)	26	-
26. Tatiana Kozmava/Aleksandr Zolotarev (GEO)	27	-
27. Cecile Postiaux/Richard Postiaux (BEL)	28	-
28. Katarina Paice/Yuri Eremenko (SUI)	29	-
WD. Penny Coomes/Nicholas Buckland (GRB)	10	-
WD. Olivia Smart/Joseph Buckland (GRB)	-	-

Sources: Entries, 2015 European Figure Skating Championships; Protocol, 2015 European Figure Skating Championships

2016 EUROPEAN FIGURE SKATING CHAMPIONSHIPS
Bratislava, Slovakia, January 25-31, 2016

European Men's Figure Skating Championships:

	SP	FS
1. Javier Fernández (ESP)	1	1
2. Alexei Bychenko (ISR)	4	4
3. Maxim Kovtun (RUS)	2	6
4. Florent Amodio (FRA)	8	2
5. Mikhail Kolyada (RUS)	9	3
6. Ivan Righini (ITA)	6	5
7. Daniel Samohin (ISR)	5	8
8. Alexander Petrov (RUS)	10	7
9. Jorik Hendrickx (BEL)	7	9
10. Michal Březina (CZE)	3	13
11. Alexander Majorov (SWE)	11	12
12. Deniss Vasiļjevs (LAT)	14	10
13. Matteo Rizzo (ITA)	12	14
14. Franz Streubel (GER)	15	11
15. Ivan Pavlov (UKR)	13	15

16. Paul Fentz (GER)	16	17
17. Felipe Montoya Pulgarín (ESP)	17	19
18. Phillip Harris (GRB)	18	16
19. Stéphane Walker (SUI)	22	18
20. Jiří Bělohradský (CZE)	19	21
21. Nicholas Vrdoljak (CRO)	21	20
22. David Kranjec (SLO)	23	22
23. Mario-Rafael Ionian (AUT)	24	23
24. Sondre Oddvoll Bøe (NOR)	20	24
25. Thomas Kennes (NED)	25	-
26. Valtter Virtanen (FIN)	26	-
27. Alexei Mialionkhin (BLS)	27	-
28. Daniil Zurav (EST)	28	-
29. Armen Agaian (GEO)	29	-
30. Patrick Myzyk (POL)	30	-
31. Slavik Hayrapetyan (ARM)	31	-
32. Larry Loupolover (AZE)	32	-
33. Alexander Maszljanko (HUN)	33	-
34. Michael Neuman (SVK)	34	-
35. Engin Ali Artan (TUR)	35	-
WD. Chafik Besseghier (FRA)	-	-

European Ladies Figure Skating Championships:

	SP	FS
1. Evgenia Medvedeva (RUS)	1	1
2. Elena Radionova (RUS)	2	2
3. Anna Pogorilaya (RUS)	3	3
4. Angelīna Kučvaļska (LAT)	5	4
5. Roberta Rodeghiero (ITA)	4	5
6. Maé-Bérénice Méité (FRA)	8	6
7. Nathalie Weinzierl (GER)	7	7
8. Viveca Lindfors (FIN)	11	8
9. Joshi Helgesson (SWE)	6	11
10. Laurine Lecavelier (FRA)	13	9
11. Ivett Tóth (HUN)	10	12
12. Nicole Rajičová (SVK)	9	18
13. Matilda Algotsson (SWE)	18	10
14. Giada Russo (ITA)	12	16

	SP	FS
15. Anastasia Galustyan (ARM)	16	13
16. Aleksandra Golovkina (LIT)	15	15
17. Anne Line Gjersem (NOR)	14	17
18. Fleur Maxwell (LUX)	22	14
19. Helery Hälvin (EST)	20	19
20. Niki Wories (NED)	21	20
21. Anna Khnychenkova (UKR)	19	22
22. Kerstin Frank (AUT)	24	21
23. Eliška Březinová (CZE)	17	23
24. Isabelle Olsson (SWE)	23	24
25. Lutricia Bock (GER)	25	-
26. Daša Grm (SLO)	26	-
27. Julia Sauter (ROM)	27	-
28. Tanja Odermatt (SUI)	28	-
29. Danielle Harrison (GRB)	29	-
30. Charlotte Vandersarren (BEL)	30	-
31. Aimee Buchanan (ISR)	31	-
32. Birce Atabey (TUR)	32	-
33. Sonia Lafuente (ESP)	33	-
34. Pernille Sørensen (DEN)	34	-
35. Daniela Stoeva (BUL)	35	-
36. Janina Makeenka (BLS)	36	-
WD. Katarina Kulgeyko (ISR)	-	-

European Pairs Skating Championships:

	SP	FS
1. Tatiana Volosozhar/Maxim Trankov (RUS)	1	1
2. Aliona Savchenko/Bruno Massot (GER)	2	3
3. Evgenia Tarasova/Vladimir Morozov (RUS)	3	2
4. Vanessa James/Morgan Ciprès (FRA)	5	5
5. Valentina Marchei/Ondřej Hotárek (ITA)	8	4
6. Nicole Della Monica/Matteo Guarise (ITA)	6	6
7. Kristina Astakhova/Alexei Rogonov (RUS)	7	7
8. Mari Vartmann/Ruben Blommaert (GER)	4	8
9. Miriam Ziegler/Severin Kiefer (AUT)	9	10
10. Tatiana Danilova/Mikalai Kamianchuk (BLS)	10	9
11. Goda Butkutė/Nikita Ermolaev (LIT)	11	11
12. Bianca Manacorda/Niccolò Macii (ITA)	12	12

13. Adel Tankova/Evgeni Krasnopolski (ISR)	14	13
14. Anna Marie Pearce/Mark Magyar (HUN)	16	14
15. Marcelina Lech/Aritz Maestu Babarro (ESP)	13	15
16. Alexandra Herbríková/Nicolas Roulet (SUI)	15	16
WD. Ksenia Stolbova/Fedor Klimov (RUS)	-	-
WD. Yuko Kavaguti/Alexander Smirnov (RUS)	-	-
WD. Amani Fancy/Christopher Boyadji (GRB)	-	-

European Ice Dancing Championships:

	SD	FD
1. Gabriella Papadakis/Guillaume Cizeron (FRA)	2	1
2. Anna Cappellini/Luca Lanotte (ITA)	1	3
3. Ekaterina Bobrova/Dmitri Soloviev (RUS)	3	2
4. Victoria Sinitsina/Nikita Katsalapov (RUS)	4	4
5. Alexandra Stepanova/Ivan Bukin (RUS)	5	5
6. Penny Coomes/Nicholas Buckland (GRB)	8	6
7. Charlène Guignard/Marco Fabbri (ITA)	6	7
8. Federica Testa/Lukáš Csölley (SVK)	9	8
9. L. Fournier Beaudry/N. Sørensen (DEN)	10	9
10. Isabella Tobias/Ilia Tkachenko (ISR)	7	12
11. Natalia Kaliszek/Maksym Spodyriev (POL)	11	11
12. Alisa Agafonova/Alper Uçar (TUR)	12	10
13. Cortney Mansour/Michal Češka (CZE)	14	13
14. Kavita Lorenz/Joti Polizoakis (GER)	13	15
15. Cecilia Törn/Jussiville Partanen (FIN)	18	14
16. Viktoria Kavaliova/Yurii Bieliaiev (BLS)	17	16
17. Barbora Silná/Juri Kurakin (AUT)	15	17
18. Tina Garabedian/Simon Proulx-Sénécal (ARM)	20	18
19. Celia Robledo/Luis Fenero (ESP)	19	19
20. Lorenza Alessandrini/Pierre Souquet (FRA)	16	20
21. Misato Komatsubara/Andrea Fabbri (ITA)	21	-
22. Olga Jakushina/Andrey Nevskiy (LAT)	22	-
23. Katharina Müller/Tim Dieck (GER)	23	-
24. Peroline Ojardias/Michael Bramante (FRA)	24	-
25. Taylor Tran/Saulius Ambrulevičius (LIT)	25	-
26. Valeria Haistruk/Alexei Olejnik (UKR)	26	-
27. Carolina Moscheni/Balázs Major (HUN)	27	-
28. Katarina Paice/Yuri Eremenko (SUI)	28	-

Javier Fernández set a record for the highest overall score awarded in the men's event at the European Championships under the IJS System (302.77).

Sources: Entries, 2016 European Figure Skating Championships; Protocol, 2016 European Figure Skating Championships

2017 EUROPEAN FIGURE SKATING CHAMPIONSHIPS
Ostrava, Czech Republic, January 25-29, 2017

European Men's Figure Skating Championships:

	SP	FS
1. Javier Fernández (ESP)	1	1
2. Maxim Kovtun (RUS)	2	2
3. Mikhail Kolyada (RUS)	4	3
4. Jorik Hendrickx (BEL)	5	5
5. Alexei Bychenko (ISR)	3	9
6. Morisi Kvitelashvili (GEO)	10	4
7. Deniss Vasiljevs (LAT)	6	6
8. Alexander Samarin (RUS)	9	7
9. Chafik Besseghier (FRA)	11	10
10. Paul Fentz (GER)	12	8
11. Alexander Majorov (SWE)	7	12
12. Michal Březina (CZE)	8	13
13. Ivan Righini (ITA)	14	11
14. Ivan Pavlov (UKR)	15	14
15. Kévin Aymoz (FRA)	13	18
16. Graham Newberry (GRB)	16	16
17. Stéphane Walker (SUI)	19	15
18. Javier Raya (ESP)	17	17
19. Maurizio Zandron (ITA)	18	19
20. Jiří Bělohradský (CZE)	20	21
21. Slavik Hayrapetyan (ARM)	21	22
22. Daniel Albert Naurits (EST)	24	20
23. Valtter Virtanen (FIN)	22	24
24. Sondre Oddvoll Bøe (NOR)	23	23
25. Igor Reznichenko (POL)	25	-
26. Nicholas Vrdoljak (CRO)	26	-

27. Alexander Borovoj (HUN)	27	-
28. Thomas Kennes (NED)	28	-
29. Anton Karpuk (BLS)	29	-
30. Mark Gorodnitsky (ISR)	30	-
31. Larry Loupolover (AZE)	31	-
32. Engin Ali Artan (TUR)	32	-
33. Daniel Samohin (ISR)	33	-
34. Michael Neuman (SVK)	34	-
35. Nicky Obreykov (BUL)	35	-
36. Mario-Rafael Ionian (AUT)	36	-

European Ladies Figure Skating Championships:

	SP	FS
1. Evgenia Medvedeva (RUS)	1	1
2. Anna Pogorilaya (RUS)	2	3
3. Carolina Kostner (ITA)	3	2
4. Maria Sotskova (RUS)	4	5
5. Laurine Lecavelier (FRA)	5	4
6. Nicole Rajičová (SVK)	7	6
7. Loena Hendrickx (BEL)	11	7
8. Ivett Tóth (HUN)	6	8
9. Roberta Rodeghiero (ITA)	8	12
10. Nicole Schott (GER)	9	10
11. Emmi Peltonen (FIN)	14	9
12. Anastasia Galustyan (ARM)	10	14
13. Matilda Algotsson (SWE)	18	11
14. Joshi Helgesson (SWE)	13	13
15. Helery Hälvin (EST)	16	15
16. Maé-Bérénice Méité (FRA)	12	19
17. Nathalie Weinzierl (GER)	22	17
18. Natasha McKay (GRB)	24	16
19. Angelīna Kučvaļska (LAT)	20	18
20. Michaela-Lucie Hanzlíková (CZE)	15	21
21. Anna Khnychenkova (UKR)	21	20
22. Kerstin Frank (AUT)	17	24
23. Viveca Lindfors (FIN)	19	22
24. Anne Line Gjersem (NOR)	23	23
25. Julia Sauter (ROM)	25	-

26. Daša Grm (SLO) 26 -
27. Yasmine Kimiko Yamada (SUI) 27 -
28. Elżbieta Kropa (LIT) 28 -
29. Antonina Dubinina (SRB) 29 -
30. Colette Coco Kaminski (POL) 30 -
31. Aimee Buchanan (ISR) 31 -
32. Birce Atabey (TUR) 32 -
33. Valentina Matos Romero (ESP) 33 -
34. Hristina Vassileva (BUL) 34 -
WD. Niki Wories (NED) - -

European Pairs Skating Championships:

	SP	FS
1. Evgenia Tarasova/Vladimir Morozov (RUS)	1	2
2. Aliona Savchenko/Bruno Massot (GER)	3	1
3. Vanessa James/Morgan Ciprès (FRA)	2	3
4. Ksenia Stolbova/Fedor Klimov (RUS)	4	4
5. Natalia Zabiiako/Alexander Enbert (RUS)	5	5
6. Valentina Marchei/Ondřej Hotárek (ITA)	6	6
7. Anna Dušková/Martin Bidař (CZE)	7	7
8. Nicole Della Monica/Matteo Guarise (ITA)	8	8
9. Miriam Ziegler/Severin Kiefer (AUT)	9	9
10. Tatiana Danilova/Mikalai Kamianchuk (BLS)	10	10
11. Rebecca Ghilardi/Filippo Ambrosini (ITA)	14	11
12. Minerva Fabienne Hase/Nolan Seegert (GER)	13	12
13. Lola Esbrat/Andrei Novoselov (FRA)	11	13
14. Zoe Jones/Christopher Boyadji (GRB)	12	14
15. L. Petranović/A. Souza-Kordeiru (CRO)	15	15
16. A.Cherniavskaia/E. Krasnopolski (ISR)	16	16
17. Ioulia Chtchetinina/Noah Scherer (SUI)	17	-
18. Goda Butkutė/Nikita Ermolaev (LIT)	18	-
WD. Mari Vartmann/Ruben Blommaert (GER)	-	-
WD. Renata Oganesian/Mark Bardei (UKR)	-	-

European Ice Dancing Championships:

	SD	FD
1. Gabriella Papadakis/Guillaume Cizeron (FRA)	3	1
2. Anna Cappellini/Luca Lanotte (ITA)	2	2

3. Ekaterina Bobrova/Dmitri Soloviev (RUS)	1	3
4. Isabella Tobias/Ilia Tkachenko (ISR)	5	4
5. Alexandra Stepanova/Ivan Bukin (RUS)	6	5
6. Charlène Guignard/Marco Fabbri (ITA)	4	7
7. L. Fournier Beaudry/N. Sørensen (DEN)	7	6
8. Natalia Kaliszek/Maksym Spodyriev (POL)	10	8
9. Alexandra Nazarova/Maxim Nikitin (UKR)	9	10
10. Victoria Sinitsina/Nikita Katsalapov (RUS)	8	12
11. Alisa Agafonova/Alper Uçar (TUR)	11	9
12. Marie-Jade Lauriault/Romain Le Gac (FRA)	12	11
13. Sara Hurtado Martín/Kirill Khaliavin (ESP)	13	15
14. Kavita Lorenz/Joti Polizoakis (GER)	15	13
15. Lilah Fear/Lewis Gibson (GRB)	19	14
16. Lucie Myslivečková/Lukáš Csölley (SLO)	17	16
17. Cecilia Törn/Jussiville Partanen (FIN)	14	18
18. Taylor Tran/Saulius Ambrulevičius (LIT)	20	17
19. Tina Garabedian/Simon Proulx-Sénécal (ARM)	16	19
20. Viktoria Kavaliova/Yurii Bieliaiev (BLS)	18	20
21. Robynne Tweedale/Joseph Buckland (GRB)	21	-
22. Jasmine Tessari/Francesco Fioretti (ITA)	22	-
23. Olga Jakushina/Andrey Nevskiy (LAT)	23	-
24. Varvara Ogloblina/Mikhail Zhirnov (AZE)	24	-
25. Victoria Manni/Carlo Röthlisberger (SUI)	25	-
26. Nicole Kuzmichová/Alexandr Sinicyn (CZE)	26	-
27. Tatiana Kozmava/Oleksii Shumskyi (GEO)	27	-
28. Hanna Jakucs/Dániel Illés (HUN)	28	-
29. Katerina Bunina/German Frolov (EST)	29	-
30. Adel Tankova/Ronald Zilberberg (ISR)	30	-
WD. Cortney Mansour/Michal Češka (CZE)	-	-

The ISU celebrated its 125th Anniversary. Vanessa James made history as the first woman of colour to win a medal in pairs skating at the European Championships.

Sources: Entries, 2017 European Figure Skating Championships; Protocol, 2017 European Figure Skating Championships

2018 EUROPEAN FIGURE SKATING CHAMPIONSHIPS
Moscow, Russia, January 15-21, 2018

European Men's Figure Skating Championships:

	SP	FS
1. Javier Fernández (ESP)	1	1
2. Dmitri Aliev (RUS)	2	2
3. Mikhail Kolyada (RUS)	4	3
4. Deniss Vasiļjevs (LAT)	3	5
5. Alexei Bychenko (ISR)	8	4
6. Alexander Samarin (RUS)	9	6
7. Alexander Majorov (SWE)	12	7
8. Michal Březina (CZE)	10	8
9. Matteo Rizzo (ITA)	6	9
10. Jorik Hendrickx (BEL)	5	12
11. Chafik Besseghier (FRA)	13	10
12. Morisi Kvitelashvili (GEO)	7	14
13. Phillip Harris (GRB)	15	11
14. Romain Ponsart (FRA)	20	13
15. Slavik Hayrapetyan (ARM)	14	16
16. Paul Fentz (GER)	11	17
17. Irakli Maysuradze (GEO)	18	15
18. Stéphane Walker (SUI)	16	20
19. Valtter Virtanen (FIN)	24	18
20. Felipe Montoya Pulgarín (ESP)	22	19
21. Daniel Albert Naurits (EST)	23	21
22. Sondre Oddvoll Bøe (NOR)	19	22
23. Burak Demirboğa (TUR)	21	23
24. Igor Reznichenko (POL)	17	24
25. Yaroslav Paniot (UKR)	25	-
26. Daniel Samohin (ISR)	26	-
27. Nicholas Vrdoljak (CRO)	27	-
28. Jiří Bělohradský (CZE)	28	-
29. Michael Neuman (SVK)	29	-
30. Thomas Kennes (NED)	30	-
31. Davide Lewton Brain (MON)	31	-
32. Larry Loupolover (AZE)	32	-
33. Alexander Maszljanko (HUN)	33	-

34. Nicky Obreykov (BUL)   34   -
35. Yakau Zenko (BLS)   35   -
36. Conor Stakelum (IRL)   36   -
WD. Peter Liebers (GER)   -   -
WD. Kévin Aymoz (FRA)   -   -

European Ladies Figure Skating Championships:

	SP	FS
1. Alina Zagitova (RUS)	1	1
2. Evgenia Medvedeva (RUS)	2	2
3. Carolina Kostner (ITA)	3	4
4. Maria Sotskova (RUS)	4	3
5. Loena Hendrickx (BEL)	8	5
6. Nicole Rajičová (SVK)	5	6
7. Alexia Paganini (SUI)	9	9
8. Maé-Bérénice Méité (FRA)	10	10
9. Emmi Peltonen (FIN)	11	8
10. Nicole Schott (GER)	18	7
11. Laurine Lecavelier (FRA)	7	12
12. Eliška Březinová (CZE)	12	14
13. Ivett Tóth (HUN)	15	13
14. Viveca Lindfors (FIN)	14	17
15. Micol Cristini (ITA)	19	11
16. Lea Johanna Dastich (GER)	16	15
17. Anita Östlund (SWE)	6	20
18. Anne Line Gjersem (NOR)	17	18
19. Giada Russo (ITA)	23	16
20. Daša Grm (SLO)	20	19
21. Pernille Sørensen (DEN)	24	21
22. Elżbieta Kropa (LIT)	21	22
23. Anna Khnychenkova (UKR)	13	23
24. Silvia Hugec (SVK)	22	24
25. Kristina Škuleta-Gromova (EST)	25	-
26. Kyarha van Tiel (NED)	26	-
27. Natasha McKay (GRB)	27	-
28. Fruzsina Medgyesi (HUN)	28	-
29. Julia Sauter (ROM)	29	-
30. Natalie Klotz (AUT)	30	-

31. Matilda Algotsson (SWE)	31	-
32. Sıla Saygı (TUR)	32	-
33. Valentina Matos Romero (ESP)	33	-
34. Elżbieta Gabryszak (POL)	34	-
35. Kim Cheremsky (AZE)	35	-
36. Diāna Ņikitina (LAT)	36	-
37. Antonina Dubinina (SRB)	37	-
38. Aimee Buchanan (ISR)	38	-
39. Presiyana Dimitrova (BUL)	39	-
WD. Charlotte Vandersarren (BEL)	40	-
WD. Anastasia Galustyan (ARM)	41	-
WD. Greta Morkytė (LIT)	42	-

European Pairs Skating Championships:

	SP	FS
1. Evgenia Tarasova/Vladimir Morozov (RUS)	5	1
2. Ksenia Stolbova/Fedor Klimov (RUS)	3	2
3. Natalia Zabiiako/Alexander Enbert (RUS)	2	3
4. Vanessa James/Morgan Ciprès (FRA)	1	4
5. Valentina Marchei/Ondřej Hotárek (ITA)	4	5
6. Nicole Della Monica/Matteo Guarise (ITA)	6	6
7. Miriam Ziegler/Severin Kiefer (AUT)	7	7
8. Annika Hocke/Ruben Blommaert (GER)	9	8
9. Paige Conners/Evgeni Krasnopolski (ISR)	10	9
10. Lola Esbrat/Andrei Novoselov (FRA)	8	10
11. L. Barquero Jiménez/A. Maestu Babarro (ESP)	11	11
12. L. Petranović/A. Souza-Kordeiru (CRO)	13	12
13. Ioulia Chtchetinina/Mikhail Akulov (SUI)	12	13
14. Sofiya Karagodina/Semyon Stepanov (AZE)	14	14
WD. Aliona Savchenko/Bruno Massot (GER)	-	-
WD. Zoe Jones/Christopher Boyadji (GRB)	-	-
WD. Anna Dušková/Martin Bidař (CZE)	-	-

European Ice Dancing Championships:

	SD	FD
1. Gabriella Papadakis/Guillaume Cizeron (FRA)	1	1
2. Ekaterina Bobrova/Dmitri Soloviev (RUS)	4	2
3. Alexandra Stepanova/Ivan Bukin (RUS)	2	3

4. Anna Cappellini/Luca Lanotte (ITA)	3	5
5. Charlène Guignard/Marco Fabbri (ITA)	5	4
6. Tiffany Zahorski/Jonathan Guerreiro (RUS)	8	6
7. Penny Coomes/Nicholas Buckland (GRB)	6	9
8. Sara Hurtado Martín/Kirill Khaliavin (ESP)	7	10
9. L. Fournier Beaudry/N. Sørensen (DEN)	9	7
10. Natalia Kaliszek/Maksym Spodyriev (POL)	10	8
11. Alexandra Nazarova/Maxim Nikitin (UKR)	11	12
12. Marie-Jade Lauriault/Romain Le Gac (FRA)	14	11
13. Alisa Agafonova/Alper Uçar (TUR)	12	13
14. Anna Yanovskaya/Ádám Lukács (HUN)	13	14
15. Cecilia Törn/Jussiville Partanen (FIN)	16	15
16. Angélique Abachkina/Louis Thauron (FRA)	15	17
17. Lucie Myslivečková/Lukáš Csölley (SVK)	17	16
18. Jasmine Tessari/Francesco Fioretti (ITA)	18	19
19. Tina Garabedian/Simon Proulx-Sénécal (ARM)	20	18
20. Viktoria Kavaliova/Yurii Bieliaiev (BLS)	19	20
21. Justyna Plutowska/Jeremie Flemin (POL)	21	-
22. Darya Popova/Volodymyr Byelikov (UKR)	22	-
23. Victoria Manni/Carlo Röthlisberger (SUI)	23	-
24. Guostė Damulevičiūtė/Deividas Kizala (LIT)	24	-
25. Cortney Mansour/Michal Češka (CZE)	25	-
26. Teodora Markova/Simon Daze (BUL)	26	-
27. Katerina Bunina/German Frolov (EST)	27	-
28. Adel Tankova/Ronald Zilberberg (ISR)	28	-
29. Aurelija Ipolito/Malcolm Jones (LAT)	29	-
30. Malin Malmberg/Thomas Nordahl (SWE)	30	-
WD. Kavita Lorenz/Joti Polizoakis (GER)	-	-
WD. Allison Reed/Saulius Ambrulevičius (LIT)	-	-

In her final trip to the European Figure Skating Championships, Carolina Kostner of Italy won the bronze medal. Kostner's career record of 11 medals in the ladies event at the European Championships has not been matched.

Sources: Entries, 2018 European Figure Skating Championships; Protocol, 2018 European Figure Skating Championships

2019 EUROPEAN FIGURE SKATING CHAMPIONSHIPS
Minsk, Belarus, January 21-27, 2019

European Men's Figure Skating Championships:

	SP	FS
1. Javier Fernández (ESP)	3	1
2. Alexander Samarin (RUS)	2	2
3. Matteo Rizzo (ITA)	10	3
4. Kévin Aymoz (FRA)	4	4
5. Mikhail Kolyada (RUS)	1	11
6. Daniel Grassl (ITA)	9	5
7. Michal Březina (CZE)	8	6
8. Alexander Majorov (SWE)	11	8
9. Alexei Bychenko (ISR)	7	13
10. Morisi Kvitelashvili (GEO)	15	7
11. Deniss Vasiļjevs (LAT)	12	10
12. Adam Siao Him Fa (FRA)	13	9
13. Daniel Samohin (ISR)	6	14
14. Maxim Kovtun (RUS)	5	16
15. Paul Fentz (GER)	17	12
16. Vladimir Litvintsev (AZE)	14	15
17. Aleksandr Selevko (EST)	16	20
18. Sondre Oddvoll Bøe (NOR)	20	18
19. Matyáš Bělohradský (CZE)	18	21
20. Luc Maierhofer (AUT)	21	19
21. Graham Newberry (GRB)	22	17
22. Ivan Shmuratko (UKR)	19	24
23. Irakli Maysuradze (GEO)	24	22
24. Davide Lewton Brain (MON)	23	23
25. Igor Reznichenko (POL)	25	-
26. Slavik Hayrapetyan (ARM)	26	-
27. Nikolaj Majorov (SWE)	27	-
28. Burak Demirboğa (TUR)	28	-
29. Nicky Obreykov (BUL)	29	-
30. Yakau Zenko (BLS)	30	-
31. Lukas Britschgi (SUI)	31	-
32. Roman Galay (FIN)	32	-
33. Conor Stakelum (IRL)	33	-

34. Héctor Alonso Serrano (ESP) 34 -
35. Michael Neuman (SVK) 35 -
36. Thomas Kennes (NED) 36 -
37. Alexander Borovoj (HUN) 37 -

European Ladies Figure Skating Championships:

	SP	FS
1. Sofia Samodurova (RUS)	2	1
2. Alina Zagitova (RUS)	1	4
3. Viveca Lindfors (FIN)	4	3
4. Stanislava Konstantinova (RUS)	11	2
5. Laurine Lecavelier (FRA)	6	6
6. Alexia Paganini (SUI)	3	7
7. Maé-Bérénice Méité (FRA)	8	5
8. Emmi Peltonen (FIN)	10	8
9. Nicole Rajičová (SVK)	5	12
10. Eliška Březinová (CZE)	12	9
11. Alexandra Feigin (BUL)	9	11
12. Ekaterina Ryabova (AZE)	7	13
13. Ivett Tóth (HUN)	13	10
14. Julia Sauter (ROM)	14	15
15. Yasmine Kimiko Yamada (SUI)	18	14
16. Nicole Schott (GER)	19	16
17. Daša Grm (SLO)	15	17
18. Anita Östlund (SWE)	17	18
19. Lucrezia Gennaro (ITA)	16	20
20. Natasha McKay (GRB)	22	19
21. Nathalie Weinzierl (GER)	24	21
22. Anastasia Galustyan (ARM)	21	22
23. Pernille Sørensen (DEN)	20	23
24. Antonina Dubinina (SRB)	23	24
25. Elżbieta Gabryszak (POL)	25	-
26. Sophia Schaller (AUT)	26	-
27. Gerli Liinamäe (EST)	27	-
28. Kyarha van Tiel (NED)	28	-
29. Lara Naki Gutmann (ITA)	29	-
30. Silvia Hugec (SVK)	30	-
31. Valentina Matos Romero (ESP)	31	-

32. Paulina Ramanauskaitė (LIT)	32	-
33. Camilla Gjersem (NOR)	33	-
34. Hana Cvijanović (CRO)	34	-
35. Elizabete Jubkane (LAT)	35	-
36. Anastasia Gozhva (UKR)	36	-
WD. Loena Hendrickx (BEL)	-	-

European Pairs Skating Championships:

	SP	FS
1. Vanessa James/Morgan Ciprès (FRA)	1	1
2. Evgenia Tarasova/Vladimir Morozov (RUS)	2	2
3. Aleksandra Boikova/Dmitrii Kozlovskii (RUS)	4	3
4. Nicole Della Monica/Matteo Guarise (ITA)	3	4
5. Daria Pavliuchenko/Denis Khodykin (RUS)	5	6
6. Minerva Fabienne Hase/Nolan Seegert (GER)	6	5
7. L. Barquero Jiménez/A. Maestu Babarro (ESP)	9	7
8. Lana Petranović/Antonio Souza-Kordeiru (CRO)	10	8
9. Rebecca Ghilardi/Filippo Ambrosini (ITA)	8	10
10. Zoe Jones/Christopher Boyadji (GRB)	11	9
WD. Miriam Ziegler/Severin Kiefer (AUT)	7	-
WD. Annika Hocke/Ruben Blommaert (GER)	-	-
WD. Natalia Zabiiako/Alexander Enbert (RUS)	-	-
WD. Cléo Hamon/Denys Strekalin (FRA)	-	-
WD. Hailey Esther Kops/Artem Tsoglin (ISR)	-	-

European Ice Dancing Championships:

	RD	FD
1. Gabriella Papadakis/Guillaume Cizeron (FRA)	1	1
2. Alexandra Stepanova/Ivan Bukin (RUS)	2	2
3. Charlène Guignard/Marco Fabbri (ITA)	3	4
4. Victoria Sinitsina/Nikita Katsalapov (RUS)	5	3
5. Natalia Kaliszek/Maksym Spodyriev (POL)	4	5
6. Lilah Fear/Lewis Gibson (GRB)	7	6
7. Sara Hurtado Martín/Kirill Khaliavin (ESP)	8	7
8. Olivia Smart/Adrián Díaz Bronchud (ESP)	6	9
9. Sofia Evdokimova/Egor Bazin (RUS)	11	8
10. Marie-Jade Lauriault/Romain Le Gac (FRA)	9	11
11. Juulia Turkkila/Matthias Versluis (FIN)	10	12

12. Adelina Galyavieva/Louis Thauron (FRA)	13	10
13. Allison Reed/Saulius Ambrulevičius (LIT)	12	14
14. Jasmine Tessari/Francesco Fioretti (ITA)	15	13
15. Shari Koch/Christian Nüchtern (GER)	14	15
16. Darya Popova/Volodymyr Byelikov (UKR)	16	17
17. Robynne Tweedale/Joseph Buckland (GRB)	18	16
18. Anna Kublikova/Yuri Hulitski (BLS)	19	18
19. Anna Yanovskaya/Ádám Lukács (HUN)	17	19
20. Shira Ichilov/Vadim Davidovich (ISR)	20	20
21. Carolina Moscheni/Andrea Fabbri (ITA)	21	-
22. Justyna Plutowska/Jérémie Flemin (POL)	22	-
23. Teodora Markova/Simon Daze (BUL)	23	-
24. Victoria Manni/Carlo Röthlisberger (SUI)	24	-
25. Katerina Bunina/German Frolov (EST)	25	-

The short dance was rebranded as the rhythm dance.

Sources: Entries, 2019 European Figure Skating Championships; Protocol, 2019 European Figure Skating Championships

Lilah Fear and Lewis Gibson, European Medallists 2023-2025. Raniero Corbelletti / Aflo Co. Ltd. / Alamy Stock Photo

THE PANDEMIC

2020 EUROPEAN FIGURE SKATING CHAMPIONSHIPS
Graz, Austria, January 20-26, 2020

European Men's Figure Skating Championships:

	SP	FS
1. Dmitri Aliev (RUS)	2	1
2. Artur Danielian (RUS)	3	4
3. Morisi Kvitelashvili (GEO)	4	3
4. Daniel Grassl (ITA)	11	2
5. Matteo Rizzo (ITA)	7	5
6. Deniss Vasiļjevs (LAT)	5	7
7. Michal Březina (CZE)	1	11
8. Paul Fentz (GER)	6	9
9. Vladimir Litvintsev (AZE)	17	8
10. Alexander Samarin (RUS)	13	10
11. Adam Siao Him Fa (FRA)	24	6
12. Alexei Bychenko (ISR)	8	13
13. Gabriele Frangipani (ITA)	10	12
14. Irakli Maysuradze (GEO)	15	14
15. Nikolaj Majorov (SWE)	14	15
16. Aleksandr Selevko (EST)	9	16
17. Mark Gorodnitsky (ISR)	12	17
18. Slavik Hayrapetyan (ARM)	20	18
19. Lukas Britschgi (SUI)	22	19
20. Matyáš Bělohradský (CZE)	18	20
21. Sondre Oddvoll Bøe (NOR)	19	21
22. Alexander Lebedev (BLS)	21	22
23. Larry Loupolover (BUL)	16	24
24. Burak Demirboğa (TUR)	23	23
25. Illya Solomin (SWE)	25	-
26. Kévin Aymoz (FRA)	26	-
27. Peter James Hallam (GRB)	27	-
28. Maurizio Zandron (AUT)	28	-
29. Davide Lewton Brain (MON)	29	-

30. Andrey Kokura (UKR)	30	-
31. Roman Galay (FIN)	31	-
32. Michael Neuman (SVK)	32	-
33. Thomas Kennes (NED)	33	-
34. Conor Stakelum (IRL)	34	-
35. András Csernoch (HUN)	35	-
WD. Daniel Samohin (ISR)	-	-
WD. Ivan Shmuratko (UKR)	-	-

European Ladies Figure Skating Championships:

	SP	FS
1. Alena Kostornaia (RUS)	1	2
2. Anna Shcherbakova (RUS)	2	1
3. Alexandra Trusova (RUS)	3	3
4. Alexia Paganini (SUI)	4	4
5. Emmi Peltonen (FIN)	5	7
6. Ekaterina Ryabova (AZE)	6	6
7. Eva-Lotta Kiibus (EST)	11	5
8. Alessia Tornaghi (ITA)	7	11
9. Maé-Bérénice Méité (FRA)	8	10
10. Ekaterina Kurakova (POL)	13	9
11. Maïa Mazzara (FRA)	16	8
12. Linnea Ceder (FIN)	15	12
13. Nicole Schott (GER)	14	14
14. Viktoriia Safonova (BLS)	20	13
15. Alina Urushadze (GEO)	12	18
16. Léa Serna (FRA)	10	19
17. Alexandra Feigin (BUL)	18	16
18. Anita Östlund (SWE)	9	21
19. Yasmine Kimiko Yamada (SUI)	24	15
20. Daša Grm (SLO)	17	20
21. Ivett Tóth (HUN)	22	17
22. Eliška Březinová (CZE)	19	22
23. Natasha McKay (GRB)	23	23
24. Olga Mikutina (AUT)	21	24
25. Nelli Ioffe (ISR)	25	-
26. Aleksandra Golovkina (LIT)	26	-
27. Anastasia Galustyan (ARM)	27	-

28. Valentina Matos (ESP)	28	-
29. Ema Doboszová (SVK)	29	-
30. Angelīna Kučvaļska (LAT)	30	-
31. Antonina Dubinina (SRB)	31	-
32. Sinem Kuyucu (TUR)	32	-
33. Jenni Saarinen (FIN)	33	-
34. Anastasia Gozhva (UKR)	34	-
35. Niki Wories (NED)	35	-
36. Klára Štěpánová (CZE)	36	-
37. Hana Cvijanović (CRO)	37	-
WD. Loena Hendrickx (BEL)	-	-
WD. Julia Sauter (ROM)	-	-
WD. Alina Iushchenkova (ISR)	-	-

European Pairs Skating Championships:

	SP	FS
1. Aleksandra Boikova/Dmitrii Kozlovskii (RUS)	1	1
2. Evgenia Tarasova/Vladimir Morozov (RUS)	3	2
3. Daria Pavliuchenko/Denis Khodykin (RUS)	2	3
4. Nicole Della Monica/Matteo Guarise (ITA)	4	4
5. Minerva Fabienne Hase/Nolan Seegert (GER)	5	5
6. Miriam Ziegler/Severin Kiefer (AUT)	6	6
7. Annika Hocke/Robert Kunkel (GER)	7	7
8. Rebecca Ghilardi/Filippo Ambrosini (ITA)	8	10
9. Cléo Hamon/Denys Strekalin (FRA)	12	8
10. Ioulia Chtchetinina/Márk Magyar (HUN)	10	9
11. Coline Keriven/Noël-Antoine Pierre (FRA)	9	11
12. Zoe Jones/Christopher Boyadji (GRB)	11	12
13. Anna Vernikov/Evgeni Krasnopolski (ISR)	13	13
14. L. Barquero Jiménez/T. Cónsul Vivar (ESP)	15	14
15. L. Petranović/A. Souza-Kordeiru (CRO)	14	15
16. Daria Danilova/Michel Tsiba (NED)	16	16
17. Dorota Broda/Pedro Betegón Martín (ESP)	17	-
18. Alexandra Herbríková/Nicolas Roulet (SUI)	18	-
DQ. Sofiia Nesterova/Artem Darenskyi (UKR)	19	-

European Ice Dancing Championships:

	RD	FD
1. Victoria Sinitsina/Nikita Katsalapov (RUS)	2	1
2. Gabriella Papadakis/Guillaume Cizeron (FRA)	1	2
3. Alexandra Stepanova/Ivan Bukin (RUS)	4	3
4. Charlène Guignard/Marco Fabbri (ITA)	3	4
5. Lilah Fear/Lewis Gibson (GRB)	6	5
6. Tiffany Zahorski/Jonathan Guerreiro (RUS)	5	6
7. Sara Hurtado Martín/Kirill Khaliavin (ESP)	7	7
8. Olivia Smart/Adrián Díaz Bronchud (ESP)	9	8
9. Natalia Kaliszek/Maksym Spodyriev (POL)	10	10
10. Alexandra Nazarova/Maxim Nikitin (UKR)	11	9
11. Allison Reed/Saulius Ambrulevičius (LIT)	8	13
12. Adelina Galyavieva/Louis Thauron (FRA)	13	12
13. Katharina Müller/Tim Dieck (GER)	18	11
14. Maria Kazakova/Georgy Reviya (GEO)	12	14
15. Evgeniia Lopareva/Geoffrey Brissaud (FRA)	15	15
16. Jasmine Tessari/Francesco Fioretti (ITA)	14	16
17. Tina Garabedian/Simon Proulx-Sénécal (ARM)	19	17
18. Yuka Orihara/Juho Pirinen (FIN)	16	19
19. Natálie Taschlerová/Filip Taschler (CZE)	17	18
20. Victoria Manni/Carlo Röthlisberger (SUI)	20	20
21. Robynne Tweedale/Joseph Buckland (GRB)	21	-
22. Justyna Plutowska/Jérémie Flemin (POL)	22	-
23. E. Kalehanova/U. Palkhouski (BLS)	23	-
24. Emily Monaghan/Ilias Fourati (HUN)	24	-
25. Mina Zdravkova/Christopher M. Davis (BUL)	25	-
26. Nicole Kelly/Berk Akalın (TUR)	26	-
27. Aurelija Ipolito/J.T. Michel (LAT)	27	-

The alarm bell hadn't yet been sounded, but the virus was already spreading at an alarming pace. During the 2020 World Figure Skating Championships, the World Health Organization's Health Regulation Emergency Committee met by teleconference and decided not to declare an emergency yet. Less than 2 months later, countries around the world were in lockdown.

A positive doping test at the 2020 Winter Youth Olympics in Lausanne, Switzerland led to the disqualification of Ukrainian pairs skater Sofiia Nesterova, and her partner Artem Darenskyi. Victoria Sinitsina and Nikita Katsalapov set a record for the highest overall score awarded in the ice dance event at the European Championships under the IJS System (220.42).

Sources: CDC, David J. Sencer CDC Museum: In Association with the Smithsonian Institution; World Health Organziation, Statement on the first meeting of the International Health Regulations Emergency Committee regarding the outbreak of novel coronavirus (2019-nCoV), January 23, 2020; Entries, 2020 European Figure Skating Championships; Protocol, 2020 European Figure Skating Championships

2021
*EVENT NOT HELD**

*The 2021 European Figure Skating Championships were scheduled to be held in Zagreb, Croatia. The ISU considered relocating or postponing the event, but ultimately cancelled the event in December of 2020, "in view of the worsening worldwide... pandemic situation and the consequent increasing risks for organizers and participants." At the time, the Arena Zagreb was being used to house patients. Over a million people had passed away as a result of complications of the virus at this time.

Sources: *Sources: CDC, David J. Sencer CDC Museum: In Association with the Smithsonian Institution; Jutarnji list, November 25, 2020; International Figure Skating Magazine, December 8, 2020; ESPN/Associated Press, December 10, 2020*

2022 EUROPEAN FIGURE SKATING CHAMPIONSHIPS
Tallinn, Estonia, January 10-16, 2022

European Men's Figure Skating Championships:

	SP	FS
1. Mark Kondratiuk (RUS)	2	1
2. Daniel Grassl (ITA)	5	2

3. Deniss Vasiļjevs (LAT)	6	3
4. Andrei Mozalev (RUS)	1	6
5. Evgeni Semenenko (RUS)	3	9
6. Morisi Kvitelashvili (GEO)	4	8
7. Kévin Aymoz (FRA)	10	4
8. Vladimir Litvintsev (AZE)	7	7
9. Gabriele Frangipani (ITA)	9	10
10. Michal Březina (CZE)	15	5
11. Lukas Britschgi (SUI)	13	11
12. Ivan Shmuratko (UKR)	8	15
13. Nikita Starostin (GER)	14	12
14. Arlet Levandi (EST)	17	13
15. Nikolaj Memola (ITA)	12	14
16. Paul Fentz (GER)	11	16
17. Maurizio Zandron (AUT)	16	20
18. Kornel Witkowski (POL)	23	17
19. Valtter Virtanen (FIN)	20	18
20. Davide Lewton Brain (MON)	21	19
21. Konstantin Milyukov (BLS)	18	21
22. Tomàs-Llorenç Guarino Sabaté (ESP)	24	22
23. Burak Demirboğa (TUR)	22	23
24. Slavik Hayrapetyan (ARM)	19	24
25. Adam Hagara (SVK)	25	-
26. Graham Newberry (GRB)	26	-
27. Matyáš Bělohradský (CZE)	27	-
28. Nika Egadze (GEO)	28	-
29. Daniels Kockers (LAT)	29	-
30. Conor Stakelum (IRL)	30	-
31. Jari Kessler (CRO)	31	-
32. András Csernoch (HUN)	32	-
33. Larry Loupolover (BUL)	33	-
WD. Nikolaj Majorov (SWE)	-	-
WD. Alexei Bychenko (ISR)	-	-
WD. Matteo Rizzo (ITA)	-	-
WD. Mikhail Kolyada (RUS)	-	-
WD. Mark Gorodnitsky (ISR)	-	-
WD. Samuel McAllister (IRL)	-	-

European Women's Figure Skating Championships:

	SP	FS
1. Anna Shcherbakova (RUS)	4	2
2. Alexandra Trusova (RUS)	3	3
3. Loena Hendrickx (BEL)	2	5
4. Ekaterina Kurakova (POL)	5	4
5. Ekaterina Ryabova (AZE)	7	6
6. Anastasiia Gubanova (GEO)	6	9
7. Niina Petrõkina (EST)	17	7
8. Viktoriia Safonova (BLS)	8	8
9. Alexia Paganini (SUI)	9	10
10. Eva-Lotta Kiibus (EST)	15	11
11. Léa Serna (FRA)	10	13
12. Nicole Schott (GER)	11	14
13. Josefin Taljegård (SWE)	18	15
14. Olga Mikutina (AUT)	12	17
15. Lara Naki Gutmann (ITA)	23	12
16. Natasha McKay (GRB)	19	16
17. Jenni Saarinen (FIN)	21	18
18. Yasmine Kimiko Yamada (SUI)	20	20
19. Alexandra Feigin (BUL)	20	20
20. Eliška Březinová (CZE)	13	21
21. Aleksandra Golovkina (LIT)	24	22
22. Regina Schermann (HUN)	22	23
23. Anete Lāce (LAT)	25	-
24. Oona Ounasvuori (FIN)	26	-
25. Lindsay van Zundert (NED)	27	-
26. Daša Grm (SLO)	28	-
27. Antonina Dubinina (SRB)	29	-
28. Taylor Morris (ISR)	30	-
29. Linnea Kilsand (NOR)	31	-
30. Marilena Kitromilis (CYP)	32	-
31. Alexandra Michaela Filcová (SVK)	33	-
32. Aldís Kara Bergsdóttir (ISL)	34	-
33. Sinem Pekder (TUR)	35	-
34. Maia Sørensen (DEN)	36	-
WD. Marina Piredda (ITA)	13	-
WD. Julia Sauter (ROM)	-	-

WD. Emmi Peltonen (FIN)	-	-
WD. Anastasia Shabotova (UKR)	-	-
WD. Mariia Andriichuk (UKR)	-	-
WD. Ema Doboszová (SVK)	-	-
DQ. Kamila Valieva (RUS)	1	1

European Pairs Skating Championships:

	SP	FS
1. Anastasia Mishina/Aleksandr Galliamov (RUS)	1	1
2. Evgenia Tarasova/Vladimir Morozov (RUS)	2	2
3. Aleksandra Boikova/Dmitrii Kozlovskii (RUS)	3	3
4. Karina Safina/Luka Berulava (GEO)	6	4
5. Rebecca Ghilardi/Filippo Ambrosini (ITA)	4	5
6. Ioulia Chtchetinina/Márk Magyar (HUN)	7	7
7. Sara Conti/Niccolò Macii (ITA)	10	6
8. Minerva Fabienne Hase/Nolan Seegert (GER)	5	9
9. Laura Barquero Jiménez/Marco Zandron (ESP)	8	8
10. B. Lukashevich/A. Stepanov (BLS)	9	12
11. Maria Pavlova/Balázs Nagy (HUN)	11	11
12. Jelizaveta Žuková/Martin Bidař (CZE)	15	10
13. Annika Hocke/Robert Kunkel (GER)	13	13
14. Camille Kovalev/Pavel Kovalev (FRA)	12	14
15. Sofiia Holichenko/Artem Darenskyi (UKR)	14	15
16. L. Petranović/A. Souza-Kordeiru (CRO)	16	16
17. Coline Keriven/Noël-Antoine Pierre (FRA)	17	-
18. Anastasia Vaipan-Law/Luke Digby (GRB)	18	-
19. Letizia Roscher/Luis Schuster (GER)	19	-
20. Milania Väänänen/Mikhail Akulov (FIN)	20	-
21. Daria Danilova/Michel Tsiba (NED)	21	-
WD. Miriam Ziegler/Severin Kiefer (AUT)	-	-
WD. Nicole Della Monica/Matteo Guarise (ITA)	-	-
WD. Zoe Jones/Christopher Boyadji (GRB)	-	-
WD. Hailey Kops/Evgeni Krasnopolski (ISR)	-	-
WD. Jessica Pfund/Joshua Santillan (USA)	-	-
WD. Anastasiia Metelkina/Daniil Parkman (GEO)	-	-

European Ice Dancing Championships:

	SP	FS
1. Victoria Sinitsina/Nikita Katsalapov (RUS)	1	1
2. Alexandra Stepanova/Ivan Bukin (RUS)	2	2
3. Charlène Guignard/Marco Fabbri (ITA)	3	3
4. Olivia Smart/Adrián Díaz Bronchud (ESP)	5	4
5. Lilah Fear/Lewis Gibson (GRB)	4	6
6. Sara Hurtado Martín/Kirill Khaliavin (ESP)	6	5
7. Diana Davis/Gleb Smolkin (RUS)	8	7
8. Allison Reed/Saulius Ambrulevičius (LIT)	7	8
9. Evgeniia Lopareva/Geoffrey Brissaud (RUS)	10	9
10. Alexandra Nazarova/Maxim Nikitin (UKR)	12	10
11. Natálie Taschlerová/Filip Taschler (CZE)	11	13
12. Katharina Müller/Tim Dieck (GER)	13	12
13. Tina Garabedian/Simon Proulx-Sénécal (ARM)	14	11
14. Natalia Kaliszek/Maksym Spodyriev (POL)	9	16
15. Sasha Fear/George Waddell (GRB)	16	14
16. Loïcia Demougeot/Théo le Mercier (FRA)	15	15
17. Mariia Holubtsova/Kyryl Bielobrov (UKR)	17	17
18. Mariia Ignateva/Danijil Szemko (HUN)	19	18
19. Jasmine Tessari/Stéphane Walker (SUI)	18	19
20. S. Mazingue/M.J. Gaidajenko (EST)	20	20
21. Carolina Moscheni/Francesco Fioretti (ITA)	21	-
22. Viktoria Semenjuk/Ilya Yukhimuk (BLS)	22	-
23. Mária Sofia Pucherová/Nikita Lysak (SVK)	23	-
24. Aurelija Ipolito/Luke Russell (LAT)	24	-
25. Hanna Jakucs/Alessio Galli (NED)	25	-
26. E. Kuznetsova/O. Kolosovskyi (AZE)	26	-
WD. A. Polibina/P. Golovishnikov (POL)	-	-
WD. Gabriella Papadakis/Guillaume Cizeron (FRA)	-	-
WD. Juulia Turkkila/Matthias Versluis (FIN)	-	-
WD. E. Mitrofanova/V. Kasinskij (BIH)	-	-
WD. M. Nosovitskaya/M. Nosovitskiy (ISR)	-	-

The International Skating Union (ISU) stopped using the term "ladies" in favour of "women" across all disciplines in the summer of 2021.

Over a dozen skaters were forced to withdraw either before or during the European Figure Skating Championships due to positive tests. Cases worldwide were at a record high, at the height of the Delta and Omricon waves. Kamila Valieva's positive doping test, a massive scandal revealed during the 2022 Winter Olympics, ultimately resulted in the ISU stripping her of her gold medal at the 2021 European Figure Skating Championships. All other skaters moved up one spot in the final standings. Ironically, Valieva set a record for the highest overall score awarded in the women's event at the European Championships under the IJS System (259.06). Anastasia Mishina and Aleksandr Galliamov earned the highest overall total ever awarded to a pair at the European Figure Skating Championships under the IJS System (239.82). Marilena Kitromilis and Aldís Kara Bergsdóttir made history as the first skaters to represent Cyprus and Iceland at the event.

Sources: Protocol, 2022 European Figure Skating Championships; Entries, 2022 European Figure Skating Championships

2023 EUROPEAN FIGURE SKATING CHAMPIONSHIPS
Espoo, Finland, January 25-29, 2023

European Men's Figure Skating Championships:

	SP	FS
1. Adam Siao Him Fa (FRA)	1	2
2. Matteo Rizzo (ITA)	2	1
3. Lukas Britschgi (SUI)	5	3
4. Kévin Aymoz (FRA)	4	4
5. Deniss Vasiļjevs (LAT)	3	6
6. Daniel Grassl (ITA)	8	5
7. Nika Egadze (GEO)	12	7
8. Mihhail Selevko (EST)	11	8
9. Andreas Nordebäck (SWE)	9	10
10. Gabriele Frangipani (ITA)	7	12
11. Maurizio Zandron (AUT)	13	11
12. Tomàs-Llorenç Guarino Sabaté (ESP)	14	13
13. Mark Gorodnitsky (ISR)	22	9
14. Valtter Virtanen (FIN)	18	14

	SP	FS
15. Nikita Starostin (GER)	10	17
16. Morisi Kvitelashvili (GEO)	16	6
17. Vladimir Samoilov (POL)	6	21
18. Adam Hagara (SVK)	21	15
19. Jari Kessler (CRO)	19	19
20. Burak Demirboğa (TUR)	23	18
21. Kyrylo Marsak (UKR)	17	22
22. Davide Lewton Brain (MON)	20	20
23. Graham Newberry (GRB)	15	24
24. Aleksandr Vlasenko (HUN)	24	23
25. Petr Kotlařík (CZE)	25	-
26. Georgii Reshtenko (CZE)	26	-
27. Larry Loupolover (BUL)	27	-
28. Samuel McAllister (ISR)	28	-
29. David Sedej (SLO)	29	-
WD. Vladimir Litvintsev (AZE)	-	-
WD. Ivan Shmuratko (UKR)	-	-

European Women's Figure Skating Championships:

	SP	FS
1. Anastasiia Gubanova (GEO)	1	1
2. Loena Hendrickx (BEL)	2	3
3. Kimmy Repond (SUI)	3	2
4. Ekaterina Kurakova (POL)	5	4
5. Nina Pinzarrone (BEL)	6	5
6. Niina Petrõkina (EST)	7	6
7. Janna Jyrkinen (FIN)	8	7
8. Lara Naki Gutmann (ITA)	13	8
9. Nicole Schott (GER)	16	9
10. Julia Sauter (ROM)	11	12
11. Sofja Stepčenko (LAT)	14	11
12. Olga Mikutina (AUT)	4	18
13. Marilena Kitromilis (CYP)	18	10
14. Lindsay van Zundert (NED)	10	15
15. Eva-Lotta Kiibus (EST)	15	13
16. Alexandra Feigin (BUL)	17	14
17. Josefin Taljegård (SWE)	12	16
18. Livia Kaiser (SUI)	9	20

19. Natasha McKay (GRB)	20	19
20. Anastasia Gozhva (UKR)	22	17
21. Daša Grm (SLO)	19	21
22. Mia Caroline Risa Gomez (NOR)	21	22
23. Júlia Láng (HUN)	23	23
24. Nikola Rychtaříková (CZE)	24	24
25. Alexandra Michaela Filcová (SVK)	25	-
26. Léa Serna (FRA)	26	-
27. Antonina Dubinina (SRB)	27	-
28. Anastasia Gracheva (MDA)	28	-
29. Alexandra Mintsidou (GRE)	29	-
WD. Meda Variakojytė (LIT)	-	-
WD. Jogailė Aglinskytė (LIT)	-	-
WD. Maia Sørensen (DEN)	-	-
WD. Aleksandra Golovkina (LIT)	-	-
WD. Barbora Vránková (CZE)	-	-
WD. Mariia Seniuk (ISR)	-	-

European Pairs Skating Championships:

	SP	FS
1. Sara Conti/Niccolò Macii (ITA)	1	2
2. Rebecca Ghilardi/Filippo Ambrosini (ITA)	5	1
3. Annika Hocke/Robert Kunkel (GER)	2	3
4. Alisa Efimova/Ruben Blommaert (GER)	3	5
5. Maria Pavlova/Alexei Sviatchenko (HUN)	6	4
6. Camille Kovalev/Pavel Kovalev (FRA)	4	6
7. Lucrezia Beccari/Matteo Guarise (ITA)	8	7
8. Nika Osipova/Dmitry Epstein (NED)	7	9
9. Violetta Sierova/Ivan Khobta (UKR)	10	8
10. Anastasia Vaipan-Law/Luke Digby (GRB)	9	10
11. Federica Simioli/Alessandro Zarbo (CZE)	11	11
12. Sophia Schaller/Livio Mayr (AUT)	12	12
13. Greta Crafoord/John Crafoord (SWE)	13	13
WD. Anastasia Metelkina/Daniil Parkman (GEO)	-	-
WD. Karina Safina/Luka Berulava (GEO)	-	-

European Ice Dancing Championships:

	RD	FD

1. Charlène Guignard/Marco Fabbri (ITA)	1	1
2. Lilah Fear/Lewis Gibson (GRB)	2	2
3. Juulia Turkkila/Matthias Versluis (FIN)	3	3
4. Allison Reed/Saulius Ambrulevičius (LIT)	4	4
5. Evgenia Lopareva/Geoffrey Brissaud (FRA)	6	5
6. Natálie Taschlerová/Filip Taschler (CZE)	5	6
7. Loïcia Demougeot/Théo Le Mercier (FRA)	7	7
8. Maria Kazakova/Georgy Reviya (GEO)	8	8
9. J. Janse van Rensburg/B. Steffan (GER)	9	10
10. Mariia Ignateva/Danijil Szemko (HUN)	10	9
11. Victoria Manni/Carlo Röthlisberger (ITA)	11	11
12. Mariia Holubtsova/Kyryl Bielobrov (UKR)	13	12
13. M. Nosovitskaya/M. Nosovitskiy (ISR)	12	13
14. Anna Šimová/Kirill Aksenov (SVK)	15	14
15. Mariia Pinchuk/Mykyta Pogorielov (UKR)	14	15
16. A. Polibina/P. Golovishnikov (POL)	17	16
17. P. Ramanauskaitė/D. Kizala (LIT)	16	17
18. Samantha Ritter/Daniel Brykalov (AZE)	19	18
19. Hanna Jakucs/Alessio Galli (NED)	18	19
20. Aurelija Ipolito/Luke Russell (LAT)	20	20
21. Arianna Sassi/Luca Morini (SUI)	21	-
22. Maria Bjorkli/James Koszuta (NOR)	22	-
23. Viktoriia Azroian/Artur Gruzdev (ARM)	23	-

Sara Conti and Niccolò Macii made history as the first Italian pair to win a gold medal at the European Figure Skating Championships and Anastasiia Gubanova was the first winner from Georgia in the women's event. The Russian doping scandal continued to be major news in the figure skating world. The ISU issued Communication No. 2469, banning all skaters from Russia and Belarus from participation in ISU Championships. The Communication condemned Russia's invasion of Ukraine "in the strongest possible terms." Russian-born Anastasia Gracheva made history as the first skater to represent Moldova at the event.

Sources: Protocol, 2023 European Figure Skating Championships; Entries, 2023 European Figure Skating Championships

Lukas Britschgi, European Champion 2025. Raniero Corbelletti / Aflo Co. Ltd. / Alamy Stock Photo.

THE NEW NORMAL

2024 EUROPEAN FIGURE SKATING CHAMPIONSHIPS
Kaunas, Lithuania, January 10-14, 2024

European Men's Figure Skating Championships:

		SP	FS
1.	Adam Siao Him Fa (FRA)	1	1
2.	Aleksandr Selevko (EST)	3	3
3.	Matteo Rizzo (ITA)	6	2
4.	Gabriele Frangipani (ITA)	4	4
5.	Lukas Britschgi (SUI)	2	10
6.	Deniss Vasiļjevs (LAT)	5	7
7.	Nika Egadze (GEO)	10	6
8.	Vladimir Samoilov (POL)	16	5
9.	Georgii Reshtenko (CZE)	13	8
10.	Nikolaj Memola (ITA)	12	9
11.	Adam Hagara (SVK)	11	11
12.	Mark Gorodnitsky (ISR)	9	13
13.	Nikita Starostin (GER)	14	14
14.	Ivan Shmuratko (UKR)	19	12
15.	Luc Economides (FRA)	7	17
16.	Vladimir Litvintsev (AZE)	20	15
17.	Maurizio Zandron (AUT)	22	16
18.	Tomàs-Llorenç Guarino Sabaté (ESP)	15	18
19.	Fedor Chitipakhovian (ARM)	21	19
20.	Makar Suntsev (FIN)	18	20
21.	Gabriel Folkesson (SWE)	17	21
22.	Andreas Nordebäck (SWE)	8	23
23.	Aleksandr Vlasenko (HUN)	23	22
24.	Davide Lewton Brain (MON)	24	24
25.	Edward Appleby (GRB)	25	-
26.	Burak Demirboğa (TUR)	26	-
27.	Jari Kessler (CRO)	27	-
28.	Alexander Zlatkov (BUL)	28	-
29.	Fedir Kulish (LAT)	29	-

30. Mihhail Selevko (EST) 30 -
31. Kévin Aymoz (FRA) 31 -
32. David Sedej (SLO) 32 -

European Women's Figure Skating Championships:

	SP	FS
1. Loena Hendrickx (BEL)	1	1
2. Anastasiia Gubanova (GEO)	3	2
3. Nina Pinzarrone (BEL)	2	3
4. Livia Kaiser (SUI)	4	4
5. Lorine Schild (FRA)	6	6
6. Sarina Joos (ITA)	9	5
7. Kimmy Repond (SUI)	8	7
8. Olga Mikutina (AUT)	5	10
9. Julia Sauter (ROM)	10	9
10. Lara Naki Gutmann (ITA)	16	8
11. Josefin Taljegård (SWE)	13	12
12. Emmi Peltonen (FIN)	14	11
13. Sofja Stepčenko (LAT)	21	13
14. Nataly Langerbaur (EST)	19	15
15. Kristina Isaev (GER)	20	14
16. Aleksandra Golovkina (LIT)	15	16
17. Nina Povey (GRB)	17	17
18. Alexandra Feigin (BUL)	12	19
19. Mariia Seniuk (ISR)	18	18
20. Anastasia Gozhva (UKR)	11	20
21. Nella Pelkonen (FIN)	7	23
22. Alina Urushadze (GEO)	23	21
23. Jade Hovine (BEL)	22	22
24. Barbora Vránková (CZE)	24	24
25. Ekaterina Kurakova (POL)	25	-
26. Mia Risa Gomez (NOR)	26	-
27. Kristina Lisovskaja (EST)	27	-
28. Regina Schermann (HUN)	28	-
29. Vanesa Šelmeková (SVK)	29	-
30. Julija Lovrenčič (SLO)	30	-
31. Antonina Dubinina (SRB)	31	-
32. Laura Szczęsna (POL)	32	-

33. Ana Sofia Beşchea (ROM) 33 -

European Pairs Skating Championships:

	SP	FS
1. Lucrezia Beccari/Matteo Guarise (ITA)	3	1
2. Anastasiia Metelkina/Luka Berulava (GEO)	1	5
3. Rebecca Ghilardi/Filippo Ambrosini (ITA)	5	2
4. Maria Pavlova/Alexei Sviatchenko (HUN)	4	3
5. Minerva Fabienne Hase/Nikita Volodin (GER)	2	6
6. Sara Conti/Niccolò Macii (ITA)	7	4
7. Annika Hocke/Robert Kunkel (GER)	6	7
8. Daria Danilova/Michel Tsiba (NED)	10	8
9. Anastasia Vaipan-Law/Luke Digby (GRB)	8	9
10. Ioulia Chtchetinina/Michał Woźniak (POL)	11	11
11. Sofiia Holichenko/Artem Darenskyi (UKR)	12	10
12. Océane Piegad/Denys Strekalin (FRA)	9	12
13. Barbora Kucianová/Martin Bidař (CZE)	13	14
14. Milania Väänänen/Filippo Clerici (FIN)	16	13
15. Lydia Smart/Harry Mattick (GRB)	14	15
16. Greta Crafoord/John Crafoord (SWE)	17	-
17. Sophia Schaller/Livio Mayr (AUT)	18	-
WD. Camille Kovalev/Pavel Kovalev (FRA)	16	-

European Ice Dancing Championships:

	RD	FD
1. Charlène Guignard/Marco Fabbri (ITA)	1	1
2. Lilah Fear/Lewis Gibson (GRB)	2	2
3. Allison Reed/Saulius Ambrulevičius (LIT)	3	3
4. Evgenia Lopareva/Geoffrey Brissaud (FRA)	4	4
5. Loïcia Demougeot/Théo le Mercier (FRA)	8	5
6. Juulia Turkkila/Matthias Versluis (FIN)	6	6
7. Natálie Taschlerová/Filip Taschler (CZE)	5	7
8. Diana Davis/Gleb Smolkin (GEO)	7	8
9. Kateřina Mrázková/Daniel Mrázek (CZE)	9	11
10. Yuka Orihara/Juho Pirinen (FIN)	10	9
11. J. Janse van Rensburg/B. Steffan (GER)	11	10
12. Marie Dupayage/Thomas Nabais (FRA)	13	12
13. Carolane Soucisse/Shane Firus (IRL)	12	13

14. Mariia Holubtsova/Kyryl Bielobrov (UKR)	14	14
15. Victoria Manni/Carlo Röthlisberger (ITA)	15	15
16. P. Ramanauskaitė/D. Kizala (LIT)	20	16
17. Phebe Bekker/James Hernandez (GRB)	19	17
18. Mariia Pinchuk/Mykyta Pogorielov (UKR)	17	18
19. M. Nosovitskaya/M. Nosovitskiy (ISR)	16	19
20. S. Mazingue/M.J. Gaidajenko (EST)	18	20
21. Charise Matthaei/Max Liebers (GER)	21	-
22. Leia Dozzi/Pietro Papetti (ITA)	22	-
23. Sofia Val/Asaf Kazimov (ESP)	23	-
24. Maria Sofia Pucherová/Nikita Lysak (SVK)	24	-
25. Mariia Ignateva/Danijil Szemko (HUN)	25	-
26. Sofiia Dovhal/Wiktor Kulesza (POL)	26	-
27. Milla Ruud Reitan/Nikolaj Majorov (SWE)	27	-
28. Layla Karnes/Liam Carr (GRB)	28	-
29. Hanna Jakucs/Alessio Galli (NED)	29	-
30. Lucy Hancock/Ilias Fourati (HUN)	30	-
31. Arianna Sassi/Luca Morini (SUI)	31	-
32. A. Carhart/O. Kolosovskyi (AZE)	32	-
33. Olivia Shilling/Léo Baeten (BEL)	33	-

Loena Hendrickx made history as the first singles skater from Belgium to win a gold medal at the European Figure Skating Championships. Aleksandr Selevko earned Estonia's first medal in the men's event.

Adam Siao Him Fa of France earned the highest overall total ever awarded to a French skater in any discipline at the European Figure Skating Championships under the IJS System (276.17).

Lilah Fear and Lewis Gibson earned the highest overall total ever awarded to British skaters in any discipline at the European Figure Skating Championships under the IJS System (210.82).

Sources: Protocol, 2024 European Figure Skating Championships; Entries, 2024 European Figure Skating Championships

2025 EUROPEAN FIGURE SKATING CHAMPIONSHIPS
Tallinn, Estonia, January 28-February 2, 2025

European Men's Figure Skating Championships:

	SP	FS
1. Lukas Britschgi (SUI)	8	1
2. Nikolaj Memola (ITA)	5	2
3. Adam Siao Him Fa (FRA)	1	3
4. Nika Egadze (GEO)	2	8
5. Matteo Rizzo (ITA)	4	6
6. Deniss Vasiļjevs (LAT)	12	4
7. Mihhail Selevko (EST)	6	7
8. Daniel Grassl (ITA)	10	5
9. Aleksandr Selevko (EST)	7	11
10. Vladimir Samoilov (POL)	3	13
11. Andreas Nordebäck (SWE)	9	9
12. Adam Hagara (SVK)	13	10
13. Lev Vinokur (ISR)	14	12
14. Fedir Kulish (LAT)	15	14
15. Vladimir Litvintsev (AZE)	11	16
16. Ivan Shmuratko (UKR)	17	17
17. Semen Daniliants (ARM)	19	18
18. Kornel Witkowski (POL)	23	15
19. Tomàs-Llorenç Guarino Sabaté (ESP)	21	19
20. Edward Appleby (GRB)	16	21
21. Aleksandr Vlasenko (HUN)	22	20
22. Kévin Aymoz (FRA)	18	22
23. Georgii Reshtenko (CZE)	20	24
24. Valtter Virtanen (FIN)	24	23
25. Davide Lewton Brain (MON)	25	-
26. Maurizio Zandron (AUT)	26	-
27. Nikita Starostin (GER)	27	-
28. David Sedej (SLO)	28	-
29. Alp Eren Özkan (TUR)	29	-
30. Alexander Zlatkov (BUL)	30	-
31. Filip Ščerba (CZE)	31	-
32. Noah Bodenstein (SUI)	32	-
33. Daniel Korabelnik (LIT)	33	-

34. Jari Kessler (CRO) 34 -
WD. Burak Demirboğa (TUR) - -

European Women's Figure Skating Championships:

	SP	FS
1. Niina Petrõkina (EST)	2	1
2. Anastasiia Gubanova (GEO)	1	2
3. Nina Pinzarrone (BEL)	4	3
4. Kimmy Repond (SUI)	3	5
5. Anna Pezzetta (ITA)	6	4
6. Lara Naki Gutmann (ITA)	5	6
7. Julia Sauter (ROM)	8	10
8. Ekaterina Kurakova (POL)	9	11
9. Kristen Spours (GRB)	10	9
10. Lorine Schild (FRA)	7	13
11. Léa Serna (FRA)	17	7
12. Mia Risa Gomez (NOR)	16	8
13. Mariia Seniuk (ISR)	13	14
14. Alexandra Feigin (BUL)	14	12
15. Linnea Ceder (FIN)	12	15
16. Jade Hovine (BEL)	11	16
17. Josefin Taljegård (SWE)	15	17
18. Janna Jyrkinen (FIN)	18	18
19. Michaela Vrašťáková (CZE)	24	19
20. Vanesa Šelmeková (SVK)	22	20
21. Anastasija Konga (LAT)	23	21
22. Julija Lovrenčič (SLO)	20	22
23. Stefanie Pesendorfer (AUT)	21	23
24. Jogailė Aglinskytė (LIT)	19	24
25. Antonina Dubinina (SCG)	25	-
26. Niki Wories (NED)	26	-
27. Anastasia Gozhva (UKR)	27	-
28. Kristina Isaev (GER)	28	-
29. Katinka Anna Zsembery (HUN)	29	-
30. Flora Marie Schaller (AUT)	30	-
31. Ana Sofia Beşchea (ROM)	31	-
WD. Loena Hendrickx (BEL)	32	-
WD. Livia Kaiser (SUI)	33	-

WD. Olga Mikutina (AUT) 34 -

European Pairs Skating Championships:

	SP	FS
1. Minerva Fabienne Hase/Nikita Volodin (GER)	1	1
2. Sara Conti/Niccolò Macii (ITA)	2	2
3. Anastasiia Metelkina/Luka Berulava (GEO)	9	3
4. Maria Pavlova/Alexei Sviatchenko (HUN)	3	4
5. Anastasia Vaipan-Law/Luke Digby (GRB)	4	6
6. Rebecca Ghilardi/Filippo Ambrosini (ITA)	6	5
7. Ioulia Chtchetinina/Michał Woźniak (POL)	7	7
8. Annika Hocke/Robert Kunkel (GER)	5	8
9. Camille Kovalev/Pavel Kovalev (FRA)	8	9
10. Daria Danilova/Michel Tsiba (NED)	11	10
11. Sofiia Holichenko/Artem Darenskyi (UKR)	10	11
12. Letizia Roscher/Luis Schuster (GER)	12	13
13. Oxana Vouillamoz/Tom Bouvart (SUI)	13	12
14. Milania Väänänen/Filippo Clerici (FIN)	16	14
15. Irma Caldara/Riccardo Maglio (ITA)	14	15
16. Sophia Schaller/Livio Mayr (AUT)	15	16
17. Greta Crafoord/John Crafoord (SWE)	17	-
18. J.S. Gunnarsdóttir/M. Piazza (ISL)	18	-
WD. Gabriella Izzo/Luc Maierhofer (AUT)	-	-

European Ice Dancing Championships:

	RD	FD
1. Charlène Guignard/Marco Fabbri (ITA)	1	1
2. Evgeniia Lopareva/Geoffrey Brissaud (FRA)	2	4
3. Lilah Fear/Lewis Gibson (GRB)	3	2
4. Juulia Turkkila/Matthias Versluis (FIN)	4	3
5. Olivia Smart/Tim Dieck (ESP)	7	5
6. Allison Reed/Saulius Ambrulevičius (LIT)	5	7
7. Yuka Orihara/Juho Pirinen (FIN)	8	6
8. Diana Davis/Gleb Smolkin (GEO)	10	8
9. Loïcia Demougeot/Théo le Mercier (FRA)	6	10
10. Natálie Taschlerová/Filip Taschler (CZE)	11	9
11. J. Janse van Rensburg/B. Steffan (GER)	9	11
12. Kateřina Mrázková/Daniel Mrázek (CZE)	12	12

13. Phebe Bekker/James Hernandez (GRB)	13	13
14. Mariia Ignateva/Danijil Szemko (HUN)	14	14
15. Victoria Manni/Carlo Röthlisberger (ITA)	16	15
16. Natacha Lagouge/Arnaud Caffa (FRA)	15	16
17. Milla Ruud Reitan/Nikolaj Majorov (SWE)	17	18
18. Carolane Soucisse/Shane Firus (IRL)	19	17
19. P. Ramanauskaitė/D. Kizala (LIT)	18	19
20. Mariia Pinchuk/Mykyta Pogorielov (UKR)	20	20
21. A. Kudryavtseva/I. Karankevich (CYP)	21	-
22. Mária Sofia Pucherová/Nikita Lysak (SVK)	22	-
23. Gina Zehnder/Beda Leon Sieber (SUI)	23	-
24. Sofiia Dovhal/Wiktor Kulesza (POL)	24	-
25. Samantha Ritter/Daniel Brykalov (AZE)	25	-
26. E.M. Ziobrowska/S.D. Judd (ROM)	26	-
27. Katarina DelCamp/Berk Akalın (TUR)	27	-
28. Hanna Jakucs/Alessio Galli (NED)	28	-
29. K. Dobroserdova/A. Pellegrini (ARM)	29	-
WD. Elizabeth Tkachenko/Alexei Kiliakov (ISR)	-	-

Niina Petrõkina made history as the first Estonian skater to win a gold medal at the European Figure Skating Championships. Juulia Turkiila and Matthias Versluis earned the highest overall total ever awarded to Finnish skaters in any discipline at the European Championships under the IJS System (205.69).

Sources: Protocol, 2025 European Figure Skating Championships; Entries, 2025 European Figure Skating Championships

APPRECIATION

This book would not have been possible had it not been for many generous donations of materials to the Skate Guard Collections over the years. A sincere and very special thanks to the following people for their special contributions:

Sandra Bezic
Yvonne Butorac
Karen Cover, World Figure Skating Museum & Hall of Fame
Matthias Hampe
Phil Hayes, British Ice Skating Historian
Elaine Hooper, Former British Ice Skating Historian
Ingrid Hunnewell
PJ Kwong
Rachel Renton
Troy Schwindt, "Skating" magazine, U.S. Figure Skating
Ken Shelley
Pauliina Vuorinen, The National Library of Finland
Benjamin T. Wright†

I am also incredibly thankful to Stefan Prodanovic, who created the fabulous cover for this book. Stefan also designed the cover for my book "Sequins, Scandals & Salchows: Figure Skating in the 1980s" and it was a pleasure to work with him again on this project.

AUTHOR'S NOTE

I genuinely hope that you have found "A Complete History of the European Figure Skating Championships" to be a valuable and worthwile resource .

I have to ask for a small favour though. Could you please spare a few minutes to write a brief review on the retailer's website where you got your copy, as well as popular book review platforms?

Reviews play a critical role in the success of all books, but they hold even greater importance for independently published ones.

I would also be extremely appreciative if you could visit your local library's website and fill out a short 'Suggest a Purchase' form.

I am grateful for your kind support in helping this important history reach the hands of more people!

BOOKS BY THIS AUTHOR

A Complete History of the European Figure Skating Championships

A Complete History of the World Figure Skating Championships.

Barbara Ann Scott: Queen of the Ice

Sequins, Scandals & Salchows: Figure Skating in the 1980s

Jackson Haines: The Skating King

Technical Merit: A History of Figure Skating Jumps

A Bibliography of Figure Skating

The Almanac of Canadian Figure Skating